WHO RUNS WASHINGTON?

WHO RUNS WASHINGTON?

Michael Kilian and Arnold Sawislak

ST. MARTIN'S PRESS • NEW YORK

F200
K52
1982

For George Washington,
who should have known better

Table of Contents

Foreword

New York sneers at the rest of American citydom, wearing its Big Apple mystique like a Gucci wardrobe. Chicago huffs and puffs about its brawn, buildings, and big money, and joyously proclaims itself No. 2. San Francisco inexplicably persists in calling itself a second Paris, while constantly carping about the real one.

Washington, D.C., in contrast, is quite modest and circumspect about itself, in all candor, with good reason. Built in a pestilential swamp, burned by the British and left for dead, for decades a ramshackle southern town noted most for its bawdy houses and slave markets, a crude hicksville that, until the Kennedys came along, lacked even one first-class restaurant, the Federal City has been for most of its life more like Paducah than Paris.

But, like a municipal Clark Kent, it lets this modesty mask a significant truth: Washington is the most powerful city on earth. There may only be 637,000 people within its limits, but there is also The Button that can destroy everything on earth and that, some assert, is all that keeps other people from destroying everything on earth. Though Washington has no voting representation in Congress, it contains the Congress. And the Agriculture Department, the State Department, the Justice Department, the Supreme Court, the department that collects our income taxes, and the department responsible for sending out our Social Security checks.

Washington is the city that saved New York from bankruptcy; that kept Detroit's Chrysler Motors alive, if barely; and that in the 1830s dispatched a young engineering officer named Robert E. Lee to keep the Mississippi River next to St. Louis. Despite the best efforts of the Reagan administration, Washington continues to touch the lives of all Americans from cradle to grave, and even then the Social Security checks sometimes keep coming. Washington sees every sparrow fall (the national inventory of zoo birds is in a computer); Washington dictates the price of everything from tomatoes to houses. Washington tells us how fast we can drive and what we can watch on television. There are Washingtonians who do nothing but worry about minnows in a Tennessee creek.

The nation's capital is all of that, and it is no longer a sleepy little place with a few stores, restaurants, mansions, and slum dwellings stuck here and there among government buildings. It's a recent development, but Washington has become a truly grand place, a real world capital, and, in the best sense of the term, America's new Second City.

No, it doesn't have towering high-rises. It is quite proud of the fact that it has outlawed them, and of the expansive views and vistas that their absence makes possible. Its broad boulevards, myriad monuments, stately facades, and countless parks and plazas give Washington the most European air of any American city.

Even mighty New York is beginning to watch Washington a little nervously over its shoulder. Though it may possess what is only the nation's second-best art museum, D.C. is, thanks to the Smithsonian, the museum capital of the country. Thanks to the Kennedy Center and a number of other first-rate theaters, it has become America's "Second City" for the stage. It was Washington's prima ballerina who won the gold medal at Moscow.

Thanks to the huge government payroll and budget (Reagan actually increased government spending, remember) and the enormous salaries and fees paid to its armies of lawyers, lobbyists, and consultants, Washington and its Maryland and Virginia suburbs are relatively recession-proof and comprise one of the wealthiest metropolitan areas in the nation, as the many expensive department stores and Mercedes-Benz dealerships attest.

Within this *grande ville* is a Washington that is not so glittery. It is a predominantly black city whose residents have higher incomes and less unemployment than most urban blacks but who for the most part still live in one of the nation's biggest slums. In fact, more black people fled Washington for the suburbs in the 1970s than did white people. When it was proposed in late 1981 that posh, luxurious Georgetown be switched from white, affluent Ward Three to the inner-city Ward Two, there were howls (although some of them came from Ward Two).

Washington has an elected and largely black local government but its only representative in Congress can't vote. There are one President, a cabinet, 100 senators, and 435 congressmen in Washington— who now allow themselves to write off local mansions and limousines as tax deductible, home-away-from-home living expenses—but their presence is often more like that of conquering generals of occupying armies than that of fellow residents. When they do get involved in local affairs, it's frequently to do something mean and nasty, such as vetoing the District of Columbia's 1981 reform of its old sexual conduct law, which had brought the city more into conformity with modern times (not to speak of Congressional life-styles).

For all its wealth, size, and power, Washington does have an air of unreality about it, and not just because it is the setting for Congress. The peculiarity was best described by veteran Washington news bureau chief Ray Coffey, who once said, "What this place needs is a couple of factories."

With this book we hope to explain this megapolis with no factories, largely through the people who run it and the rest of the nation. We'll show you how they do it. We'll also tell you who ranks at the top and who doesn't, in areas ranging from White House power brokers and influential diplomats to the city's top cops, sports impresarios, and society figures.

Heads do roll in government, and a few may be lopped off between the time this book rushes to press and the time it reaches the stores. But every effort has been made to keep every chapter as timely as the morning gossip, one of the city's most important products.

M. K. and A.S.
The Old Ebbitt Grill
Washington, D.C.
May 1982

I

THE HONORABLE BODIES

The White House Gang

RONALD REAGAN may have already announced he will not seek a second term as President.

This possibility arises from no whispered word from some anonymous White House source. It came from Reagan, who mentioned in an offhand way shortly after taking office that his role model in the Presidency was not Abraham Lincoln, not Teddy Roosevelt, not even Dwight Eisenhower, all esteemed Republican Presidents, but Calvin Coolidge.

Those who took note of the remark interpreted it to mean that Reagan, who like many public men looks for example in the past, intended to be a hands-off President. But it more likely means that like Silent Cal, and despite what his intimates say, Reagan will declare, "I do not choose to run."

Omen-reading aside, it should be no surprise when any President decides to pack it in short of the permitted two four-year terms. Almost every President, asked how he likes the White House after a few weeks on the job, replies with some variation of the familiar comment that it does offer the advantage of living close to the office. But within a year or two, almost every President has begun to liken the White House to a prison, echoing Thomas Jefferson's lament about "the splendid misery" of the Presidency.

There is, of course, a reason for this disillusionment. From the outside and during the first heady months of the typical Presidential "honeymoon," the White House offers an almost perfect environment for executive efficiency and successful national leadership.

For starters, the country really seems eager to give new Presidents the benefit of the doubt. When Richard Nixon took office in 1969, an ancient enemy, *Washington Post* cartoonist Herblock, drew a barbershop interior with a sign over the chair saying, "All new Presidents get a free shave." During the honeymoon, a new President has almost complete freedom to select his advisers, his associates, and his staff. It is true that Jimmy Carter had to dump Ted Sorenson and Reagan jettisoned Ernest Lefever early on and gave Richard Allen the boot after the first year, but all three men, Sorenson, Lefever, and Allen, had already made their own implacable enemies.

3

A new President, no matter what was said during the campaign, has almost limitless opportunity to throw out old policies, embrace new ideas, and ignore his own promises—unless, like Carter, he has made a fetish of pledges in the heat of political competition. The promise of a balanced budget is a good example. Carter insisted he would do it for almost three years; Reagan faced facts and abandoned it before his first year ended.

New Presidents have at their beck and call the largest concentration of news media in the world. If they don't like what is written and said about them, or can't bend it to their wishes with well-placed news leaks, they usually can commandeer the television and radio channels to take their case directly to the public.

Best of all, or so it may seem, new Presidents can set their own agendas and pace and style, working and thinking free from the interruptions and irritations of life beyond the high iron fence that separates the White House from the rest of the world. Of course, there are some unavoidable ceremonial duties, but if they become really onerous, there is always the Vice-President standing around waiting for something to do.

The problem with all of this is that the honeymoon always ends, as Reagan discovered at the end of his first summer in Washington. This inevitability illustrates the folk saying that you tend to forget that your original purpose was to drain the swamp when you find yourself up to your ass in alligators.

Even if he has no domestic or international crises in his first year, a new President is almost never prepared for the intense scrutiny and overblown expectations that will be imposed on himself, his family, his friends, and his coworkers.

Washington, Reagan complained, is "one giant ear," and everything, from feuding associates to a new set of dishes the President's wife buys with private funds, seems to become a major issue.

Nor are new Presidents, whether as experienced as Lyndon Johnson or as green as Carter, really aware of how hard it can be to make things happen in Washington. Congress and the bureaucracy have metabolisms of their own, and watching them work can be like observing a python digesting a pig. The President, meanwhile, walks into the White House to be faced with national problems that may have been festering for years and is expected to begin solving them the morning after Inauguration Day. Small wonder that so many Presidents come to think of their terms as sentences and the White House as a gilded jail.

It is a nice enough 132-room house. Standing on 18 acres in downtown Washington, the Executive Mansion—its proper name—was getting to be a decrepit relic until Margaret Truman's piano almost fell through an upstairs floor about 30 years ago. That did it for father Harry, who moved his family across the street to Blair House for a couple of years while the White House interior was gutted to the outside walls and rebuilt to modern standards. The place also offers some recreational extras: a small movie theater, the tennis courts whose use Jimmy Carter so carefully monitored, a bowling alley just a few steps away in the rococo Old Executive Building where Richard Nixon worked off some of his aggressions, and a swimming pool on the grounds. (The pool was built with donated funds for Jerry Ford after the old indoor pool, used by the polio-crippled Franklin Roosevelt for his only physical exercise and by John F. Kennedy and Lyndon Johnson for skinny-dipping, was covered and converted into space for the burgeoning White House press corps.)

Even so, living in the White House has to be frustrating for families who like privacy and freedom of movement. The President and his family do have spacious and comfortable private quarters upstairs, but they can hardly come to the first floor in their bathrobes when, about three hundred days every year, several thousand strangers are tramping through the rooms. Even when the White House isn't open for tours, people line the fences hoping for a glimpse of someone important—a practice LBJ rewarded by periodically strolling out to talk to the gawkers but that Nixon disliked so much that he once ordered demonstrators chased off Lafayette Park, all the way across Pennsylvania Avenue from the mansion grounds.

Presidents and their families find diverse ways to cope with the fishbowl life. One First Lady, Mrs. Franklin Pierce, so detested the environment that she refused to move to Washington, leaving her husband to drink himself into stupors in the White House. Truman, who refused to be shackled by protocol or security, liked to take early morning strolls through the city. Dr. Eugene Myer, a local chiropodist who had treated Truman when he was in the Senate, looked up one day to see the President, unannounced and unaccompanied, walking into his downtown office. Myer asked where the Secret Service was, and HST gleefully replied, "I gave them the slip!" About five minutes later, two worried and puffing agents arrived to stand guard over the trimming of the Presidential corns.

In addition to being a tourist attraction and a home, the White House is an office building. Although only the top Presidential aides are quartered in the White House's west wing near the Oval Office, it was estimated that when Reagan took over, about 500 people were attached to the White House itself and another 1,500 were working for the Executive Office of the President in the nearby Old Executive Office Building and a newer EOB across the street. *Inquiry* magazine recently estimated it costs at least $150 million a year to pay and support the President and his staff.

If he permitted it to happen, the President would be a man under the spout of a funnel disgorging the work product of all these people—numbers, words, arguments, analyses, proposals, recommendations, appeals, options, and brainstorms.

No President can look at, let alone read and digest, all the paper that comes to the White House or out of its staffs. "His choice is to run or be run by his office," Harvard professor Hugh Heclo wrote as Reagan was coming to office.

Every President has his own way to deal with the nitty-gritty of his office. He is required, for example, to produce more than 40 major reports each year, ranging from the State of the Union to the volume of U.S. weapons sales abroad, plus thousands of executive orders, proclamations, legislative messages, and vetoes. Further, he is responsible, politically at least, for what the cabinet secretaries and agency heads he appointed are doing—it was a low-level Department of Agriculture official who decided that catsup could be classified as a vegetable in school lunches, but it was the President who got the blame and the White House that had to answer the questions when that dumb idea got out in public. The ruling eventually was "withdrawn," which means dropped like a hot potato.

Dwight Eisenhower kept on top of his Presidency by installing the military staff system he knew best and by moving very slowly into new areas of presidential activity. John Kennedy had a good enough staff, but sometimes grew impatient with the sedate pace of the bureaucracy and tried to speed things up by personally phoning slow-moving officials. That caused some excitement, but had little effect on the government's response time. Jimmy Carter thought speed-reading would help. It didn't much, except perhaps on election night in 1980 when he was able to ascertain very quickly that he had lost.

Reagan has a close in staff of 50 people, which includes the top-ranking group of White House Counselor Edwin Meese, Chief of Staff James Baker, Deputy Chief of Staff Michael Deaver, and national security adviser William Clark, about a dozen assistants to the President, 19 deputy assistants and counsels, and the same number of special assistants. These are the people who winnow the problems and the paper they generate and pass what they can't dispose of upward toward the Oval Office.

Meese is the issue man in the Reagan White House, the President's closest adviser on policy. Baker runs the apparat, seeing to it that the work gets done and the paper keeps moving. Deaver is Reagan's personal aide, guarding his time and directing his attention to the priorities of the day. Clark replaced Dick Allen early in 1982, with an important extra tool—direct access to the President.

The President sits atop this pyramid of people and, when the system works right, has only to give his attention to the major decisions of statecraft and politics. But Murphy's Law ("If anything can possibly go wrong, it will") applies to the White House as well as to the rest of life, and Presidents often get involved in the most minuscule issues. Some Presidents, of course, are incapable of keeping hands off minutiae. Lyndon Johnson once telephoned United Press International late at night to complain that a story on the UPI ticker said there would be "fee" rather than "free" admission to his childhood home in Texas.

At the same time, there are occasions, such as at their news conferences, when Presidents seem to be expected to know about every sparrow that falls in the federal forest. When Eisenhower first got a helicopter for official travel, he was taken aback (and infuriated) by a reporter who asked if it was going to be used to fly him to the golf course, and Kennedy, asked about a couple of bureaucrats at the Pentagon the questioner described as "un-American," covered his lack of knowledge about the men by giving the reporter hell for engaging in McCarthyism. But that is why Presidents are briefed by their press secretaries before news conferences and why they value press secretaries who can guess what wicked curveball is going to be thrown during that ordeal.

Presidential news conferences have changed radically since the days when Herbert Hoover used to receive written questions and answer only the ones he thought merited replies. Franklin Roosevelt held news conferences twice a week in his office during most of his 12 years in the White House, but his responses could not be quoted verbatim except in special circumstances. Ike was the first to have filmed meetings with the press, but the sound and pictures were held back until reviewed by press secretary Jim Hagerty. Kennedy, relishing the challenge, went on live television, and every President since has felt bound by the precedent, although most of them, including the camera-seasoned Reagan, have had some of their worst public moments during those sessions.

The news conference is one of the elements of a relatively recent presidential role, that of the only national leader accountable to and capable of marshaling support from the public at large. The framers of the Constitution would not have liked the idea, but universal suffrage and mass communications probably made the "maximum leader" Presidency inevitable.

This is where Reagan cashed in on his much-discussed ability to communicate. Actor or not, Reagan was able to project himself as an unpretentious, honest man who believes what he says and is able to poke mild fun at himself without appearing to grovel.

Reagan also does well as a practical politician, as he showed by choosing George Bush as his running mate despite the shrieks of the far right-wingers among his supporters. And, soft as it may have been, his promise to go easy on Democratic congressmen in 1982 if they supported his programs in 1981 speaks of a man cognizant of the immutable political truth that no one gets something for nothing.

An unexpected quality was Reagan's ability to keep cool in a time of intense personal stress and trauma. Actors are not trained to joke with doctors after they are shot with real bullets, and Reagan's performance after the attempt on his life in March of 1981 has to be regarded as a measure of personal grit, not occupational know-how. As the whole country saw at the time, even four-star generals can become unstrung under less difficult circumstances.

None of this means that Reagan is ready to be measured for enshrinement at Mount Rushmore. In fact, some of the same qualities that served him well in the first stages of his term could cause him big problems before it ends.

One is what could be obsessive insistence on a particular plan to achieve a specific goal. Depending on circumstances, that could be commendable determination or blind obstinacy. The test of that will be Reagan's capacity to adjust to losing a few major battles with Congress over foreign policy initiatives.

Another potential problem is isolation, which goes directly to the issue of working and living in an airtight capsule such as the White House can be. No President now is likely to get feedback directly from those who elected him, as Lincoln did when he received all comers at the White House. But some Presidents are more sheltered than others—whether by overprotective staffs or their own inclinations—and Reagan appears to be one who has built exceptionally heavy buffers between himself and the world outside the White House.

Ned Sparks, a speech writer in the Johnson White House, wrote a book after he left entitled *Who Spoke to the President Last?* Others who have served in the White House have agreed that the answer to the question asked by Sparks' title often helps to explain the origin of a presidential decision.

Access to the President is not all there is to White House influence, but it is important enough to make the Oval Office appointment schedule must reading for those who have to know what is happening in Washington. It is almost as important and much harder to find out who arranged the appointments.

That is relevant in Reagan's case because, like Carter, he did not have a network of confidantes or former colleagues in place in Washington when he came to office. There are few old hands in the capital likely to get calls from Reagan soliciting advice; likewise, who can ring up the President and offer it? Which probably means that what you see is what you get: the White House staff, a few cabinet members, and an even smaller number of congressmen are Reagan's links to the outside.

Unlike Carter, Reagan does not have a wife who plays a daily role in decision making. Nancy has her say on matters of style and in some personal choices, but the country is not likely to hear that she was taking the notes at some future crisis conference. Nor is there any strong evidence that the Reagan circle of friends—the Walter Annenbergs, Justin Darts, or Holmes Tuttles—is calling many shots. The Rodeo Drive crowd had a voice during the transition, but when the show began in earnest, they were frozen out by the White House staff. In fact, Reagan's buddies were evicted from office space in the Old EOB.

The holy warriors of the political and religious right wing were in a slightly different category. They helped Reagan win the Republican nomination and the Presidency, but got very few patronage plums for their efforts. James Edwards, a longtime Reagan enthusiast who had gone back to dentistry when he left the South Carolina governorship, was rescued from the drills and sputum cups to become secretary of the Energy Department. But the real tigers of the New Right—Phyllis Schlafly, Richard Viguerie, Howard Phillips, Paul Weyrich, and Terry Dolan—were not brought into the administration.

Richard Allen was one favorite of the New Right inducted into the inner circle, but he came to grief before he could really consolidate his position as national security adviser. First, he bumped heads with that consummate bureaucratic infighter, Secretary of State Alexander Haig, and then lost his job when it was revealed he had forgotten to turn in a $1,000 "thank you" left by Japanese magazine journalists for whom he had arranged an interview with Mrs. Reagan.

The Reverend Jerry Falwell and his fundamentalist brethren of the electronic church came later to the Reagan crusade and got less from its 1980 triumph. Moral Majority Bible-thumpers received few appointments and even less access to the decision-making machinery. The same was true for Pro-Lifers, as was demonstrated by the selection of Sandra Day O'Connor for the Supreme Court. The volatility of the antiabortionists was also demonstrated: the day after the appointment was announced, a picket showed up outside the White House with a sign declaring that Ronald Reagan had put "a curse on the United States" by naming a woman for the high court who favored "the murder of babies."

That kind of superheated rhetoric, increasingly characteristic of the "hot button," single-interest politics of recent times, is one of the reasons such groups are kept outside government. As Interior Secretary James Watt has discovered, people who frame public issues in absolutes lose the ability to negotiate differences. They also have trouble winning confirmation from a closely divided Senate, as the Lefever case showed.

Most of the people close to Reagan are cool, sometimes icy. They fall into two general categories—those who have been with Reagan since he broke into big-time politics as governor of California, and those who have made an impression, frequently as opponents, during Reagan's drive to the top. Meese, Deaver, Clark, and Caspar Weinberger are three of the tried-and-true veterans of the California days. Baker, Bush, and Budget Director David Stockman are "outsiders" who moved into the inner circle because of perceived competence, experience, or connections.

Just outside the inner circle is a group with previous White House experience—from the Nixon administration. These include Martin Anderson, who worked for Arthur Burns on domestic policy and now heads that operation under Meese; Fred Fielding, one of the White House lawyers then and now chief counsel; and David Gergen, first staff director and now communications director under Baker. While none of them were sucked under by Watergate, all have memories of those nightmare days, and Dick Allen, who was another Nixon staff retread, told a writer long afterwards that he once stumbled on the EOB basement room occupied by the infamous "Plumbers" and wondered, "My God, what are they doing?" It now seems odd that a man who had been so close to the flame could not recognize the danger of fire when he was handed an unmarked envelope with $1,000 inside.

As an illustration of the staff's political ecumenism, Richard Darman, another of Baker's men who is regarded as a whiz at keeping the paper flow moving at the White House, was a protégé of Elliot Richardson, and Joe Canzeri, Deaver's deputy, was a personal aide to Nelson Rockefeller.

The common denominator of these people is that all are seasoned veterans of high-level office politics, and Reagan's plaintive claim that "we're all one happy family" during the "guerilla war" between Allen and Haig convinced no one who was familiar with the roster of players involved. It is also from this level of staff that news leaks spring, as in the steady flow of anti-Haig, pro-Allen items that showed up in the Evans and Novak column during that hassle.

Every President in living memory has come to office saying he intended to make cabinet government really work, but in fact no one since Eisenhower really did so. Under Kennedy, Johnson, Nixon, Ford, and Carter, the White House staff grew in both size and power, with the national security adviser in at least three of those administrations all but taking over the policy-making functions of the Secretary of State.

Allen was unable to do that with Haig at State, but there was a period in the Reagan administration when it appeared Stockman had undertaken to swallow Treasury, Defense, Energy, and a couple others. The hyperambitious budget director won a couple of skirmishes but met his match in Cap Weinberger, and just about blew his chance to remain out front in the administration with his babbling confessions of figure-juggling and uncertainty about supply-side economics to *The Atlantic Monthly*. He wasn't fired because the President didn't have anyone ready to step into his job . . . then.

Reagan's staff hasn't seized control of the Cabinet departments because their boss probably doesn't want to deal with all that work. His leisurely work habits—no 7 A.M. office show-ups for him—have evoked memories of Eisenhower, who was criticized for paying more attention to his golf scores than his "out" basket. (It should be noted that students of the Presidency who dismissed Ike as a lazy President now appear to be coming around to the opinion that the canny old soldier was keeping the White House out of trouble it didn't have to get into and operating on the rural injunction: If it ain't broke, don't fix it.)

Reagan's staff may be smart enough to see that the President doesn't have to get involved in every twitch of the body politic, but it—specifically Meese—did not serve him well in several cases. It can be debated whether Reagan should have been routed out of bed when U.S. Navy fighters shot down two Libyan jets, but those around him should have realized how bad it looked to publicly declare that the President had slept blissfully through the whole affair.

Even worse was the damage Reagan took from the hasty proposal to cut Social Security benefits. Reagan's approval ratings in the national polls plummeted more than 10 points in two weeks (well below Bush's, in fact) because his people had failed to clear the plan with at least the Republicans on Capitol Hill, or at least set up someone like Health and Human Services Secretary Richard Schweiker as a lightning rod for the reaction. The same Social Security balloon was floated during the Carter Presidency, but in a rare instance of smelling trouble in advance, Carter made sure that Joseph Califano would take the heat.

This tactic of diverting hostile fire was used during the early budget battles. Stockman was allowed to be the heavy in calling for cuts in food stamps and tuition loans, and Reagan got the credit for converting supposedly wavering members of Congress. Actually, most of them had been promised rewards, such as favored treatment for programs benefiting their constituents, before they ever arrived at the White House to have their pictures taken with the President. That operation, and the switching of the Senate on the AWACS sale that followed, were masterful jobs of building Reagan's image.

Reagan, who had one nasty staff shake-up when he first became governor of California in 1967, obviously doesn't like to have to chuck people out the front door. He let a fierce struggle go on inside his campaign staff in 1980 until he was almost forced to choose between Meese and his political strategist John Sears (Meese won). Some of his predecessors would have cashiered both Allen and Stockman at the first whiff of indiscretion. Eisenhower dropped Sherman Adams for taking gifts, and Carter let Dr. Peter Bourne go when it was found he was too quick to write prescriptions for other staff members, although he did wait too long to say good-bye to Bert Lance and never did punish Hamilton Jordan for his barroom shenanigans.

Both the strengths and the weaknesses of the Reagan staff were demonstrated by the traumatic events of March 30, 1981. An assassination attempt is a profoundly shocking event for anyone, let alone the men and women who work with the President, but the White House, like the Pentagon, is supposed to be ready to take emergencies in stride. In this case, because all the senior members of the staff rushed to the hospital, the White House was left apparently rudderless, at least in the eyes of the public.

With Meese, Baker, political director Lyn Nofziger, and assistant press secretary Larry Speakes at the hospital with Deaver, Haig was left as "contact man" in the White House situation room. That produced at least one nasty quarrel among the cabinet members and Haig's horrendous "I am in control here" appearance before the TV cameras.

The White House press, excitable in far less trying circumstances, was left in the hands of staff people with little or no experience in the press-room bear pit until Nofziger took over briefings at the hospital and Speakes returned. By that time, the place was a seething cauldron, and Speakes and Gergen had to cut off one briefing when the questioning reached the level of an inquiry by one reporter whether steps had been taken to prevent a "coup d'etat" by Haig.

To its credit, the staff rallied overnight, and by next morning someone with a good memory had found a document for the President to sign—not because it was urgent government business, but because it presented tangible proof that Reagan was able to function. That is exactly what Jim Hagerty did when Eisenhower had his heart attack in 1955, and as then, it helped sustain the authority of the Presidency.

Any list of the most important people at the White House is bound to be based on judgments and perceptions that differ according to the vantage point of the observer. The revelations of future memoirs may change what looks right now, but until then, here is a look at the inner circle from just outside the door.

THE WHITE HOUSE TOP TEN

1. Ronald Reagan

If there were no other reasons, the President would be first because, in the words of Lyndon Johnson, he is the person who can "mash the button" to unleash the planet-flattening destruction of the United States' nuclear arsenal. It may be that no other single person, not even in the Kremlin, has that power alone.

But the power to make war does not describe the Presidency or measure its effectiveness. The great task of the office is national leadership—more a state of mind than a set of facts—and it is there that recent Presidents have faltered. In the face of public skepticism that has been hardening into cynicism for several decades, the successful President must project a sense that he knows where he wants to lead the nation and how he intends to get there. Reagan certainly accomplished some of that in the first year of his Presidency.

His notion of dividing top staff responsibility among three people gave some management experts pause, and there was some trial-and-error with his "collegial" cabinet concept. Using cabinet meetings as free-for-all policy forums gave everyone a say, but the members found it tied them up so long that they didn't have time for their departments. A series of cabinet councils was substituted so that members would be working mainly in areas of interest to their departments, and that seemed to succeed.

This freed the President from the kind of detail work that tied up Carter. It also permitted Reagan to concentrate on major goals, such as economic programs and the AWACS sale in 1981. But even with all this delegating, Reagan does make the "go or no-go" decisions on the major issues. Baker told one audience, "The President wants no 'yes men' around. When he says 'no,' we all say 'no.'" Slightly more disinterested testimony came from Representative Sonny Montgomery, a Democrat, who said, "No doubt about it, he is the boss. I have been at the White House when he has demonstrated it."

Reagan has made the most of the ability to be seen as a President who is on the side of the public rather than of the government. Carter projected that in 1976, but once in office became preachy and tedious. Reagan's hardest job, made tougher by the luxury and deference that comes with the job and which he seems to enjoy, will be to avoid the appearance of having lost touch with the problems of ordinary people. That is particularly true in a time when it is his policies that are closing parks, cutting out established benefits for veterans and the elderly, and being blamed for increasing unemployment.

Reagan's conduct in the Presidency alone gives only fragmentary clues of his intentions for 1984, when he will be 74 years old. To avoid the inevitable loss of clout suffered by lame-duck Presidents and to keep both Republicans and Democrats from starting to campaign immediately, the Reagan staff has had to say he plans to run for a second term.

But there are contrary signs, not all of which are as faint as the suggested Coolidge parallel. Reagan has set out in his first term to make a major change in the direction of the government and the country, and it was apparent very quickly that the "Reagan Revolution" was going to be difficult and divisive. Even if he gets what he wants before 1984, Reagan may have to use up so much political capital that a second-term campaign would be doomed. Surely knowing this, Reagan still has pulled very few punches in seeking his goals.

Coolidge quit at a time when he probably could have been reelected. The question is whether Reagan will have that option, or, like Truman and Lyndon Johnson, will be faced with the prospect of a shattering rejection by the same voters who had embraced him just four years before.

2. Edwin Meese III

Ed Meese looks like a beer drinker. That is relevant because some of Reagan's opponents portray Meese as a Rasputin, the evil genius who really runs the White House. (Governor Jerry Brown, mad as hell when Washington insisted on aerial spraying of the fruit fly in the summer of 1981, made just such a pitch.) But Ed Meese looks and acts a little like Ed McMahon, and who would buy the claim that the jolly Budweiser man really pulls the strings of Johnny Carson?

In truth, Meese is Reagan's first-ranking aide, the acknowledged leader of the group that dominates the White House staff and the only one with cabinet rank. His title is Counselor to the President (salary $60,662 a year), but if that evokes the image of a pipe-smoking pundit locked away in some cubbyhole to ponder the Big Picture, it is misleading.

Meese runs the White House "policy shop." He controls the development of policy studies and proposals and their flow to Reagan's desk. That makes him a most important man on the staff of a President who has never been accused of being an original thinker.

Shortly after Dick Allen, whose neck Meese tried to save, was dumped, stories surfaced that Big Ed himself was to be moved out of the White House inner circle in a lateral arabesque that would give him the post of attorney general as soon as a Supreme Court seat opened for William French Smith.

"Preposterous" was the mildest official White House reaction to this scenario, but Washington entrail-readers, long accustomed to vehement denials of impending changes that later take place, noted that the story was broken by reporters who ordinarily have good sources and that Meese did appear to be losing some of his preeminence at the center of power toward the end of Reagan's first year.

Bigger men at the White House have fallen faster, and so could Meese—perhaps even before the ink has dried on these pages.

There is little doubt that Meese is a conservative—that much can be deduced from his utterances about law enforcement, which was his line before he joined the Reagan staff in 1967. Further, the high priests of the New Right, who probably are suspicious of the fact that the Army requires its soldiers to step off on the left foot, have had no beef about Meese. Born in 1931, he went to the University of California at Berkeley (it was different in those days). He also went to Yale Law.

At the same time, Meese is results-oriented, and that has put him into a mediator's role when strong opinions have clashed in the White House. Such was the case early in the administration when Reagan's campaign promise to help the slumping U.S. automobile industry collided with the free-market theories that are the centerpiece of the President's economic policy.

Some of Reagan's advisers, led by Transportation Secretary Drew Lewis, wanted the administration to back import restrictions on Japanese cars. His economic advisers, including Murray Weidenbaum and Dave Stockman, counseled a hands-off policy. It was Meese who helped develop the final policy: prodding the Japanese to adopt "voluntary" curbs on their own industry, a feat of apparent altruism impelled by the sure knowledge that Reagan would let Congress clamp down on imports if Tokyo didn't.

Meese has caused Reagan some embarrassment: It was he who told the press he felt no need to awaken the President the night U. S. Navy fighters downed two Libyan planes and who, without telling Baker and Deaver, let (or encouraged) the Internal Revenue people restore tax exemptions to private schools that bar blacks.

Meese usually remains in the background at the White House, although he was the spokesman during the Carter-Reagan transition and surfaced quickly the day after the assassination attempt to give Haig absolution. He is regarded as unflappable—"It's just out of character for Ed Meese to throw his hat on the floor," said longtime aide Ed Thomas in a Meese profile. "I've seen him upset only on rare occasions."

But Meese obviously is nobody's patsy. In 1980, campaign chief John Sears was able to shoulder Mike Deaver and Lyn Nofziger out of the show, but Meese survived to emerge on top and welcome Deaver and Nofziger back when the night of the long knives arrived for Sears.

3. James Baker III

On paper, Jim Baker looks like the last man who would end up as Reagan White House chief of staff. Not only is he a Texan in a grove of Californians, but Baker was the main man in Gerald Ford's 1976 nomination campaign that beat Reagan, and in the George Bush 1980 effort that represented the only serious challenge to the eventual winner.

A year older and considerably leaner than Meese, Baker did have a minor role in the Reagan campaign in negotiating the ground rules for the Anderson and Carter debates, but he expected to return to his law practice in Houston after the election. Instead, he is now running the operating part of the White House, which includes supervision of the big staff functions such as liaison with Congress, political affairs, speech writing, and media relations. Some actually think Baker has more power than Meese, though he must be circumspect in its usage.

Baker is no stereotype Texan of the J.R. Ewing type. Tall and clean-cut, he is more likely to be seen in three-piece suits of Ivy League cut than western-style togs (except when he is back home hunting the elusive wild turkey). A Houston corporation lawyer educated at Princeton and the University of Texas, Baker has a passion for politics and a flair for administration, assets that have made him in the eyes of some at least as important to Reagan as Meese. He also has an advantage over some of the careerists on the White House staff: he has enough money of his own not to need his government salary and a good job to go back to if he wants to walk away from the intrigues of the Washington fast track.

Baker got into politics by joining Bush's ill-starred 1970 Texas Senate campaign and came to Washington in 1975 to serve as Undersecretary of Commerce. After heading the losing Ford campaign in 1976, he tried the political waters himself, running for attorney general in Texas in 1978. He lost but got a record 46 percent of the vote as a GOP candidate for the office.

Because of the Ford and Bush connections as well as his former links to Commerce Secretaries Rogers Morton and Elliot Richardson, Baker was regarded as a liberal or, at best, a moderate Republican. That image persists—after the Sandra Day O'Connor Supreme Court nomination, the antiabortion "Life Letter" referred to him as head of the "Moderate Mafia" in the White House.

But in fact Baker passes muster with more sophisticated conservatives, such as Republican Senator Jesse Helms of North Carolina and New Right campaigner Terry Dolan, who was quoted in January 1981 as saying, "He's [Baker] more of a Reaganite than most people around Reagan."

Baker told an interviewer after he was handed the chief of staff assignment, "My job is to make the train run, and I go on disclaiming any intentions of formulating policy because you can't be an honest broker and push policy." The job also involves appointments and political work, which, Baker admitted and all of Washington knows, put him into the policy-making business. But none of the available evidence indicates that Baker uses that entrée to push his own group—it was Baker who installed Lyn Nofziger in the top political slot to screen appointments after conservatives complained too many people of suspect ideological loyalty were getting government jobs. And, according to testimony, it was Meese who decided on Bush as the administration's "crisis manager" instead of Haig, who thought he was going to get the job.

4. Michael K. Deaver

Mike Deaver, the youngest of the White House inner circle at 43, holds the title of deputy chief of staff. But he doesn't really work for Baker; his boss is Ronald Reagan, and he spends more time with the President than anyone else on the top staff.

Deaver has a job that is called in political parlance, "Keeper of the Body." Wherever Reagan goes, Deaver follows, keeping the schedule up to snuff and prompting the President when places and people begin to blur. Deaver was on the sidewalk at the Washington Hilton when Reagan was shot and, in fact, checked the President into George Washington University Hospital. Once, in the 1976 campaign, Deaver literally saved Reagan's life by applying the Heimlich manuever to dislodge a peanut that had caught in the candidate's throat.

Deaver, like Meese, goes back to Reagan's first term as governor of California, and another veteran of that long association, Nancy Reynolds, has been quoted as saying, "I think Mike has telepathy with Ronald Reagan. He understands what he's going to say, think and do sometimes before the man himself does."

Although listed as Baker's deputy, Deaver is close to equal in standing with him and Meese. He meets with them every working morning at 7:30, and they confer again before the day ends. Deaver has been described as the "wild card" in the group, drawing emergency jobs such as preparing the briefing papers for the Ottawa economic summit meeting after others assigned to the job had come up with a mass of complicated material that left Reagan dizzy.

Deaver also is close to Nancy Reagan and serves a function that every staff needs and no one wants to perform. "If I ever had any bad news to give the President, I'd like Mike to deliver it," a former White House speech writer told a reporter.

Deaver, a public relations man who earns the same $60,662 as Meese and Baker, has said he will be leaving the White House late in

1982 because he can't support his family on the salary—which unlike others at top federal levels did not go up after the administration's first year. (He gets the same pay as a member of Congress, and no federal employees except cabinet members, Supreme Court justices, and a few others are allowed to draw more.)

In any case, there are a number of people at the White House who think it will take only one thing to get Deaver to stay—a personal request from Reagan. And because of the President's almost fatherly regard for Deaver, there are plenty who think that will soon be forthcoming.

5. *George Bush*

In the musical comedy *Of Thee I Sing,* Vice-President Alexander Throttlebottom was so far removed from the action of the administration that he had to take the public tour to get into the White House. That was fiction, but it agrees with the perception of reality most Americans have had about the Vice-Presidency. "Cactus Jack" Garner, who gave up the job of speaker of the House to become Franklin Roosevelt's first Vice-President, once told Lyndon Johnson the position "ain't worth a cup of warm spit." It ruined Hubert Humphrey's presidential ambitions and made a pathetic pasture for Nelson Rockefeller. Ronald Reagan hasn't emulated Carter in much, but the place he has given George Bush in his administration does follow the Walter Mondale precedent, which is to give the Vice-President grown-up work to do.

Bush, the New England blue blood who moved to Texas after World War II to make his own name and fortune in oil drilling machinery, has become a member of the White House inner circle for several reasons. First, he is immensely likable and Reagan likes him. Second, he knows more about government close up than practically anyone else close to the President. Third, he protects Reagan's Republican flank on the left and gives the White House a link with what used to be called the Rockefeller wing of the GOP.

When Reagan agreed to designate Bush as the administration's crisis manager, the fact that the Vice-President had served in Congress, directed the Central Intelligence Agency, served as U.S. envoy to China and ambassador to the United Nations, and headed the Republican National Committee got lost in power-happy Washington's fixation with the selection as a defeat for Secretary of State Alexander Haig. What went unnoticed in that view of the decision as a struggle for turf was the probability that Bush was better qualified for a job that may involve domestic problems as well as international crises.

In any case, that episode gave Bush cachet that he did not really need. Reagan from the start has cut Bush in on the action at the White House, and the Vice-President has responded by becoming a Reagan loyalist to the degree that he hardly blinks when reminded that he once called the President's tax proposal "voodoo economics" and never objects when reporters suggested he made so much of his jogging during the 1980 campaign to remind the voters that he was the young-and-fit candidate.

Bush has the same office in the White House that Mondale used, but he has an even bigger prize: a standing date for lunch alone with the President every week. Like most Vice-Presidents, he draws the "scut" work of greeting visiting delegations of spelling-bee winners and hog-calling champions, but he also is there when kings and presidents call at the White House.

Least known is his work for the administration on Capitol Hill. He seldom presides over the Senate, which is the only job he has, but he usually spends one morning a week playing paddleball with old colleagues in the House gymnasium. "He has been very helpful to the President there," one of his congressional buddies said.

6. Paul Laxalt

Laxalt, the Republican senator from Nevada, is a gutsy gambler. As campaign chairman, he put his money on Ronald Reagan in 1976 and lost. He doubled the bet in 1980, when he took the same job even though he was up for reelection himself, and won. Now he is the President's friend in the Senate, and that means considerably more at the White House than a couple of tickets for constituents who want to take the VIP tour.

Laxalt, now 59, probably could have had Reagan's support if he had chosen to challenge Howard Baker for the Senate Republican leadership. He passed up the chance, whether out of unwillingness to take on the extra work or because he believed he would be more effective outside the formal leadership structure. In any case, he is a man with clout at both ends of Pennsylvania Avenue.

How much? When Bob Gray, a public relations man and lobbyist with GOP links back to the Eisenhower White House, threw a party for Laxalt in a tent on the Capitol lawn, several hundred people, including most of this list, attended. It was a full dress affair, and the temperature and humidity both were in the high 90s.

7. Caspar Weinberger

"Cap" Weinberger is another Reagan associate from the California days and made his mark, the story goes, by discovering a section of federal law that would let Reagan finance a state health program for the poor with federal money. That, of course, is the Medicaid program Reagan is now trying to cap, but Weinberger has moved on to the Pentagon as secretary of defense.

Weinberger is no soldier and Reagan is no psychic, but the President knows if you give bureaucrats money, they will dispose of it—down rat holes, if necessary. Reagan came to office determined to give the Defense Department a lot more money than it had been getting in recent years, and he chose Weinberger, who had a similar assignment from Richard Nixon at the Health, Education, and Welfare Department, to mount guard on the rat holes. Weinberger instead became a "more, more, more!" government spender, but that happens.

When Reagan was shot, another duty of the Defense secretary came to light. Under a little-known but long-standing executive order, when the President is incapacitated, as Reagan was during surgery, and the Vice-President is not on hand, as Bush was not for several hours that day, the secretary of defense has the nuclear button. That information surprised a lot of people, possibly including Haig.

8. David Stockman

Should the 34-year-old director of the Office of Management and Budget be higher on this list? Should he be off it after his *Atlantic* confessions? The ambitious former Michigan congressman was the most visible manifestation of the Reagan assault on big government in the opening weeks of the administration because he had been practicing for it. (He drafted an austerity budget while he was in Congress in 1980, but it never got past the Budget Committee door.)

The White House was delighted to have a point man for the budget and gave Stockman his head until the rest of the Reagan team was up to speed. Then it let cabinet members, Haig and Donald Regan at Treasury, for two, wrestle Stockman for the chunks of their turf he was happily appropriating.

Stockman is highly valued for his encyclopedic knowledge of federal spending. If he sticks to budget cutting, he probably will be around for the duration. If he goofs again, don't be surprised to see the White House announce, regretfully, of course, that Stockman is departing to run for the Senate.

9. Bill Clark

Bill Clark may well move up the ladder at the White House. He didn't move into the West Wing until the second year of the Reagan administration, when he replaced Dick Allen as national security adviser.

But his previous experience as a close Reagan associate—he was the original chief of staff in California who brought both Meese and

Deaver into the circle—and the enhanced position given him in the security job puts him into the top ten.

Clark, 50, was anything but eager to come to Washington when Reagan won the Presidency. He was happy as a justice of the California Supreme Court, even as an out-numbered conservative, and delayed his resignation to become deputy secretary of state under Haig as long as possible. And when he got to Washington, senators thoroughly ventilated his freely admitted unfamiliarity with foreign policy by asking him questions about countries and leaders whose location and names he could not supply.

But Clark was confirmed and turned out to be a good working partner with the temperamental Haig, turning his talents for mediation and administration to good use. And, by the time he was called over to the White House, Clark was able to say that he not only could identify Robert Mugabe but actually had met the Zimbabwean leader.

Clark has one thing to prove at the White House—that he can survive the spears and arrows of the roughest bureaucratic jungle of them all.

10. Edward Rollins

Ed Rollins also was new to his job, White House political director, in 1982, but not unfamiliar to the place or the work because he spent the first year of the Reagan administration as Lyn Nofziger's deputy.

Rollins, like Nofziger, is bearded, balding, and tough. A Massachusetts native, he was reared in California and literally fought his way to recognition: he was an alternate member of the 1964 U.S. Olympic boxing team who outgrew his 165-pound class and had to settle for becoming a sparring partner for the likes of Joe Frazier.

Now 39, equipped with a doctorate in political science and a decade of experience in the California political cauldron, he is the White House point man in the effort to retain a loyal Reaganite Republican majority in the Senate and produce party control of the House. He will work with Baker in this and try to establish a coherent campaign for the midterm elections, when members of Congress frequently try to cut themselves loose from their own Presidents.

A note about Nofziger. The rumpled and often irreverent former newsman who left the business in 1966 to tie his career to Reagan will remain a political power even after leaving his job (under his own power), because in a real sense he is the keeper of the President's conservative credentials. The New Right, the Pro-Lifers, and the Moral Majority may think they own a piece of Reagan, but their access to the Oval Office goes through Nofziger.

The Hill

PIERRE L'ENFANT, commissioned by George Washington to transform a swamp into a capital for the fledgling United States, had his problems. But when the temperamental French engineer spied a 90-foot elevation with the inelegant name of Jenkins Hill near the eastern edge of the tract, L'Enfant called it "a pedestal waiting for its monument," and reserved it for a "Congress House."

The rise of land above the Potomac floodplain became known as Capitol Hill, and on it stands the gleaming white-domed building that, with the Washington Monument at the opposite end of the national Mall, symbolizes the seat of government of the United States for Americans and the world.

But the Capitol atop its hill is more than a symbol. It is a factory as well as a monument and the centerpiece of a city within a city. There, gathering from the states and territories, 100 senators, 435 representatives, and 4 nonvoting delegates make law for the nation and preside over a unique community of 225 acres with 20 buildings and a daytime work force of about 23,000 people.

In addition to about 17,000 aides and secretaries for the members of Congress, congressional committee staffers, legislative researchers, and legal draftsmen, there are also a 1,200-member police force—as big as Atlanta's—and nearly 3,000 other employees whose duties range from leaf raking to computer servicing, from guiding the Capitol's 1.4 million visitors to hoisting and lowering thousands of flags every year to be sent to organizations and individuals who have asked for an Old Glory that has flown over the Capitol.

Congress has its own restaurants and stores, barber shops and beauty salons, an immense power-generating plant and a fully equipped medical clinic that could serve as a small-town hospital. It has airline and railroad ticket agencies, television and radio studios with the most up-to-date equipment and a closed circuit broadcasting system, a highly sophisticated computer network, a coeducational high school for its teenaged pages, and half a dozen post offices. It has three subway lines and a shuttle-bus system, its own greenhouse and nursery, a first-class gymnasium and several swimming pools and the largest library in the world. During Prohibition, it had its own resident bootlegger—memorialized by a nearby pub called "The Man in the Green Hat"—and now, some say, its own thriving numbers operation.

When the legislative branch budget went over $1 billion in 1976, some members, particularly those who fill the *Congressional Record* with daily diatribes against profligate government spending, were mortified. So when the Republicans took control of the Senate in 1981, they announced its budget would be cut 10 percent. They undertook to accomplish this by hiring fewer committee aides than the 1,200 the Democrats had on the payroll and by reducing the number of operators who have been running automatic elevators on Capitol Hill for years. The most drastic retrenchment was to turn over the Senate's barber shops to private enterprise, ending forever the tradition of free senatorial haircuts. But it still costs more than $1 billion a year to run Capitol Hill.

This hilltop citadel is just about independent of Washington, D.C. It is run by the leadership and several committees of the House and Senate, and they are exceedingly jealous of their jurisdiction. The District of Columbia police department dares put no flat foot on the Capitol grounds without permission, although the local gendarmes are called in to help the Capitol cops when big events like inaugurations or demonstrations bring huge crowds to the Hill.

No local sales taxes are collected in congressional eating places or stores (a carton of cigarettes cost $5.35 late in 1981 at Capitol tobacco counters), and members of Congress usually do not pay income taxes to the District of Columbia, Maryland, or Virginia, even though most of them and their families are full-time residents using state and local government services. ·

As an employer, Congress has exempted itself from the labor and antidiscrimination laws it passed to cover the rest of the country, and members can hire and fire without explanation or cause. However, after repeated newspaper stories about nepotism, members now are forbidden to put close relatives on their payrolls.

Members of Congress justify giving themselves what amounts to a kind of divine right of employment with the argument that their staffs are an extension of themselves and, like themselves, responsible only to the voters every two or six years. But this also carries an element of political paranoia: members, especially in the House, are forever worried about their next opponent and shudder at stories of aides who have plotted to sabotage their bosses and seek their seats.

This has produced some classic tyrants. Members have used their employees as baby-sitters, chauffeurs, and janitors. One New Jersey congressman required a congressional intern to act as a bartender for office visitors, and there was a spate of stories a few years back about congressmen from Ohio, Illinois, and Texas who hired women to provide themselves with nothing more than a regular roll-in-the-hay at taxpayer expense.

But most congressional employees are happy to have the work, and the rewards for satisfactory service are considerable. Salaries for top aides exceed $50,000, and anyone who lasts 20 years can retire with a sizable pension paid from a retirement system that exempts them, along with other federal workers, from Social Security taxes.

Congressmen love to rail about the growth of bureaucracy, but there is no place in Washington where it has mushroomed more than on Capitol Hill. Senators and House members, for example, had about 5,800 people on their personal staffs in 1967; by 1978 that number had increased to more than 10,200. The same House and Senate committees that employed about 900 people in 1960 boomed to about 3,000 in less than 20 years.

For some of this "stafflation" there is justification. Senators and House members are representing 40 million more Americans than they were 20 years ago, and the concept of constituent service has changed vastly. The increase in Social Security beneficiaries alone has had a marked effect on congressional office caseloads, while the recent emphasis on "grass roots" letter and postcard lobbying by interest groups has tripled the volume of mail to and from Capitol Hill each year. House Postmaster Robert Rota in 1981 gave what he called "a very, very conservative estimate" of the total mail volume—120 million items.

The explanation for larger committee and research staffs may be even more compelling. Until the 1960s, Congress was almost totally dependent upon federal bureaucrats, private business, and academics for the facts and figures to back up arguments for and against legislation.

As the role of the federal government increased, the lawmakers saw that the material they got from government sources or the universities could as easily be stacked as that from industry. So they hired their own experts.

Most of these committee staffs gather information and keep their noses out of policy, but some are so expert and persuasive that they are regarded as having more impact on legislation than the elected officials they work for. That was said to be the case during the years that the late Colin Stam and Laurence Woodworth directed the influential Joint Committee on Taxation and when Michael Pertschuk headed the Senate Commerce Committee staff. Richard Sullivan of the House Public Works Committee is a current staffer with a strong influence on legislation.

Sometimes committee staffs get out of hand, as in the case of Roy Cohn and David Schine, the two young investigators for the late Senator Joseph R. McCarthy, who terrorized U.S. embassies abroad in madcap searches for Reds under the beds in the early 1950s, or the committee staffer 20 years later who created 12 days of hearings by sending a stack of written statements to the printers in the form of testimony delivered by live witnesses. He was sacked.

But the committee staffs, which not only investigate issues and draft legislation but sometimes conduct questioning at hearings, are a proven career stepping-stone for the brightest talents.

Three examples among many over the years: Michael Pertschuk became chairman of the Federal Trade Commission; Nancy Teeters of the House Budget Committee became a member of the Federal Reserve Board; and a young lawyer who worked for a House Judiciary subcommittee in 1950–51 is now Mr. Justice John Paul Stevens of the U.S. Supreme Court.

In addition to the 40 House and Senate committees, members of Congress have access to even more specialized expertise from the staffs of the General Accounting Office, the Library of Congress' Congressional Research Service, the Congressional Budget Office, and the Office of Technology Assessment. An estimated 2,800 people in these organizations funnel their work to Congress.

The tangible product of all these people is paper, hundreds of tons of it. William "Fishbait" Miller, for years doorkeeper of the House, spent most of his time supervising a crew of patronage go-fers and door-openers, but counted it as one of his proudest accomplishments that he organized a system of collecting, baling, and selling scrap paper from Capitol Hill that returned thousands of dollars a year to the Treasury.

But much of the paper leaves the Hill in envelopes, some 48 million a year. Besides the countless official letters and publications that flow out of the congressional and committee offices, members mail millions of newsletters to their constituents each year. Most of the newsletters are printed at the members' expense, but they go through the mails free under the congressional "frank"—a privilege all members have and most use to glorify themselves in regular mass mailings to the folks back home. Only openly political material and campaign season newsletters are out of bounds for use of the frank, but for many members, that is a distinction without much of a difference. Periodically, efforts are made to police abuses of the frank, and once in a while a member of Congress is billed for postage on a mailing that has bent the rules.

All of this bespeaks a huge capacity to reproduce words, and Congress has it. Members' offices are equipped with the latest in typewriters, word processors, and letter folding and envelope stuffing machinery. To handle mass letter and postcard campaigns for and against legislation (the House post office once received 55,000 pieces of mail in a half hour addressed to Speaker Tip O'Neill during debate on a labor bill), both the House and Senate have basement rooms filled with high-speed automatic robot typewriters and machines that sign members' names with real ink.

The real heavyweight printing for Congress is done down the street from the Capitol at the massive red brick Government Printing Office. GPO does much more than congressional printing—among other jobs it spews out several hundred million income tax forms every year. But Capitol Hill gives it $91 million worth of business annually.

It prints bills, resolutions, amendments, legislative calendars, and committee reports by the hundreds of thousands, and it publishes the equivalent of a daily magazine in the *Congressional Record.* Into the *Record,* available every morning Congress is in session, goes every word spoken in the previous day's House and Senate sessions, the text of major legislation under debate, the backup committee material that goes with it, and an absolutely bewildering collection of often totally irrelevant information that can range on any day from a tribute to a senator's daughter who established a new record for standing under a shower (Lisa D'Amato, 112 hours) to a voluminous report on the domestic production of tung nut oil. It even prints poetry, usually from members' constituents. An all-time favorite was a long ballad appealing to Congress to require fire departments to adopt uniform hose couplings and concluding:

> Beware of disaster and accompanying dreads,
> Without national standard threads.

About 32,000 copies of the *Record* are printed from transcripts prepared by "official reporters" who work on the House and Senate floor with shorthand pads and stenotype machines. They usually clean up members' grammar and syntax and sometimes change their meaning. The late Representative Adam Clayton Powell was frustrated in an effort to get the Speaker to admonish a southerner who repeatedly used the word "nigger," because the transcript always showed the man had said "Negro." Powell finally made his point by declaring, "Mr. Speaker, the gentleman from Mississippi did not say 'Negro.' He said 'nigger.' N-i-g-g-e-r."

Many "speeches" in the *Record* are never made. Typically, a member will speak for about a minute and ask permission "to revise and extend" his remarks. The next day, the 1-minute talk may come back as a 60-minute stem-winder. This got so confusing and costly (each page of the *Record* costs $480 to produce) that Congress ordered black dots printed next to speeches that were never spoken.

Phantom speeches are only one problem. Visitors to the congressional galleries, finding business being conducted in nearly empty chambers, often wonder aloud what the hell happened to the senator or House member they elected to represent them. There are reasons for this hooky-playing, a few of which are actually valid.

Civics textbooks notwithstanding, there is very little actual lawmaking done on the House and Senate floors. Major bills usually are explained and discussed on the floor, and once in a while, amendments are written and debates conducted that affect the outcome.

The reason for this is that legislation that has survived the complex, often agonizing process of reaching the House or Senate floor already has had the intense scrutiny of both legal technicians and politicians, and whatever compromises are needed have already been struck.

Members of Congress introduce bills in the tens of thousands every session, but the committees, organized according to subject matter (for example, education, armed services, agriculture), seldom conduct hearings on any besides those known to have significant or influential support. Once a bill is scheduled for a hearing, the committee members start hearing from the advocates and opponents, and by the time they are called upon to consider a bill—in sessions called, appropriately, "mark-ups"—amendments usually have been drafted, deals for votes have been made, and the fate of the measure has been settled.

Sometimes it takes years for legislation to pass because it embraces a new idea or shatters some existing tradition. If it has strong backing, it reappears every session like a crocus in the springtime, and eventually gets to a floor vote. The Equal Rights Amendment is an example—it took decades to get through Congress and was the focus of feminist lobbying efforts long before it began its apparently ill-starred ratification journey through the state legislatures.

So most bills that come to the floor are passed or killed in the form they came from the sponsoring committees without change or more than perfunctory debate, and except for members who have a specific interest in the legislation, few bother to come except to vote. At that, a lot of legislation is disposed of by voice vote: there were only 966 roll-call votes taken to pass 1,643 measures in the 1980 congressional session.

These conditions tend to hold down attendance during sessions, especially when members have desks loaded with correspondence and anterooms crowded with visitors at their offices, as well as committee hearings and sessions. However, members do not like to miss recorded votes, since political opponents often make much of members' absenteeism. Before it installed an electronic voting system, the House used to spend 45 minutes or longer on every roll call, but with the new machinery, the votes take only 15 minutes. Instead of having to wait for a clerk to call their name, members now vote by inserting plastic cards into terminals placed around the House chamber, and their votes are registered in lights on the wall over the press galleries.

This is fast, but not foolproof. No one has been caught at it, but there is gossip that some members give their cards to colleagues to cast votes for them. Even in the days when the roll was called, there were cases of "ghost voting." Some years back, a tally clerk was fired when it appeared he was—at the request of members—entering their names on the roll-call sheets when they were no closer to the House floor than Cleveland.

Members are called to the floor by a system of bells, buzzers, and lights built into wall clocks all over Capitol Hill. It is often possible to tell where they were when the vote was called—those who rush in clutching napkins probably were at lunch; those with damp hair and wearing sneakers probably were in the gym.

Entrances to the House and Senate chambers are closely guarded, but for many years there was only the lightest security for the galleries. Visitors must have passes, but these are given out freely by members' offices, and sometimes crackpots or demonstrators get in.

It is a rare year when someone in the galleries does not rise to give a speech or argue with a member of Congress on the floor below, and during the 1960s, it was popular for demonstrators to chain themselves to the gallery railings. But there also are plainclothes policemen in the galleries, and they can usually quell the disturbances quickly.

Yet gallery outbreaks can be serious. In the mid-1950s, a group of Puerto Rican nationalists got into the House gallery and began firing automatic weapons at the members. Five were seriously wounded.

When the shooting started, members ran for cover, and when former Representative Frank Boykin burst out of the chamber, a doorkeeper asked, "Where are you going, Congressman?"

"To get mah gun," the portly Boykin puffed.

"Where's your gun?"

"In Alabama," replied Boykin as he vanished down the corridor.

Nowadays, the galleries are guarded by airport-type metal detectors as well as doorkeepers, and Capitol cops inspect handbags, briefcases, and parcels at the entrances to all the buildings on the Hill.

Even with these implements of modern security, and with the arrival of electronics—television cameras panning the House chamber and digital scoreboards to tally votes—Congress manages to retain some of the rituals and traditions of its eighteenth century origins. In the Senate, the members' desks still are equipped with receptacles for ink and sand to blot it, and snuffboxes are kept in niches in the chamber. The House still begins its sessions with the appearance of a sergeant-at-arms carrying the ceremonial mace, a brass and wooden battle club that is supposed to be a reminder to the members that they are to persuade with words, not fists.

Before the Civil War, the House was the scene of some epic brawls, including one in which a Wisconsin congressman snatched off a Mississippi colleague's wig and shouted, "Hurrah, boys! I've scalped one!" There hasn't been a good bout on the Hill since Representative Henry "Hammering Hank" Gonzalez, taking exception to being called a "pinko," punched out Representative Ed Foreman in the Speaker's Lobby a few years back.

But for the most part, the Capitol is sedate as a cathedral, with the members, often trailing retinues of aides and attachés, treated with the deference given visiting cardinals at the Vatican.

The comparison of Capitol Hill to Vatican City is tempting, but limited by the facts. It is true that the institutions that occupy both enclaves exercise jurisdiction far beyond their own borders, depend upon faith and consent to achieve obedience, and have given their constituencies ignorance and prejudice besides wisdom and courage.

But the parallel shatters on the issue of ideological steadfastness. The Roman Catholic Church has been known to dig in for centuries against what it has declared to be error or sin, but it only takes one day—the one on which elections are held—to spin Congress around like a well-oiled weathercock in a light breeze.

That is what happened in 1980. Even though the House leadership remained in control of the Democratic liberals and the Senate went Republican by only three votes, Congress took a sharp turn to the right. There are a number of explanations that have been offered for this phenomenon, but the one that fits best is fear.

In the first instance, the fear stemmed from the realization that Congress, which had become the preeminent branch of government when the Presidency proved first corrupt and later bumbling in the 1970s, had failed to solve the nation's nagging economic and social problems. When the New Right said the 1980 election was a conservative mandate, all but the most steadfast liberals on Capitol Hill were ready to believe it.

There also was widespread fear among members of Congress that they would lose their jobs. While many members have strong public service and/or political motives, careerism—simply, job-holding for its own sake—seems to have increased on the Hill. While it is often said that many members of Congress could make a lot more money in business or a profession, there are plenty who couldn't earn anything near the $60,622 congressional salary in private life, nor command the perks offered by the Hill.

The upshot of all this was, at least in the early months of the Reagan administration, a near collapse of coherent and constructive opposition. What Reagan and whiz kid Budget Director David Stockman demanded between January and August of 1981—budget cuts for social programs, spending increases for the military, and tax breaks for business and wealthy individuals—they got.

But when the leaves began to turn, so did Congress. Wall Street, which was supposed to turn cartwheels to celebrate the introduction of supply-side economics, instead panicked, and the administration had to concede the onset of recession. Suddenly, Democrats (and some urban northeastern Republicans) who had been in full flight turned and put up some resistance, handing the administration its first really significant defeat by refusing to go along with a $13 billion cut in the 1982 budget they already had reduced by nearly $35 billion.

Reagan's early triumphs featured a level of presidential "hands-on" congressional lobbying that exceeded anything in the recent past, but it was notably absent during the autumn budget struggle that culminated in a White House–Capitol Hill deadlock and a six-hour shutdown of some federal activities. While the media gave itself goose pimples writing and talking about the government "closing shop," actually only 20 percent of the federal work force was involved, and most Americans probably wouldn't have known the difference if the stalemate had lasted a week or so.

Reagan did go back to one-on-one lobbying when the House rejected the AWACS radar plane deal with Saudi Arabia. To get it through, he needed the approval of only one house, and he got it from the Senate by twisting the arms of reluctant Republican senators. It was an impressive win, though costly in terms of political capital expended.

But as Reagan's first year in office ended, it was clear he had lost the momentum of the previous spring and summer and would have to compromise on some of his stated budget and defense goals. House Republican Leader Bob Michel, for one, said late in 1981 that the White House had "rolled over" too often in negotiations with individual members and had few goodies left to offer for future votes.

The effect will be a restoration of some of the power congressional leaders lost during the months when Reagan was jiggling the House and Senate like a master puppeteer.

Most foreigners, accustomed to the rigid party discipline of parliamentary government, and many Americans cannot understand why Democrats vote with Republicans and vice versa in the U.S. Congress. The short answer is that both parties, but particularly the Democrats, have tried to straddle too broad a range of issues in seeking national dominance. Members of Congress, who are supposed to represent national interests but must respond to regional or even local needs to stay in office, almost always choose personal survival over party loyalty.

As a result, coalitions have been pivotal in Congress for several decades and probably will be for some time to come. Thus Speaker Tip O'Neill knows that Michel is likely to get 20 or 30 "Boll Weevil" votes from conservative southern Democratic districts, but should be able to count on some Republican defections from the Northeast. That didn't happen early in 1981; it was beginning to as the year ended, and the election year may accentuate it.

Overlaid on the demands of party and regional loyalty are the personalities of the members. A statistically composite member of Congress probably would be a white Protestant male lawyer from a small town or suburb in Illinois, but in the flesh they span a spectrum that includes bookish former professional basketball players (Senator Bill Bradley of New Jersey), sleepy former professors (Senator S. I. Hayakawa of California), refugees from the Nazi holocaust (Representative Tom Lantos of California, a Democrat, and Senator Rudy Boschwitz of Minnesota, a Republican), and astronauts (Senator John Glenn of Ohio, a Democrat, and Senator Harrison Schmitt of New Mexico, a Republican.) Congress is no cross section of America, but it is an interesting mishmash.

Congress is, of course, short on women (18 in the House, 2 in the Senate) and minorities (18 blacks and fewer Hispanics and Orientals), but it is far more diverse now than it was in the past. Former Representative John Brademas of Indiana looked around the House when he arrived in the late 1950s and discovered that he was the only Greek-American in the place, just as Jacob Javits was the only Jew in the Senate for much of his long service.

It takes special people to lead in Congress. Experience is vital, and it takes a safe electoral base to get that in most cases. The ability to negotiate and the capacity to accept compromise are important. Dependability is absolutely essential: double-dealers are shunned. Exceptional intelligence is not necessary and in fact can cause resentment. And, as in most things, luck helps—some of the men in the list that follows do not have all of the qualifications of the model leader, but all have been fortunate enough to be members of Congress at a time when the talents they have were in demand.

THE TOP FIFTEEN ON CAPITOL HILL
1. Howard H. Baker Jr.
Americans make much of their distaste for the Old World notion of hereditary aristocracy, but a stranger studying the country's history and the people who shaped it might wonder if they meant it. For

decades or even centuries, certain families—the Adamses, Lodges, and Kennedys of Massachusetts, the Harrisons and Byrds of Virginia, the Tafts of Ohio, and the Browns of California, for a few—keep turning up in the high places of American government. One such family is the Bakers of Tennessee.

Howard Baker's father and stepmother were members of the House from Tennessee. His father-in-law, Everett M. Dirksen of Illinois, was the Senate Republican leader for 10 years, and Baker's daughter, Cynthia, wants to return the family name to the House.

Baker skipped that step. Elected to the Senate at 41 in 1966, he became the Republican leader in 1977 and in 1981 became the majority leader of a Senate divided 53–47 in favor of the GOP. It was the first time in a quarter of a century that the Republicans controlled the Senate.

And, with a popular Republican President in the White House, a three-vote majority in the Senate, and a conservative mood in the country, Baker would appear to have had a piece of cake. But the party division in the Senate can be misleading because, among other factors, there is nothing like a six-year term to make a politician feel as independent as a hog on ice. Baker, for example, has to lead about a dozen senators of both the new and old right who regard him as suspiciously liberal and about half that number who think he is far, too far, to the right.

To complicate matters, Baker made a stab at the Republican presidential nomination in 1980, and that makes some of his colleagues believe he is interested in the Senate only as a springboard to the White House (the same beef Senate careerists cite against the Kennedys), while Reagan zealots at both ends of Pennsylvania Avenue watch him narrowly for the least sign of disloyalty to the President.

But Baker took over and ran the Senate with skill and aplomb. The White House wanted no diversions from the budget and tax bills, and Baker kept the Senate's nose to the economic grindstone while fending off panting right-wingers who demanded action yesterday on such explosive and time-consuming issues as abortion and busing. Environmentalists may have been outraged by his fast shuffle on the Tellico Dam amendment, but few in Congress were.

Although operating with a far less open show of partisanship than the House GOP leaders, Baker still kept all but one or two of his people on the reservation while luring a dozen or more Democratic votes across the party line on key votes. In all, as good a job of Senate leadership hasn't been seen since Lyndon Johnson himself stalked the chamber. Baker sometimes leads not by looking ahead but by looking back to see where his followers are going, but that has been true of many in the pantheon of American political leadership.

2. Thomas P. O'Neill Jr.

Some might regard this as comparable to giving the captain of the Titanic an award for seamanship, but in fact Tip O'Neill is and will be the most important member of the House of Representatives as long as he is Speaker. (That might not be so long—even if the Democrats retain control of the House in 1982, Tip is pushing 70 and has had some health problems that—along with both justified and cheap-shot criticism from his own side of the aisle—might persuade him to chuck the job.)

In any case, Tip's biggest problem is that there are a lot of people who remember Sam Rayburn—in many cases inaccurately.

The rap on O'Neill is that he can't seem to hold the House Democratic majority against Reagan in key confrontations. The widely-held belief is that Mr. Sam was able to control his troops during the Eisenhower years, but the truth is that Rayburn did business with the White House whenever he could and often lost—to the same kind of Republican-southern Democratic coalition that has been bedeviling O'Neill—when he or Lyndon Johnson couldn't cut a deal.

Furthermore, Rayburn had a far more moderate GOP administration to deal with, and, except for the Communist-hunters who were in full cry then, fewer right-wing avenging angels in the House. Rayburn also had far more control over congressional perquisites such as committee assignments and foreign travel than Tip has, and had to deal with fewer special interests that now can pull members away from their party leaders.

But the Speaker does still control the program and pace of the House, and O'Neill probably could have given the White House fits in 1981 if he and his committee chairmen had come down with a case of the congressional "slows" on the Reagan economic bills. That weapon might still be unsheathed as the President and his advisers dig even deeper into social programs and try to wipe the slate clean of Democratic legislation dating back to the New Deal.

Tip is a cartoonist's dream. His heavy frame, rubbery face, and shock of white hair make him a living caricature of the old-time comic strip politician, and, of course, he comes directly from the James Michael Curley tradition of Boston. (This image is so pronounced that the Republicans in 1980 hired a portly professional actor who looked like O'Neill to portray in TV commercials all that they hoped voters would reject in Democratic political dominance.)

Actually, O'Neill is no mere hack politician. His congressional district is the one represented for two terms by John F. Kennedy and his constituents include the faculties and students of Harvard, Radcliffe, Massachusetts Institute of Technology, and Boston University—not the kind of people who can be herded to the polls by cigar-chomping ward bosses. Tip was one of the first leading House Democrats to oppose the Vietnam War, but because the district also contains an ethnic and economic mix that makes Irish stew as plain as vanilla custard, he speaks out for the blue collars as well as the tweed jackets.

O'Neill makes a good target for Republicans and frustrated Democrats alike, but he probably has been as good or better a Speaker as Carl Albert or John McCormack. As a party leader, he certainly has done better than his opposite numbers in the Senate, who appeared in the first year of the Reagan Presidency to have joined hands and inelegantly dived into the tank.

3. Robert H. Michel

Bob Michel looks like a Peoria insurance man, which is what he was before he got a job on the staff of Representative Harold Velde, as avid a Red-baiter as ever peered into a pumpkin. Michel succeeded Velde after 1956, but concentrated on becoming a political and legislative workman.

His labors paid off in 1981, when, at age 58, he won the House Republican leadership in a contest against the flashier Representative Guy Vander Jagt of Michigan. Since then, he has done just what a minority leader is supposed to do—hold his votes solid and try to make defectors from the majority welcome when their votes are needed.

No one could have done the first part of the job better; Michel frequently had all the Republicans lined up and ready to vote for Reagan legislation. But the Illinois Republican is a fierce partisan and several times had difficulty restraining the impulse to gloat over the Democratic disarray in the House.

Michel actually had little to do with luring the Democratic Boll Weevils who gave Reagan his budget and tax victories in 1981. The credit for that went to the Great Communicator himself, with the skilled hand-holding of White House congressional lobbyist Max Friedersdorf as backup. Michel concentrated on keeping the small band of moderate Republicans—"Gypsy Moths"—happy and is credited with getting them some concessions on the tax bill. Too bad for him they didn't stay happy.

4. Gillespie V. Montgomery

If you have never heard of "Sonny" Montgomery, that's fine with this shrewd and courtly Mississippi Democrat. He is the all-but-invisible leader of the House Boll Weevils and as such ranks right up there with the official party functionaries in congressional clout.

Montgomery, a 16-year House member and chairman of its

Veterans Committee, is listed only as a member of the 40-plus-strong Conservative Democratic Forum (two-term Representative Charlie Stenholm of Texas is the official leader), but almost everyone involved with the group points to Montgomery as the principal adviser and tactician. His position was more or less established early in the year when Tip O'Neill made a special appeal to "the [National Guard] general from Mississippi" for party unity. O'Neill got a smile as Montgomery led his southern Democratic cohorts over to the Republican side.

Montgomery, sixtyish and bearing a fleeting resemblance to Laurence Olivier, has been voting conservative ever since he came to Congress but never had the opportunity to be on the winning side before. Like the leader of the Boll Weevils in the 1950s, Representative Howard Smith of Virginia, Montgomery prefers inside work and helped negotiate a private deal in 1980 under which the southerners got several key committee assignments in return for a solid vote to elect O'Neill as Speaker. He hoped to the end that the Reagan administration would have cut a deal on taxes with the House Democratic leadership, but when negotiations foundered, he went with the President.

Montgomery's White House contact is Vice-President George Bush, with whom he came to Congress in 1967 and also with whom he regularly engages in sweaty paddleball matches in the House gym.

5. Robert J. Dole

Bob Dole has been around national politics for a long time, but the 58-year-old Kansas Republican senator has enjoyed precious few big victories. He went to the Senate in 1969 after eight years in the House, served as GOP national chairman in 1971–72 (knowing nothing about Watergate), ran with Jerry Ford as vice-presidential candidate in 1976 (and was accused of hurting the ticket with his hobnail debate tactics against Fritz Mondale). He reached for the brass ring himself in 1980 and quickly fell off the merry-go-round.

He finally got some critical acclaim in 1981 when he took over chairmanship of the Senate Finance Committee and steered the biggest and most heavily-contested tax bill in a quarter century to passage.

Dole is extremely bright and well-connected (his wife, Libby, is one of Reagan's top aides), but he has a tongue sharp enough to shave cactus. For the first time in local memory, however, he didn't say anything to lose votes in the tax battle and got the bill through without having to trade away nearly as much to oil state senators—Russell Long of Louisiana and Lloyd Bentsen of Texas rank high on his committee—as the House stewards of the Reagan measure.

He is no doctrinaire right-winger and has been a longtime supporter of the food stamp program (though this is hardly a leftist stance to the farmers of Kansas). He remains in a key position because it is his committee that has jurisdiction over Social Security, health insurance, and welfare, as well as international trade issues.

6. Jesse Helms

A reconstructed Democrat who stepped directly from a television studio (his commentaries were a conservative smash hit on North Carolina TV screens) to the Senate as a Republican in 1972, Helms is the radical right's most strategically-placed member of Congress.

He became chairman of the Agriculture Committee in 1981 (the better to protect tobacco subsidies from Dave Stockman's busy axe), but his impact is much wider than on farm issues. Helms, perhaps more than any other New Right figure in Washington, is able to bring pressure to bear on the White House and congressional Republicans alike to redeem the promises made in 1980 on "hot button" social, economic, and foreign policy issues.

Helms is not one of those senators who mellows once he gets to Washington. He proved his ideological purity by calling Nixon an appeaser for going to Peking, and the Reagan administration treats him with the respect due an unexploded bomb.

Almost as seasoned and successful a "communicator" as Reagan himself, the 60-year-old Helms probably has the influence to lead the New Right out of the President's camp if he concluded Reagan was straying from the starboard course of the true faith. And there are few people in Washington who have watched him who think Helms hasn't got the gall to do it.

7. Dan Rostenkowski

There was a time when many in Washington had Danny Rostenkowski pegged as six feet two inches and 225 pounds of political lightweight.

That was when Richard Daley was running Chicago in person and the city's big congressional delegation by long-distance telephone. Rostenkowski, just 30 when he arrived in 1959 to represent a Northwest side district, spent years on the Washington end of that phone connection relaying Da Mare's instructions.

But Rostenkowski turned out to be more than just a Daley creation. In the 1970s he was pushed aside in maneuvering for House leadership posts, but he came back at the end of the decade as chairman of the tax-writing Ways and Means Committee; he is an intimate of Tip O'Neill and Democratic Leader Jim Wright of Texas and a speculative contender for the speakership in the not too distant future.

Rosty's first big legislative test was the 1981 tax cut, and he did his damnedest to put a Democratic label on it. He was, in fact, more willing to compromise with the President than were Reagan's own men when negotiations broke down into a bidding contest for oil and other special-interest support.

The Republicans won after a Reagan-induced deluge of mail, telegrams, and phone calls hit Congress from outside Washington—but Rostenkowski came out of it having tried to help the lower middle class and with an issue that the Republicans will be hearing a lot more about in 1982. Rosty took his lumps with the other Democratic leaders, but no one believed the former messenger boy had disgraced himself or hurt his chances to continue up the ladder in the House. At age 54, he still has lots of time to climb.

8. Pete V. Domenici

Pete Domenici is a handsome and affable fellow from Albuquerque who ended a 36-year Democratic grip on New Mexico's Senate seats when he was elected in 1972 to succeed the venerable Clinton Anderson. Until 1981, that was about it for Domenici, but at 49 he became chairman of the Senate Budget Committee and delivered a virtuoso performance.

With half his 12-member Republican majority consisting of freshmen and with only one other GOP senator besides himself with more than four years of experience, Domenici started work even before the 97th Congress convened to master the staggering detail that was required to reverse a 50-year trend of spending increases by the federal government.

When he was finished, Domenici had not only given Reagan the $35 million-plus in budget cuts the President requested, but had effectively established his own independence by summarily rejecting Budget Director Stockman's push to have the Senate accept the House-passed bill, which was covered with the budget chief's fingerprints.

The House-Senate conference on the bill involved more than 270 members—nearly half the total Congress—but Domenici kept the legislation moving in a hectic two-week series of meetings and held the line against more experienced House Democrats. He also made a big move toward the top in the Senate.

9. Russell B. Long

Huey Long's boy Russell never duplicated his daddy's fame, but at 64 he has achieved a lot more than inveterate detractors of the Louisiana Democratic dynasty would have conceded when he came to the Senate in 1948.

Long was, during Democratic control of the Senate, its most

powerful committee chairman, and he retains considerable influence now as ranking minority member of the Finance Committee.

Puffy and porky like his father, Long hurt himself during the 1960s with what was described (but seldom in that era's kinder press) as a drinking problem and in fact probably blew a chance to become Democratic leader of the Senate. But after taking over Finance in 1965, he was almost all business—a tough advocate for home-state gas and oil and, like Huey, for government benefits for the elderly.

Russell got much of what he wanted in the 1981 tax bill and didn't add much to the weak Democratic presence on the legislation. But Reagan and his men should regard Long as a pushover only at their own grave risk. He will be heard from.

10. Phil Gramm

Phil Gramm, not yet 40, is the closest to a media star the new southern Democratic bloc in the House can boast. A former professor of economics at Texas A&M University, Gramm has represented an east-central Texas district since 1979, but it wasn't until 1981 that he came to public attention as the Democratic cosponsor of the "bipartisan" administration budget bill.

Tall, tousled, and rumpled, Gramm may appear to some to be unorganized, but in fact he has a sharper mind and wit than about 90 percent of his House colleagues, and he is always ready to prove it in debate.

Some Democrats feel Gramm sold out his party by making common cause with the Republicans on the budget cuts, but Tip O'Neill is too smart to countenance a witch-hunt to purge dissenters. Gramm, who will tell anyone with a camera, microphone, or notebook exactly what is wrong with liberalism in several thousand well-chosen words, probably would love to be read out of the national Democratic Party. That would give him the opportunity to run in either party in Texas and as a martyr to boot.

Gramm, a member of the Budget Committee, probably is not fated for bigger things in the Congress, where his style of showboating is considered bad form. But he could go on to bigger things in Texas or even national government . . . if supply-side economics really works.

11. Edward M. Kennedy

Teddy Kennedy, although judged a better senator than either of his brothers, and after 20 years in government probably better qualified for the Presidency than they were, is on this list as a symbol that may have become a historical curiosity.

Teddy was supposed to have completed the work that Jack and Bobby started. But his own appetites and a lot of bad luck have left Kennedy, now 51, with only a slim hope of restoring Camelot.

When the Republicans took over the Senate, Kennedy abandoned his top spot on the Judiciary Committee to become the ranking Democrat on the Labor and Human Resources Committee. From that redoubt he hoped to fight off Reaganite attacks on the social programs installed by liberal Democrats, whose champion he remains.

The Republicans outflanked him and other Senate liberal tigers by cutting and eliminating the programs through the budget process, leaving Kennedy with little recourse other than delaying tactics that only made Democrats as well as Republicans angry.

Few doubt he will try to lead a liberal resurgence in the 1984 presidential year, fueled with the blood, sweat, and tears of victims of Reagan's spending cuts.

12. Paul Laxalt

The Republican senator from Nevada has some unique claims to fame. He is the first senator of Basque extraction and the first, at least on the record, to own part of a gambling joint. And, when he was governor of Nevada, Laxalt actually talked to Howard Hughes . . . on the phone.

He also is a personal friend of Ronald Reagan, having served as his campaign chairman in 1976 and 1980, and was one of three senators invited to the President's first birthday party in the White House. In Washington, all of this means that Laxalt appears to have influence in the White House, and in Washington, the perception of power usually becomes the reality thereof.

It appeared for some time this would be tested by the White House decision on locating the MX missile, but when the governor came forward with an offer to accept the weapon despite previous objections, a confrontation was avoided. Some people saw a fine Basque hand in this development.

His wife, Carol, is something of a society figure and has modeled bathing suits for charity fashion shows.

13. James R. Jones

Jim Jones learned his way around Washington as a congressional aide for three years and then in a four-year stint at the feet of Lyndon Johnson in the White House. He also learned something about politics from LBJ.

He proved that, after winning his fifth term in an Oklahoma House seat in 1980, by leapfrogging several senior Democrats to win the chairmanship of the powerful Budget Committee. Jones, like Rostenkowski, lost his first battle to the surging Republican-Boll Weevil combine in 1981, but handled himself with enough class and know-how for most observers to put him on their list of comers.

Only 43, Jones is no political glamor boy, but he is said to be in good shape politically in his hometown of Tulsa despite efforts by the ultraright National Conservative Political Action Committee to picture him as a liberal.

14. Barber Conable

Barber Conable, a safe, sound, and solid Republican, represented an upstate New York House district in and around Rochester for 16 years without attracting too much attention. But in 1981, as ranking GOP member of the Ways and Means Committee, it became his job to beat O'Neill and Rostenkowski on the tax bill.

He carried it off, though some who knew him said Conable was queasy about the idea of a supply-side tax cut in the first place and not happy about all the deals that had to be made to corral the needed votes. But Conable, 59, now should be a key man in the GOP House hierarchy, especially if the Republicans take control in 1983.

15. Guy Vander Jagt

If the Republicans do end 30 years of minority status by taking over the House in the next election, Guy Vander Jagt will get a lot of the credit.

A 50-year-old lawyer who also had theological training and is regarded as the House GOP's best speaker (he delivered the keynote address at the 1980 Republican National Convention), Vander Jagt has made his mark as chairman of the House Republican Congressional Campaign Committee since 1978.

Vander Jagt has the campaign committee so well organized that the Democrats openly admitted in 1981 that they were going to start copying his methods. If Vander Jagt really can beat the tradition that the party in the White House loses congressional seats in midterm elections, he may be in a position to make another bid for the top rungs of the House GOP leadership ladder—as floor leader or perhaps even as Speaker.

Black Nightshirts

THE FEDERALIST PAPERS described the Supreme Court as "the least dangerous branch" of the federal government. The argument was that it can't tax, it doesn't control the army, and it is beholden to the rest of government for the enforcement of its rulings.

Indeed, when Chief Justice John Marshall came down on the side of the Indians in the famous 1831 *Cherokee Nation* v. *State of Georgia,* President Andrew Jackson is reported to have said, "Marshall has made his law; now let him enforce it." He could not. A year later, the Congress passed the Indian Removal Acts, and the poor Cherokees were dragged off and set forth on the Trail of Tears.

Times have changed, especially as concerns minority rights. The Court's 1954 *Brown* v. *Board of Education* school desegregation ruling was enforced by President Eisenhower and the U. S. Army. A federal judge in Chicago recently took over local police hiring powers to assure black representation on the force. With its 1973 abortion decision, the high court found itself looking into the womb of every woman in America. In a nation of lawyers, courts don't need taxes or armies to be powerful.

There has been a movement in recent years to curb the powers of the federal judiciary, and more than 30 pieces of legislation were introduced in 1981 designed to remove court jurisdiction from a number of aspects of American life, most of them matters dear to right-wing zanies like prayer in the schools.

It is unlikely they will come to anything. The Supremes would simply declare any measure limiting their jurisdiction unconstitutional, and the ensuing clash would be more than any but the most ardent right-winger would want to endure.

Of course, Washington does enjoy a good fight, and it hasn't had a really good time since Watergate.

Washington is home to the two most important and powerful court jurisdictions in the nation: the Supreme Court of the United States and the U.S. Court of Appeals for the District of Columbia.

The workings of the Supremes have been amply documented, or at least rumored, in best-selling books, newspaper and magazine articles, television commentaries, learned bar journals, and the sermons of the Moral Majority. All that's known for sure about what goes on back there where they put on those black nightshirts comes from their opinions and public comments, along with whatever divinations can be made from their backgrounds.

In addition to the sage jurists' knowledge of the law and the Constitution, their principal tool is time. As befits a group dominated by graybeards, there is a great deal of waiting involved in the job. It's been said by legal scholars that the high court's virtue is a passive one, that it has the mechanism "to avoid deciding the great issues in great terms" and makes good use of it, putting off momentous decisions until it feels the country and its institutions are ready. It was Abraham Lincoln, not the Supreme Court, who abolished slavery. The federal income tax had to be put back on the books through a constitutional amendment after the Supremes ruled it unconstitutional.

It's easy for the justices not to decide things. Of the thousands of cases appealed to it, the court agrees to hear only about 160 a year.

With the exception of the aging William Brennan, there is no one now on the court of the stature of an Oliver Wendell Holmes or Felix Frankfurter. Whatever Richard Nixon had in mind for it, the Burger court is in no way a conservative version of the liberal Warren court, and in no way an activist court. Yet, neither is it complacent and passive. Rather, it's a confused court. It always seems to be coming down foursquare for disagreement. In one case, it tendered seven different opinions. Its landmark death-penalty decision at once upheld the constitutionality of capital punishment and made it almost impossible to carry out. Its landmark 1973 abortion decision required numerous fix-up landmark abortion decisions. The last one, a ruling that the federal government is not required to pay for abortions, was rendered with a typically narrow vote of five to four.

As it stands, the Burger court is likely to be remembered most for its latest addition, Sandra O'Connor, the first lady Supreme. But she will more properly belong to what may come to be known as the Reagan court. With five of the justices at least as old as he is, Reagan may have an excellent chance to "pack the court" constitutionally.

The trouble is, as Dwight Eisenhower discovered with Earl Warren, once they get on the court, the leopards always seem to change their spots, deferring more to posterity and the constitution than to their ideology. And there's absolutely nothing the President can do about it. The Supreme Court, like the District Court of Appeals just beneath it, has this strong advantage in terms of maintaining the balance of powers: it is utterly lobby-proof. No other branch of government can say the same.

Often called "the little Supreme Court," the U.S. Court of Appeals in the District of Columbia is without question the second most important in the land. It is the court of the Administrative Procedure Act, the chief screening house for the Supremes, the court people turn to when they wish to contest new federal laws and regulations, the court in which the federal government defends itself. Its 11 full-time and 2 senior judges take on as many as 8 cases a day, or between 1,500 and 2,000 a year, of which only about 10 percent reach the highest court. The little Supremes have also dealt with a large body of criminal law, setting all sorts of precedents in cases involving insanity, search and seizure, and arrest procedures.

The local federal district court gets a few government regulation cases and an awful lot of drug busts. One of its more interesting burglary cases eventually made household words of the names of Judges John Sirica and Gerhard Gesell and a building called Watergate. A little-known but extremely powerful judicial group are the federal administrative law judges, some 1,200 in number, who decide civil cases involving federal agencies like the Federal Mine Safety and Health Review Commission. Even less known, in fact, downright secret, is the Federal Foreign Intelligence Surveillance Court. We can't tell you exactly what it does. The first question that George Hart, the secret court's head judge, faced in an interview with the *Washington Star* was: "Would you discuss, at least in general terms, the new Foreign Intelligence Surveillance Court that you will head?" His reply: "No, I'm not at liberty to discuss that."

There are some local city courts, but they largely handle petty crimes and police matters. You hardly ever see one of the pin-striped, vested-suit boys in them, unless some pooh-bah client is trying to fight a traffic ticket—which, incidentally, is extremely difficult to do in Washington.

The cases that come the Supreme Court's way are not all *Brown* v. *Board of Education,* or *United States* v. *Nixon.* A more typical case, now six years old and still struggling through the courts, is the one brought by the small Fleer Corporation of Philadelphia against the giant Topps Chewing Gum Company of Brooklyn, both of them purveyors of chewing gum baseball cards still collected by children in the hundreds of thousands. The case, naturally, is almost incomprehensibly complicated, but the main issue is Fleer's contention that Topps (which sells 500 million baseball cards annually) has cornered the baseball card market with its long-standing practice of signing up hordes of minor league players for nominal sums for exclusive rights to their bubble gum cards, then holding them to it should any of them make the majors and become famous. Fleer charged that this violated the antitrust statutes. Federal Judge Clarence Newcomer agreed, allowing Fleer to sign its own contract with the Major League Baseball Players Association. But, predictably, Topps appealed. The lower court proceedings thus far have included testimony from a drug store pharmacist who sells baseball cards, a great deal of judicial passing around of baseball cards, and, for some reason, a statistical presentation by a nuclear physicist.

A lawyer lobbyist fixer might have suggested simplifying things by just going to The Hill and getting a law changed, or passed. Or, better, getting the Congress to create a Bubble Gum Baseball Card Commission.

But then, that might only mean more lawsuits. Suing the government has become a national craze, or, in lawyers' terms, a highly profitable new industry. In 1980, for example, the Justice Department found itself involved in 97,205 cases, ranging from old swine flu complaints to civil rights problems concerning Cuban refugees. Complicating matters are the endless oars stuck in by amicus curiae or "friend of the court" groups, who love to intrude in disputes involving others. The American Civil Liberties Union is one of the busier of these busybodies.

As cannot be said of all federal jurisdictions, there have been very few really bad judges on the Washington bench, and an exceptional number of quite good ones. If the ghost of John Marshall came around, he would not be disappointed by the people on the following list. In fact, he'd probably wish one or two had been around in his time.

THE TOP FIVE JUDGES IN WASHINGTON

1. Justice William Brennan

Any one justice on the Supreme Court of the United States is perforce more powerful, influential, prestigious, and presumably more able than anyone else involved in American law. As all the justices have an equal say and vote, they should all be included as No. 1 here, and in a sense they are.

But William Brennan, the senior justice after Burger, is the giant among equals, the heavyweight on the highest bench. That he is often in the minority is perhaps further testament to this. A Harvard man appointed by Eisenhower in 1956, Brennan is a liberal with a strong sense of decency and devotion to the Constitution. A painstaking scholar, he writes the best and most studied opinions on the court. His only drawbacks are age and failing health, which may bring about his retirement far too soon for the good of his court and his country.

Chief Justice Warren Burger is a better judge than his liberal critics allow, perhaps a good judge, but he is not the great judge that his position or that No. 1 ranking require. Sometimes he is as cantankerous in his legal opinions as he is with the press, and he's more a legal handyman than a craftsman. However, he deserves credit as a major driving force for sensible and overdue courtroom and law practice reforms, and he sure does look like a chief justice.

Harry Blackmun, like Burger a Nixon appointee from Minnesota, has shown considerable independence from his statemate. A moderate, he is very conscientious and works very, very hard to compensate for his less than brilliant legal scholarship. He seems not to understand the lawmaking process entirely.

Thurgood Marshall, an LBJ appointee, is the most liberal member of the court and its only black. His opinions reflexively bring forth doctrinaire liberal views but not overwhelming arguments in support of them. They are greatly steeped in compassion, however.

Lewis Powell, yet another Nixon appointee, is a courtly, gracious southern gentleman, noted for the intellectual consistency of his views. He is as fond of corporate America as Justice Marshall is of black people.

William Rehnquist, also appointed by RN, is a brilliant legal scholar and craftsman and one of the most popular fellows on the court. His conservatism can get a trifle out of hand, though, such as when he supported District police in their activities during the 1971 Washington antiwar disorders, despite their rounding up of hundreds of people at random and throwing them into what amounted to concentration camps.

John Paul Stevens, Gerald Ford's only Supreme Court appointment, is a nice fellow with a good mind. He bothers some people, though, for so frequently taking great pains to posit himself in the ideological middle and on neutral ground constitutionally. The middle ground is often behind the eight ball, especially with this court.

Byron "Whizzer" White, by far a better football player turned judge than Congressman Jack Kemp is a football player turned economic genius, was deputy attorney general under Bobby Kennedy when Bobby urged brother Jack to put him on the Supreme Court. JFK agreed, but subsequently told Arthur Goldberg it was his biggest mistake. Whizzer isn't *that* bad. He was a Rhodes Scholar, after all. Not many Detroit Lions or Pittsburgh Steelers can say that.

2. Sandra Day O'Connor

Sandra O'Connor, the new girl on the bench, is certainly more intellectual, personable, and attractive than the character played by Jill Clayburgh in the ridiculous movie *First Monday in October,* about a fictitious first woman on the Supreme Court. But there are more important reasons for Mrs. O'Connor to warrant her own place and second place on this list.

She must bear the constant burden and discipline of coming to the high court in one of the Reagan Republican Party's few affirmative-action programs and of largely fulfilling one of Reagan's more intelligent campaign promises. She was chosen with great care. Her qualifications are sound and respectable. But they would not have been enough to put a man in her seat—certainly not with the extraordinary ease with which her own appointment was secured. The slipshod work and opprobrious behavior that some of her colleagues have been able to get away with from time to time will never be tolerated on her part. She will be closely watched for years.

But thus far her grades have been A +. There has been a diligence, care, and thoughtfulness to her work remarkable for any judge. And there is also a highly visible streak of strong and honorable character.

Yet if her chief qualifications seemed to amount only to having been a classmate of Justice Rehnquist's at Stanford and a state court judge, she brings a highly valuable strength to Supreme Court deliberations, an advantage that very few justices have had in recent decades: as a former Arizona state legislator, she has actually had some long and hard experience with making laws.

3. Abner Mikva

The U.S. Court of Appeals for the District of Columbia isn't, of course, Abner Mikva's court, or Skelly Wright's court, or Carl McGowan's court. It remains, likely for eternity, David Bazelon's court. Appointed to it by Harry Truman in 1949 and its chief judge from 1963 until he assumed senior status in 1979, Judge Bazelon transformed it into one of the great forces for social change in the nation and, with the explosion of government occasioned by the Great Society, the second most powerful judicial jurisdiction of them all.

Skelly Wright, who served as Bazelon's successor until stepping down upon reaching the age of 70, has remained on active status and continues to be one of the most highly regarded judges on the court. The court's scholarly Judge Carl McGowan, who served briefly as Wright's successor, is another heavyweight. It is not a court noted for weakness.

Mikva, a Carter appointee, stands out not only because of his relative youth (he was born in 1926) or because he was a liberal activist (liberal judges are of considerably more consequence during conservative Republican administrations than liberal Democratic ones), but because he's the only judge on the D. C. Appeals Court with legislative experience, having been a state legislator like Justice O'Connor and also a highly regarded member of Congress.

Half the cases to come before the Supremes and the D. C. Court of Appeals involve legislation and statutory construction. An understanding of the legislative process, or, more to the point, the congressional process, is imperative and ought to be required.

Justice Blackmun, for one, is frequently complaining about the vagueness of the laws Congress passes: "Why can't they state it more clearly?" What he fails to understand is that legislation, especially controversial legislation, must of necessity be somewhat vague if it is to pass. You don't go out of your way to reveal all its true intents, purposes, and possibilities, and thus scare away potential supporters. You offer it as "merely" a bill.

Also, there is a great deal of rhetoric incorporated into legislation that is not intended to be taken completely literally. Congress writes laws that promise or hint at more than Congress really has in mind. In a recent case involving a Department of Transportation requirement that cities install elevators for the handicapped on all city buses—when cities were willing to provide other means of transportation—judges more conservative than Mikva were siding with the DOT because they thought it was the express wish of Congress. Mikva knew better, and decided against DOT. Taxpayers were saved millions of dollars a year, and the handicapped still got rides.

When next there's a liberal Democrat in the White House, presuming the Reagan epoch is not eternal, and a vacancy among the Supremes, the studious yet savvy Mikva will be a much-mentioned candidate.

4. Robert Bork

The man most likely to be Ronald Reagan's next Supreme Court appointment, Robert Heron Bork is the brightest and soundest Republican legal mind around, a credit to his great friend and mentor, the late and much-revered Professor Alexander Bickel of Yale University. Bork, solicitor general in the Nixon administration, was the leading candidate for Reagan's first appointment to the Supreme Court on the basis of legal qualifications alone. But Reagan felt it necessary to fulfill his promise to seek a woman. Bork was put on hold, which is to say his name immediately went up for appointment to the D. C. Court of Appeals—a great ladder step, as Mikva might tell him, from which to ascend to the Supremes. Burger himself stood upon that step before his glorious ascension.

Famous for carrying out Nixon's orders to fire Watergate prosecutor Archibald Cox when Elliot Richardson wouldn't, Bork is a conservative intellectual widely respected as a constitutional scholar. Born in Pittsburgh in 1927, he is a University of Chicago grad who went on to become one of the heavies at Yale Law, as well as at Kirkland Ellis and the American Enterprise Institute.

5. Harold Greene (not June)

In a recent survey of federal judges throughout the country, *American Lawyer* magazine picked Harold H. Greene as the very best judge on the D.C. United States District Court, narrowly beating out the very able and respected Gerhard Gesell. Two of the factors considered in awarding Greene first place were his temperament and lack of ego.

We'll say. Most listees in *Who's Who in America* go on and on about their schools, accomplishments, clubs, and honors. Here is Greene's entire entry: "Judge, B.S., J.D., George Washington U. Judge, U.S. Dist. Ct. for D.C., 1978—Office: U.S. Dist. Ct. 3rd and Constitution Ave. N.W. Washington D.C. 20001."

The judge often is, but should not be, confused with Judge June Green, whom *American Lawyer* declared the worst federal trial judge in the District. It's not at all such a problem for him to be confused with the court's Judge Joyce Green, a much-respected fellow alum of George Washington University, who came to the federal bench after distinguished service with the D.C. Superior Court, and who has handled with great judicial skill and aplomb some of the hottest legal potatoes Washington can serve up.

Brass Hats, Dr. Strangeloves, and Spooks

I F IT weren't for the fact that it costs so horrendously much and is supposedly all that keeps us from being blasted into radioactive crisps, the American defense establishment would seem just another dull, sluggish bureaucracy. As it is, it embodies the largest bureaucracy in the federal government. About three-fifths of the federal payroll works for the Department of Defense and its ancillary agencies, 2.2. million in uniform and some 984,000 as considerably higher-paid civilians. Defense spending accounts for more than 25 percent of the federal budget and is bounding higher and higher.

Back in the 1950s, President Eisenhower complained that Washington looked like an armed camp and had orders issued that permitted and encouraged the wearing of civilian clothes. Disguised in civvies or not, Washington *is* a military camp. Not counting the Pentagon, there are 14 major military installations in the metropolitan area, including four army forts, two air force bases, a naval air base, and the U.S. Naval Academy at nearby Annapolis.

The Federal City is hardly impregnable, but the British would think twice about trying to burn it again. The Defense Department has 132,000 people laboring in the area, 56,000 of them active-duty military. Of the 40,000 working in the Pentagon building itself, 22,000 are saluters. When the spit-and-polish Reagan administration, shortly after taking office, huffily ordered everyone out of Eisenhower civvies and back into uniforms, some terrified commuters wondered if the country had suddenly gone on full alert.

Your run-of-the-mill Washington bureaucrat's occupational skills may run to calculating crop subsidies or pondering actuarial tables. That nice colonel riding the Metro to work may have in his briefcase neat stuff on better ways to vaporize Omsk. The American military has at its—if not our—disposal 500,000 times the nuclear destructive power we had in hand in 1945. The fabled "Triad" of missile-firing submarines, bombers, and ICBMs theoretically can wipe out 80 percent of the Soviet Union's industrial base and government centers

49

and all sorts of other juicy targets, and still have a thousand weapons left in case World War III has a second act.

Aside from maintaining hundreds of highly labor-intensive military installations throughout the United States (about the only vote Bella Abzug ever cast for a defense bill in Congress was in favor of a measure to keep the all-important Fort Drum and Watervliet Arsenal in New York State), the DOD operates a far-flung empire of bases in 25 foreign countries or possessions, including such hardship posts as Bermuda. And in all these places it runs hospitals, restaurants, laundries, movie theaters, grocery stores, tennis courts, saloons, swimming pools, bowling alleys, clothing stores, yacht harbors, riding stables, and no fewer than 300 golf courses.

As awesome as the military's power and size is its cost, which, until America is "rearmed" to the Reagan administration's satisfaction, may be the most terrifying thing about it. Admittedly, the generals and admirals have reason to gripe that these are not the gravy days. In 1952, the $46 billion defense budget amounted to 49 percent of federal spending. In 1976, we were spending $90 billion on the military, but it was only 26.9 percent of total outlays. Jimmy Carter's last military budget was $130 billion, but only 22.9 percent of total spending. At its most optimistic, the paradise promised the military by the Reagan administration comes to a 32.4 percent slice of the federal pie.

Yet the cost of individual items nowadays is enough to make a World War II-era congressman do laps around the ceiling of the Armed Services Committee hearing room. The revived B-1 (variant) bomber, the modern-day strategic equivalent of the B-17, costs $250 million (each!), something like 10,000 percent more than the Flying Fortress cost. An airplane like that, the American taxpayer would like to see exhibited behind bulletproof glass in the Smithsonian, not up in the sky where someone can shoot at it.

Most of the other weapons cost less, but not that much less. Killer satellites, which, given the balance of technology, can be knocked down by the Russians as quickly as we can knock down theirs, run between $80 and $100 million each, depending on extras. A jet fighter costs some $40 million. In the 1950s, we were able to outfit the fly-boys with 3,000 new fighters a year. Tops, now, is 400 a year, and so many of those go to the Arabs and Venezuelans. Helicopters? Now more than $30 million each, and we knocked off three in the Iranian desert doing nothing more aggressive than trying to carry out President Carter's peculiar refueling plans.

The humble tank is now a $2 million to $3 million vehicle, and any one of them can be knocked out at night by a $1,000 parachute bomb.

The trend is not what taxpayers' groups consider a happy one.

According to the CIA, whose top bureaucrats understand budgets if not international politics, the Soviets have been outspending us by 50 percent a year on arms, lavishing between 11 and 12 percent of their gross national product on them since 1970. The best we did since 1964 was 8 percent, and we were down to 5.7 percent when Reagan came in.

There's a problem with the kind of catch-up that's being played: it's easy to match the Soviets dollar-for-ruble (if you don't mind giving up a few food stamps), but will that match them weapon-for-weapon? After the Vietnam War, the defense industry atrophied and diversified into nonmilitary manufacturing to the lamentable point where the only thing it was prepared to produce in a real hurry was cost-overruns. Hence such interesting high-level notions as having the mighty United States buy its submarines abroad. Defense remains the most inflation-prone major segment of the national economy.

And inflation has been killing our military (in terms of desert rescue missions, quite literally). Cost-of-living pay increases and zooming fuel costs add billions to the defense budget every year without adding a single weapon. As it is, our pilots are allocated enough fuel only for about 10 hours of flying a month. Israeli pilots fly 30 hours a month. According to the American Enterprise Institute, which knows at least as much as the CIA, our antitank gunners have been firing only one missile a year in training; some pilots have fired an air-to-air missile only once in their careers, and were probably surprised that it worked.

To supply combat squadrons with enough ordnance to fly roughly a month of missions, compared to the two weeks or so they can fight now, would run us an additional $30 billion. It's no wonder Reagan picked budget expert Caspar "Cap the Knife" Weinberger as secretary of defense.

Naysayers have always thrived in the Federal City. Safe is always better than sorry. If evolution had worked the way Washington does, the highest form of life on our planet would be the slug. But nowhere do naysayers predominate as they do in the defense establishment. A subcommittee chairman in the Congress can get a farm subsidy increased with the roll of a log. A shrewd staff director on a regulatory commission usually can get a new rule imposed whether his commissioners understand it or not. The Federal Reserve can make interest rates jump up or down with the flick of a finger.

The military thinker must function rather like a Canadian goose on the opening day of hunting season. To put it another way, more American weapons systems have been shot down by Americans than by any enemy. The Russians had no defense against the neutron bomb but one: Jimmy Carter's fear of looking like a mad nukester.

If a scientist in the Defense Advanced Research Projects Agency were to come up with an idea for, say, neutralizing Soviet warheads with rocket-fired wads of Silly Putty, his brainstorm would not simply be sent up to the White House for a yea or nay. It would have to survive the opinions of the National Security Agency, the Defense Intelligence Agency, the Aerospace Defense Command, the Strategic Air Command, the secretary of the Air Force, the secretary of the Navy, the secretary of the Army, the Joint Chiefs of Staff, the undersecretary of defense for research and engineering, the assistant secretary of defense for program analysis and evaluation, the under-secretary of defense for policy, the deputy secretary of defense, the secretary of defense, the Central Intelligence Agency, the National Security Council, the assistant to the President for national security affairs, assorted White House aides, the White House chief of staff, the Vice-President (in the Reagan administration), the kitchen cabinet, the President, and probably the President's wife.

That would be before a single consultant, think tank, MIT professor, congressional staff, industry lobbyist, labor union, *Washington Post* editorial writer, NATO ally, scientific advisory board, State Department official, law firm, or environmental protest group had a shot at it.

It could be years before such a weapon went into production, as history attests. When the parachute was developed in World War I, the Germans rushed it out to their squadrons as a heaven-sent protector of their most valuable aerial asset, experienced pilots. Not us. The War Department held it back in the belief that timid pilots would too hastily abandon their aircraft. The Gatling gun was patented in 1862, but by 1876 had achieved no wider use than as a cavalry weapon mounted on camel saddles. For suggesting that the airplane could destroy actual warships, not to speak of entire cities, Billy Mitchell was given the bum's rush.

The "naysayer syndrome" has produced an unfortunate con-ditioned reflex in our military. In the hopes of getting something, the services ask for everything imaginable, including far-out weapons systems that may never work. The land-sea-air nuclear Triad evolved, not because it was necessary, but because the Army, Navy, and Air Force all wanted a piece of the atomic action. And when a "yeasayer" like Ronald Reagan gets into the White House, everything imaginable can get approved.

Ours is foremost a civilian-run military, and defense policy tends to emanate from the White House or congressional staffs more than from within the department itself (in the regulatory agencies, it tends to be the opposite). Since the late and great George C. Marshall, defense secretaries have tended to function mostly as bureaucrats, and as one senior official put it: "Bureaucrats generally start dead in the water." Eisenhower's Charlie Wilson and Kennedy's Robert McNamara were whizzes at running their automobile companies (in the days before serious Japanese competition) but were awful policy makers and not terribly good bureaucrats. Nixon's Melvin Laird and Ford's Donald Rumsfeld turned out to be pretty good bureaucrats. Though he probably had more influence over defense matters as a recognized genius in the nuclear science community, Carter's Harold Brown was an excellent bureaucrat, protecting and expanding his agency despite White House military attitudes that ranged from benign neglect to outright hostility (he ruined an otherwise blameless reputation by blatantly involving his department in Carter's reelection campaign; the good bureaucrat avoids politics the way he should the General Accounting Office).

Service secretaries function largely as spokesmen for their branches, and often come by their jobs as political rewards accorded much like ambassadorships (John Warner, Navy secretary under Nixon, is a good example). Sometimes they come to their posts simply by progressing up the Washington ladder (Cyrus Vance and Harold Brown were service secretaries before reaching the top). Sometimes they are picked because they serve some useful political purpose (like many soldiers, Clifford Alexander, Carter's Army secretary, is black). With presidential indulgence, service secretaries occasionally are allowed to set policy, as with Alexander's turning the Army into a Job Corps with guns, and Reagan's Navy secretary, John Lehman, having the notion of bringing back two World War II battleships to haunt the high seas (manpower shortages are so acute that some critics wondered if Lehman planned to have these dreadnoughts float about empty like the Flying Dutchman).

Whatever is dreamed up, the Joint Chiefs and the service high commands are usually very compliant. When Air Force General David "Davey" Jones, chairman of the Joint Chiefs of Staff, got the word that Carter had decided against production of the B-1 bomber, he may well have done six laps around the ceiling, as there was no more ardent supporter of that supersonic money bag than he. But within three hours he had orders cut declaring the B-1 a dead issue and telling everyone to get on with the Cruise missile instead.

The Joint Chiefs obediently follow the party line (one of the many problems in Vietnam), and just as obediently shift to a new party line when a new administration takes over (as when the B-1 was revived by Reagan). When asked directly by a congressional committee for their candid opinion, however, they invariably give it. Giving it without being asked remains a serious no-no. When General John Singlaub declared Carter's plan to withdraw troops from South Korea near idiocy—an opinion which shortly became almost universal—his ouster as troop commander in Korea was viewed as necessarily automatic. General Edward Rowny, a much respected figure who served as our chief military arms negotiator during Salt II, felt Carter had abandoned the goal of trying to achieve mutual, equitable arms reduction for one of simply trying to get any kind of treaty. But, to say this, Rowny had to resign. Reagan took quite a shine to him when he did.

The Navy, the most socially prestigious of the services, has been the boldest and most forthright of the three, and the most successful at getting what it wants from the White House and Capitol Hill (certainly no one would let the Air Force bring any mothballed World War II bombers back into active service). It helps that Presidents Roosevelt, Kennedy, Johnson, Nixon, Ford, and Carter were Navy men.

The Air Force, the most boy-scoutish of the three, has a reputation for building the best case for its wants and needs, and for saluting smartly and getting on with the job when it's turned down, which occurs more than it likes. Though Lyndon Johnson got his Silver Star for riding in an airplane that flew over an island believed to be occupied by the Japanese, no President has been an Air Force man.

As for the Army, which got absolutely everything it wanted in Vietnam, including airlifts of cold beer, it no longer always has its way. Tanks, rocket launchers, assorted electronic whizzies, it can have. But not what it wants and needs most: reinstitution of the draft.

The poor little Coast Guard, which is an adjunct of the Department of Transportation in peacetime, was terror-stricken at the prospect of Reagan's budget cuts, fearful that it would be treated as some sort of civilian frill like the National Endowment of the Arts. It was right. The administration stripped a thousand men and an entire officers' graduating class from Coast Guard ranks. After all, they dealt with mere drownings, not Russkies.

Especially powerful in the defense establishment are the numerous scientific and technological boards scattered over the Washington landscape. Cautious, prestigious, sophisticated, and steeped in all the latest technology and mumbo jumbo, these cerebral tag teams can derail even the soundest proposal with the arch of a brow and delay the most major decisions almost interminably with the profundity of their yak.

Another obstacle to carrying out our national policy is that national policy is usually proclaimed in the vaguest, broadest possible language—something that sounds nice on television but doesn't necessarily commit the proclaimer to anything specific enough to be acted upon or to go wrong. Just how rapid is a rapid deployment force?

How is one to respond to Carter's ringing call for "adequacy"?

The military-industrial complex that worried Eisenhower has become the military-industrial consultant think-tank academic complex. Consultants are to Washington what dandelions are to lawns. The Beltway Bandits, as the Pentagon calls them, clustered in sparkly new office buildings out in the grassier Washington suburbs, are specialists who can help the Defense Department with everything from small-arms procurement to upholstery color for killer satellites. But the grandmother of them all, the redwood among dandelions, is the California-based Rand Corporation, an amalgamation of specialists so inextricably linked to the defense establishment's power centers that the DOD probably couldn't function without it.

Rand came into prominence in the 1950s by introducing the American military to what was to become the computer age. If the Pentagon wanted to know how many unmarried Japanese-American sergeants it had on active duty in west-central Mississippi, Rand, and seemingly only Rand, could find out. Its first major project was the DEW-line early warning system, and since then the DOD has hardly made a move without Rand.

There is, as one Pentagon planner put it, "this neatly incestuous relationship." Officers not only work side by side with Rand men but enter the Rand fold themselves either through fellowships or after retirement. Sometimes very early retirement. Rand grads go back into the Defense Department, usually into such high-level jobs as program analysis and evaluation. One of the more formidable Rand grads is a chap named James Schlesinger. After he became Secretary of Defense, some of his thoughtful papers from the early 1960s were rounded up and redistributed by the Rand folk and circulated in the defense community as really neat stuff.

When Schlesinger ultimately left the Carter administration, it was to go to another Washington institution as pervasive and incestuous as the consulting firm, the think tank. Schlesinger chose a well-respected academic one, Georgetown University's Center for Strategic and International Studies. Some are not so respected. In fact, there's a think tank of some kind in Washington for almost every shade of opinion. If you want to support a theory that the 16 missiles on a single Polaris submarine can destroy life as we know it, there's an obscure think tank somewhere that will happily whip something up for you. If you want to press the notion that an all-out nuclear exchange will hardly muss our hair, you won't want for some supportive thought, either.

The think tank most Republicans listen to is the American Enterprise Institute, a World War II-era creation noted for its conservative mien and sound thinking that has come to serve as the principal intellectual and informational resource for the GOP on Capitol Hill and in the White House. Its Public Policy Project on National Defense, a continuing effort begun in 1976 and headed by former Defense Secretary Melvin Laird, got heavily into the MX missile debate, providing a forum for both sides. Both sides, of course, represented by Republicans.

The Democratic counterpart of the AEI is the long-revered Brookings Institution, whose word was always taken as gospel until the Republicans took control of the Senate in 1980. The two think tanks ride a teeter-totter, rising and falling according to elections, suffering losses of influence but never prestige. Not all that far apart on defense matters, especially as far as factual data are concerned, the two have all sorts of competition but no real rivals.

On Capitol Hill, congressional influence over defense policy derives from the principle that knowledge is power. The military and appropriations committee chairmen of necessity have power, but rely heavily on the knowledge and advice of their expert staffs. A number of other senators and congressmen have achieved a great deal of stature and influence in the field simply by becoming interested and educated in defense matters all on their own. Senators John Warner of Virginia, Gary Hart of Colorado, Sam Nunn of Georgia, and Jake Garn are stand-out examples. Hart, who directed George McGovern's pacifist, anti-Vietnam War campaign in 1972, curiously joined the Navy Reserve at the age of 43 as a lieutenant j.g. Some opined this was just so he could wear an American Legion cap should he want to enter the presidential competition.

At the White House, influence on defense matters as on all matters depends on proximity to the President. Brother Bobby helped call JFK's shots during the Bay of Pigs fiasco. Jimmy Carter bounced military stuff off the not-very-military minds of adman Gerald Rafshoon and Ham Jordan during some of the more hot and heavy moments in Iran. Ronald Reagan made it clear early on that he felt more comfortable with the opinions of aides Ed Meese and Jim Baker and Vice-President Bush than with those of anyone on the National Security Council, and happily so. It was the NSC's Richard Pipes who asserted that the United States had only two alternatives in the 1980s: Persuade the Russkies to abandon Communism, or go to war with them.

There is an old-boy network at work in the military, of course. The required steps to the top of the heap traditionally have included four years at one of the service academies, some "ticket punching" combat experience, some time at a command or staff college, assignment to the Pentagon, and attendance at the National War College at Washington's Fort McNair. Those who share these experiences remain on the lookout for one another for the rest of their careers. Pentagon duty also mingles one with powerful civilians who can be a help, as Henry Kissinger was a help to Alexander Haig. The National War College fosters school ties as strong as those at the academies, but they are formed at a much more advanced and useful career stage. Of the 160 graduated by the NWC every year, 25 to 30 percent are important civilians, mostly from the State Department, CIA, Congressional committee staffs, the OMB, and other key agencies. Not only does an up-and-coming brass hat make powerful contacts at the NWC, he learns how the civilian side of government really functions. And he learns the shortcuts.

Civilians will always have the last word, however. Military men may chafe that that word is so frequently "no," but that's the American way. There's something in the nature of this country that hates a military, at least, a Prussian-style professional one. Between wars, the Army and Navy have historically been given the shortest of shrift. In 1790, just nine years after Yorktown, we were down to exactly 80 enlisted men. After 1800, despite the constant danger of war with either Britain or France, President Jefferson allowed troop strength to decrease to only 2,732 men, whom he scattered to some 43 posts, including one at strategic Frederick, Maryland, that had two officers and just one enlisted man, a rather hen-pecked private.

We produced 38,000 troops for the War of 1812, then cut the Army back to 6,000. In 1846, General Zachary Taylor went off to fight the war with Mexico with just 4,000 men. The Spanish-American War began with our marching 28,000 soldiers off to fight 100,000 Spaniards. Pearl Harbor speaks for itself.

The problem is that World War III is to be what the generals call "a come as you are war," one in which a Pearl Harbor might be the only battle fought. The United States in this circumstance hasn't the luxury of mobilization or crash weapons development. We have to do with whatever is at hand. That is why, in both the nuclear and conventional modes, our military is supposed to be at all times equal to the other guy's. Yet, after the Vietnam War, it was allowed to go to hell almost as thoroughly as it did after the Revolutionary War.

Richard Nixon ended the draft, not because it wasn't needed, but because his action might defuse the often violently hostile antiwar movement at home. Gerald Ford declined to reinstitute the draft. Jimmy Carter made much ado about not bringing back the draft, though at the end of his term he brought back draft registration. Ronald Reagan, while promising to make the American military the mightiest in the world, vowed not to bring back the draft as well, although he went back on his word and continued draft registration.

The all-volunteer military has had a dozen years to prove itself. By the end of Carter's term it was what Senator Sam Nunn called no better than "an armed WPA." The number of functional illiterates was such that Army Secretary Clifford Alexander had intelligence scores removed from soldiers' files. A government study found only one out of ten infantry divisions, the 82nd Airborne, fit for combat. Sixty percent of our tank crews in Europe could not operate their battle sights. In 1965, 28 percent of Army draftees were high school dropouts. By 1980, no less than 46 percent of new recruits lacked high school diplomas. Six thousand sergeants in Europe and 900 in Korea had to be shipped home to take conditions in hand in stateside posts.

In 1964, our Navy had 803 ships. By 1980, it was down to 418. A support ship that had the previous year won the Navy's award for most efficient vessel had to balk at sailing orders in 1980 because it didn't have enough trained crew aboard.

The Air Force was just as bad. A readiness test of the First Tactical Fighter Wing at Langley Air Force Base in 1980 showed only 23 of the wing's 66 F-15 fighters were "mission capable," with the blame placed on a lack of trained personnel. A combat exercise staged out in the western desert (and, some say, rigged to favor the F-15) saw the F-15 clobbered by the smaller, cheaper, and supposedly out-of-date F-5. The huge C-5 transport, which is supposed to be the backbone of our Rapid Deployment Force, had to be grounded because of a structural flaw that could make the wing come "unzippered" while flying in heavy weather. The aging Titan missile began blowing up in its silos.

Reagan came into office prepared to deal with all these problems by stealing a page from the liberals: he would throw money at them. He might say "no" to the draft, but he was prepared to say "yes" to practically everything else the military wanted.

Carter had left a sandbag for his successor. After the 1980 election, the defeated Democrat proposed an exceedingly generous defense budget for 1981 (which many cynics said he would never have proposed if he had won). If Reagan called for anything less, he would be accused of being as "soft" as Jimmy Carter.

Reagan called for more, an increase from Carter's last defense budget of $171.2 billion to $226.3 billion in a single year. By 1986, he wanted $374.3 billion a year for defense. Some $1.6 trillion was to go for new weapons systems alone. It was to be a military buildup bigger than that of the Vietnam War.

During Vietnam, LBJ made the mistake of going for both "guns and butter." Reagan certainly had no interest in more butter, but he did something just as daft. While embarking on one of the biggest defense spending sprees in history, he also set about cutting federal income taxes, by a whopping 25 percent over three years. Combined with the huge fixed costs of Social Security and federal debt service, this led to the eminently predictable—an estimated budget deficit that quickly rose from $50 billion to $100 billion, and in an administration that was supposed to be the most fiscally conservative since Coolidge.

Budget cutter David Stockman saw no reason why the Defense Department should be immune from his axe, especially when the GAO and Republican congressional studies were putting waste, fraud, and mismanagement in Defense at a cost of better than $15 billion, including $6.9 million on improper, unjustified, nonmilitary use of aircraft. Caspar Weinberger, who incidentally used a military plane to repeatedly visit the vacationland of Bar Harbor, Maine, in 1981, persuaded the Old Man to tell Stockman to keep hands off.

Congress was equally respectful. The huge Pentagon waste was well documented. The administration was slashing domestic spending where constituents were telling congressmen it hurt: schools, Medicaid, highways, law enforcement, urban redevelopment, mass transit, consumer protection, and safety. Why should military procurement officers be allowed to spend as profligately as Jackie Onassis, who is said to have her silk sheets changed every time she leaves her bed?

Because there are times when it doesn't pay to be a naysayer; George McGovern and a flock of other congressional doves had gone down in flames in the 1980 election, after all. The Congress rolled over and voted the largest defense bill in history. What happened to the following weapons systems was in part the result.

The MX missile: In the 1950s, the going concept in nuclear warfare was Mutual Assured Destruction, or MAD, which meant, according to General Curtis LeMay, depopulating "vast areas of the earth's surface, leaving only vestigial remnants of man's material works." This gave way to the "no cities" approach, in which each side concentrated first on wiping out the other guy's ICBMs, and only then maybe blowing up his population centers. This led to the MIRV or multiple warhead fad and a race to build bigger and more accurate antimissile-silo missiles. By the late 1970s, the Soviets had advanced sufficiently in this race to scare American World War III experts into worrying about a "window of vulnerability"—a period of years in which the Russians probably could wipe out our land-based ICBMs before we could do much about it.

The Ford administration came up with the MX, missile experimental, in response. It was an extremely accurate new ICBM, but its chief advantage lay in what the Pentagon called its basing mode. Two hundred of these killer rockets were to be constantly rotated among 4,600 holes in the ground out in Utah and Nevada, compelling the Russians to fire off 4,600 of their own ICBMs if they wanted to get ours. (The Brookings Institution, incidentally, said that if the Russians did, the radioactive death cloud would drift east all the way to Virginia.)

The Carter administration went along with the MX, though not very enthusiastically until the 1980 campaign got underway and the need arose to compensate for Jimmy's wimp military image. The Reagan administration was at first supportive of the MX, not even blinking an eye at the $500 million in roads it would have to build to drag the missiles around on.

Others blinked. Air Force Chief of Staff General Lew Allen went out to sell the good folks of Utah and Nevada on the idea. Demonstrating why generals aren't elected President anymore, he told them they should take the MX so they could serve as a "nuclear sponge" and absorb enemy warheads. Notions like this, and the fact that the MX project would use up much of the scarce water in the vicinity, prompted such otherwise superhawk conservatives as Reagan's good friend, Nevada Senator Paul Laxalt, and the Mormon Church to think better of the MX, and inform Reagan accordingly.

Ultimately, the administration came out for only 100 MX missiles. A third were to go into existing Minuteman silos, which were to be hardened at a cost of $7 billion or more. The rest would go, well, that would be decided after the 1984 election. Would this substitute plan still confound the enemy? Well . . .

The B-1 bomber: Though missiles perform by far the major role in the nation's defense and offense, and the tactical air stuff is handled largely by the Navy, Marines, and Army, nearly all the general officers of the Air Force are pilots. This is in part responsible for the fact that we still have so many 25-year-old B-52 bombers flying around.

To replace the B-52, the flying generals proposed the B-1, a sleek, supersonic aircraft that could carry a nuclear bomb at twice the speed of a B-52 and, because of a supersecret terrain-following radar-controlled guidance device, do this at treetop level. In other words, it could do everything the Cruise missile could do—yet carry pilots, too!

The Carterites toyed with the B-1 proposal, then junked it in favor of the Cruise after a capital thriller best described as the War of the Lobbyists. The National Taxpayers Union, SANE, Environmental Action, Common Cause, the Council on Economic Priorities, the National Association of Social Workers, the Oil, Chemical, and Atomic Workers Union, assorted other unions, the Women's International League for Peace and Freedom, the Federation of American Scientists, and even former Defense Secretary Clark Clifford came out strongly against the B-1. The United Auto Workers and Rockwell International, with 140,000 stockholders, came out just as strongly for it.

So did the Reagan administration when it took office, deciding to give the Air Force's flying four-stars the B-1, some stretch F-111 bombers, and the wonderful new Stealth bomber. But by that time, the unit cost of the B-1 was up to a projected $250 million, a hundred times the cost of a World War II B-17, and the Russians were perfecting defenses that, according to some experts, could shoot down the B-1. So what? The Air Force got its planes.

ELF: The third leg of the United States' "triad" of nuclear defense and deterrence is the fleet of missile-carrying Polaris and Trident submarines. One of the drawbacks of these vessels is that, for them to communicate with home base or each other, they have to rise near the surface and trail a long antenna that can be sighted by the enemy. To overcome this difficulty, the Navy hit upon the idea of constructing a huge Extremely Low Frequency, or ELF, radio antenna grid, which could send messages through the earth itself to subs lying deep beneath the surface of the ocean.

The transmissions might be a bit slow—some 20 to 30 minutes for a four-letter word—but as a four-letter word like STOP, FIRE, or something less printable would suffice, it was deemed worth it.

The ELF grid originally was to cover about 6,600 square miles of the Upper Peninsula of Michigan and northern Wisconsin. The local residents were not keen on having the landscape hum all the time, however. The Carter administration backed away from the project, and the Navy itself backed off.

The Reagan administration started marching ahead with it, then paused. Ultimately, it came out for ELF, all right, but, as with the MX, on a slightly reduced scale. Instead of 6,600 square miles of antenna grid, there would be just two little stretches of it, one 56 miles long and the other 28 miles.

Antique battleships: If the Reagan administration stumbled a little while marching into the bold future, it did right well marching into the past. To instantly help remake the U.S. Navy into the powerful force it was in World War II, Navy Secretary John Lehman decided to bring back some actual World War II battleships. With the enthusiastic approval of the 70-year-old President, and of a somewhat bewildered but patriotic Congress, work began to recondition and recommission the U.S.S. *New Jersey* and the U.S.S. *Iowa*, along with an old aircraft carrier. That 17-inch steel plate can stop anything, Lehman boasted (without adequately explaining how it can stop a nuclear warhead), and, though you'd want to load the battlewagons up with modern missiles, rockets, and stuff like that, they would still have those swell 16-inch guns! Of course, the 40-year-old ships would cost between $500 million to $1 billion each to restore and would require trained crews of 1,500 each, plus 1,000 support personnel on shore. And, of course, most of the battleships that engaged in naval combat in World War II were sunk. But who can stand in the way of progress, even if it does take you backward?

One of the more interesting examples of how the American military functions, or doesn't, occurred in March 1981, consequent to the shooting of President Reagan at the Washington Hilton. With everyone rushing off to the hospital, the Air Force colonel carrying the black bag or "football" of nuclear war command responses was left on the sidewalk and separated from the powers that were for half an hour. Incidentally, that's about the flight time of a Russian ICBM from launch to impact.

Liberals have long carried on as though the CIA were still functioning like Wild Bill Donovan's old Office of Strategic Services, dropping provocateurs and diabolical agents behind enemy lines almost hourly and causing endless mayhem and mischief. Thus was the United States responsible for all the political catastrophe in the world. The trouble with that neat liberal orthodoxy is that it presupposes a competence far beyond what one could reasonably expect from a government agency, even a good one like the CIA.

Not all CIA covert actions have been so clumsy as to feature E. Howard Hunt disguising himself in a red wig for bedside chats with ITT lobbyist Dita Beard. But consider some of the whoppers. In 1963, the South Vietnamese generals preparing to knock off President Diem went through the CIA to get President Kennedy's permission. With CIA counsel, it was granted. As a result of the coup, South Vietnam lost all hope of governmental stability for years, inflation and corruption ran riot, the Viet Cong overran the countryside, and our massive involvement and ultimate defeat became inevitable.

The three words, "Bay of Pigs," are another testament to the agency's genius, however "evil." So is the fact that, as Lyndon Johnson reportedly discovered shortly after assuming the Presidency, Kennedy had also given the CIA the go-ahead to terminate with extreme prejudice one Fidel Castro. They had been at it three years, with some 600 case officers in Florida and an array of agents coming up with such ingeniously ridiculous schemes as doing in the bearded one with poisoned cigars and exploding seashells. Kennedy's men failed. According to some theories, Castro's men didn't, although it's as likely the Mob had a hand in Kennedy's departure as well.

An evolutionary product of Wild Bill Donovan's World War II OSS, the CIA was born with passage of the National Security Acts of 1947, just in time for the Cold War. A year later, the National Security Council authorized the agency to undertake covert activities. The idea was that if the Russians were doing it, we should be doing it, too. Even in this, they have achieved superiority.

Over the years, the CIA has been periodically if temporarily reformed. Covert activities have been halted or restrained. Congress has attempted to make the Agency more accountable (mostly by giving more congressmen and committees oversight powers). Domestic spying has been curtailed (although the Reagan administration was able to restore that practice to some degree). Restraints like the "Bush rule" banning the use of journalists as spies have come into force. But there has never been the slightest likelihood the Agency would be merged or junked. It performs its primary mission too well.

That mission is intelligence gathering and analysis. Nixon didn't think much of the agency's performance in this regard. "What use are they?" he asked aide John Ehrlichman once. "They've got 40,000 people over there reading newspapers."

Even were this nasty exaggeration true, the CIA would be worthwhile having for its assessment of what it read in the papers. In September of 1980, the White House was still puzzling over the "mystery flash" detected in the South Atlantic a year before. The Navy and the Defense Intelligence Agency, whose spy satellite observed the flash, were convinced it was a nuclear explosion, probably a South African one. The White House Office of Science and Technology decided it was a weather freak or some other mysterious phenomenon. The CIA cast its deciding vote with the DIA and the Navy, issuing a thoroughgoing secret report describing the flash as a small, tactical nuclear weapon exploded by South Africa in probable collaboration with Israel and Taiwan. The CIA conclusion prevailed.

Admiral Stansfield Turner, Jimmy Carter's unhappy choice for CIA director, never did get to realize his grandiose plan to amalgamate all American intelligence agencies under his command. He never really got to run the CIA for that matter. But he was able to get the agency reorganized into four directorates that oversee an assemblage of activities that covers everything imaginable, including two separate sections for photo analysis. The names of most of the sections, weapons intelligence, political analysis, economic research, and national intelligence officers for warning, are fairly self-explanatory. Others, such as imagery analysis, human intelligence, and national intelligence officers, are a little more vague. Human intelligence means spies.

Though comparatively tiny, the CIA remains one of the government's most powerful bureaucracies because its director, and also its deputy director, always have direct access to the President and can circumvent the almighty Joint Chiefs if it has to. Even a President who despises the CIA, as appears to have been the case with Carter, knows he ignores its intelligence at his peril.

In its first 25 years of existence, the Agency was run largely by the eastern establishment elite, an old school not unlike that of Britain's upper-class MI-6. William F. Buckley, a CIA alumnus, is typical of that CIA breed, though much more conservative than most. A surprisingly large number of CIA veterans of that vintage are liberal Democrats and *New Republic* readers. Nowadays, they tend to be less leisure-class and more middle-American professionals; high school, not prep school.

Directors Allen Dulles and Richard Helms, and counterspy James Angleton, were absolute professionals. The politicizing of the agency was actually the result of post-Watergate attempts to reform it. Of the political-appointee directors, George Bush was easily the most popular with staff and by far the most able. Dumped into the hot-seat job by Ford White House chief Donald Rumsfeld, who always liked to keep his track clear of rivals, Bush pulled the agency out of its morass and greatly improved morale, putting it back to work in a clean professional manner that satisfied both the urgent need for intelligence and the agency's horde of critics. When Bush commenced running for President in 1979, his bumper stickers sprouted all over McLean and Langley like dandelions.

Admiral Turner was considered singularly incompetent and so unpopular that some agents probably would have preferred to see Leonid Brezhnev running the place. At times it seemed as though he was. In his "October massacre" of 1977, Turner summarily fired, retired, shelved, shifted, or otherwise shafted more than 800 spooks, some of them the best in the business. By May 1979, he had gotten rid of more than 300 of the agency's top brass and top brains. If it weren't for his deputy, Frank Carlucci, the agency would have fallen apart. As it was, Carlucci, who, as a Nixon administration budget and HEW official, had had no intelligence experience, ended up in effective control.

Reagan's choice of his campaign manager, William Casey, to succeed Turner startled and irritated many (though not so much as his notion of putting the Peace Corps under the command of a former Army intelligence officer). But in fairness, Casey was a grade-A spook in his time, running the OSS's entire spy network in France and Germany during the last years of World War II. Of course, the war was a long, long, long time ago, and Casey's subsequent service with Richard Nixon and later Reagan may have bent his judgment a little. He got singed by Nixon's ITT scandal and, shortly after taking over the CIA job, was criticized in such nonleftist public forums as *US News & World Report* magazine for the churlish and sometimes snarling way he dealt with intelligence conclusions that differed with

Reaganite national security theology. His selection of sewing machine mogul Max Hugel as chief spy almost cost him his job.

Fortunately, Casey was also given a first-rate, highly respected deputy, Admiral Bobby Ray Inman. It was Inman, backed up by some outraged congressman, who ended up shooting down a proposal floated by Casey and a study group headed by CIA counsel Daniel Silver for a full-scale return to domestic spying on U.S. citizens.

At times, the CIA can be inexplicably obvious. In 1980, for example, it placed help-wanted ads in the *New York Times* and elsewhere to recruit would-be agents. "It's not a job for everybody," the ad said. And then there are those cute little blue buses that shuttle up and down the George Washington Parkway between CIA headquarters at Langley and the District of Columbia. If the Russians have not, most auto commuters on the parkways have figured out that the jitneys, identified only with the destination sign "Rosslyn" or "Crystal City," are not carrying Sunday school children. There's a highway sign in Virginia telling people where to turn off for the CIA.

In keeping with America's pre-Reagan "peaceful use of space" ethic, the National Aeronautics and Space Administration has had a largely civilian emphasis. Hence the orbital selling of Tang and the selection, as first man on the moon, of civilian Neil Armstrong, who went on to sell Chryslers. But NASA's primary mission is military, especially now that we have entered the fun-filled age of space-borne death rays, charged particle beam and laser projectors, which can fry an ICBM in flight or exposed in its silo from 23,000 miles away. The military also depends heavily on NASA technology and logistics for its early warning, reconnaissance, navigation, command control, and communication satellites. Indeed, now 80 percent of U.S. defense communications are carried by satellite.

When all our killer satellites are ready for deployment, NASA will put them there. Or will it?

After Americans got so bored with the Apollo successes that a lunar orgy wouldn't have kept them at their television sets, congressional interest in our manned space program was about as keen as that in aboriginal flower arranging. Between January 1975 and April 1981, the Russians flew 21 manned space missions compared to our none. NASA struck back with the remarkably successful mission of the Columbia space shuttle, a feat which put us years ahead of the Soviets in terms of our ability to hammer together killer satellite space platforms in a hurry. And for all the talk of more orbiting TV towers and weightlessness experiments with sex-happy frogs, killer satellites is the name of the space-shuttle game. The rub for NASA is this: If the space shuttle works so well, why should it stay in the hands of mere civilians? The effort to give the military complete control of space-borne weapons projects and the attempt to relegate NASA to inconsequential concerns like finding life on other planets were under way even before the Columbia's landing-gear tires so neatly touched the ground. And then Reagan killed the program seeking intelligent life in outer space.

A CIA official predicted to us one evening back in the 1970s that one of the most important and powerful defense agencies would shortly be the Department of Energy. It was already providing the military with all its weapons-grade uranium and other nuclear goodies, incorporating as it did the old Atomic Energy Commission. With the focus of our strategic and national security concerns shifting to the vital oil sources of the Middle East, the prediction seemed natural. Had the formidable James Schlesinger not been bounced as energy secretary by Carter, and had Carter not been bounced by the American people, it might well have come true. Schlesinger could have ended up the most powerful man in the cabinet.

But the ultimate say on this question was given to Reagan, whose friends in the oil industry convinced him that the Energy Department was a dangerous nuisance that ought to be abolished (just as they easily convinced him that a good way to fight inflation would be to decontrol domestic oil prices). The secretaryship was given to the hapless James Edwards, a former dentist and South Carolina governor who, at the end of Reagan's historic first 100 days, had been able to fill only one of the department's 19 top policy-making positions: his own. Eventually, Reagan decided to abolish the department and transfer its nuclear warhead manufacturing activities to, of all places, the Commerce Department.

The authors searched through the Pentagon and the defense establishment for a *Catch 22*–style Pfc. Wintergreen, or even a General Wintergreen—a little-known master manipulator sitting at some key crossroads of power or communication who is able to cut through the red tape and bureaucratic bloat, outfox the defense industry lobbyists and think tank theoreticians, outflank the legions of naysayers and jealous administration warlords, and Actually Get Things Done.

With the possible exception of the man who runs America's defense establishment, Frank Carlucci, we could find no one like that—only red tape and bloat, lobbyists and theoreticians, naysayers and jealous warlords.

But there is a *group* of insiders who are coming to exert an increasingly significant amount of influence on defense policy. Their enemies among Pentagon brass hats call them "the Reformers." Their premise is that defense spending, especially under the Reagan administration, has become too uncontrolled, too wasteful, too squandered on high tech, complex junk that is unnecessary or, worse, unusable in the stress of combat. Their message is that, if the United States is to maintain a position of strength in this hostile world, it should apply its increasingly limited resources only in the most intelligent and effective ways, and not throw them into the procurement process simply in an effort to outspend the Russians.

In sum, if an F-5 can outfight an F-15, why keep building F-15s, especially at $38 million a copy? If the crew of a $3 million battle tank can't use their gunsights and have to wear leak-prone vests filled with chemical coolant to withstand the heat, what good is it, especially if its exhaust fumes make it impossible for infantry to use the tank for protection in an assault? Why keep something that doesn't work just because it has survived the naysayer process and reputations will suffer if a mistake is admitted?

Pentagon brass are very, very nervous about the Reformers. They have identified the ringleaders as former White House speech writer James Fallows, author of *National Defense,* one of the most influential and widely read books on defense policy published in recent times; former fighter pilot and retired Air Force Colonel John Boyd, famous for measuring defense policy against the lessons of history; the brilliant Charles Spinney, a former Air Force engineering officer now working as a top civilian analyst for the Pentagon; a former Pentagon analyst named Pierre Sprey who has important connections throughout Washington; and William Lind, an aide to Senator Gary Hart.

Other members of the group include aides to Secretary of Defense Weinberger, journalists, think-tank thinkers, consultants, a number of other congressional staff members, and at least one OMB staffer. OMB Director David Stockman is said to be a sycophant, and White House Chief of Staff Jim Baker appreciates many of the Reformers' ideas.

Lieutenant Colonel Walter Kross, a critic of the Reformers, wrote about them this way in a recent article in *Air University Review:*

> Their professed purpose is to change U.S. military strategy, planning, tactics, and force structure in order to fight and win a modern theater war. They would markedly alter the way DOD prepares for war, establish significantly different war-fighting concepts and attendant force structure, and change the way weapons are developed and procured. Their motivation is simple: they are patriots who believe the United States will lose the next war unless their ideas are adopted. . . .
>
> These defense critics have survived through several administrations. Last spring, their influence grew widespread because they were able to

seize upon the major initiative of the Reagan administration: large increases in defense spending. Turning the issue to their advantage, the Reformers argue that blind increases in defense spending will not guarantee greater military capability. Instead, they say more spending could yield even less capability if we continue to buy expensive, complex, vulnerable weapons that are costly to operate. Our military leaders, they assert, are transfixed on a losers' game: attrition warfare.

The Reformers suggest a different approach to modern war. First, military operations should rely on maneuver, deception, decentralized C3, and exploitation of the enemy's weaknesses. Second, force structure should be recast to emphasize simpler, cheaper, more easily supportable weapons that really work in combat. In this way, the Reformers hold out the promise of more capability for less cost. There it is—more or less—a fiscal aphrodisiac guaranteed to gain widespread support, both inside government and with the public.

None of the Reformers outrank those who appear on the following list. Yet. In a few years, this may change, and there are many in Washington in both political parties who think that could be a very good thing.

THE TOP FIFTEEN MEN IN THE
AMERICAN DEFENSE ESTABLISHMENT
1. Frank Carlucci
Frank Carlucci, deputy secretary of defense; former deputy CIA director; former ambassador to Portugal; former deputy secretary of health, education, and welfare; former deputy director of OMB; former director of the Office of Economic Opportunity; and former State Department African specialist, is a survivor. He is also a shrewd operator, a "Mr. Inside" with connections deep within the defense, diplomatic, intelligence, and Republican establishments; and probably the most effective bureaucrat in Washington. Four Presidents considered him indispensable. Tough enough to stand up to Henry Kissinger and the right-wing zanies in the Reagan camp and triumph, he is the only power player in Washington who was ever stabbed in the back with a real knife.

Like Alexander Haig, Carlucci went three times into a fight ready to resign if he lost. Unlike Haig, he didn't lose. As was made clear at his confirmation hearings, Cap Weinberger couldn't run the Defense Department without him. Though the two are very close, it's clear to everyone that Carlucci could run Defense without Weinberger, and often does.

A rugged, self-possessed little fellow who slightly resembles Police Captain Frank Furillo in television's "Hill Street Blues," Frank

Charles Carlucci III was born in 1930 in the Pennsylvania coal country around Scranton. A Princeton collegiate wrestler, he graduated in 1952, served as a Navy gunnery officer in the Korean War, went to Harvard Business, and signed up as a management trainee with the Jantzen bathing suit firm. It wasn't his cup of tea.

He became a foreign service officer in 1956 and was sent to Africa. In 1960, when an accident involving a car he was riding in sparked a riot in Leopoldville in the then Belgian Congo, he fended off the shrieking mob until he and his party could escape. Upon reaching safety, he discovered he'd been stabbed in the back.

He worked the African and Latin American beat until 1969, when his Princeton wrestling teammate Donald Rumsfeld brought him into the OEO as his right-hand man, a description that would follow him for years. He succeeded Rumsfeld as head of the OEO, then moved to the OMB and proved such a star that Weinberger took him on as No. 2 at HEW, where they became known as "Cap the Knife" and "Carlucci the Cutter." In 1975, he was made ambassador to Portugal. Though he has never revealed the three occasions on which he was prepared to resign, one may well have been in Lisbon. Kissinger, distracted as always by more cosmic concerns, had taken the position that the new revolutionary Portuguese government was doomed to go Communist and should not receive either U.S. friendship or assistance. Carlucci said the hell with that and, working with NATO commander Alexander Haig, forged new ties with Lisbon that have lasted unto this day.

Jimmy Carter had brains enough to see that Carlucci, though a conservative Republican, was the ideal man to keep the CIA on an even keel no matter which way Admiral Turner spun the helm. It was a job Carlucci performed ably enough to win him a devoted following within the agency rank and file, and a great many admirers throughout the defense community. At times, Carlucci seemed to some the only sane man in the Carter administration.

Weinberger virtually made Carlucci's appointment as deputy a precondition of his own acceptance of the top post, but the right-wing zanies were apoplectic. Though Weinberger had a very large, warm place in his heart for things like the neutron bomb, they considered him too dangerously liberal. With Carlucci, they feared they'd get more of the same, as well as a superefficient administrator and cost-cutter who might play havoc with grandiose military spending plans. They raised the now all-too-familiar hue and cry that Reagan was choosing someone insufficiently Reaganite, but Carlucci easily won. He always does.

An advocate of the not-so-liberal doctrine of the thinkability of nuclear war, Carlucci has been a forceful spokesman for a U.S.

"nuclear war fighting capability" on The Hill and elsewhere. With Weinberger so much involved in policy bickering at the White House and foreign trips to shore up our military alliances, and not all that energetic in the first place, Carlucci has been in effective charge of the shop from the very beginning. If there is one man running the American defense establishment, it is Carlucci, who is the indispensable man.

2. Caspar Weinberger

Cap Weinberger is another of Washington's master bureaucrats, a brilliant survivor and governmental tactician whose experience has been as wide, deep, and varied as Carlucci's, though little of it has been in defense, intelligence, or foreign affairs.

Put into the top defense job as the best man the Reagan team could think of to spend the administration's lavish military largess intelligently, he has proved a quick study, as always. His nomination rankled the right-wing zealots, who seem to think that everyone who served in the Nixon administration is somewhat to the left of Thomas Hayden, but the Russians hardly think so. Weinberger had barely taken the oath of office before he was off trying to push the neutron bomb on the Europeans, much to the distress of the supposedly hawkish General Haig. He is another advocate of the thinkability of war with the Russians, not just the nuclear kind but a protracted conventional kind as well.

While leaving much of defense operations to Carlucci, Weinberger has found frequent occasion to stray onto Haig's turf, meeting with allied defense ministers as peripatetically as Haig does with his striped-pants counterparts. Speaking for Europe, Haig was able to shove Weinberger into the ditch on the neutron bomb issue, but lost out to the defense secretary on the White House decision to sell AWACS radar planes and F-15 jets to the Saudis. Weinberger speaks softly, but directly into the President's ear. No matter what any booby said or did, Weinberger was going to get Carlucci because Weinberger wanted Carlucci.

Born in San Francisco in 1917, the diminutive Weinberger is what might be called an "eastern establishment" Californian. Graduating magna cum laude from Harvard in 1938, with Elliot Richardson and *Chicago Tribune* editorial-page editor John McCutcheon as campus buddies, Weinberger went on to Harvard Law and then to World War II, working his way up in four years from private to infantry captain and winning the Bronze Star to boot. Joining one of California's bigger three-piece-suit law firms in 1947, he was elected to the state legislature in 1952, serving until 1958. Chairman of the state Republican central committee by 1962, Weinberger established a reputation as a government fiscal whiz and served as then Governor Ronald Reagan's state finance director from 1968 to 1970, when another Californian named Richard Nixon brought him to Washington.

Weinberger spent his Nixon years as chairman of the Federal Trade Commission, deputy director and director of OMB, counselor to the President, and secretary of HEW. Between 1975 and Reagan's inaugural, he labored as vice president of California's mighty Bechtel Corporation and as a director of a slew of other companies, making very big bucks.

Treasurer of the Episcopalian Diocese of California, Weinberger was an active member of the Trilateral Commission, which may be why the zanies think he's simpatico with Jane Fonda. Like Reagan and George Bush, he's a member of the Bohemian Club, which holds fun romps at its Bohemian Grove retreat in which members often dress up as women but which excludes female members because the boys get drunk and like to pee on trees. It stretches the imagination overmuch to envision Cap the Knife in such a setting. Weinberger has also put his hand to writing a newspaper column on government and serving as host of a TV panel show, which isn't easy to envision, either.

3. John Tower

The Senate Armed Services Committee chairmanship was considered all-powerful before John Tower swaggered into it, but he's been expanding its reach and influence wherever and whenever possible ever since. The top jobs in foreign arms sales, for example, had always come under the purview of the Senate Foreign Relations Committee, though appointments to fill them did not require Senate confirmation. Tower quickly moved to have confirmation required— by the Armed Services Committee. He is a chairman who sees the smallest sparrow fall. When an Annapolis midshipman from Texas was ordered by the Naval Academy commandant not to wear cowboy boots off duty because they were "inappropriate civilian attire," Tower hurried to the rescue with a pointed note reminding the admiral that the commander-in-chief himself thought cowboy boots appropriate enough attire to wear off duty. The midshipman got to keep his boots, provided they were properly shined.

Technically, the admiral far outranked Tower, who is a petty officer in the Navy Reserve and the only enlisted reservist in the Congress. A veteran of World War II, he used to wear cowboy boots on board ship in interesting places like Saipan.

A man as short if broad in the beam as Senate Majority Leader Howard Baker, Tower is noted as an elaborate if somewhat rustic dresser with an admiring eye for the ladies. Twice married, he was born in Houston in 1925, went to college at Southwestern University and Southern Methodist, and after acquiring his master's degree in political science studied at the London School of Economics. He followed peculiar stepping-stones to the Senate, working as a radio announcer, college professor, and insurance man before winning his first Senate election in 1961.

Senators Paul Laxalt, John Warner, Mark Hatfield, and other Republicans have taken prominent roles in defense matters, but with the House Armed Services Committee in the hands of opposition Democrats and led by the feeble Representative Melvin Price, Tower remains in absolute control and the administration's No. 1 defense man on The Hill. His voting record rates 100 percent from the American Security Council.

4. David Stockman

A Vietnam-era draft resister once as devoted to the peace movement as he is now to getting the untruly needy off food stamps, young David Stockman would seem an odd inclusion on this list, but the director of OMB ranks near the top of the defense establishment. Born in Fort Hood, Texas, in 1946, Stockman survived the pacifist past acquired at Michigan State and Harvard, and the experience of working for liberal John Anderson as a congressional aide, to evolve into a pretty fair conservative himself when he finally arrived in Congress in January 1977. His last American Security Council rating was 88 percent, thanks to such votes as his support for the B-1 bomber and defense spending increases beyond President Carter's.

Though a staunch defender of Reagan's more lavish defense programs and a man prudent enough to keep out of Cap Weinberger's way, Stockman has been as commendably severe with the demands of the generals as with those of the untruly needy. With defense demonstrably the most wasteful, inefficient, and inflation-prone branch of the federal government, this was essential if Reagan's grandiose economic plans were not to be drowned immediately in a tidal wave of deficit, as may still be the case.

"There's a kind of swamp of $10 to $20 to $30 billion worth of waste that can be ferreted out if you really push hard," said Stockman in his famous *Atlantic Monthly* article. Of the defense budget debate, he said: "The whole question is blatant inefficiency, poor deployment of manpower, [and] contracting idiocy." Fighting words.

5. Alexander Haig

It must always be remembered that Al Haig is your quintessential military man, even if he is also your quintessential scheming office politician. Born in Philadelphia in 1924, he graduated from West

Point in 1947 and went on to all the right military schools, graduating from the Army and Navy war colleges in addition to studying at Notre Dame and Georgetown. A Vietnam veteran and enough of a combat commander to win the Silver Star, Bronze Star, Air Medal, and Purple Heart, he has seemed to thrive most assisting superior officers. He married Patricia Fox, daughter of General Douglas MacArthur's chief of staff, a month before the Korean War began and has never had to labor out of sight of the mighties and worthies since. His career posts included staff officer for the deputy chief of staff for operations, military assistant to the secretary of the Army, deputy special assistant to the secretary of defense, military assistant to the presidential assistant for national security affairs (Henry Kissinger), vice chief of staff, and assistant to the President (Richard Nixon in the talking-to-the-portraits-on-the-wall period). Many who followed his career before and since were surprised that he performed so superbly all on his own as supreme commander of NATO forces from 1974 to 1978.

Though he has not been able to intrude himself in defense matters as much as he'd like, or as much as Cap Weinberger seems to intrude in foreign policy, Haig remains a major power in the defense establishment because, as secretary of state as much as general, he personifies NATO. Extremely well-liked and respected by European leaders, he has effectively represented their views in American councils and functioned as a persuasive spokesman for Reagan's policies in European capitals. With the two main thrusts of Reagan's defense policy the defense of Europe and the defense of Middle East oil resources, Haig's role continues to be major, if not general.

6. General David Jones

You don't get to be the highest ranking man in American uniform just by being a good saluter, but General Davy Jones is also a good saluter. An ardent and articulate spokesman on the need for the B-1 bomber, he saluted smartly when Carter dropped the project and became a spokesman on our lack of a need for it. And when Reagan took office, there was Jones talking about our need for the thing all over again.

Chairman of the Joint Chiefs of Staff since 1978, Jones was born in Aberdeen, South Dakota, in 1921, sought higher learning at Minot State College, and then went off to Army Air Corps flying school in 1943. Later stops included the National War College, University of Nebraska, and Louisiana Tech, and as deputy commander for operations in Vietnam, commander-in-chief of the U.S. Air Force in Europe, and as chief of staff of the Air Force.

Jones won the Legion of Merit, Distinguished Flying Cross, Bronze Star, Air Medal, and a chestful of others slightly less significant. A quintessential representative of the fly-boy general clique that has dominated the Air Force despite the enormous importance placed on missiles, Jones would doubtless be very unhappy if, as some have suggested, the Air Force were put out of the flying business and concentrated on rocketry.

7. *Admiral Bobby Ray Inman*

With CIA Director William Casey an over-the-hill politicized ex-spook who some say sneers at intelligence that conflicts with his preconceptions, it is imperative that the nation have a first-rate man in the No. 2 spot. To Reagan's lasting credit, it does. Admiral Bobby Ray Inman is playing as vital a role in keeping Casey's CIA alive and well as Frank Carlucci did in keeping Turner's afloat. And Inman is much the superior intelligence man.

Born in Rhonesboro, Texas, in 1931, he graduated from the University of Texas in 1950 and got an ensign's commission in 1952, serving in the Korean War on the carrier *Valley Forge.* Despite never having gone to Annapolis, though he did go to the National War College, Inman rose all the way up to vice admiral in 24 years. Serving as assistant naval attaché at the U.S. embassy in Stockholm in the late 1960s, Bobby Ray went from that key Soviet-watcher's nest to the post of assistant chief of staff for intelligence for the Pacific fleet and on up to director of naval intelligence, vice director of the Defense Intelligence Agency, and director of the National Security Agency, which is principally involved in monitoring foreign communications and codes and protecting ours from being monitored in turn. He was in the NSA job, preparing for an early retirement, when Reagan plucked him for the CIA, to what amounted to a standing ovation on Capitol Hill and throughout the defense and intelligence community.

Inman is a determinedly objective and apolitical sort of intelligence operative, telling superiors not what they want to hear but what they must. It was Inman who learned that the Libyans were planning to "lend" Billy Carter $200,000, and he passed the news through channels right on up to the White House without hesitation or any untoward "discretion." Despite his code and electronics background and his never having served as an undercover agent himself, Inman is a strong believer in human spies as opposed to computers and electronic gadgets as the agency's best tool. Though it might have set a few of the "old Navy" Annapolis types to gnashing their teeth, one of Inman's rewards for taking the CIA job was being made a full admiral. He deserves it more than most.

Inman helped Casey out during the Max Hugel fiasco, and probably saved Casey's job. He deserves it himself.

8. George Bush

Former Lieutenant (j.g.) George Herbert Walker Bush's chief claim to military fame in the 1980 presidential campaign was his starring role as the Navy's youngest combat pilot in World War II, which won him the Distinguished Flying Cross, three air medals, and the mixed blessing of being shot down in flames, both by the Japanese and, later, by Ronald Reagan.

But you pick up a thing or two as director of the CIA and envoy to China.

The Reagan apparat came to appreciate this. Over the head and objections of career military man Al Haig, Bush was made "crisis manager" at the White House. When Reagan was shot and hospitalized, Bush took over and functioned as de facto commander-in-chief, an arrangement complete (finally) with the colonel with the nuclear "black bag." Should there be another Mayaguez or desert rescue attempt, Reagan would, of course, make the required appearance in the situation room, and make his wishes known.

The man to look for at the head of the big table, however, poring over maps and dispatches long into the night, would be the one-time teenage war hero who, only 17 at the time of Pearl Harbor, went off to fight the foreign scourge. As though anticipating this important role in the Reagan administration, Bush signed on his old CIA deputy as his chief of staff after he was elected Vice-President. He has maintained close contact with some of the more cerebral members of the defense establishment's old-boy network and sits in on every defense and national security meeting of consequence. Reagan values his opinion and the neutral position he occupies between the NSC, Haig, Weinberger, and the agency.

It was Bush who was put in day-to-day charge of dealing with the explosive situation in Poland.

9. Paul Nitze

Reagan made veteran defense policy advisor Eugene Rostow head of his Arms Control Agency. He appointed former General Edward Rowney, who had retired to protest what he viewed as Jimmy Carter's sellout to the Russians in SALT II, his chief arms control negotiator. But when it finally came to talk turkey with the Russkies about a mutual reduction of nuclear arms in Europe in the late fall of 1981, Reagan chose the wisest old war-horse around, 74-year-old Paul Nitze, to be his chief negotiator at Geneva.

An Amherst, Massachusetts native, Harvard graduate, and onetime New York investment banker, Nitze joined the Roosevelt administration in 1940, becoming director of the Strategic Bombing Survey in

1944 and head of State Department policy planning in 1950. It was at that time he authored the now famous National Security Council memo NSC-68, which proposed a four-fold increase in defense spending and, some say, launched the Cold War.

Though writing some more explosive papers on his own, Nitze stayed out of government during the Eisenhower administration, of which he may have disapproved as being too soft. He came back with Kennedy in 1961 and stayed through the Johnson administration, serving as assistant and then deputy secretary of defense. Nixon made him his chief arms-control negotiator for SALT I, but Nitze resigned in 1974, complaining Watergate was making Nixon too anxious for a deal with the Soviets.

During the late 1970s, Nitze was policy chairman of the Carter-baiting Committee on the Present Danger, and in 1980 wrote yet another bombshell demanding that defense spending be increased by a minimum of $260 billion by 1984. He is the one probably most responsible for the "Window of Vulnerability" theory that gave us the MX, after a fashion.

His wife, Phyllis, is the granddaughter of a founder of the Standard Oil Company and of the world-famous Pratt Art Institute in New York.

10. Donald Rumsfeld

Don Rumsfeld is back, though not quite the imperial pooh-bah he once was and may become again. The former Illinois congressman, Nixon war on poverty and wage-price control czar, ambassador to NATO, Ford White House chief of staff, and secretary of defense was expected to get something fairly juicy from the newly-elected Reagan administration. If he didn't get the secretary of state slot, his friends presumed that at the least he'd get his old defense job back. Reagan thought otherwise, but Rumsfeld has returned as a major power in defense matters despite the lack of a public post.

Long a director of the Rand Corporation, he was in early 1981 made chairman of Rand's board of trustees, a position that in some circumstances gives him twice as much power as Weinberger or Carlucci. People may joke that "Rand" is an acronym for "research and no development," but that ultimate in defense think tanks is the most indispensable component in the American military, and the shrewd Rumsfeld has been busy making it more so.

Born in Chicago in 1932, Rumsfeld was a wrestling star at Princeton. Having abandoned his crew cut in middle age for longish hair and aviator glasses, the youthful looking "Rummy" remains archetypical of his erstwhile North Shore constituency. He also remains president of the giant G. D. Searle drug company, which he restored to profitability, mostly by jettisoning products and operations that weren't making money.

Whenever Reagan gets around to fine-tuning his cabinet with some shuffles and replacements, Rummy may well be the first one out from the wings. During Watergate, there was a Republican joke that went like this:

1st Republican: Don Rumsfeld is the smartest man in Washington.
2nd Republican: But he's not in Washington. He got himself made ambassador to NATO in Brussels.
1st Republican: See?

See.

11. Professor William Kaufmann

One of the happiest happenstances for the American defense establishment is that Professor William Kaufmann is still willing to take one or two days off every week from his duties in the political science department at the Massachusetts Institute of Technology and fly down from Cambridge to Washington to lend a bit of his wisdom toward the goal of American military survival.

Born in New York City in 1918, the discreet Dr. Kaufmann acquired his bachelor's, master's, and doctoral degrees from Yale; he taught at Yale and Princeton before joining the MIT faculty in 1961. That same year, he also signed on as a heavy thinker with the Rand Corporation, where he remained until 1976. A former member of the U.S. Air Force Science Advisory Board and the author of two very important books on national security, Kaufmann has also been a consultant for the Hudson Institute and the Institute for Defense Studies. One of the heaviest thinkers now at the Brookings Institution, Kaufmann may well be the only Brookings man Reagan and his apparat care to listen to. And they do listen to Kaufmann.

Renowned as one of the coolest, clearest, and most rational of voices on defense matters, Kaufmann had much to do with the formulation of our nuclear strategy policies of the 1960s and early 1970s, and has been extremely useful as an apolitical sage in the reordering of American defense priorities for the 1980s and 1990s. Few generals could ever dream of possessing the power manifest in one of Dr. Kaufmann's quiet observations.

12. Senator Sam Nunn

The Democratic Party's battery of defense experts includes House Armed Services Chairman Melvin Price, who was born at the time of Czar Nicholas' war against the Japanese; Senator Henry Jackson, who is getting to be almost as old and is lacking a committee chairmanship; and young Senator Gary Hart, the onetime manager of George McGovern's antiwar presidential campaign who recently joined the Navy Reserve.

But what the Democrats have mostly is Georgia Senator Sam Nunn. A farmer-lawyer from Perry, Georgia, where he was born in 1938, the balding, bespectacled Nunn came to the Senate with no more military experience than a two-year stint in the Coast Guard. But he studied and learned. If knowledge were all there was to power on Capitol Hill, supremely expert Nunn would be the ranking military type in the Congress. And he almost is. Civilians and brass hats alike tremble before his questioning on military matters, as did his fellow Georgian, Jimmy Carter.

13. General Russell Dougherty (Ret.)

The highly cerebral General Russell Dougherty has probably been even more influential since he retired from the Air Force than when he was in, and when he was in, he held such posts as director of strategic target planning and commander-in-chief of the Strategic Air Command. Now executive director of the Air Force Association, among many other things, he was the one called upon by the American Enterprise Institute to make the case for the MX, and no one has made it better, before or since.

A lawyer who practiced before the U.S. Supreme Court, Dougherty was born in Kentucky in 1920, acquired a second lieutenant's commission in 1943, and acquired degrees ranging from bachelor's to doctor's from Western Kentucky University, University of Louisville, University of Akron, University of Nebraska, and Westminster College. He did time with the National War College and the Rand Corporation, and otherwise punched his ticket with a number of top staff assignments, most notably in Europe.

A military man's intellectual with a forthright writing style—"the MX missile system is so fundamental to U.S. security that it must be removed from domestic politics"—Dougherty serves on the boards of the Atlantic Council of the United States, the U.S. Institute of Defense Analysis, and the U.S. Strategic Institute. He also holds the Distinguished Service Medal, the Legion of Merit, and the Bronze Star.

14. John Lehman

Admiral Hyman Rickover, legendary father of the nuclear Navy and a 1922 graduate of the Naval Academy, had charmed or intimidated so many Presidents and congressmen it seemed he would stay on active duty all the way to the grave, or at least until age 100, despite the many mutterings about his taking shaky actual command of nuclear submarines and almost sinking them. He was still wearing his admiral's uniform at age 82 when, in November 1981, septuagenarian Ronald Reagan finally retired him on the interesting grounds that he was too old.

The man who really did Rickover in, curiously enough, was John Lehman, at 38 one of the youngest secretaries of the Navy in history. Lehman had felled one of the toughest trees in the defense establishment. Witness the time when an engineer seeking a position on Rickover's elite team explained he had been interested in electrical engineering ever since his father gave him an electric train as a boy for Christmas. The kindly Rickover replied: "If you were ten and got a pile of horseshit for Christmas, would you want to be a cowboy?"

Lehman, a bright, witty, assertive, and well-groomed fellow who served as one of Henry Kissinger's NSC whiz kids in the Nixon administration, deserves a ranking on this list just for the coup de grace to the aged admiral, but he has achieved much more than that.

In a job that has all too often gone to well-heeled campaign contributors with experience in small boats (though one of his predecessors was named Franklin D. Roosevelt), Lehman has played such a dominant role in the rearming and refitting of the U.S. Navy that the Reagan administration's crusade in that direction is now called the Lehman Doctrine.

Lehman has been able to bring giant contractors like General Dynamics to heel with threats to go to European arms manufacturers if necessary. He deflected David Stockman's budget-cutting blade with more skill than even Weinberger has mustered. And he always seems to have his way with Congress. Who else could push through such a costly, idiotic scheme as putting two obsolete, 40-year-old battleships to sea?

When Lehman swears we will have a 600-ship Navy by 1989, people believe him, even if they fear that Navy may end up including a refitted Old Ironsides. When Lehman swears we will have a fleet strong enough to tangle with the Russians in the Arctic waters near Murmansk, the Soviets may not believe him, but they probably should.

15. John Warner

John Warner was written off almost immediately by a great many Washington hard cases as a rich pretty boy who had to wear weights in his shoes to keep his feet on the ground and who made it to the Senate mostly through a fluke and the campaign draw of his famous wife, Elizabeth Taylor. After all, the guy went to the same Georgetown hairstylist his wife did to have his hair blowdried.

But in three years in the Senate, the 54-year-old Warner has proved himself surprisingly expert on defense matters, which is why he is now chairman of the Senate Subcommittee on Strategic and Theater Nuclear Forces. He is as knowledgeable and useful an adjunct to the Republican Party on defense as Gary Hart is to the Democrats, and it's the Republicans who are running things. It was Warner who made the complex SALT II dispute most understandable to Republican groups during the 1980 presidential campaign. If Howard Baker had consulted Warner more, he wouldn't have stumbled so badly over the issue.

A World War II Navy vet who worked as an attorney and assistant U.S. attorney when he wasn't marrying pretty rich girls, Warner served as secretary of the Navy for Nixon from 1972 to 1974, though he is better remembered for his stellar performance as director of the American Bicentennial Commission, one of the few federal agencies actually to be abolished as soon as its usefulness was ended.

The Bureaucracy

THE FEDERAL BUREAUCRACY is a creature one part sloth, one part dinosaur, one part wolverine, and one part bucking bronco. It is demonstrably more than is necessary to attend to the affairs of this nation and its inhabitants, yet it is also all that we have, and for legions of constituent groups throughout the country, it doesn't provide enough. The President and the Congress run the United States of America only insofar as they can control the federal bureaucracy, and they don't control it much. The inclination of most Presidents and Congresses has been to expand the bureaucracy, but if they do nothing it always manages to expand itself. Attempts to curb its size are seldom successful. Witness Jimmy Carter's streamlining effort that accomplished nothing more than the creation of two new Cabinet departments.

The Reagan administration tried the devilishly clever technique of bringing the bureaucracy to hell by slashing budgets, appointing government-hating businessmen to key administration posts, replacing competent personnel with incompetents, and generally using mismanagement to trash the bureaucracy from within. But this didn't bring the bureaucracy under control; it merely made a big mess and provided a rationale for the next Democratic Congress to give us more government than ever before.

This isn't quite what the Founding Fathers had in mind. Having fought a long unpleasant war against one, they were not too keen on creating a strong central government of their own. Many, like Thomas Jefferson, envisioned a loosely federated republic run largely on the local level. But government abhors a vacuum as much as does nature. In the 1819 *McCulloch* v. *Maryland* decision, John Marshall's Supreme Court ruled that the federal government was limited only by the Constitution and that its powers had supremacy over the states.

In 1824, Marshall put the feds into the business of regulating commerce with a vengeance, and it was downhill from there. Abraham Lincoln used the Civil War to exert federal authority almost everywhere and establish the nation's first federal income tax. The Interstate Commerce Commission, the nation's first regulatory agency, was created in 1887. The federal highway program began in 1916. Franklin Roosevelt brought forth everything from rural electrification to aid to dependent children, increasing federal aid payments from $232 million in 1932 to more than $1 billion in 1934. Urban renewal came along in 1949. School desegregation followed in 1954. And, in the 1960s, all hell broke loose.

Graphs reflecting the upward trend of federal involvement all look like cliffs, as seen from the bottom. The amount of federal aid went from less than $10 billion in 1940, 1950, and 1960 to $12 billion in 1965 to $40 billion in 1970 to $94 billion in 1981. The number of grant-in-aid programs went from 50 in 1965 to 550 in 1974. The percentage of state agencies receiving federal aid went from 35 percent in 1965 to 70 percent in 1980. Funding for the budgets of regulatory agencies increased from $1 billion in 1970 to $6 billion in 1980. The number of pages in the Federal Register went from 15,000 in 1960 to 60,000 in 1975.

Not uncoincidentally, congressional staffs increased from 6,000 to 13,000 in the same general period. Not uncoincidentally at all, federal spending as a percentage of total U.S. output rose from 17.9 percent in 1965 to 22.9 percent in 1980.

The first year of the Reagan administration saw the federal budget exceed $700 billion, compared to $232 billion just eight years before. In the intervening period, federal pensions and Social Security alone rose nearly 300 percent, with Social Security amounting to a $155 billion chunk of the budget. Interest on the public debt went up 341 percent, reaching $68.4 billion for fiscal year 1982 and still climbing, what with 20 percent interest rates and $80 billion deficits haunting the Treasury. Defense spending, including payments on prior contracts, reached $170 billion. There's an old Washington joke quoting the late Senator Everett M. Dirksen as saying, "A billion here, a billion there. Pretty soon you're talking about real money." The Reagan era gave currency to a new term: "Trillion." No less than $1.6 trillion asked for new arms procurement alone. The very real prospect of a trillion-dollar federal budget before Reagan left office, budget cuts and tax cuts notwithstanding. And, for the first time, the national debt went over a trillion. Lyndon Johnson had a fit when the budget topped $100 billion in 1965.

According to a study by *US News & World Report,* no less than 77.6 percent of federal spending the year Reagan took office was required by law and beyond the control of the White House.

Of the total budget, around 38 percent goes for health and human services, education, and Social Security, with some 25 percent allocated to defense (although Reagan is changing that). Thirteen percent goes to Treasury, most of it for interest on the federal debt.

Transportation, at a time when the nation's federal highways and bridges are falling apart at an alarming rate, gets just 3 percent. Though the federal government now owns one-third of the land in the United States, the Interior Department is allocated only .7 percent. The Justice Department gets .5 percent, the State Department .4 percent.

Not counting men and women in uniform, the federal bureaucracy now employs 2.8 million people, including 984,000 civilian Defense Department workers, and 650,000 postal workers. Reagan cut 44,000 from the payroll his first year, but this was 26,000 fewer than he tried to fire.

More than half of all Americans are now dependent on government—either federal, state, or local—for paychecks, pensions, or other benefits as either wage earners or dependents.

It should be noted that federal employees now constitute just 1.2 percent of the population, compared to 1.3 percent in 1960. But they remain extremely powerful, their civil service protection such that, in a recent 12-month period, only 9,000 of the 2.8 million civilian and nonpostal federal employees were fired for cause.

When the Democrats still controlled both houses of Congress, repeated efforts were made to make public employees as strong offensively as they are defensively by repealing the Hatch Act protection that prevented them from doing political work, voluntarily or otherwise. With civil service, no patronage boss could push them around. With political power, they could push anyone around. Consider the effect of 650,000 postal workers deciding to back or oppose a candidate—on the single ground of whether the candidate supported a postal rate increase.

The Reagan administration fought tooth, nail, and elbow—and took considerable liberal heat—just to effect some $35 billion in program budget cuts, nearly all of them from social service, environmental protection, education, science, public transportation, the arts, and government regulation programs. According to the General Accounting Office, those cuts were offset by continuing waste and fraud. When Reagan tried for deeper cuts, he got heat. But he never really tried to eliminate waste and fraud; he just cut programs.

Of some $51 billion to $77 billion in waste and fraud identified in 1980, an estimated $25 billion was in the form of embezzlement from local federal-aid programs, sale of property mortgaged to the government as collateral for loans, theft of office equipment and supplies, the taking of bribes, and sale of such valuable items as contraband food stamps.

Another $2 to $4 billion was lost to the unnecessary use of consultants. Despite the huge federal payroll, federal agencies hire consultants the way trucking companies hire day laborers—except they don't pay them like day laborers. Some 87 percent of the budget of the unadmired Department of Energy was found to go for contractual services and consultants. The DOE had some 21,000 people on its regular payroll in 1980. At the same time, it was found to have 200,000 outside workers under contract, doing such highly skilled work as typing and stamping folders.

The Department of Education spent $17,416 to hire an outside firm to "manage" an agency conference. Basically, they provided paper, pens, and coffee. The Department of Commerce spent $25,000 on consultants to study department stores. The job ultimately was completed by Commerce Department employees themselves.

Senator David Pryor of Arkansas, sharing a cab unrecognized with two federal consultants, listened as they debated whether to charge the government $12,000 or $25,000 for their work. With almost the flip of a coin, they settled on the 25 big ones.

The former Health, Education, and Welfare Department paid one consultant $440 for work performed on September 31, 1978. There are only 30 days in September.

Another nifty little dodge for hiding people getting paid by the feds is the part-time worker—"part-time" meaning every workday of the year but one, the one being the day that the count of federal workers is taken to see that the number doesn't exceed the official ceiling.

The GAO found some $34 million in waste lying about in such places as the GSA purchasing department, which acquired pocket calculators for a discount price of $110 each when they could have been bought at any retail store for $89. The Energy Department stapled the wrong covers on 8 million booklets. Instead of replacing the covers with the right ones, the department destroyed all the booklets. For 136 youths enrolled in a conservation camp program, the Interior Department bought 1,072 pairs of cowboy chaps, 3,736 pairs of work gloves, 112 ladders, 54 wheelbarrows, 1,509 desk calendars, and 126 lawn mowers. Military reservists collected $744 million in pay for exercises they never attended. A clerk at the EPA stuck 900 unused airline tickets in cardboard boxes instead of returning them for refunds.

And so it goes. It really goes at the end of the budget year, when the GAO estimates an additional $2 to $4 billion is spent for no other reason than to use up all the funds in various budgets. Thus did the Pentagon buy $119,074 worth of magazine subscriptions on the last day of one fiscal year, and a U.S. ambassador ordered his staff to throw parties until the entertainment budget was used up; more liquor was bought than could be drunk.

Travel waste is good for more than $750,000 a year, not merely the "fact-finding" junkets congressmen always find some way to justify, but excursions such as Jimmy Carter, Bert Lance, and friends "finding facts" at the 1980 Sugar Bowl, at a cost to the taxpayers of $20,000 (or Ron and Nancy Reagan hitting the public trough for $100,000 in air travel every time they go home for the weekend to their California ranch). Though not as flagrant, lesser bureaucrats pull off the same thing. The GAO found 17 percent of federal travel "not essential."

Failure to collect debts, like some 700,000 outstanding student college loans, is another item worth at least $6 billion, according to the GAO.

Then there's the question of competence. In 1980, the GSA was sending out "dawn patrols" of energy investigators looking for lights left on, coffeepots plugged in, windows left open, and other sources of energy waste in federal buildings. This is the same GSA that since 1973 has been unable to control the temperatures in the Dirksen and Kluczynski Federal Buildings in Chicago, inflicting freezing temperatures on one courtroom and unbearable heat on another.

Federal studies have kept Senator William Proxmire and his "Golden Fleece" Award in business for years. Everyone has his favorite. Ours is the $124,000 study that in 1974 somehow proclaimed that trucks traveled through New York City at an average speed of 68 miles an hour.

Paperwork takes its toll. When have words carried such import as in the following, culled by the *Washington Monthly* for its Memo of the Month:

To: All Executive Staff
From: Herbert R. Doggette, Jr., Deputy Commissioner (Operations)
Subject: Program Misuse and Management Inefficiency—Information.

In a recent meeting, Secretary Harris informed us that in the future, rather than using the phrase, "fraud, abuse, and waste," she would prefer "program misuse and management inefficiency." I agree that the Secretary's terminology more accurately reflects what we are measuring and working to eliminate. The change is effective immediately; please see that it is effected in your areas of responsibility.

And, sometimes as early as two years before the next presidential election, there's the government generosity and largess inspired by practical political concerns. In 1980, Jimmy Carter could not call on the army of federal workers the way a Mayor Daley could marshal city payrollers, but he could reach into the federal till, and go tossing federal contracts and loans around key primary states like a billionaire Santa Claus.

A typical bureaucracy, the Agriculture Department devotes its valuable time to such enterprises as trying to figure out the optimum time to make French toast—measured not in ordinary minutes and seconds but in something Ag calls MTMs—and carrying on price-support programs for obscure crops like the Tung nut, which grew only in Louisiana and Texas and was wiped out by hurricanes years ago.

But there's always time for other things. Senator Edward Zorinsky, in one probe, found enough hanky, panky, and whoopee going on in the Ag's Federal Crop Insurance Corporation to make Hugh Hefner salivate. According to sworn testimony, FCIC officials were trading promotions for sex; making employees contribute to an illegal entertainment slush fund used to buy liquor and throw parties at which to entertain women; falsifying employee work records; ordering subordinates to destroy civil service records involving a higher-up's girlfriend; and sexually harassing female employees, denying them promotions if they resisted advances. Some lower ranks were reportedly sent out to buy X-rated cassettes for the department video equipment. Employees who displeased the ringleaders of this "fun" bunch were allegedly dispatched to what was called "the bone yard"—an office in Kansas City where they were given nothing to do but sit on a folding chair in a hallway all day.

Federal sex is not confined to the Agriculture Department, however. According to an investigation by the Merit Systems Protection Board, some 42 percent of female federal employees have complained of sexual harassment on the job, with 1 percent of those surveyed saying they'd been the victims of rape. Another study found that government officials negotiating contracts with consultants often find themselves with cuddly companions for an evening—hired by the consultants at rates exceeding $500 a, er, throw.

The bureaucratic life-style has other advantages. Aside from federal pay averaging some $5,000 more a year than in the public sector, there are 41,000 free parking spaces available in Washington for federal payrollers (a $1.5 million a month subsidy) and retirement at age 55 at levels far exceeding Social Security. A retired colonel nowadays can draw more in retirement pay than a serving colonel does in active duty pay. Some 200 or more government officials rate chauffeur-driven limousines, de rigueur in the Reagan administration, and, for the weary bureaucrat, the government maintains five leisure spas, extending from the Blue Ridge Mountains to the Grand Tetons and including one in Florida.

Never models of efficiency—no one ever made a study to determine the optimum time to make a study determining the optimum time in which to make French toast—bureaucrats formerly used to work nine to five, or the equivalent. The Carter administration instituted something called "flexitime," which required workers in some agencies to hang around only for their "core" hours of ten to three. Radios and tape recorders were permitted at desks to help pass the "core" time. For a while, so were television sets, so workers wouldn't miss their soap operas.

One of the authors, seeking to renew a glider pilot's license, went, logically enough, to the Federal Aviation Administration building just off the Mall. It took him more than an hour of being passed around from department to department and person to person until a supervisor, called out of an office party, finally informed him that he would have to go to an office at National Airport to obtain one.

There are ways to keep a bureaucrat in line. When Defense Department employee Ernest Fitzgerald blew the whistle on more than $2 billion in cost overruns on the C5A transport project in the late 1960s, the Air Force, with Richard Nixon's approval, abolished his job. It took Fitzgerald 10 years of fighting with the Civil Service Commission and in the courts to win back an equivalent job and the money due him.

Otherwise, job tenure is eternal, unless one terminates an entire agency, as Reagan loves to do. Those 9,000 fired individually every year almost have to steal all the office furniture to get the boot.

Carter came to Washington specifically vowing to reduce the number of government agencies and programs from 2,000 to 200. Hah. At one point, he claimed he had eliminated 760 units of government, adding only 348. Don Lambro of United Press International discovered that 677 of the 760 were largely informal advisory committees with little or no staff or significant mission. Of the remaining 83, most were simply merged with other agencies or programs, along with their missions and staff. Carter actually added 34,000 workers, while creating two new cabinet departments.

The Reagan team came in vowing to tear the bureaucracy limb from limb, ordering an absolute freeze on new hiring and new rules and regulations. The short-term result was chaos, as employees caught in midhire found themselves without a federal job to come to though they'd already left their old ones. The administration also made the amazing discovery that the rule freeze was obstructing its regulatory-reform drive because it takes a new rule to abolish an old one.

Longer term, they made some even more amazing discoveries. Of the 2.8 million employees in the federal bureaucracy, the incoming administration had the power to replace only a little more than 4,000, because they were under civil service protection. These included most of the policy-making positions, but policy made is not necessarily policy carried out. Justice Department attorneys, for example, went on doing liberal things long after the Reaganites and Reaganuts took over.

The most important discovery they made was what should have

been a most obvious political one: for all its wastefulness, inefficiency, arrogance, and sheer mass, the federal bureaucracy is there to serve the American people. Every federal program has a constituency, whether it's the small hardware owners protected by the FTC's Bureau of Competition; the Pope County, Illinois, sheriff's police that paid most of its patrolmen's salaries with CETA funds; or the intellectuals who love National Public Radio's "All Things Considered." With Social Security, federal debt service, and defense all but immune to slashes, cuts elsewhere would come hard.

A favorite word of the Reaganites and Reaganuts was the verb "to ding," as in "I dinged him," translated by William Safire, among others, as "I made known my displeasure." The Reagan administration "dinged" the federal bureaucracy, but it didn't hurt as much as they hoped, as many of those on the following list will agree.

THE TOP TEN MEN IN THE BUREAUCRACY
1. Charles A. Bowsher
The second most powerful post in the federal government after President is that of comptroller general. The comptroller runs the mighty General Accounting Office, has jurisdiction over the entire federal bureaucracy, and reports directly to Congress. Better than that, the comptroller has complete independence and serves a 15-year term.

Appointed by Reagan to replace the retiring Elmer Staats, Charles Bowsher came to the comptroller's job as managing partner of the huge Arthur Andersen & Company accounting firm, whose audits have uncovered as much fraud and waste in private industry as the GAO should be finding in the public sector.

Born in Elkhart, Indiana, in 1931, Bowsher is a product of the University of Illinois and the University of Chicago and looks much the hard-nosed accountant he is supposed to be. His suitability for the comptroller's job is based not only on his long service with Arthur Andersen's Washington office. He was a bureaucrat from 1967 to 1971: assistant secretary of the Navy for financial management.

Bowsher faces only one disadvantage as the nation's most powerful accountant: reporting directly to Congress is fine, if Congress pays attention.

2. David Stockman
All of Bert Lance's bounced checks and other fascinating business habits might never have come to much public light if Jimmy Carter had given him a job as a mere White House advisor. Instead, Carter made him director of the Office of Management and Budget, which

certainly rivals the GAO as one of the most powerful and influential agencies in the bureaucracy.

OMB has its finger in everything. Every budget program, every word of congressional budget testimony, every new rule and regulation must pass the scrutiny of OMB. Confronted by cabinet departments run by undersecretaries and less, and manned by people immune from firing, the Reagan administration has found the budget process its only means of controlling programs and policies.

Joining the cabinet at 34, David Stockman lost not a minute in exploiting the opportunity to become the administration's boy wonder. If he didn't quite bring the bureaucracy to heel, he certainly got its attention, and proved himself one of the President's most effective and hard-working lieutenants.

Unfortunately, one makes more enemies than friends slashing budgets, especially if one swaggers into congressional committee hearings with all the humility of Attila the Hun riding into Europe. As Republican Congressman Barber Conable noted: "He's flashing like a meteor across the sky. I hope he lasts longer than the average meteor." Not long after, Stockman was quoted in the *Atlantic Monthly* calling Reaganomics "a Trojan horse," and Reagan put him on probation.

Whatever happens to him, Stockman won't starve. No Bert Lance, Stockman came into the administration as the poorest member of the cabinet, listing assets of less than $50,000. Any big consulting outfit should now find his knowledge of the bureaucracy and the working of the White House worth at least $50,000 a month.

3. Frank Carlucci

The Defense Department may be the protector of the Free World and possess more military might than any other nation, save the Soviet Union, in history, but basically it's a bureaucracy, and the nation's largest. Our military has many more typewriters and file cabinets than guns. If George Washington had had to contend with as much paperwork, he'd still be at Valley Forge, filling out forms.

Carlucci has some of the best bureaucratic credentials in the Federal City, having served as operations director of the Office of Economic Opportunity, deputy director of the Office of Management and Budget, undersecretary of Health, Education, and Welfare, and deputy director of the CIA, before joining the Reagan team at the age of 50 in 1981. The Navy veteran and Princeton and Harvard man is a champion bureaucrat for another reason. He held all those jobs in both Republican and Democratic administrations.

He and his boss, Caspar Weinberger, were the most successful bureaucrats in resisting Stockman's budget cuts.

4. Richard Schweiker

When Carter stripped Education from the Health, Education, and Welfare Department, it became Health and Human Services (if it had been left Health and Welfare its acronym would have been HAW). It did not become much diminished. HHS still spends about a third of the federal budget, is the second largest cabinet bureaucracy after Defense, and touches more Americans' lives than any other cabinet department, cradle to grave.

Former Pennsylvania Senator Richard Schweiker, Reagan's choice for head of HHS, has proved himself an effective bureaucratic warlord, especially when one considers the nature of the mission. His mandate from Reagan was to get HHS to touch Americans' lives as little as possible. Given the noisy constituencies HHS has and the predilections of most of its employees, this was rather like asking the chief chef in an Italian, French, or German restaurant to serve nothing but low-calorie meals.

Most famous as the liberal Republican who was Reagan's bold-stroke choice for running mate in his nearly successful 1976 challenge to Jerry Ford, Schweiker was born in Norristown, Pennsylvania, in 1926, served in the Navy in World War II, and graduated from Penn State. He is also one of three Reagan administration kingpins who belong to the little known Schwenkfelder Church.

A congressman or senator since 1960, he was no stranger to the vast HHS empire. He was ranking Republican on the Senate Labor and Human Resources Committee, serving on subcommittees dealing with the handicapped, education, arts and humanities, health, and scientific research. His ADA (liberal) and COPE (union) voting ratings ranged as high as the 80s and 90s, respectively, but it's doubtful his administrative decisions at HHS would get such favorable marks. Especially with the social life he leads.

5. William Bolger

The United States has had 65 postmaster generals, dating back to Benjamin Franklin in 1775. William Bolger is only the second career postal employee to have been given the top job.

Born in Waterbury, Connecticut, in 1923, Bolger joined the Postal Service in 1941 as a clerk. Except for brief service as a clerk for the FBI and with the Army Air Corps in World War II, he's been with U.S. Mail ever since, ultimately rising to deputy postmaster general in 1975. Carter made him No. 1 in 1978.

A friendly, easy-going fellow who would look at home behind the postal counter back in Waterbury, Bolger has resisted efforts in Congress to deprive the Service of the semiautonomous status it was given in 1971. He has kept rate increases as reasonable as inflation will allow, continued the Service's program of eliminating unprofitable branches and services, and proved master enough of his 650,000 employees to help the Reagan administration head off a threatened strike in 1981. Bolger met his wife, Margaret, when she was a postal clerk.

6. Gerald Carmen

The General Services Administration provides all the other bureaucracies the wherewithal to function: paper for the paperwork, offices for the desks and file cabinets, and every color of tape. With 33,000 employees in Washington and in 11 regional offices, the GSA is a big bureaucracy in itself.

It is arguably also the most scandal-ridden and wasteful. In 1977, an IRS investigation uncovered widespread instances of GSA employees taking bribes and kickbacks from suppliers and contractors. Eighty-four employees were convicted. The waste is legendary, typified by its spending $915,000 a year to lease a building in California the government has never used. Pilfering from GSA stocks of adding machines, camera film, and office supplies has been legion. Estimates of GSA losses from waste, fraud, and theft have exceeded $100 million a year, but no one can say for sure because the agency doesn't employ enough auditors to make an accurate accounting. A GAO report in 1980 found things little changed from 1977.

Gerald Carmen, the man Reagan hired to clean up this mess, was a Reagan political operative in New Hampshire for the 1980 primary and earlier served as New Hampshire GOP chairman. He had bureaucratic experience as chairman of the New Hampshire Housing Authority and the state Vocational Education Committee as well as with the Manchester Housing and Urban Renewal Authority. Born in Quincy, Massachusetts, in 1930, Carmen is essentially a businessman with no experience in government procurement. White House Press Secretary James Brady cited as his chief qualification for the job that he is a "straight, tough, no-nonsense guy—someone who will kick tail and take names." Among his first acts as GSA administrator was to restore the agency's top investigator and auditor to the power they used to enjoy before being sat on by the Carter administration after complaining about the scandals. An abrasive, outspoken flinger-forth of criticisms, Carmen was transferred from the Republican National Committee to the Reagan-Bush campaign staff during the 1980 election to keep peace in the GOP family. His traits have proved more useful at the GSA, where he is the seventh administrator in the past 10 years.

7. John R. Block

When not subsidizing tobacco smoking, making whoopee in FCIC conference rooms, and studying fry cooks, the huge empire that is the

Agriculture Department oversees nearly everything we eat from earth to mouth. It also doles out food stamps, runs the United States Forest Service, and messes with the sex lives of insects in Mexico.

John Block, the man who runs the place for Ronald Reagan, typifies what has happened to American agriculture in the past 20 years. Born in 1935 near Galesburg, Illinois, he took what was then just another family farm and built it into a 3,000 acre corporate enterprise valued at $10 million. A West Point graduate and former Army paratrooper, Block served as Illinois' agriculture director from 1977 until tapped for the Reagan cabinet in 1981. He has received very high marks for his conduct of the office and has been rated the second most effective man in the cabinet after Treasury Secretary Don Regan.

Block has made it clear he speaks mostly for his farmer constituents, but thus far consumers have found more complaint with the Mediterranean fruit fly than with him. His principal chinaman on Capitol Hill is Senator Robert Dole.

8. Robert Nimmo

Early in 1981, rumors spread among veterans' groups that the Reagan administration planned to dismantle the long-troubled Veterans Administration—rumors not a little encouraged by the knife job David Stockman was doing on it. Robert Nimmo, Reagan's VA administrator, allayed those fears as much as could be.

He won the unanimous support of veterans' groups at his confirmation, though Michael Kogutek, national commander of the American Legion, held out the reservation of "a potential conflict between the President's desire for fiscal austerity and the administrator's responsibility to seek full funding for those programs that have been mandated by Congress for the welfare of veterans and their families."

Nimmo, a World War II bomber pilot, served as a fiscal adviser to Reagan when he was governor of California. Born in 1922, he also served three terms in the California legislature and is a close friend of Ed Meese.

After fulfilling "a solemn obligation" to provide service to veterans, Nimmo declared his second priority would be curbing the VA budget, which had increased from $11.5 billion to $24 billion in the preceding 10 years. Yet, at the end of 1981, there were 20,000 more employees in the VA than were authorized.

9. James Watt

In a curious way, in terms of fulfilling his department's mission, Interior Secretary James Watt is one of the most effective men in the federal bureaucracy.

Interior's mission is to conserve our natural resources and preserve and protect our environment. On most domestic issues, Reagan has been content to be a benign, soft-soaping spokesman for the segment of big business that put him up for office. On the environment, however, he has behaved with such hostility the *Chicago Tribune* denounced the President as "a menace."

Had Reagan put some affable, unassuming professional bureaucrat into the Interior job to carry out his antienvironment policies—such as tearing up the Alaskan interior and putting the blame for pollution on trees—with quiet discretion, he might have caused some really terrible damage. Instead he picked the incredible Watt, who quickly established himself as a man who believed in the industrial exploitation of the wilderness with the same fervor as he did in his religion. Watt, who is said to "speak in tongues," told a congressional committee concerned about preserving the wilderness for future Americans that "we don't know how many generations there will be before the Lord comes."

His policies have been so outrageous, his administrative conduct so flagrant, and his attitude so arrogant and combative that his opponents among environmental groups and in the Congress were galvanized as they could have been by nothing else. Newspaper editorial pages turned against Watt all over the country. So did American public opinion, which repeated polls showed had never supported Reagan's positions on environmental issues. Watt's most ambitious proposal—opening the California coast to widespread oil drilling—ended up having to be withdrawn in a personal debacle when oil companies complained it was far too ambitious and GOP leaders in California warned the controversy was destroying their party.

Watt has thus proved to be one of the most effective men in America at saving the environment from the policies of the Reagan administration.

Born in Lusk, Wyoming, in 1938, the bald, bespectacled born-again Christian served previous Republican administration in middle-echelon jobs at Interior, but it was as head of the anti-environmentalist Mountain States Legal Foundation that he first came to the approving attention of Reagan's close friend, Senator Paul Laxalt.

"This is the first time in my memory," said former Senator Gaylord Nelson, now with the Wilderness Society, "that the country's chief conservation officer has been an antienvironmentalist."

Watt neither smokes nor drinks, abstaining even from coffee, and disapproves of pantsuits for women. Having noticed a few worn by some women attorneys in his department after taking office, Watt issued an edict banning them immediately. The next day, every one of the women lawyers showed up in a pantsuit.

And they're still wearing them.

10. General Mark Clark

Old soldiers never die. Neither do most governmental commissions. The American Battle Monuments Commission, whose members and staff get to tour such unpleasant places as the Normandy Coast to see that everything is neat and tidy, has been a recurring target for administrations bent on beating back the superfluity of needless commissions, despite its tiny budget and staff. The Carter administration thought it was an especially juicy target.

No, sir. The cushy commission, the penultimate resting place of the career bureaucrat, lives on and on.

The General, Hero of Rome and now well past 80, is a fitting chairman for the commission and quite a monument himself.

The Regs

IN DRAFTING the Constitution, the Founding Fathers pulled off the neat trick of separation of powers, an ingenious squaring off of the White House, the Congress, and the courts through a system of checks and balances that ultimately kept Franklin Roosevelt from packing the Supreme Court and sent Richard Nixon back to hearing train whistles in the night on New York's Upper East Side.

But with all their sagacity, they failed to foresee a development that would send some of their best laid plans ganging aft agley: the evolution of a fourth and nearly autonomous branch of government called the Regulatory Agencies. Had Thomas Jefferson the slightest glimmering of what was to come to pass, they would have had to haul him away in a padded carriage.

Created by Congress, administered largely by the executive, and overseen by the courts, the Regs have managed to elude the control of all, and in large part still do, despite the best efforts of the regulation-hating Reagan administration.

There are 43 major regulatory agencies in the federal government, 20 of them independent agencies and the remainder units of larger departments. They reach into every imaginable aspect of our lives: the labels on our whiskey bottles, the number of sheep we can graze on our land, the price of our airline tickets, the speed we travel water skiing, the price of meat, the amount of interest earned by our savings, what toys we can buy for our children, what we can buy abroad, the cost of gasoline, the color of the water we drink, the color of the air we breathe, the color of the people who work for us, what crops we're going to grow, how high we can fly in a small airplane over Chicago, what we can watch on television, who can run for public office, how hot our homes should be, how quickly we can drive to work, the size of our mortgage payments, what ships can tie up in our ports, whether there shall be passenger trains, the rate of inflation, what kind of television commercials we can see, the kind of pills we can take, the color of hot dogs, the color of eggs, the speed of our cars, whether we can make rain, whether cowboys need outhouses,

95

who can live next to us, what stocks we can buy, what fish we have to throw back, and so on, and on and on.

Like the Congress, the Regs are almost entirely run by staff. Unlike the Congress, the commissioners and administrators they answer to are not elected. Much of the work done and actions taken by the staff never come to the attention of the commissioners anyway, and at best it is often for a pro forma, after-the-fact endorsement.

Regulatory agencies are empowered to promulgate rules that have the force of law. The Congress can overturn them only with great difficulty, and in a number of cases, the courts have ruled that the Congress lacks the technical expertise to interfere in any way. There is, of course, judicial review, but it is a long, usually costly, litigious process that seldom results in anything being rescinded.

Once a rule is in place, it is enforced by commission or agency staff. Those charged with violation of a rule have commission staff for judge and jury. Often they end up paying penalties without being officially charged with anything at all. And if a company or individual doesn't carefully follow industry trade journals or subscribe to the *Federal Register,* it or he may never know a new rule has been adopted at all— until it's too late.

Under the provisions of the 1946 Administrative Procedure Act, which governs all the Regs, a new rule comes into being something like this:

A staff assistant at the federal Ice Cream Control Commission (ICCC) decides he does not like the taste of tutti-frutti ice cream and that eating it makes him irritable. He concludes that eating tutti-frutti ice cream causes irritability and gets permission from the staff director, who has a weight problem and doesn't eat ice cream, to initiate proceedings to deal with the matter. Shortly afterwards, the commission officially proposes a new rule banning the manufacture, distribution, and sale of tutti-frutti ice cream throughout the United States.

The proposed rule is published in the *Federal Register,* a daily publication not exactly in the circulation league of *TV Guide* and *Reader's Digest.* This is all the notice the public gets. The staff man has the option of directly informing all the ice cream manufacturers, distributers, and retailers, but ICCC prefers an item in the *Register.* How informative an item would that be? Here's one picked at random by the *Washington Monitor* as an illustration for its clients.

(4110-03)
1 (2) CFR Part 680)
2 (Docket No. 78N-0172)
3 ALLERGENIC PRODUCTS

4 Proposed Limit of Maximum Volume in Multiple Dose Containers

5 AGENCY: Food and Drug Administration.

6 ACTION: Proposed rule.

7 SUMMARY: This is a proposal to amend the biologics regulation to limit the permitted maximum volume contained in multiple dose containers to 30 milliliters thereby reducing the potential danger of contamination of allergenic products by limiting the available number of injectable doses in the container. The proposal would make the requirements for manufacturers of allergenic products consistent with the U.S. Pharmacopeia ("U.S.P.") regarding maximum volume of product for multiple dose containers.

8 DATES: Comments by September 12.

In other words, if the ice cream dealers didn't employ a National Ice Cream Purveyors Association to sit in Washington and comb the *Federal Register* every day for interesting items like that, the tutti-frutti ban could sail through unimpeded.

Which is almost what happens. All the Administrative Procedure Act requires is that the ICCC accept written data, views, or arguments from interested parties before adopting the new rule. It may hold a public hearing or hearings if it wants to, but it doesn't have to. If it does elect to hold a hearing, the roles of prosecutor, judge, jury, and bailiff will be performed by ICCC staff. The staff also has the power to decide who will testify in opposition to the new rule. If from a hundred prospective opposition witnesses they pick a known fool with a long arrest record, that's their privilege.

After the hearing or written arguments, the staff makes its report and recommendations, which—surprise!—are to press on with the ban on tutti-frutti. This is published in the form of a general statement about the need and purpose of the rule along with a statement of 30 days' notice before the rule is to take effect. A summary of the rule in its final form is also published in the *Federal Register*. Here's an example of how informative that can be.

SUMMARY: The Commodity Futures Trading Commission ("Commission") is revising regulation 1.50 to permit the Commission periodically to review the designations of contract markets more efficiently. Regulation 1.50 previously required each contract market to demonstrate to the Commission at least once every five years the provisions that it had made to comply with the conditions and requirements for designation as a contract market set forth in sections five and five A of the Commodity Exchange Act, as amended. The automatic five-year filing requirement has been deleted. A contract market will be required to file a report upon the request of the

Commission to demonstrate compliance with all or a specified portion of the conditions and requirements of sections five and five A.

If all else fails, including the most expensive efforts of lawyer and/or lobbyist, there is always "Judicial Review." All a plaintiff has to prove is that the agency's regulatory action is arbitrary, capricious, an abuse of discretion, unconstitutional, in excess of statutory jurisdiction, taken without following proper procedure, or unsupported by evidence. Ronald Reagan has carried on as though every regulation ever adopted in the history of the U.S. government was all of those things, but the courts are not similarly inclined.

If the rule makers have extraordinary power, the rule enforcers are no wimps, either. Consider the not atypical case of Joseph Sugarman, president of the JS & A mail order firm of Northbrook, Illinois.

In January 1979, two killer blizzards struck the Chicago area, a near cataclysm that, among other things, made an angry lady named Jane Byrne mayor. It also prevented nearly all of Sugarman's employees from getting to work. As a result of that, and a near catastrophic computer breakdown, Sugarman encountered serious delays in shipping out his merchandise—as did firms all over Chicago. He was also unable to fully comply with a Federal Trade Commission rule that requires mail order firms to send customers a written notice if their goods are going to be delayed in shipment more than 30 days.

A month or so later, as he and his staff were struggling to catch up with their orders, an investigator from the Chicago office of the FTC came by and asked how things were going. He was told JS & A was making progress but that there were 3,166 orders still stuck in the computer. The next thing Sugarman knew, he was advised that he was in violation of the 30-day notice rule and that, unless he wanted to go through a long, arduous, and extremely expensive process of adjudication and review by the FTC staff and commissioners and ultimately the courts, it would be nice if he signed a consent order agreeing not to be so nasty ever again—and also, cough up $100,000 in the way of a fine.

Sugarman's response was belligerent, always a mistake with regulatory agencies. In time he found that FTC staff had embarked on a fishing expedition to unearth complaints against his firm as a means of bolstering the agency's case (as an FTC official subsequently put it, "What's wrong with fishing expeditions?"). The agency also subpoenaed several hundred documents, including what amounted to Sugarman's mailing list.

It was never for a moment suggested by Sugarman that he wasn't in violation of FTC rules. What got to him was the immense raw power that a handful of agency staff would wield on their own volition. The

$100,000 fine was the sort the FTC usually reserves for really sleazy, unscrupulous bad actors. Sugarman's is a first-rate firm, marketing chiefly pocket computers, tape recorders, and other expensive electronic items to businessmen and professionals. So large a fine could have ruined his company's reputation just because of its size. The man-hours his company would lose producing the requested documents constituted another severe penalty. Worse, competitors might use the federal Freedom of Information Act to gain access to his subpoenaed mailing list records. In direct mail advertising, your mailing list is everything.

An advertising man, Sugarman fought back the best way he knew how—with advertising. Buying space in the *Wall Street Journal* and other national publications, Sugarman launched a long advertising campaign setting forth his case against what he charged was an egregious abuse of power by the FTC.

Ultimately, and predictably, he lost. The FTC's Washington office and the courts upheld the action taken by the local staff in Chicago. But his campaign attracted widespread attention and support, and proved a portent. Two years after Sugarman fell victim to the Chicago blizzard, the FTC itself came in for a bit of trouble—that almost cost it its existence. Ronald Reagan became President.

The regulatory burden, as the Reaganites called it, grew with every Congress and President since Abraham Lincoln took the oath of office in 1860. As the Reaganites like to ignore, most of the environmental protection effort by the federal government was brought about by the Nixon administration, and it was the most popular and worthwhile enterprise Nixon ever attached his name to.

There were excesses, however, and it can be safely said that in the 1970s, many of the Regs simply ran amok.

The FTC stepped over the line with an assault on "kidvid" advertisers who aimed television programming and commercials at little tykes in the presumption they were easy marks. The television industry screamed censorship. Cynics noted that if the FTC really wanted to get something unfair, misleading, and exploitive off the television screens, it would outlaw political advertising.

The Consumer Product Safety Commission, which seemed bent on locking everyone in America in safe rubber rooms complete with directions on how to use the rubber padding, proposed a rule to require manufacturers of swimming pool slides to cover their products with diagrams and written instructions on how to use them. "Put your left foot on the flat place. This is the first step. Then, put your right foot in the next flat place. Stand up fully on your right foot. Move your left foot to . . ."

The Occupational Safety and Health Administration came up with a nifty proposal to require portable outdoor toilets within a 15-minute walk of every agricultural worker in the country when he was at his place of employment. That works out to about one portable toilet every half mile. Over amber fields of privies, etc. . . . . Cowboys are agricultural workers.

The horror stories were legion and universal. Wisconsin Governor Patrick Lucey compiled a massive volume of federal rules and regulations his own state government had trouble complying with. One required the windows of a state hospital to be ripped out and reconstructed because they didn't meet exact federal width specifications. Another required the state to hire two workers to stand at the gate of each state construction project and count entering and exiting dump trucks. A dump truck, apparently, could escape one man's notice.

US News & World Report made a survey of one town, Cape Girardeau, Missouri (pop. 35,000), and found that nearly everyone in the community had a gripe about federal and state regulations. The local hospital, for example, had to hold five public hearings and produce 120,000 pages of data, documents, and testimony to justify a $6.7 million expansion of its critical-care center.

Reagan made a hugely successful campaign issue of these excesses. Alarmed, if not actually cackling fiendishly, Jimmy Carter's Democratic regulators moved swiftly after Reagan's election to enact some 847 last-minute "midnight regulations" before the new administration could take power.

When the Reaganites at last did enter the corridors of regulatory power, they were about as discreet and merciful as drunken Visigoths. The only good rule was a dead rule. Free enterprise was going to burst its chains.

They advanced along a multipronged front. In the Congress, Reaganite lawmakers worked to exempt specific businesses and industries from regulatory rule (most notoriously, the funeral industry), an effort that drew forth hordes of salivating lobbyists like ants to a big picnic. There was also a move to increase Congressional veto power over rule making. An immediate freeze was ordered halting implementation of all the Carter "midnight regulations," pending further review. OMB Director David Stockman, comporting himself like St. George the dragon killer, authored a budget that explicitly and rather unconstitutionally sought to curb regulatory agencies and alter their policies through executive slashes in their operating funds—even though the agencies were created by Congress and supposedly independent of the executive. Publicly disdaining any need for the Federal Trade Commission whatsoever, Stockman tried to cut its budget by 25 percent and eliminate all funding for the FTC's Bureau of Competition, its antitrust arm, leaving all federal antitrust powers in the hands of Reagan-buddy William French Smith's Justice Department.

The FTC was to play the principal dragon to Stockman's St. George. From the very first, the Reaganites made it blood-curdlingly clear they wanted the head of FTC Chairman Michael Pertschuk.

The Reaganites also terrorized the agencies with a bewildering new concept in rule making. Henceforth, rules had to be cost-effective. The agencies somehow had to show that new rules were worth all the money they were costing industry.

For all Reagan's success in getting his budget and tax cut legislation through Congress, his assault on the regulatory agencies had to run heavy fire. The Reaganites discovered, among other things, that it most usually takes adoption of a new rule to eliminate or weaken an existing one. They also discovered that, for every rule, there is a voluble if not powerful constituency. Regulation of funeral directors, for example, has long been supported by an increasingly powerful group of voters known as senior citizens.

The FTC's Bureau of Competition was there to protect (largely Republican) small businessmen from the clutches of big business. With the help of Vice-President Bush and several key Republican members of Congress, Stockman was stopped dead in his effort to abolish the Bureau of Competition. Of the 847 "midnight regulations," Bush's Task Force on Regulatory Relief and Stockman's OMB were able to review 725 by the time the freeze ended. They let 669 go into effect. No industry was fully exempted from federal regulation. Not from the Consumer Product Safety Commission's rules, though they were made subject to congressional veto, nor the FTC's, though Pertschuk was deposed as chairman. All on their own, the Civil Aeronautics Board and the Federal Communications Commission deregulated themselves, dramatically relaxing federal control over public air routes and air waves, but this effort was begun before Reagan came into office.

As for cost benefit, the cost of all regulations to American business in 1980 was more than $100 billion, a figure rising to $150 billion by 1982, largely through the process of inflation. But how do you assess the value of their benefit? James Worsham, regulatory correspondent for the *Chicago Tribune,* put it this way:

> Air pollution curbs mean $5 billion to $58 billion in annual benefits because of lower death rates and less disease; twenty-eight thousand lives were saved from 1966 through 1974 because of passenger safety

features on autos; and hundreds of children's deaths were avoided because of safety rules for such items as cribs and medicine container caps.

Even by the Reagan administration's figuring, OSHA regulations produced benefits of $6.4 billion in 1978 in terms of lower insurance rates, fewer accidents, and fewer medical problems. Their 1978 cost was $4.3 billion. The Environmental Protection Agency produced $23.3 billion in benefits in 1978 for $22.7 billion in cost, with $50.3 billion in benefits expected by 1985. The National Highway Traffic Safety Administration's rules cost $4 billion for $6 billion in benefits.

In its first four and a half months, Bush's Regulatory Relief Task Force identified $18 billion in what it deemed unnecessary regulations. The Reaganites were able to retard somewhat the growth of new regulations, stop the excesses, and send most of the zealots running for cover.

But in neither their initial or subsequent efforts were they able to slay the dragon. With good reason. As Pertschuk told us in an interview: "The answer to bad regulation is not no regulation."

Were there no regulatory agencies, private citizens would have to rely on the honesty, compassion, concern, and competence of private industry. Such sorry sagas as Love Canal, the Scott Paper Company's Wisconsin Oconomo River plant, Ford's exploding Pintos, General Motors' Oldsmobiles with Chevrolet engines, combustible children's pajamas, Three Mile Island, and countless purveyors of botulism testify to the fact that mere profit too often comes first.

The following individuals are representative of all we have to protect us.

THE TOP TEN POWERS IN REGULATORY GOVERNMENT
1. James C. Miller III
One of the biggest guns ever to come out of the American Enterprise Institute, Jim Miller was the executive director of Bush's Regulatory Relief Task Force and a natural choice for Reagan's chairman of the FTC, the mightiest of the Regs. As his books, articles, monographs, and voluminous congressional testimony make clear, there are few people wandering around Washington as predisposed against big government and the uneconomical nature of government operations. As even his critics will admit, he is one of the most scholarly, rational, and reasonable man of that bent holding office in the Reagan administration.

Born in 1942 in Atlanta, Miller earned a BA in economics from the University of Georgia and a doctorate from the University of

Virginia. He taught for a year at Georgia State, then joined the Nixon administration in 1969 as senior economist at the Department of Transportation. He left the Nixon scene in 1972, a wise time to do so, becoming a research associate first at the infidel Brookings Institution and then at the comfortably orthodox AEI. From September 1972 until June 1974, he served as a consultant to the feds while a professor of economics at Texas A&M, rejoining the administration as Nixon was leaving it as senior economist for the Council of Economic Advisors. In 1975, President Ford put him on his wage-price control team as his chief regulatory expert.

Miller sat out the Carter administration, doubtless wincing, as a resident AEI scholar and then codirector of AEI's Center for the Study of Government Regulation. Reagan had to look no further for a gunslinger to take on the Regs.

In all fairness, the right-wing zanies should note that his tenure at Brookings in 1972 was only a month.

2. Annie Gorsuch

In 1978, a group of field marshals of industry organized as the Business Roundtable surveyed 48 leading American companies and found that it cost them $2.6 billion in 1977 to comply with the regulations of six major regulatory agencies. Three-quarters of this cost came from compliance with Environmental Protection Agency rules.

In issuing its first report, the Bush Task Force mentioned one agency above all others in terms of negative comment: the EPA.

Largely the creation of the Nixon administration, the EPA has been one of the most powerful and probably the most effective regulatory agency in the federal government. It saved the Great Lakes at a time when Lake Erie was slipping into the grave and Lake Michigan was on the critical list. It came too late to prevent Love Canal, but it averted thousands of toxic-waste dump atrocities just like it. It dragged the American automobile industry kicking and screaming into viable competition with environmentally safe and fuel-efficient Japanese and German cars.

Annie Gorsuch was an obvious choice for a Reagan administration that considered Interior Secretary James Watt "an environmentalist." A protégé of Watt who, as a Colorado state legislator, fought legislation curbing toxic waste, she lost no time as EPA director coming forth with proposed changes in the Clean Air Act that among other things doubled the allowable amount of nitrogen oxide and carbon monoxide pollution from automobile exhaust. Her changes also called for more study rather than quick action on acid rain.

Though thousands of Canadian lakes were dying from sulphuric and nitrogen pollutants in the air coming from the United States, she said the causes of acid rain were "largely speculation."

"Whether you contact my friends or my enemies, they'll tell you two things: I'm intelligent, and I'm capable of making hard decisions."

Born in 1943, she graduated from the University of Colorado at the age of 19. Finishing law school there in 1964, she went off to India on a Fulbright, teaching English and studying Indian prisons. Before her election to the Colorado legislature, she worked as a lawyer for a bank and a telephone company and as an assistant district attorney. The divorced mother of three, she is a close friend of former Colorado House Speaker Robert Burford, a cattle rancher whom Reagan made head of the Bureau of Land Management.

And she has this to her credit, at least in Reagan's eyes: the EPA is perhaps the most chaotically and ineffectually run agency in the government. Mismanagement is just as crippling as a budget cut.

3. David Stockman

The ubiquitous young (born 1946) David Stockman has his sharp-nailed thumb on the regulatory agencies as much as he does on the rest of the federal bureaucracy. When, as the new OMB director, he expressed the opinion that there was no need at all for the FTC, no one thought he was kidding.

Occasionally, he got too far out in front, as in his attempt to kill the FTC's Bureau of Competition and turn over all antitrust power to Justice. He hadn't consulted Reagan before floating his plans in the press, and got no support from the White House when powerful Republicans on The Hill and elsewhere rose to the Bureau's defense.

Stockman also discovered that, while a slashed budget can be intimidating, it doesn't necessarily stop an agency from doing what Congress has ordered it to do. Nevertheless, though Stockman's axe didn't cut off any heads, it sliced off a lot of limbs. He has captured the attention of the once all-powerful regulatory warlords as has no one in recent governmental history.

4. Tommy Boggs

As former FTC Chairman Mike Pertschuk noted once in an interview, there are Washington lawyers who fight the Regs in the courts and those who fight them on The Hill, with those going the Hill route often the most successful. No one has been more successful than Tommy Boggs, the most effective regulatory agency specialist in town. A former congressional staffer whose late father was powerful Louisiana Congressman Hale Boggs and whose mother, Lindy Boggs, still holds the seat, Boggs knows precisely whom to go to no matter what the problem. It was he who was credited with organizing the steamroller of a lobby that so successfully threw "kidvid" back in the FTC's face.

Born in 1940, Boggs graduated from Georgetown University in 1961 and has stayed in Washington ever since, except for such occasional jaunts as his serving as a member of Jimmy Carter's trade delegation to China in 1979 and with the delegation marking the independence of the Solomon Islands. A high-ranking honcho of sorts in the Lyndon Johnson and Hubert Humphrey campaigns, Boggs was made a charter member of the Democratic National Committee in 1973. He ran for Congress from Maryland in 1970 and lost. A number of regulators probably wish he had won. He has infinitely more power and influence on the outside.

5. Jack Anderson

As Mike Pertschuk sees it, columnist Jack Anderson is a more important figure on the regulatory battlefield than even Ralph Nader, than perhaps anyone. Nader holds press conferences to which no one comes, and in fact has largely abandoned lobbying for grass-roots organizing. Anderson's column runs in 1,100 newspapers. When he exposes a dangerous automobile defect, the world knows. It's not the same with items in the *Federal Register* or Nader's harangues in commission hearings. What industry fears most is publicity, and there is no one in the country to provide it the way Anderson can. In the *Washington Post,* his column appears on the comics page instead of the editorial page. Anderson has said he doesn't mind at all: The comics page has many more readers.

Some complain that Anderson is spreading himself too thin, what with his newspaper column, *Parade* pieces, exhausting lecture tours, investigative magazine, network television appearances, talk show guest shots, and many coauthored books. Much of the research and preparation for the column is done by young assistants and interns not long out of college. Indeed, his Victorian headquarters on 16th Street could double for one of Nader's outfits. But for all their youth and the disdain shown for them by the more pompous members of the Washington press corps, they are among the most powerful people in Washington. And Anderson is their leader.

A Mormon born in Long Beach, California, in 1922, the mildly eccentric Anderson attended the University of Utah, Georgetown University, and George Washington University. Starting as a reporter with the *Salt Lake Tribune,* he served as a war correspondent for the *Deseret News* after a stint in the Merchant Marines and considers himself an old China hand. He joined Drew Pearson's "Washington

Merry-go-Round" as a reporter in 1947, became a partner in 1965, and took over the column entirely in 1969, after Pearson's death. He has nine children and has written or been coauthor of twelve books. He also won a Pulitzer Prize.

6. Thorne Auchter

If the mention of any government agency can prompt a captain of industry to hit the roof of his club, it's the Occupational Safety and Health Administration. Plant managers dread OSHA inspectors the way Frank Nitti used to fear Elliot Ness and his Untouchables. And with few exceptions, OSHA inspectors are untouchables.

Many of President Reagan's close friends and supporters would be just as happy if OSHA suddenly went the way of the Philippine Alien Property Commission, but nothing doing. It has too many friends on The Hill—and in coal mines and factories.

Assistant Secretary of Labor Thorne Auchter, the man Reagan put in charge of OSHA, is no James Watt, but he's no Ralph Nader, either. A Florida construction executive before joining the Reagan administration, he is not exactly the sort of fellow to allow OSHA to promulgate any rules for portable toilets for cowboys, although he seems a reasonable enough sort to keep them for construction workers.

Born in 1945, Auchter graduated from Jacksonville University, and at one time worked as an apprentice carpenter.

7. George Bush

The Vice-President entered the White House having done practically everything there was to do in government, but the Reagan boys managed to hit him with a first assignment for which he had no background or preparation or experience: chairman of the presidential task force on regulatory reform. Some newsmen thought he was being set up as a patsy, that Haig men, Casey men, and Allen men wanted him kept away from intelligence and foreign affairs—despite his eminent qualifications—and that it would be just dandy for him to take the heat for what would ultimately prove a highly unpopular emasculation of the regulatory agencies.

But Bush was able to reduce appreciably the scope and cost of government regulation, and without committing the axe murder that so many had feared and so many Reaganites seemed to desire. His decisions were rational, reasonable, responsible, and—in keeping with the essence of the man—very fair. It was he as much as anyone who kept Stockman from butchering the Bureau of Competition.

However, he lacked the guts, inclination, or power to restrain the ruthless likes of James Watt and Annie Gorsuch in their terrorist campaign against the environment and environmental protection regulation.

8. Ray Peck

No one knows the regulatory business like a Washington lawyer or association lobbyist, and Ray Peck, Reagan's administrator of the all-powerful National Highway Traffic Safety Administration, has been both, working as an attorney both in and out of government and as vice president in charge of regulatory affairs for the National Coal Association, not the Regs' best pal. But now, as they say, he is one. He is responsible for the safety and good mileage of the American automobile, a post that gives him a very long reach into the lives of nearly every American.

Born in 1940, the New Jersey native obtained his law degree from New York University. His previous experience in government includes director of energy regulatory and legislative policy for the Treasury Department from 1974 to 1975 and deputy assistant secretary for energy and minerals in the Interior Department.

Not exactly a Joan Claybrook, his predecessor in the safety post, Peck is emphasizing "raising America's level of awareness" about things like seat belts and child restraints. And maybe raising speed limits, too.

9. Senator Bob Packwood

Bob Packwood is chairman of the Senate Commerce Committee, the most important and effective congressional brake on excessive regulation and on right-wing efforts to abolish government regulation. Packwood, one of the leading Republican moderates, is perfect for the role, his ascension to the chairmanship one of the few occasions when the committee seniority system worked. His ADA (liberal) and ACA (conservative) ratings have both been in the low to middle 40s. If his COPE (labor) rating has been as high as the 60s, the record shows he was for deregulation of natural gas.

Born in Portland in 1932, the Oregonian graduated from Willamette University and received his law degree from New York University in 1957. Before his election to the Senate in 1968, he worked as an attorney and member of the Oregon House of Representatives.

10. Mike Pertschuk

The bespectacled, thoughtful-looking Mike Pertschuk, who has been seen lunching at Dominique's in tweed jacket and checkered sport shirt, has been demoted from FTC chairman to mere commissioner. The car and driver are gone, as is the power to take on a major industry like the funeral directors single-handed.

But he remains the conscience of the commission, a professional bureaucrat so able he was considered probably the best appointment made by Jimmy Carter. When Reagan first attempted to oust him upon taking office in January 1981, Patricia Bailey, one of the sitting Republican members of the commission and Reagan's choice for acting chairman, made an impassioned defense of Pertschuk and lost her job as a result. One of her chinamen had been Senate Majority Leader Howard Baker.

A Yale man born in London in 1933, Pertschuk was on the staff of the Senate Commerce Committee from 1964 to 1977, the last nine years as the powerful chief counsel and staff director. Carter named him FTC chairman in 1977. More than any of the Reagan men, he knows how it all works. Despite such stumblings as "kidvid" and the Sugarman case, he also knows how it all should work. As long as he is on the commission, David Stockman will not have an easy life.

Moneymen

WASHINGTON IS not a money town in the usual sense of the term. True, it has those $60,000-and-up government salaries, and there are jokes about $50,000 a year being the Washington minimum wage. Lawyers and lobbyists often pull down 10 times that much. The metropolitan area's cost and standard of living have ranked near or at the top. Its housing costs are third highest in the nation and are ahead of New York's. Mercedes Benzes, BMWs, and Volvos are as common as Volkswagens. French restaurants seem to sprout on every corner and in every suburban shopping center. Since the advent of the Reagan administration, capital ladies go about wrapped in all the furs and jewels they can buy or borrow, even in the dreadful heat.

But it's not a money town like New York, Chicago, or even Pittsburgh. There's next to nothing in the way of "old family" wealth, and most of what there is belongs to third-rate relatives of other cities' "great families" who came to Washington to find a pond small enough to make a splash in. There's no way to make a fortune except in real estate, law, or car dealerships. There are no major industries. There's no New York Stock Exchange, no Chicago commodity, options, or other high-roller futures markets. No far-flung business or financial empires are headquartered in Washington. It has no Citicorp or Bank of America and the only bank of major stature it does possess—Riggs—hardly compares with Chicago's First National or Continental.

But it's a money town in a way that no other city in America is. It decides how much money everyone is going to have.

By taxing and borrowing, it sucks up nearly $800 billion from the rest of the country every year and, in one form or another, spews it back, as it sees fit (in the Reagan administration's case, less now spewed on northern cities and more on Sunbelt defense industries). It hands out $160 billion a year to people all over the country, and world, in Social Security payments. With the advice and consent of the Senate Finance Committee, the House Ways and Means Committee decides how much federal taxes we'll have to pay (although the Reagan administration's federal tax cuts were wiped out for most people by state and local tax increases necessitated by the Reagan administration's budget cuts).

The biggest say, though, belongs to a peculiar institution known as the Federal Reserve, a sort of Supreme Court of the economy, a police force against inflation. Through a system of Federal Reserve main and branch banks in 12 Federal Reserve districts throughout the country, it quite literally controls the flow of money into the economy.

The method is a trifle mysterious. It can enlarge the amount sloshing about in the economy by floating checks on its own account. It can shrink the money supply by calling up federal notes lent to banks. It can affect the level of interest rates by increasing the interest it charges banks for money lent. The effect is dramatic. By increasing the amount of money available for capital development and expansion, and for spending, the Fed can of its own volition heat up the economy. By curbing the supply, it can curb inflation—and put a lot of people out of work. By curbing the money supply, it also drives up interest rates, as it has been insistently and stubbornly doing for the past several years.

The secret of its power is its autonomy. Its economic policies and monetary decisions are set and made by its 7 governors, and 5 of the 12 presidents of its Federal Reserve banks. The governors are appointed by the President, but serve 14-year terms. The bank presidents, who rotate the five voting seats among each other, are totally subservient to the board.

The Fed often cooperates with the White House—sometimes too well. Though he vehemently denies it, former Fed chairman Arthur Burns' easy money policies in the inflationary year of 1972 didn't hurt Richard Nixon's reelection chances. According to financial columnist William Neikirk, Burns' successor, G. William Miller, pursued looser money policies when tighter ones were needed. Miller was close to the Carter administration and subsequently was made treasury secretary, a job with less power but more glamor.

But the Fed just as often acts independently. Miller's successor Paul Volcker endorsed a bail-out loan for the high-roller Hunt brothers when they went bottom up in the silver market to keep their bankers from going bottom up, too. At the same time, farmers, housing developers, small businesses, and car dealers were begging for more loan money, and not getting a penny.

The Fed can also operate in direct opposition to the White House. The Carter administration went out yelping about high interest rates. The Reagan administration at least made a public pretense of complaining about them. Half the government heads of Europe screamed about them. And all with good reason.

The prime rate in 1974, when the Fed was successfully fighting a terrifying bout of double-digit inflation, was 12 percent. As inflation subsided in 1975 and 1976 to 4.8 percent, the prime fell to 6.5 percent. By 1979 it was up past 15 percent. It hit 20 percent in 1980, fell briefly back to 11, then zoomed back up to 20. Volcker's Fed was going to ride herd on inflation come what may.

What came most recently was the Reagan administration and the holy gospel of the Kemp-Roth tax cut. By 1981, a tax cut was certainly justified. Inflation had driven the middle class into the tax brackets of the rich. But Kemp-Roth wasn't brought forward as legitimate tax relief accompanied by corresponding cuts in federal spending. It was Keynesian pump-priming (for a favored class of citizens) accompanied by a massive shift in federal spending from admittedly wasteful social programs to equally wasteful and highly inflationary defense programs, with the equally inflationary federal deficit zooming to more than $100 billion.

The Kemp-Roth zealots argued that President Kennedy had successfully pulled off such a tax cut. But Kennedy did that at a time when the government was running a budgetary surplus and the inflation rate was less than 1 percent. His cut was followed by a progressive rise in inflation. The Kemp-Roth fanatics also contended that taxpayers would put their tax-cut money into savings, making money available for capital development. But the majority put their money into increased state, local, and Social Security taxes, continued inflation, and—if anything was left—consumer goods. Industries seeking capital for expansion had to deal with that, as well as the fact that the Reagan administration was borrowing huge amounts of capital to finance its huge deficits. Also, Volcker's Fed was not relenting in its policy of tight money, even if it meant continued high interest rates. These made it that much more difficult for industry to get capital and also added to the federal deficit by increasing the government's cost of borrowing money.

As the Fed saw it, the nation's long-term interests were best served by curbing inflation first. If the Reagan administration wanted to throw some capital to industry, it could cut its real spending and eliminate those huge federal deficits that Reagan used to complain about when he was campaigning. As always, the Fed knew best.

What commended Reagan's economic prosperity plan most to the Congress—aside from the obvious allure of handing the voters a big tax cut—was the skillful lobbying effort of Treasury Secretary Donald Regan. As much as congressmen went all soft and helpless at the President's stroking, or terrified at the prospect of being gunned down in the next election by right-wing PAC hunter-killer squads, they had to wonder why Wall Street was reacting to the President's panacea with wails, shrieks, hair-tearing, utter confusion, and precipitous drops in the Dow-Jones. Regan, former chairman of Merrill Lynch, and the highest-rated cabinet officer in a *US News & World Report* survey, was reassuring, even though the stock and bond markets continued to confound him.

Treasury secretaries have long been among the strongest members of the cabinet, as the records of Regan, Miller, William Simon, and John Connally most certainly attest.

It goes with the territory. Treasury is to the economy what Defense is to World War. Though White House economists and the folks at the Fed like to horn in, Treasury is the principal formulator of American fiscal policy. It is the printer, circulator, and defender of the American dollar. Its jurisdiction includes trade, taxes, investment, commodities, natural resources, developing nations, international affairs, budget and program analysis, revenue sharing, state and local finance, industrial economics, and financial institutions. It has an office of New York finance and a post called deputy assistant secretary for Saudi Arabian affairs.

Treasury runs a friendly little agency known as the Internal Revenue Service. It runs the Mint; the Bureau of Engraving; the U.S. Customs Service; the Comptroller of the Currency; and the U.S. Secret Service.

After the Capitol, it is the most imposing federal building on Pennsylvania Avenue and next-door to the White House. New Presidents riding along in their inaugural parade quickly learn why.

This isn't quite what the Founding Fathers, most particularly Alexander Hamilton, intended. For the first few decades, financial power in this country resided largely in the hands of a quasipublic but mostly private institution known as the Bank of the United States, in Philadelphia, run by an insufferable would-be aristocrat named Nicholas Biddle. Though Biddle protected his interests in the Senate by doling out annual $23,000 bribes to Daniel Webster, among others, to keep U.S. deposits in his bank, Andrew Jackson was able to bring the bank down by abruptly withdrawing federal deposits. Disliking paper money as well, which then was issued solely by banks, Jackson also issued his Specie Circular requiring that all federal land purchases be paid for with gold and silver coins.

The immediate consequence was a depression and much chaos and confusion. Banking power shifted from Philadelphia to New York. Ultimately, though, Jackson's protégé James K. Polk was able to establish an independent treasury and concentrate the nation's financial power in Washington, for good.

If the Fed and the Treasury spoon-feed money into the economy, the World Bank—Washington's third leading financial institution— throws it around all over the world.

Perhaps more accurately described as the Third World Bank, the bank was founded in 1944 along with the International Monetary Fund. Its initial purpose was to provide development capital for the rebuilding of postwar Europe, but it quickly became a major conduit of foreign-aid loans and credits to underdeveloped nations.

One recent $615 million batch of loans and credits included $32 million to Burma to improve the efficiency of its teak industry, $14 million to Egypt for a fish farm, $3.2 million to Haiti for agricultural hurricane recovery, $30 million to Pakistan for small industries (atomic bomb factories?), and $9 million to Uganda for expansion of water systems.

Occupying one of the more palatial structures in Washington (its employees have salaries to match), the World Bank has 139 member nations and assets of $40 billion. Because it supplies some 20 percent of the $12 billion or so the Bank shells out every year, the United States has long had the major say in Bank operations, though the Bank is totally independent.

When former Defense Secretary Robert McNamara retired after 13 years as president of the Bank in late 1980, some member nations started muttering about replacing him with former British Prime Minister Edward Heath or another non-American. The Third World members wanted former United Nations ambassador Andrew Young. Fat chance.

The Export-Import Bank, headquartered in posh digs across Lafayette Park from the White House, is a federally-funded institution that lends money to foreign companies and countries to buy American goods. It often gets paid back.

Loans have been running as high as $5 billion a year. Some of the more notable ones recently have included $504 million to South Korea to buy nuclear power plants from Westinghouse, $97 million to Angola for a gas reinjection project, $50 million to Taiwan for a gas and oil plant, and $87 million to Britain's Laker Airways to buy five DC-10s.

In the spring of 1981, the ExIm suffered its first losing quarter in its history. Unless it got help, there were predictions it could go out of business in four years. Instead of first aid, the bank got mostly snarls from the Reagan administration, which had called it "inefficient" and "market distorting." OMB Director Stockman started yapping at its heels with talk of cutting its operations back by 40 percent. In some quarters in Washington there was talk about abolishing ExIm altogether.

But the Reagan administration balked at anything so drastic, finding—as it has with so many of its attempts to cut budgets—that the bank has a big Republican constituency. Westinghouse, McDonnell Douglas, Boeing, and General Electric are names to get the President's attention.

Local banks don't always have an easy time of it in Washington, as the sorry tales concerning the Diplomat National Bank and the National Bank of Washington attested. Not so Riggs. Housed in an imposing stone structure just down the street from the White House and across the street from the Treasury, with branches all over the city, it is the Citicorp or Morgan Guaranty Trust of Washington. It is, of course, nothing at all like Citicorp or Morgan Guaranty, but, with assets exceeding $3.5 billion, it is the largest bank in town and getting larger.

Established in 1836, it has long been one of the thickest pillars of the city's conservative establishment, but came in for more exciting times in 1981, when high-flying Texas multimillionaire Joe Allbritton took it over, buying up 40.1 percent of its stock for $70 million. Allbritton, who owned the *Washington Star* from 1975 to 1978, bought a small suburban bank in Houston in 1976 and in four years doubled its deposits. If only he had done as well with the *Star*.

He certainly merits inclusion on the following list.

THE TOP FIVE MONEYMEN IN WASHINGTON
1. Paul Volcker
The Secretary of the Treasury has power, prestige, cabinet rank, and his own police force, but the President can always tell him no. Paul Volcker, the President has to ask. Or beg.

Born in Cape May, New Jersey, in 1927, just in time to be around for the Great Crash, Volcker has always been a commanding presence. At six-feet-seven, he's so tall no one can tell he's balding. With one of his long, two-dollar cigars in his mouth, he's been described as looking like an inverted L. But people would listen to him even if he sucked lollipops and was shorter than Howard Baker.

Volcker entered the world of finance through Princeton, Harvard, and the London School of Economics. From there he became an economist with the Federal Reserve Bank of New York in 1952, and switched to the Chase Manhattan Bank in 1957. Joining the Treasury Department in 1961, he rose to the rank of undersecretary, and became president of the New York Federal Reserve Bank in 1975 and top man at the Fed in 1979.

His appointment and tight money policies were cheered by conservative economists and Republicans everywhere. Reagan himself cheered them, until it finally dawned on him what would happen when Kemp-Roth collided with them.

The Fed's headquarters at 20th and Constitution are in a relatively small building, but the boardroom has been described as something approximating the inside of a cathedral and the board table as possibly the biggest in Washington. Fits exactly.

2. Don Regan

Like an inordinate number of Reagan's cabinet members, Treasury Secretary Don Regan is Irish, hard-driving, and something of a self-made man. He was born in Cambridge, Massachusetts, a month after World War I ended, and got out of Harvard in time to join the Marines in World War II and rise to the rank of lieutenant colonel.

A careerist, he joined Merrill Lynch in 1946, becoming its president in 1968 and chairman in 1971. Considered one of the brightest men on Wall Street, he expanded Merrill Lynch into the biggest brokerage house in the country, with 600 offices and more than 8,000 account executives. He also diversified the firm into banking, real estate, and insurance.

Regan has set the example for intellect and skillful management in the cabinet, and expanded his power and influence deep into other areas such as regulatory reform, to the consternation perhaps of young Stockman.

For all his drive, Regan is a man who, like Reagan, is fond of keeping proper business hours. He is a golfer, a clubman, and the author of *A View from the Street,* published in 1972.

3. A. W. Clausen

The man Jimmy Carter picked to run the World Bank, with the approval of Ronald Reagan, is no Andy Young. He had probably thought he was already running the World Bank.

Alden Winship Clausen took over the World Bank after 10 years as chief executive officer of BankAmerica Corporation and Bank of America, which are to world banking what Boeing is to world aviation.

A bespectacled, stern-faced man who looks every penny the banker, Clausen was born in Hamilton, Illinois, in 1923, went to Carthage College and the University of Minnesota, and thought of becoming a lawyer. Moving to San Francisco in 1949, he took his first job with Bank of America.

An expert on Asia, he came to the World Bank with experience as a member of the Japanese-California Association, the Japan-U.S. Economic Relations Group, and the National Council for U.S.-China Trade.

4. William H. Draper III

The Reagan administration did reduce somewhat the scope of the ExIm Bank's operations and generosity, but put what remained in the hands of entrepreneur William Draper III with instructions to make a going concern of the place again.

Born in White Plains, New York, and a product of Yale and Harvard Business, Draper went west to make his fortune, and did. His most successful enterprise was Sutter Hill Ventures of Palo Alto, California, a venture capital firm specializing in providing capital and management expertise to new companies in high-technology fields. His career in private enterprise was much like that of his friend George Bush.

He was chairman of the Bush presidential campaign's finance committee and served as a California fund-raiser for the Reagan-Bush general election effort.

5. *Joe Allbritton*

Born in D'Lo, Mississippi, in 1924, Joe Lewis Allbritton went to Baylor University and, like many a Texas millionaire, started out as lawyer, beginning practice in Houson in 1949. After that, he just started buying into companies. How he acquired them all is as confusing as his empire's organizational chart, but everything he touched seemed to prosper.

With a net worth exceeding $200 million (some five years ago it was only $100 million), Allbritton has holdings that include 100 percent of Houston's University Bank, 60 percent of Houston's First Bank of Alief, and 40 percent of Washington's Riggs.

He is chairman, president, and 100 percent owner of the Perpetual Corporation, a holding company through which he owns all or part of an English capital investment firm, a big California real estate company, a life insurance company, a string of funeral parlors, a group of newspapers, and the *Washington Star*'s former broadcasting properties.

When he bought the *Star* in 1975, he gave the dying paper its last best shot, hiring a genius editor named Jim Bellows who turned it into a saucy, irreverent, digging, and altogether appealing alternative to the *Post*. The paper might have survived if he had not sold it to Time, Inc., who smothered it in stodginess, but it was no business for a man who likes to double his money.

Dips

EARLY IN HIS FIRST TERM, George Washington noted that the Constitution required him to seek the "advice and consent" of the Senate on all treaties. As he was about to negotiate a treaty with the Creek Indians, he took the proposed text to the Senate chambers and proceeded to ask the Senate members their advice. Vice-President John Adams read the text of the treaty, but there was so much carriage traffic outside no one could hear him. "I could tell it was something about Indians, but was not master of one sentence of it," complained one senator. All the windows were closed and it was read again.

"The business is new to the Senate," the senator said. "It is of importance. It is our duty to inform ourselves." He then proceeded to call for the reading aloud of a number of documents pertinent to the matter. Then random discussions broke out among the senators on the floor. Confusion mounted. Washington glowered. He acceded to a request that action on the first paragraph of the treaty be deferred. Then someone asked for deferment of the second paragraph. Finally, in typical senatorial fashion, they struck the ultimate insulting blow: Could the entire treaty be submitted to a committee for study?

Washington rose in what was described as "a violent fret." "This defeats every purpose of my coming here!" Giving the Senate only until the following Monday to complete their perusals, he angrily departed, muttering: "I'll be damned if I ever go in there again."

He didn't. Perhaps the incident had something to do with his strong words about avoiding foreign entanglements in his Farewell Address.

The conduct of foreign affairs hasn't changed much in 200 years. The State Department has evolved into an enormous bureaucracy that often gets in everybody's way, but it was that way when Thomas Jefferson was secretary of state. Other cabinet departments horn in, but so did Alexander Hamilton's Treasury Department and Henry Knox's War Department. Foreign ambassadors and agents and their hired American lobbyists swarm all over the State Department, Capitol Hill, and the White House. Washington had to contend with

Citizen Genêt. And on most matters of state, modern-day Presidents get along with the Senate about as well as Washington did.

Sometimes it seems a wonder that we get along with any country at all. To see how clever our foreign policy folk can be, consider what happened to our relations with Mexico during the Carter administration. The Yankee-baiting Echeverria had left the Mexican presidency in 1976, replaced by the friendlier and much more moderate José Lopez Portillo. Mexico was just then discovering it had become a major oil power, and was negotiating a deal with American energy companies for long-term supplies of Mexican oil and gas. A pipeline from Mexico's oil fields had been built to within 50 miles of the U.S. border.

Carter's new ambassador to Mexico, Patrick Lucey, was a political appointment. A two-term liberal Democratic governor of Wisconsin, he was a good friend of Minnesota's Walter Mondale, who helped arrange Lucey's selection. Lucey spoke poor Spanish, and was more an administrator than diplomat, but he got along well with Santiago Roel, Mexico's foreign minister. He repeatedly sent cables to Washington apprising the President of the potential for energy and long-term improved relations and warning Washington not to do anything to irritate the Mexicans.

Right. The irritations the United States then inflicted upon Mexico barely stopped short of a declaration of war. At the urgings of labor unions, among other ungenerous groups, we sought to stem the flow of illegal aliens by a knife-edged "tortilla curtain" along our southern border. The arrogant James Schlesinger, fired by Jerry Ford but rehired by Carter as his energy secretary, abruptly vetoed the Mexican gas deal out of hand. Mexico, furious, halted construction of the pipeline.

Carter went down to Mexico desperate to make friends. Instead, he made the horrendous gaffe of telling a Montezuma's revenge joke in a toast at a Mexico City state dinner.

It went from bad to horrible. The ailing Shah of Iran took refuge in Cuernavaca. Henry Kissinger, according to reports, encouraged him to come to the United States for treatment, and lobbied the Carter White House to admit him. Lopez Portillo urged him not to go, saying he might not be able to let him back into Mexico if the Iranian ayatollahs raised hell. The Shah went anyway, and all hell broke loose.

Later, a Carter White House operative planted a ridiculous story with a friendly Washington correspondent that claimed that Lopez Portillo had begged the Shah to go to New York so he could get decent medical care not available in Mexico, an utterance Lopez Portillo vehemently denied.

In trying to bring the staff of his embassy—our largest—firmly under his control, Lucey stepped on a number of Gucci loafers in the chancery and in Washington. His outspoken egalitarian wife, Jean, disliked the rich aristocrats of Mexico's ruling classes and was not fond of the enthusiasm with which embassy staff frolicked in their midst. So she put a damper on embassy parties.

Seizing upon this, and abetted by the Carter White House, career foreign-service types Lucey had stepped on struck back, planting news stories in Mexico and the United States to the effect that the Luceys hated Mexicans.

Lucey had tired of serving the Carter administration in Mexico long before this and arranged to be transferred to Washington as a coordinator of Mexican-American affairs, an administrative post he could perform well. Texas Democrats leaped at the opportunity, as much as Robert Strauss ever leaps, and put up for Lucey's replacement as ambassador a former Texas congressman and failed senatorial candidate, Robert Krueger. Lucey was house-hunting in Washington when word came that Krueger had failed to win the approval of Carter's own ambassadorial screening committee. So Krueger was given the coordinator job and Lucey was told to stay in Mexico.

Krueger still had to be confirmed by the Senate. Bipartisan forces led by Republican Richard Lugar of the Senate Foreign Relations Committee challenged the appointment on the grounds Krueger was unqualified. After a noisy, nasty fight, which the Mexicans followed intently, Krueger was confirmed by a considerably less than routine vote of 45 to 38. He proceeded to spend much of his time in Texas— some said laying the groundwork for another Senate run. During a dispute involving a Mexican oil spill and fire in the Gulf and American pollution of a Mexican river, Krueger was quoted as calling Lopez Portillo a liar. The strongest a diplomat is ever supposed to get is "deeply concerned."

Two more shoes dropped. At the behest of Florida produce growers, factions in the Congress and the Carter White House tried to curb the import of Mexican winter vegetables, including edible, non-plastic, tomatoes.

And when Lucey resigned to help run Teddy Kennedy's presidential campaign in 1980, Carter selected as his replacement a popular Mexican-American school board official from Los Angeles, Dr. Julian Nava. Dr. Nava was a good choice but the Mexicans cold-shouldered him, in part because Mexican aristocrats don't like American Chicanos, in part because they knew it was a cynical ploy to appeal to the Los Angeles Hispanic vote, and in part because they hated Carter so much.

When Reagan named as his ambassador to Mexico John Gavin, an aging movie and television actor who was starring in rum commercials on Mexico City television, he was welcomed warmly. He was a good friend of the new President, which helped, but anything Reagan did was bound to be an improvement.

Like Montezuma, Lucey got his revenge by becoming the vice-presidential candidate on John Anderson's independent ticket. Anderson ran in the strange, vain hope that he might somehow win. Lucey ran for a number of personal satisfactions, chief among them that the Anderson-Lucey ticket took 6 percent of the vote and made Jimmy Carter's political extinction a certainty. Lopez Portillo must have smiled, too, as may have Montezuma.

Lucey's only flaw was that he failed to understand that the State Department and the American foreign policy establishment do not function administratively the way regular government departments do, or as did the real estate business Lucey used to run. Foreign service is a priesthood, a collegial fraternity, a band of brothers no less insular than the OSS eastern establishment liberals who used to run the CIA. Their similarities in dress, speech, tone, manner, and thought are subtly apparent, but pervasive. They are master manipulators of the interoffice stiletto, but they also look out for their own. Should someone do them dirty from the outside, they'll pleasantly bide their time. But at the first opportunity, snicker snack the vorpal blade runs through and through.

Like the old eastern establishment CIA spooks, foreign service officers consider themselves the government's elite. They think they know more about any given area of the world than anyone else. And they're probably right. They also think they should always have their way. They're wrong.

Happily, and unhappily, much intrudes between a policy decision made in the Oval Office and its implementation in some chancery in Africa or Europe. Likewise with the flow of information and opinion from the field back up to the Oval Office. The organizational chart of the State Department is remarkably vertical for a Washington bureaucracy, but between State and the White House, the lines get bent.

The uninitiated in the White House love to take part. Pierre Salinger, mere press secretary, became a major operative in Jack Kennedy's dealings with Khrushchev. Jimmy Carter turned White House oversight on foreign policy over to Ham Jordan. Gerald Rafshoon, Carter's ad man, and Patrick Caddell, his pollster, were part of the Iran hostage–crisis deliberations.

Even more can be done by the initiated. Henry Kissinger turned the relatively unimportant staff post of national security adviser into that of all-powerful chief presidential foreign policy adviser. When, almost as an afterthought, he took over the title of secretary of state as well, he didn't really become secretary of state in the sense of running the department. He mostly took the office and title to prevent any rival from assuming them. He functioned much the same as before, absorbed with such preoccupations as the Middle East while totally ignoring such urgent matters as the 1975–1976 "Cod War" between NATO allies Iceland and Britain. As a consequence, we almost got thrown out of our key air base in Iceland, something the Soviets have been seeking for decades.

Zbigniew Brzezinski, Carter's NSA, was a second-rate Kissinger who never got to be secretary of state, but he messed up much for Cyrus Vance and his successor, Ed Muskie, as the election year "new nuclear strategy" and other fiascos attest. And Reagan's NSA, Richard Allen, all but declared war on Secretary of State Alexander Haig, though, this time, the State Department won.

Other cabinet secretaries are always sticking in their oars. Sometimes, this is to the good. While Henry the K was busy elsewhere, Defense Secretary Donald Rumsfeld played a major role in getting Britain to stop beating up on Iceland in 1975. Carter's Defense Secretary, Harold Brown, was a coconspirator in the "new nuclear strategy" carnival. Caspar Weinberger had big trouble prevailing on the MX question, but none at all selling superarms all over the globe.

Defense and State were strong supporters of the Law of the Sea Treaty because it would restrict sovereign territorial waters to 12 miles or less and would guarantee us the right of peaceful access to all the world's key straits and passages. The treaty was opposed by outfits like Kennecott Copper, who feared it would place too much international control over their deep seabed mining operations. It was Kennecott's friend, Interior Secretary James Watt, who did the most to get the treaty derailed.

As with everything, OMB has a role in foreign afairs. David Stockman, not the most tutored foreign policy analyst, made major decisions concerning foreign aid, and slashed accordingly. He made cuts in the State Department operating budget. As a consequence, the Ireland desk officer was not permitted the travel money to visit Ireland. Nothing going on there. Just ask the Irish Republican Army.

Congress involves itself in foreign policy the way termites involve themselves in home construction. Under such powerful Democrats as former Senators William Fulbright and Frank Church, the Senate Foreign Relations committee not only advised and consented (or refused to), but embarked on foreign policy of its own. Compared to what's happened to the Committee since Republican Charles Percy became chairman, the Reagan people may now think Frank Church looks pretty good.

With Percy the ranking Republican member as well as chairman, the Reagan administration thought it might be nice if Percy could work out an agreement with the White House and other GOP committee members on Reagan's proposals and, in some orderly fashion, work for their passage from the committee to the Senate floor. Instead, Percy has conducted the committee much like the trial scene in *Alice in Wonderland.*

Presiding over an assemblage that includes the disparate likes of the superultraconservative Jesse Helms, flighty liberal Republican Larry Pressler, the sleepy S. I. Hayakawa, the nitpicking Nancy Kassebaum, and loner Charles Mathias—pitted against a phalanx of such tough-minded Democratic liberals as Paul Tsongas, Christopher Dodd, and Paul Sarbanes—Percy seemingly sought to achieve a consensus before taking almost every vote. Assisting him in this ludicrous enterprise was the committee's ranking Democrat, Claiborne Pell, who often looked as though he thought he was serving on the house committee of the Princeton Club.

Percy's committee meetings became some of the high entertainments on Capitol Hill, with the most entertaining part the way Reagan staff would depart screaming and tearing their hair. Despite Republican control of Senate Foreign Relations, the White House often ended up accomplishing more through its GOP minority on the House Foreign Affairs Committee.

More annoying can be the freelancers—members of Congress who conduct their own foreign policy. In 1975, former Senator Dick Clark of the then Democratic-controlled Foreign Relations Committee went to Angola to observe CIA efforts to halt a Communist takeover first-hand. Shortly after his return to the United States, the CIA operation was shut down. The Communists were not shut down, and by late 1981, an African shooting war involving Russian and South African troops was a real possibility.

Senator Howard Baker, his eyes fixed on the 1980 presidential race, went down to Panama and personally renegotiated Jimmy Carter's floundering Panama Canal treaties. As a consequence, they passed, and Baker become a hero to his party's left wing, but a villain to its right. So, when Carter just as fecklessly came forth with his SALT II treaty, Baker tried to renegotiate that, too. All he contributed to the debate was more confusion. The complexities of nuclear warfare were far beyond the grasp of his staff. When some of them went to the Pentagon seeking data to justify a position Baker had taken, the Air Force could only shrug. The Russians weren't about to renegotiate anything anyway. Baker went into the primaries still a villain to the GOP right wing. SALT II died.

Jesse Helms sent "observers" to the British-sponsored Rhodesian peace talks in London. British diplomats in Washington complained they came to disrupt the proceedings and prevent a black government from taking power. For his part, liberal Democratic Congressman Stephen Solarz of New York worked for the creation of a Mugabe Patriotic Front Zimbabwe government so diligently he might as well have been a British agent.

Congressman Paul Findley is the Palestinians' friend on Capitol Hill. Congressman Mario Biaggi of New York has been accused of being the Irish Republican Army's. Congressman Ed Derwinski of Illinois is the champion of the South Korean and Taiwanese governments and the captive nations' governments in absentia of Eastern Europe. The ambassador of Ireland to the United States traditionally reports first to Senator Edward Kennedy and Speaker Tip O'Neill, then to the President.

Few are higher or mightier in their own perception than ambassadors, career or political, ours or other nations'. It is an education to stroll by a congressman's office and see them sitting meekly, striped suits and all, in the reception area, waiting their turn. Sometimes for an hour or more.

As much as they can, foreign diplomats try to formulate our foreign policy for us, an opportunity afforded them in few other countries. We can reach the policy makers in the Kremlin only through their ambassador, or ours, or, in a crunch, through the hotline. In addition to our own dips, other countries have ready access to members of Congress, White House staff, assorted cabinet departments, assorted American lobbying and public relations firms, society leaders, religious groups, unions, and the almighty American news media. They spend vast amounts of money in this effort; honorably, as with Canada's recent lobbying efforts to make the White House and the Congress realize how much American power plants are killing Canadian (and American) lakes and trees with acid rain, or not so honorably, as with Libya's interesting "loan" to Billy Carter.

Sometimes they don't have to spend anything. American-accented Soviet propagandist Vladimir Pozner not only makes regular appearances on ABC-TV's "Nightline" from Moscow, but he gets paid for it. He splits the take with the Kremlin.

Give or take a disaccredited Libyan mission or two trying to sneak into rented offices in McLean, across the river, there are 143 foreign embassies in Washington.

They are staffed by some 2,500 diplomats, the nucleus of a foreign enclave that, with dependents, numbers 17,000. The World Bank, with 2,400 people, adds to this, as do the Organization of American States, the local United Nations office and library, the International Monetary Fund, and myriad small organizations like Ireland's "Cooperation North." Counting foreign students, 6 percent of all those in the country, many of whom have strong or interesting connections to local embassies, there are more than a quarter of a million foreigners in the Washington metropolitan area, probably 10 percent of the population. If nothing else, it makes for some wonderful restaurants. Washington has three featuring Afghan cuisine (Russe flambé?).

The most influential embassy in Washington is perforce the Soviet one. The British and French are supposed to be the next most influential, but they're not. The Brits always make much of their "special relationship" with the United States, but because the relationship is "special"—"special" indeed between ideological soul mates Maggie and Ron—nearly all important matters are handled at foreign secretary and secretary of state level, if not directly between President and PM.

Where the Brits do succeed most splendidly is socially. They are the top snob draw in town, and an invitation to gobble at the ambassador's table or frolic at a gala means you've arrived—as the arrivistes in the Reagan entourage like to say. Protocol chieftess Lee Annenberg didn't curtsy to Prince Charles for nothing.

The French are the British peers on the social front, ranking higher for people who like food. The only decent grub served at the British ambassador's table is French. But, politically, the French are relatively inconsequential. The "special relationship" between Washington and Paris has often been an unpleasant one.

Some of the most effective foreign missions are among the smallest. Because of their large or powerful American constituencies, the Israeli, Irish, and Greek throw around weight many times their own poundage, especially up on The Hill.

Some embassies are so small they are neither very effective nor in Washington. Congo, Equatorial Guinea, Fiji, Guinea-Bissau, Saint Lucia, the Seychelles, and Western Samoa all operate out of their United Nations embassies in New York. The ambassador of Nauru, Mr. H. E. T. W. Star, works out of Melbourne, Australia.

Ambassador Hans Andersen of Iceland serves simultaneously as envoy to the United States and a number of other countries and at the same time has been busy in New York and Geneva as one of the leading figures in the Law of the Sea Conference. The Irish ambassador is simultaneously envoy to the U.S. and to Mexico.

If understaffed, foreign embassies can always hire outside help. Prerevolutionary Iran hired then Senator Jacob Javits' wife as public relations counsel. Former Senate Minority Leader Hugh Scott of Pennsylvania ended up a registered agent for Pakistan. Brother Billy Carter had to register as an agent for Libya to avoid a worse fate.

Overstaffed embassies employ other kinds of agents. Estimates on the number of spies and operatives working out of the Soviet embassy and its Washington satellites range from 30 to 200, although it's small potatoes compared to the hordes they run out of their United Nations operation in New York. Foreign spooks in Washington spy not only on us but on other countries' spies. Israel's Mossad seems to spy on everyone, trusting no one. Exile groups spy on their own country's embassy. It can get very crowded in Washington's museums and other drops.

The principal tool of a practicing dip in Washington, though, is the party. In terms of liver disease, Washington is a more hazardous duty post than Uganda. There is some sort of diplomatic function every night of the year, including the soggy, desolate nights of superheated August. At the height of the season, most particularly approaching Christmas, it's commonplace for some Washingtonians to take in two or three of these do's a night. It was not at all unusual for one of Washington's all-time champion party-goers, Manuel Ramirez, chief of protocol for the fun-loving OAS, to take in four or five. A typical night one recent June (another high season) saw him at a party for U.S. senators, an F Street Club reception, a decorating ceremony at the palatial Pan American Union, and a supper for a departing Belgian ambassador.

The names change, but the guest lists stay the same: fellow diplomats, State Department types, members of Congress, White House types, prominent foreign nationals, prominent Americans of the embassy's nationality, journalists American and foreign, occasional military men, and, if possible, a celebrity (Elizabeth Taylor, Charlton Heston, Maureen Reagan, Prince Charles).

Parties are often given for the most trivial reason: a departing cultural attaché, an obscure national holiday, some visiting unknowns from the home country. The Irish embassy recently threw a lawn party for some visiting Presbyterian ministers from Northern Ireland. But the true purpose is never trivial. The Saudis wanted AWACS airplanes. The Israelis wanted the Saudis not to have AWACS airplanes. The Irish want the Congress and the White House to pressure the British into effecting a political settlement to bring peace to Northern Ireland. Making friends helps.

British and French parties may carry the most prestige, but until 1979 the reputation for the most extravagant and frequent parties went to former Iranian Ambassador Ardeshir Zahedi. In addition to his endless succession of big blasts, he had, according to a congressional report, a "secret fund" of $25,000 a month to be used to make friends for the Shah. Zahedi was most generous, dispensing bottles of Dom Perignon champagne and $200 tins of caviar like so many Christmas cards. Once he felt so generous as to bestow a $6,000 diamond watch on one network news lady, but she returned it. According to a list Zahedi left behind when he fled the embassy, he had 648 big news media names targeted for friendship. Of these, 284 were sent handsome gifts.

Zahedi's purpose with all this extravagant generosity was to try to shore up imperial Iran's public image and American support at a time when many in Congress and the news media were portraying the Shah as a bloodthirsty monster and the Ayatollah Khomeini as just an interesting guy. Zahedi's successor as Washington's most extravagant party giver, Count Wilhelm Wachtmeister, the Swedish ambassador, is no Santa Claus but certainly never lets any of the guests at his sprawling estate at Nebraska and Massachusetts go hungry or thirsty. What no one can figure out is why. What can the Swedish government, which has taxed its citizens to death and has otherwise made Sweden the great pinch-penny of Europe, be after?

Foreign embassies put much more store in American journalists than most Washingtonians do. Washingtonians might dismiss the *New York Times'* James Reston's latest column as just a rehash of Henry Kissinger's lunchtime thoughts. The diplomatic community is interested in Kissinger's thoughts. Evans and Novak were often put down as trumpeters for White House national security adviser Richard Allen. Foreign dips studied every word. Mary McGrory's latest column on Northern Ireland may seem perfectly predictable, but she gets to sit near the ambassador himself at British embassy luncheons and is Queen-of-the-May at any Irish embassy do.

American journalists are constantly sought out for their political opinions, even if they're frequently wrong. Foreign ministries back home have an insatiable appetite for analyses of American politics, and their dips in Washington have to get them somewhere.

As few realize, the most important and powerful American journalists in the diplomatic community's scheme of things are not columnists or correspondents or foreign desk editors. They're editorial writers. The foreign ministries back home will yawn at a Joseph Kraft column while reading a *New York Times* editorial on the same subject with trembling awe, even though Kraft may know twice as much as the editorial writer.

To the ministries back home, the editorial speaks utterly for the newspaper and the newspaper speaks for the city and region—in the *New York Times'* case, for the entire eastern establishment. Telexes daily hum across the Atlantic with the latest opinions of the *Chicago Tribune, Boston Globe, Philadelphia Inquirer*—and, of course, the *Washington Post.* The editorials are read on high, circulated among various sections, kept, and filed. Good editorials bring smiles. Many bad ones bring transfers to Bermuda or Bangladesh.

Foreign diplomats have the same kind of symbiotic relationship with Washington journalists that the politicians and ranking bureaucrats do. Because foreign dips invite them to nice parties and hand them hot news tips, there's a tendency among some members of the Washington press corps to "protect their sources" by printing the hot (and often self-serving) tips and also write nice things about the dip. Because the journalist shows such good news judgment and writes such nice things, he gets invited to the soirées and keeps getting "the inside dope."

Not all influences on American foreign policy are so opprobrious. One very high-ranking State Department official returns every year to the small town in New York where he grew up and always makes a point of having a long talk about what's going on in the world with his childhood best friend, now a local policeman.

"If I can't answer his questions, then there's something wrong with our foreign policy," he said.

Would that all the ranking diplomats in Washington thought the same.

THE TOP FIFTEEN POWERS IN THE FOREIGN AFFAIRS COMMUNITY

1. Al Haig

As much as it makes White House aides sometimes grit their teeth to admit it, Al Haig still runs the foreign policy machinery of the United States. He is not the "vicar" of foreign policy he claimed to be. He had to stay clear of that nasty Richard Allen and the other gleaming-eyed righties in the National Security Council, though he finally bested Allen. He has to be appropriately deferential to CIA chief and Reagan friend William Casey. He failed to get the "crisis manager" job that went to George Bush. He has to be ever so careful now, every step of the way.

But he is still secretary of state. He has survived. Shortly before Reagan was shot in early 1981, one of Reagan's ruling White House triumvirate reportedly told a friend, "Haig is down to his last mistake." A few hours later, there was Haig in the White House press room making his most colossal mistake, proclaiming in quavering voice the obvious untruth of "I am in control here at the White House." Yet he survived.

But the Philadelphia-born West Pointer did not go leaping over the heads of others to such exalted ranks as deputy national security adviser, White House chief of staff, four-star general, NATO commander, and secretary of state—all by the age of 57—without knowing a little diplomacy.

His chief asset, of course, is Europe. He made lasting friendships in the highest of places as NATO commander, and they continue to pay off. Maggie Thatcher may have it hot and heavy with Reagan, but much of Europe considers him a dangerous dolt. With the possible exception of Vice-President Bush and Caspar Weinberger, Haig is the only top man in the Reagan administration most European leaders really trust.

Haig is also the unquestioned chief executive officer of State, commanding respect and loyalty throughout the entire department. He's probably the most popular secretary the department has had in modern times, protecting its interests, fighting for its prerogatives, being damn decent to its staff. When the White House persuades Haig of something, it can assume it has persuaded the entire foreign policy mechanism.

The general has also moved to expand his political base. He was backed for the post by right-wing Jesse Helms, but has attracted many moderates in Congress to his cause and, skillfully employing both charm and belligerence, neutralized his remaining critics. He has reached out to the Trilateral Commission and *Foreign Affairs* component of American international thought, and discreetly kept open ties to his one-time boss and mentor, der good Henry. After his "I am in control here" blunder, he's worked quite successfully at establishing some useful symbiotic relationships in the Washington press corps, and has made himself very popular with foreign diplomats in Washington, remaining unusually accessible and indefatigably making the rounds of parties and receptions. His longtime wife, Patricia, far more attractive, charming, and politically adept than your usual Army brat, is a very definite asset.

Having finally learned to mind his assertive manners, Haig has this decided advantage in Reagan administration power struggles: unless they were to bring former Defense Secretary Donald Rumsfeld back as secretary of State they really don't have anyone suitable to replace him with. There was talk of moving Weinberger over to State and promoting Carlucci up to No. 1 at Defense, but that was before Weinberger came up with the idea of dangling MX missiles from slow-moving airplanes.

There is only one problem with Haig's preeminence in the American foreign policy establishment: He's had to work so hard at office politics to maintain his position, he hasn't been able to formulate much foreign policy.

2. James Baker III

The triumvirate of Ed Meese, Mike Deaver, and Jim Baker runs the White House, the administration, and supposedly the nation.

Meese is the senior partner in name because he has for so long functioned as Ronald Reagan's right-hand man, but the edge in foreign policy has to go to White House chief of staff Jim Baker because of the truth in the aphorism, "knowledge is power."

Michael Deaver, the third member of the triumvirate, is a loyal Reagan family retainer whose foreign affairs experience is limited. Meese isn't much better grounded in such matters as, say, the "X, Y, Z Affair." In fact, his chief governmental preoccupation is law and order. Baker, who as George Bush's campaign manager ran the best political organization in the 1980 election, knows about foreign affairs, and what he doesn't know he can always stroll down the hall and ask Bush about. William Clark, the old Reagan chum who had been made deputy secretary of state and then promoted to national security adviser when Richard Allen was fired, is popular, effective, and a quick study. But he hasn't studied as much as Baker and Bush.

Born in 1930 and the product of Princeton, the Marines, and the University of Texas Law School, Baker is as superior an intellect as he is an administrator. He is a master of such diplomatic skills as subtlety, timing, and knowing just how far to sink the blade. He knew just exactly when to pull Bush out of the 1980 Republican race, winning his White House job and Bush's place on the Reagan ticket as a result. He headed off Haig's attempt to preempt the crisis-management field, installing his old friend Bush in the post instead. He put a quick end to the 1981 Max Hugel–CIA scandal by getting Casey to dump Hugel immediately and then persuading Casey-critic Barry Goldwater to lay off for the good of the President. He was mostly responsible for keeping the in-house MX debate from becoming a real public fiasco.

The macho triumph (as the Reaganites saw it) of the United States shooting down two Libyan fighters in 1981 degenerated into a sort of joke when the press learned that "President" Meese had failed to awaken the real President and tell him about it. White House staff complained that, if Baker had had anything to say about the matter, Reagan would have been awakened.

Now he has a lot to say.

If Baker were to launch an all-out struggle for power against Meese, such as was always going on in the Nixon administration, he'd of course lose. But Baker is much too smart for that, which is why it's always others who lose.

3. George Bush

With George Bush, appearances have always been deceiving.

Shortly after the Reagan team moved into the White House, Bush was asked by a friend if he wasn't being set up as a fall guy to take the heat for dismantling popular regulations while being kept at arm's length from his area of greatest expertise: intelligence and foreign affairs.

He replied that he was not being kept at arm's length on foreign affairs, that he sat in on national security meetings and cabinet meetings, that he conferred with every state visitor either with the President or privately, that he conferred with Reagan privately on foreign affairs, and that he expected some significant overseas missions. He said he had absolutely nothing to gain from publicly tangling with Al Haig, William Casey, or Richard Allen to make a display of being a big deal on foreign policy.

Two weeks later, he was appointed White House "crisis manager." Two weeks after that, when Reagan was shot, he was handed his first crisis, and it was Bush who ended up "in control here at the White House." It was Bush who went to France to meet with François Mitterand after the Socialists took over and who took over the Polish situation.

If only he hadn't made the silly toast to dictator Marcos about the high quality of democracy in the Philippines. . . .

4. William Clark

A rancher-lawyer born in Oxnard, California, in 1931, Judge William Clark knows a lot more about cows than foreign affairs, and would be the first to admit it. When Reagan nominated his former California chief of staff for deputy secretary of state, many Republicans on The Hill winced. When Clark completed four hours of confirmation hearings before the Senate Foreign Relations Committee, practically everyone was wincing.

He had said, "I don't know," "I'm sorry" or something equally useless to the most elementary questions, displaying an ignorance about the world around him equal to that of his boss, who during the 1980 campaign had assured reporters that he would be younger at 70 than all the world leaders he'd be dealing with. At least one strong Reagan supporter on the committee privately allowed as to how he hadn't seen anyone less qualified come before the committee in all his time in the Senate.

But, like Reagan, Clark is a nice guy, and he had the President's strong support and friendship. The committee gave him the benefit of the doubt, and he's proved worthy of it. As Haig's No. 2, Clark has done much to keep good relations between the White House and State, and has helped maintain the unique collegial atmosphere now operative in the department. Though sent to State as Reagan's political commissar, Clark has become a great admirer of Haig and one of the team.

In his new, more powerful post as national security adviser, Clark is increasingly finding himself operating in competition with Haig. Whether this strains their warm relationship remains to be seen. In any event, he's learned the answers to all those questions the senators asked him.

5. Caspar Weinberger

The secretary of Defense has become involved in foreign affairs to a degree Henry Kissinger would have found intolerable. He has tromped all over Al Haig's backyard—Europe—meeting with defense ministers and prime ministers as though he were the United States' principal spokesman. He has pushed Haig aside on such matters as development of the neutron bomb and arms sales. He stood by smiling ever so sweetly when Eugene Rostow, head of Reagan's arms control agency, balked at dealing with Haig and insisted upon reporting directly to the White House.

But Haig has found ways to fend him off. And it appears unseemly for Weinberger to be intruding so much in foreign policy decisions when his own defense policy decisions on where to stick the MX and such have been ridiculed and in some cases overturned. And, with elements in Congress hungering so after the juicy ledger items in the defense budget, Caspar and his deputy Frank Carlucci have enough work to do defending home turf.

Still, though a Harvard man, the California-born Weinberger was an original Reaganite and is still close to the President. As long as Reagan's foreign policy centers mainly on defense, if not offense, Cap Weinberger will have a major say in it. He would even if Kissinger were secretary of state. Cap the Knife doesn't mind a little screaming.

6. Richard Lugar

The President's main man on the Senate Foreign Relations Committee, Indiana Senator Richard Lugar, sometimes seems the only sane man on the Foreign Relations Committee.

With the help of his brilliant young foreign policy assistant, Jeffrey Bergner, Lugar has often been all that has kept the committee on the President's course, or at least some sort of course. He was the key man in getting through the nominations of Bill Clark and many other major Reagan appointments. He led the fight against Carter's Robert Krueger and played a major role in restoring friendliness to Mexican-American relations. A pragmatic conservative, he is a close ally of Majority Leader Howard Baker and, like Baker, a man who can deal amiably and effectively with opposition Democrats, and with moderates and liberals in his own Republican Party.

Born in Indianapolis in 1932, Lugar is a short, quiet-spoken, rustically cerebral sort of fellow, looking much the Eagle Scout he once was. A graduate of Denison University, he was a Rhodes Scholar at Oxford, and later served as Admiral Arleigh Burke's staff intelligence officer. A gentleman farmer, such as they have them in Indiana, he served two terms as mayor of Indianapolis, his performance winning him a great deal of national prestige, along with the unfortunate sobriquet "Nixon's favorite mayor," which was created by an imaginative newspaperman, not Nixon.

Lugar is the Reagan team's favorite member of Foreign Relations, in any event. How they must wish Charles Percy would run for mayor of Chicago.

7. Walter Stoessel

Deputy Secretary Walter Stoessel is by far the heaviest of the State Department heavies standing behind Al Haig. His specialty is political affairs. His background and expertise are in European affairs, most particularly Soviet ones. As long as the Soviet Union remains the principal focal point of American foreign policy, Walter Stoessel is the most indispensable man at State.

He is also a career man. Born in Kansas in 1920, he graduated from Stanford University in 1941 and went immediately into the foreign service, posted shortly afterwards to Caracas, Venezuela. Taking two years out to serve in the Navy, he returned to the foreign service in 1946. In 1947, he was sent to Moscow for two years, upon his return studying at the Russian Institute of Columbia University.

He subsequently served as director of the State Department's Soviet affairs office, as a foreign policy adviser to President Eisenhower, and assorted other high-ranking posts. Stoessel was ambassador to Poland from 1968 to 1972, ambassador to Moscow from 1974 to 1976, and ambassador to West Germany from 1976 until 1981. He was undersecretary to Haig until tapped as Bill Clark's replacement in January 1982.

The only cold warriors who know the Russians better than Stoessel are characters in spy novels.

8. Anatoly Dobrynin

One of the greatest shocks dealt the Washington diplomatic community in recent years occurred in early 1981, just after the Reagan people moved into the White House. Ever on the lookout for macho gestures with which to impress the world, Reagan yanked the special underground garage parking privileges of Soviet Ambassador Anatoly Dobrynin, making him walk through the State Department front door just like all the other dips. All the other dips were stunned. In the past, no one would have dared do that to Dobrynin.

The dean of the Washington diplomatic corps, Dobrynin has been Moscow's man in the American capital since 1962, when he figured largely in those interesting Cuban missile crisis conversations. Most Russian dips avoid Congress, preferring to do their mingling and missionary work in private homes and at other embassies' parties. Dobrynin goes to The Hill, where he is a major presence. He is also a major presence in his own country, being a member of the Soviet Politburo.

Highly regarded by Americans as well as Russians for the accuracy of his reporting, Dobrynin has a perceptive political eye and is quick to seize upon and exploit such schisms as developed between Cyrus Vance and Zbigniew Brzezinski, and as initially developed between Haig and the White House.

Born the son of a plumber in a village outside Moscow in 1919, at the raging height of the Russian Civil War, Dobrynin originally studied to become an engineer, and did. But he was plucked for the diplomatic service in 1944, largely on the basis of his demonstrable skills at office politics. Known for his crafty eyes, friendly smiles, and hefty bulk (he's six foot one and obviously doesn't use the Russian embassy's private volleyball courts up in Maryland very much), Dobrynin is fond of Washington's fast-food joints. He got along very well with Kissinger, who later wrote favorably of him.

People are always interested in Dobrynin's health. On December 10, 1979, he cancelled a number of social engagements with the excuse that he needed a checkup. While he was supposedly being checked up, the Russians invaded Afghanistan.

9. Jeane Kirkpatrick

Dr. Jeane Kirkpatrick is one of those right-wing academic intellectuals most used to haranguing the world from the confines of her lecture hall and treating everything beyond the body of her own ideological concepts as a hostile wilderness. She would still be flailing out from her Georgetown University classroom had she not written an article in *Commentary* magazine that Ronald Reagan, not exactly a bookworm, chanced to read. According to legend, he decided upon her for ambassador to the United Nations on the spot.

Andrew Young was an awful world spokesman for Jimmy Carter's (and his own) foreign policy but was an excellent ambassador to the UN, where he quickly had erstwhile Yankee-baiting Third Worlders eating out of his hand. Dr. Kirkpatrick articulates Ronald Reagan's xenophobic anticommunist doctrine superbly, but was an awful choice for the UN, where she's about as useful as Jane Fonda would be running the Defense Department.

But she's Ronald Reagan's friend, and the Third Worlders are sufficiently terrified of her to remain relatively circumspect even when she says something nice about South Africa, or has a South African intelligence officer to tea. Al Haig and William Casey are wary of her, too. So is George Bush, probably.

Born in Oklahoma in 1926, the daughter of an oil drilling contractor, Jeane Jordan emerged from Barnard and Columbia in the early years of the Cold War. Embarking on a career as a political scientist, she married a colleague, Dr. Evron Kirkpatrick, in 1956.

Though she's extremely fond of Latin American dictators, she says she doesn't like guns, which she maintains is one of the reasons she's a Democrat. The other reason is that she's very prounion, she says. Ronald Reagan loves guns and gave a 1981 Labor Day speech that never once mentioned the word "union," but he's extremely fond of Latin American dictators, too. Whatever works.

10. Ed Derwinski

With the Senate Foreign Relations Committee such a zoo, Reagan foreign policy operatives and other sane people have come to make more and more use of the House Committee counterpart. Ed Derwinski, second-ranking Republican on the House Foreign Affairs Committee and ranking minority member on the International Operations Subcommittee, is the committee's most useful GOP member and one of the most skillful foreign relations men on The Hill.

As with George Bush, Derwinski's appearance can be deceiving. A big, jovial, jowly fellow with horn-rimmed glasses and a crew cut, Derwinski looks like the head of a suburban savings and loan, which is what he was. To foreign officials all over the globe, he is quite something else.

He is closer to the governments of South Korea and Taiwan than anyone on The Hill. He is the spokesman for the Eastern European "Captive Nations," which include Poland, where Derwinski's cousin is a local leader of Solidarity and through which Derwinski traveled widely as just another Pole. He has contacts in places as far-flung as Iceland and Southeast Asia. One of the most rational Russophobes in Congress, he also functions ably and affably as an administration spokesman who can speak convincingly to both hard-line right-wing loons and moderates.

Born in Chicago in 1926, Derwinski has represented his south suburban Illinois district since 1958. He graduated from Loyola University. His wife, Patricia, is known to many on The Hill because she sold them their houses. She's one of the top real estate saleswomen in Northern Virginia.

11. Bobby Ray Inman

Admiral Bobby Ray Inman, the deputy CIA director whom the young professionals in the agency hope will soon become No. 1, is a key man in the foreign policy establishment for the simple reason that the most intelligent foreign policy depends on good, clean, honest, objective, and reliable intelligence. Texas-born and a Korean War veteran (though a young one), Bobby Ray provided this kind of intelligence as director of the National Security Agency, and he's been trying to do it as William Casey's deputy. If the White House chooses to base foreign policy on Reagan's campaign pronouncements instead, it's their lookout.

12. Sean Donlon

Sean Donlon came to Washington at the age of 38 in 1978, taking over the Irish embassy from a man who went on to the Vatican and was happier there. Young Donlon, a career diplomat with powerful friends in both of Ireland's major political parties, had two principal missions beyond the usual encouragement of American capital investment in Ireland and entertainment of visiting Irish bards: He was to draw American public and congressional opinion away from support of Irish Republican Army terrorists while at the same time bringing it to bear on Britain to help pressure Her Majesty's Government toward reaching a political settlement in the north of Ireland.

Within three years, with a small staff and a minimal entertainment budget, Donlon had established himself as one of the most effective ambassadors in the history of the Washington diplomatic corps, a sort of Irish Benjamin Franklin. Not only did he accomplish his twin missions, but he had established such clout with powerful Irish-American politicians that newly-elected Irish Prime Minister Charles Haughey found himself outgunned and overruled when he attempted to transfer Donlon to placate some pro-IRA elements back home.

Aside from making lasting, solid friendships throughout the State Department, press corps, and Congress, Donlon was able to pull off an extraordinary coup when Ronald Reagan came to his house for a 1981 St. Patrick's Day dinner, the first embassy Reagan visited as President. Donlon wasn't able to nudge Reagan into telling Margaret Thatcher to get off her duff and start negotiating, but he did elicit an offer from Reagan to use the United States' "good offices" in working out a solution. And Margaret ultimately got off her duff.

With the election of Dr. Garret FitzGerald as prime minister in the summer of 1981, Donlon was promoted back to Dublin and the top career job in the foreign ministry. But knowledge is power, even at several thousand miles remove, and Donlon still knows more than most in Washington precisely how the place works. Before he left, he gave his powerful friends in Washington his Dublin phone number.

His replacement, Ambassador Tadhg O'Sullivan, is a formidable diplomat and among the best in Washington, as is his counselor, James Sharkey. But Donlan's phone in Dublin still rings.

13. John E. Carbaugh

The Senate Foreign Relations Committee, it seems, is too much of a zoo even for Jesse Helms. He spends much of his time in Senate Agriculture, which he heads, and which deals with matters of even more life-or-death consequence to his North Carolina constituents than who rules Zimbabwe. To keep an eye on things in Foreign Affairs, he can always rely on staff.

"Staff" means mostly John Carbaugh, Helms' foreign policy adviser. He may lack the brilliance and historical perspective of, say, Lugar's Bergner, but he's a terror around the Foreign Relations Committee, the State Department, the National Security Council, the CIA, and all over the world, because, like his demagogic boss, he's shrewd, cunning, ruthless, and knows all the ways to get things done.

Not content to work behind the scenes at Foreign Relations (and what's the point of seizing the helm of a ship that has no rudder?), chubby, bespectacled young Carbaugh makes his moves all over town. If he were a professional lobbyist for private industry, he'd be a millionaire by the time he's 40. Without him on Foreign Relations, Helms would be just another colorful character.

Acting in Helms' name, and with methods of his own devising, Carbaugh last March was credited with compelling the cutoff in American aid to Nicaragua.

Dozens of important foreign service appointments were blocked, deflected, or endlessly delayed because Carbaugh deemed the nominees too liberal or, worse, too close to Henry Kissinger. At the same time, Carbaugh was able to lobby both State and the White House into accepting hard-line righties for sensitive posts in the Arms Control and Disarmament Agency and other important outfits.

A man with a taste for good eats and pleasant surroundings, young Carbaugh's expenses are picked up in part by four tax-exempt foundations that he helped found. They provide the wherewithal for his interesting journeys, such as when he turned up at the Rhodesian peace talks in London in 1979 and enraged the British, as they complained to then Secretary of State Cyrus Vance, by urging former Rhodesian Prime Minister Ian Smith to hold fast against the black fellows, a move that would have ruined the proceedings.

Carbaugh was part of Reagan's foreign affairs transition team. It was not known if he was hoping for a post like undersecretary of state for African affairs, but all he was reportedly offered was ambassador to Paraguay, a favored refuge for failed dictators like Anastasio Somoza. Carbaugh, then a mere 35, declined. Why go to paradise before your time?

14. Stephen Solarz

If there is a liberal version of John Carbaugh, it is New York Congressman Stephen Solarz. Though only eighth-ranking Democrat on the House Foreign Affairs Committee, he has wandered the world acting like a one-man State Department—representing a one-man country. He holds the congressional record for most trips taken.

One moment he's popping up around the Horn of Africa, warning the U.S. to stay out of Somalia. The next, he's in Pyongyang, North Korea, announcing that Kim Il Sung would now like closer ties with the U.S. Three months later, he's in Moscow, announcing that Leonid Brezhnev would like closer ties. Then he's in Japan, announcing that U.S.-Japanese ties are strained.

Sometimes he hitchhikes. In 1975, Kissinger gave the young, then first-term congressman a lift from Syria to Israel. Solarz told him he had been encouraged by Syrian President Hafez al Assad.

If any American undid Carbaugh's maneuvering at the Rhodesian peace talks, and prevented Congress from ruining everything, it was Solarz. The British love him. Perhaps he could go to Northern Ireland, and announce closer ties there.

Born in Brooklyn in 1940, Solarz graduated from Brandeis and Columbia and went almost immediately into the state legislature, moving up to the Congress in 1974.

His wife is quite a tough customer, too. A McLean writer was driving in from the suburbs recently when she cut in front of him with her Volkswagen. Too closely, he thought, and did the same to her. Enraged by that, if not the George Bush bumper sticker he had on his car, she chased him onto the George Washington Parkway and all the way into the District, abandoning the chase only after she had passed him at a stoplight and left him in the dust.

15. Allan Gotleib

If you were to draw up a list of the brightest men in Washington, you'd quickly write down Canadian Ambassador Allan Gotleib and then might wonder who next to put in that league. A Rhodes Scholar like Senator Lugar, Gotleib has been considered the most cerebral man in his country's foreign service. One colleague in Ottawa, recalling an occasion when Gotleib was mulling over a particularly serious problem, said he stood at a crosswalk, lost in thought, as the traffic lights went through three cycles. When he finally did step off the curb, it was against the red light.

A native of Winnipeg who sounds more American than many a member of the Reagan administration, the professorial, bespectacled Gotleib rose to the highest civil rank in Canada's foreign service before being appointed to Washington. Unlike anyone in the Reagan White House except possibly George Bush, he is well aware of Canada and the United States' extreme importance to each other—and threat to each other. Such major disputes as the acid rain issue, the Alaskan-Canadian pipeline, the Canadianization of American energy interests north of the border, and myriad fishing and boundary disputes have given Gotleib a full plate. His task is greater than even the Israeli ambassador's. The Reagan administration at least defends Israel's right to exist; it thinks pollution comes from trees and ignores Canada's pleadings to stop acid rain. The Canadians have found that acid rain is killing trees.

Gotleib's wife, Sondra, is one of the most charming and least pretentious ambassadorial wives. She's written two novels that have had Canadians eagerly turning pages for hot stuff about Canadian foreign service and political figures, including extramarital affairs. Wowee! Eh?

II

THE DEPENDENCIES

Influence Traders

There is, in fact, no reason for confusing the people and the legislature; the two, in these later years, are quite distinct. The legislature, like the executive, has ceased, save indirectly, to be even the creature of the people; it is the creature, in the main, of pressure groups, and most of them, it must be manifest, are of dubious wisdom and even more dubious honesty. Laws are no longer made by a rational process of public discussion; they are made by a process of blackmail and intimidation, and they are executed in the same manner. The typical lawmaker of today is a man wholly devoid of principle—a mere counter in a grotesque and knavish game. If the right pressure could be applied to him he would be cheerfully in favor of polygamy, astrology, or cannibalism.

THESE WORDS SOUND EXCEEDINGLY TIMELY, a diatribe that might well have come from the mouth or pen of any of the reformers or crusaders who inhabit the nation's capital as numerously as the lobbyists and influence peddlers they so revile.

They were written, however, by neither reformer nor crusader but by the conservative iconoclast H. L. Mencken, and they were written in 1930.

Time has not diminished their truth. In the Republic envisioned by our Founding Fathers, the congressmen and the President were to serve as the people's representatives. But the vast aggregate of individual special interests referred to as "the people" was not satisfied. Through the years, decade by decade, the people have gone out and hired their own representatives, who do their bidding for the simple reason that they are paid to. There are lobbyists in Washington representing the interests of every human being (not to speak of every animal) in America—from senior citizens to unborn fetuses, from captains of industry to winos. Never-to-be-born fetuses have a lobbyist, too: Zero Population Growth. There are registered lobbyists for the Pribilof Islands, the Chilean Army, the Ute Indians, and the producers of fertilizer. The Aras Psychomotor Domain of Self of Bar

Harbor, Maine, has a registered lobbyist in the capital. So, too, does Uganda.

The list of names of the lobbyists registered with Congress is 108 pages long. In the 1970s, more than 800 trade associations moved their headquarters to Washington. Of those who didn't, most maintain an office or hire a Washington lobbyist, even if only when they have a serious problem. Also in the 1970s, the number of public-interest lobbies increased from 15 to 112. There are now more than 15,000 men and women employed as lobbyists. It's gotten to the point where even the lobbyists have their own lobby: the American Society of Association Executives, which has more than 8,500 members. Lobbying is the fourth largest industry in town, after government, printing, and tourism. If current trends continue, and the number of associations in Washington reaches and surpasses the 4,000 figure by 1990, as predicted, lobbying could become No. 2.

In many ways, it's already the preeminent industry. The member associations of the ASAE had combined operating budgets of more than $11 billion in 1980. The Congress, with all its self-indulgent waste, operates on about $1 billion. Lobbyists out number congressmen by 38 to 1.

Money is far from the lobbyists' only tool, but it is a most useful one. It is an irony of the Watergate scandals, which in part involved illegal contributions from influence-seeking corporations and lobbyists, that they inspired reforms that gave birth to the Political Action Committee, which allowed corporations to seek influence through legal contributions. The first year, 1974, 89 PACs were formed. By 1980, the total had reached 954 corporate PACs, compared to 240 for labor. There are now more than 2,500 PACs of all kinds, and they handed out some $55 million in the 1980 elections alone.

According to Common Cause, the largest PAC contributor in 1980 was the American Telephone and Telegraph Company, which gave away $652,679 through 23 different PACs. The recipient of the most PAC money was Senator John Tower, now chairman of the Senate Armed Services Committee, who hauled in $382,992. Or take Senator Howard Baker, the new majority leader, who received $341,743 in PAC money.

Common Cause detailed his contributors, the list running seven-and-a-half pages. Agriculture chipped in $17,950, including $8,000 from Associated Milk Producers and $4,750 from Dairymen, Inc. Business dropped $268,993 into the kitty, including $5,000 from Grumman, $2,200 from United Technologies, $10,000 from the National Automobile Dealers Association, $2,800 from AT&T, $2,400 from the American Petroleum Refiners Association, $2,500 from the International Association of Drilling, $3,000 from the

National Rural Electrification Cooperative, $5,000 from the American Bankers Association, $2,100 from the U.S. League of Savings Associations, $9,400 from the International Paper Company, $5,000 from the Aluminum Company of America, $3,500 from the Insurance Public Affairs Council, $9,600 from the American Association of Realtors, $3,000 from Republic Steel, and $3,100 from the American Trucking Associations. In health, $5,000 came from the American Dental Association, $15,000 from the American Medical Association, and $3,000 from the American Federation of Hospitals. The National Rifle Association dropped in $2,200, the International Airline Pilots Association gave $5,000, and the Association of Trial Lawyers of America tossed in $5,000.

In rather marked contrast to Baker and nearly everyone else was Congressman Carl Perkins of Kentucky, chairman of the House Education and Labor Committee. He ran unopposed in 1980, raised $3,750 in contributions, spent $3,695, and returned the rest.

The PAC reforms at least required public disclosure, so we all know that the AMA handed Baker 15,000 big ones. Lyndon Johnson's former Senate aide, Bobby Baker, has written lengthily and almost lovingly of the fat crinkly plain white envelopes that get handed around without our knowing about it. As we saw on the Abscam videotapes, congressional bribees nowadays are still pretty blasé about pocketing wads of cash, especially former Congressman Richard Kelly, who loaded himself up like a pack mule. Foreign governments, to whom bribery is an official way of life, don't necessarily change their ways when they send ambassadors to the United States. The Dom Perignon the late Shah of Iran's Ardeshir Zahedi handed out may have been only $50 a jug back then, but his gifts of caviar and diamond watches were a trifle more costly.

A great many Washington lobbyists are actually honorable people performing honorable work. A lobbyist painstakingly reading through the *Federal Register* every day is the only defense a hardware store owner, schoolteacher, or farmer might have against a big federal regulatory agency bent on making mischief. As anyone who has ever sat through a routine congressional committee meeting will attest, the average member of Congress can be woefully uninformed about technical matters, especially if he never comes to the meetings. Expert testimony from lobbyists can be quite legitimately educational, and important to the survivability and workability of new legislation.

Lobbyists provide their constituencies with direct access to the democratic process, an access that on Capitol Hill may not exist otherwise. Taxpayers fought the American Revolution to gain representation, but instead they gained Congress. So they've gone and created taxpayer lobbies. Lobbyists have another very valuable function: they protect their constituents from other lobbyists. Much of what is produced by Congress—or, for that matter, by the defense industry—is the result of wars between opposing lobbyists or coalitions of opposing lobbyists.

Louisiana's Huey Long first got elected to public office by making an issue out of oil company lawyers drafting the legislation that gave the state its first tax on oil companies. But lobbyist expertise is often called upon in this manner nowadays without causing many raised eyebrows, sometimes to good effect, sometimes not. The U.S. Chamber of Commerce did not try to kill the FTC, but it had a heavy hand in the drafting of the legislation that gave the Congress a 90-day veto period over new FTC rules.

In addition to money and expertise, lobbyists wield a mighty pen. The NRA's hysterical letter-writing salvos are infamous. President Reagan used a barrage of letters and phone calls to bring Congress around on his 1981 tax bill and first round of budget cuts. The Democrats could have organized the same amount of mail and calls easily, but they did not. Perhaps, given the mess Reagan's economic plan eventually became, they didn't want to.

Computer and mailing list wizard Richard Viguerie made himself into a significant political power just by mastering the art of high-tech propaganda distribution. The U.S. Chamber of Commerce's $1.3 million computer setup is one of the best in the capital. In 1979, it produced 250,000 letters against a single FTC bill. One committee member cast a crucial vote that killed a National Land Use Planning Act bill the Chamber didn't like—not because it lobbied him personally, but because it was able to generate 15,000 letters against the bill from the congressman's home district.

A new and increasingly effective lobbying technique is to produce constituents in person and en masse. Associations are not only moving offices to Washington, they are holding conventions and annual meetings there, usually at hotels quite convenient to The Hill. Whatever association business is conducted is usually perfunctory; the main thing is to round up the local folk and unleash them on the House and Senate office buildings. A congressman need only glance out his office window at the waning winter to know that the robins and his home-district bankers will soon be arriving.

A typical home folks blitz was staged by the Illinois Hospital Association when the Carter administration was trying to get legislation passed to put a lid on hospital costs. The Associaton rented a room in a House office, put on a big luncheon spread complete with fancy wine, and invited in the Illinois delegation, including such powerhouses as Bob Michel, now House Republican leader, and

Danny Rostenkowski, now chairman of the Ways and Means Committee. It was come as you are and come or else. The Association had brought with it powerful or socially prominent members of hospital boards from each of the congressmen's districts. One board member was a well-known newspaper columnist. The congressmen, who at least made an appearance if they didn't stay for the eats, got sandwiched in between the locals, photographed, and hectored. The main event was a show-and-tell in which the Association produced a graph indicating that hospitals were doing everything humanly possible to keep costs down, and warning, in so many words, that if Carter's bill passed, people in their home districts might die. The bill didn't pass.

Lobbying associations are also incessantly putting on after-working-hours receptions and feeds on The Hill, generally a waste of their money. Most of the people who go to the things are underpaid congressional staffers who get their food that way. One powerful congressman makes a practice of going to all he's invited to, but only to pick up his name tag from the reception table and move on to the next affair to do the same thing. That way, they never think he's stiffing them.

Lobbyists actually do spend a lot of time in the Capitol's hallways and lobbies, snatching at senators' and congressmen's sleeves as they rush to the floor to vote or move from committee to committee. Tourists often wonder at the purpose of the red velvet ropes strung along stanchions in the corridors near the chambers. When either house is in session, crowds of lobbyists stand behind those ropes, constituting a formidable gamut to run.

All kinds of people become lobbyists. Former members of Congress are always joining the ranks because it provides a means of staying in Washington and of making the kind of money they've never been able to earn in public life, at least honestly. A goodly portion of the teeming thousands of lawyers in Washington are nothing more than lobbyists, and freely admit it. They're easily able to make the $500,000 annual salaries that senior partners of major firms in New York, Philadelphia, and Chicago do by actually practicing law. Campaign staffers whose candidates lose, or are unwilling or unable to hire them if they win, often become lobbyists if they've made a few connections or are still on friendly terms with the winner. Former White House aides who've learned how the joint works are in big demand as lobbyists, or consultants, which is often much the same thing. Retired military officers find lucrative employment with defense contractors working The Hill or the Pentagon. Retired foreign service officers can be found doing the same thing with former associates at State, on The Hill, or in the White House. Sargent Shriver, once our ambassador to France, had to register as an agent and lobbyist for France.

The position of lobbyist is a prestigious one within corporate hierarchies, with pay scales ranging from $40,000 to $125,000-plus and averaging $70,000. Goggle-eyed young idealists come to Washington as crusaders and end up as lobbyists, pulling many of the same tricks and speaking the same language as the hard cases from the corporate sector. Many former journalists join association and corporate public relations staffs, only to find they've become lobbyists.

Lobbyists can accomplish a great deal of civic good while pursuing narrow, selfish interests. With inflation as horrendous as it is, it's universally accepted that federal deficits should be drastically reduced if not eliminated. The powerful National Association of Realtors, with 750,000 members and a 1980 campaign war chest of $1.5 million, has been lobbying like crazy for a balanced budget—so Paul Volcker of the Federal Reserve will lower interest rates and let them sell houses again.

Just as often, civic good does not result. The less-than-savory National Conservative Political Action Committee, which is supposed to be upholding traditional conservative constitutional principles, instead was lobbying to uphold lucrative tax-law loopholes for commodity brokers, and was found out by the *Washington Post*.

William T. Coleman, Gerald Ford's secretary of transportation, was hired by Ford Motor Company to fight the National Highway Traffic Safety Administration's efforts to get Ford to recall 20 million vehicles with transmissions that supposedly went from "park" into "reverse" all by themselves.

The American Petroleum Institute, a formidable outfit with 350-member oil companies and a 600-member staff, had a fairly easy time of it lobbying with the incoming Reagan administration for early decontrol of oil and gas prices, so early it hit many New Englanders in the midst of a cold winter. Shortly afterward, 23 big-time oilmen contributed more than $270,000 to the special fund Nancy Reagan used to redecorate the White House family quarters to her expensive taste.

According to a 1981 Common Cause report, defense contractors have not only been waging a massive lobbying campaign to keep defense spending as high, wasteful, and inflationary as possible, but have been routinely passing the lobbying costs on to the taxpayers.

But the other side, if that's the proper term, can be less than pure. The maritime unions, generous supporters of Jimmy Carter's 1976 campaign, were rewarded with the notorious and inflationary "American bottoms" bill. The National Education Association, the powerful schoolteachers' lobby, all but hugged and kissed Carter, and got its very own very unnecessary cabinet department.

The National Organization for Women was absolutely brutal with some of its lobbying, replete with coercive and unfair boycotts against entire states. One NOW lady in Illinois was charged with trying to bribe a lawmaker with a campaign contribution on behalf of the ERA.

Now that he's calmer and devotes his energies to more reasonable causes, Ralph Nader is gaining back some of his old respect. But for a time, when he was carrying on like a self-proclaimed one-man government, he was universally considered the biggest pain-in-the-ass in Washington, a city noted for many. Millions of Americans to this day curse Nader every time their seat-belt buzzers go off.

Most Washington lobbyists are rational, reasonable sorts. Lew Regenstein of the Fund for Animals is one of the most effective environmentalist lobbyists in town, though he almost never raises his southern-accented voice. Instead, he marshals facts, frequently employing economic arguments to defend environmental causes. His articles appear with great regularity in the space prized most by any capital lobbyists: the Op-Ed page of the *Washington Post*.

Maggie Kuhn, the 76-year-old head of the Gray Panthers, and all the other senior citizen lobbyists are a well-behaved and much respected bunch—and devastatingly effective. Not even Ronald Reagan's beloved Defense Department was able to emerge totally unscathed from Budget Director David Stockman's scalpel attacks. Yet, when Reagan tried to lower Social Security benefits for some recipients, he was defeated in the Senate virtually unanimously. When he then came back with a "merely" plan to defer Social Security cost-of-living increases for just three months, he was told flatly by his congressional leaders simply not to bother. He didn't.

You'll even find Washington lobbyists who are not only much respected but exceedingly refined—some might say, insufferably refined. To ward off the specter of budget cuts, the pooh-bahs of the financially embarrassed National Symphony had a herd of congressfolk up to the Kennedy Center for a free performance of Rimsky-Korsakov's Symphony No. 2, followed by free drinks and elegant eats across the street at the Watergate. Not much later, the Friends of the Kennedy Center hosted a freebie performance of *The Little Foxes* for members of Congress, topped off with a soirée afterward at which they could chat with the star, Elizabeth Taylor, always a treat. Other arts lobby parties, performances, and receptions attracted even President and Mrs. Reagan, which is more than the National Solid Wastes Management Association can say for their soirées.

The tab for the National Symphony reception was picked up by

Texaco as a tax-deductible contribution. A number of Washington arts organizations, including the almighty Smithsonian Institution, are forbidden by law from undertaking organized lobbying efforts, but they explain there is a need to keep members of Congress "informed" about things—such as the best available vintage of Dom Perignon.

Candlelight and music go hand in hand with lobbying in another sense—and it usually amounts to more than just hand in hand. If there are votes to be had in consideration of money, favors, gifts, parties, and reciprocal votes, there are also votes to be had in consideration of sex. All kinds of sex.

For those who have no scruples about negotiating their vote between the sheets, it is much better to use the lobbyist as a middleman to procure the very best sex partner available, the most suitable for, er, one's needs. Why settle for a female lobbyist, like Paula Parkinson, however buxom, who might get you into trouble, when you can have the 18-year-old, 6-foot redhead of your dreams, a redhead who specializes, and all free of charge? Except, of course, for your vote.

A famous sex figure of the 1970s used to do lobbying work for a congressman—on his houseboat. He'd invite other congressmen or influential friends over for a good time, she'd provide the good time, trying not to capsize the houseboat, and the legislative process would take its natural, or unnatural, course.

There are stables of such young ladies about, most of them available for Washington's many out-call services, which seem to thrive despite numerous police crackdowns on mere streetwalkers. These young ladies provide many specialities. One, who used to carry her coiled whip about in a Gucci shoulder bag, was hired by the CIA to entertain a Russian defector.

The first function of the lobbyist is to fulfill a congressman's needs. In most cases, that means providing technical information or a detailed explanation of a client's point of view on a given bill or issue. But there are congressmen with illicit if not perfectly unspeakable needs, and there are respectable lobbyists—or at least lobbyists with respectable clients—more than willing to fulfill them. If that's what it takes, then so be it.

The slimy underside of a very large rock was turned over following the murder of Alexei Goodarzi, flashy headwaiter of Capitol Hill's Rotunda Restaurant, in 1977. It was never officially determined why someone fired three bullets into Goodarzi's head, in his very own Porsche, but police were intrigued by the man's reputed lust for expensive clothes, fancy cars, good-looking women, and gambling. They learned that he frequently bragged about having congressmen and important bureaucrats for friends and performed many favors for them, including fixing them up with "dates." According to a "mystery woman" who was interrogated and later identified as a madam, Goodarzi was involved in a ring that supplied call girls to corrupt or corruptible government officials. There was evidence that a number of lobbyists were involved—along with those always fascinating gentlemen in the crime syndicate. The Justice Department also found possible links to Merle Baumgart, onetime lobbyist for the American Bankers Association and former aide to Congressman Peter Rodino of New Jersey. Baumgart had been killed in a 1975 automobile accident, 10 days after he had complained that two thugs had smashed all the windows in his car with a baseball bat. Shortly before the fatal crash, Baumgart had been drinking in the Rotunda Restaurant.

As happens when rocks are turned over, the little creatures mostly scampered under other rocks. As also happens when the crime syndicate might be involved, there weren't exactly a lot of arrests. But there were some interesting questions raised, such as, of what possible use would it be to the syndicate to compromise congressmen with call girls? Was this sort of thing pervasive, or was it only an isolated incident? Such as when a friend of Frank Sinatra said she started sleeping with a President of the United States at the same time she was a mistress of crime syndicate chieftain Sam "Momo" Giancana.

The Rotunda Restaurant has since been taken over by the Democratic Club, where only the most refined and respectable forms of lobbying take place, but where there's a rule against repeating what you hear there.

An increasingly popular form of lobbying is the mass march or demonstration. It's not particularly new, dating back as it does at least to the Bonus Army encampment of the Depression (which was put down, incidentally, with troops led by one General Douglas MacArthur and one Colonel Dwight Eisenhower).

More successful was the civil rights march led by Martin Luther King on the Washington monument in 1963. Its sequel, the "Resurrection City" encampment that followed his assassination, was largely a flop. The subsequent mass antiwar demonstration that struck the capital in 1971 proved a disaster for almost everybody concerned, including Richard Nixon, who came on like Czar Nicholas, and the demonstrators, more than a thousand of whom got thrown into detention camps just as in Argentina.

Jane Fonda's 1979 antinuclear rally on the Capitol Mall was an exercise in comic futility. Jane screeched that she was going to stop Jimmy Carter from being reelected. She was right, and her new President was Ronald Reagan. The farmers' invasion of the capital that same year was an utter fiasco. The farmers caused so much trouble by tying up traffic with their tractors, setting fires, urinating on hotel and public building floors, and in a couple of cases hassling young women, that they were a dirty word in Washington for months, especially on Capitol Hill.

Call them marches or demonstrations, if you will; they are a form of lobbying, perhaps the most honest form of lobbying, the people organizing themselves visibly and dramatically to express dissatisfaction with a policy or with the kind of representation they're getting. When these gatherings are law abiding and well behaved, they can be extremely effective. Labor's Solidarity Day demonstration, which drew 250,000 well-organized American workers to the Capitol Mall in 1981, rallied as nothing else could Democrats in Congress to oppose Reagan's second round of budget cuts, while firmly demonstrating that Reagan had lost a major part of his supposed "mandate" constituency.

The weakness of these marches is that there are now so many of them—Free Ireland marchers one day, NOW ladies on another, Indians the next—that they begin to pall. On one recent afternoon, someone burst into a news bureau to announce that seven women had chained themselves to the White House fence. Without looking up, a correspondent asked if it was a bondage demonstration.

The clergy can be enormously effective lobbyists. A Methodist minister from the South was chiefly responsible for getting the Volstead Act through Congress. The Catholic Church played a key role in enactment of the Hyde Amendment that prohibits the use of federal funds for abortions. A gang of Bible Belt, Moral Majority TV preachers persuaded Congress to overturn Washington's locally passed sexual conduct reform law because it allowed homosexuality and teenage sex.

The problem with lobbies is not that so many of them are corrupt or evil or excessively powerful; it is simply that there are so many of them, and that they are powerful in the aggregate. They exert their power at every level of government, in every agency of government.

Fred Wertheimer's Common Cause, itself a lobby, has long recognized this. In a 1979 speech, Common Cause's David Cohen expressed the point this way:

> As long as the nation was experiencing economic expansion and abundant resources, the growth in numbers and influence of the special interests was scarcely noticed. Now, in a period of inflation, unemployment, and finite resources, it has paralyzed national decision making. Each special interest—the dairy industry, labor unions, airlines, truckers, professions, and a host of others—has a particular set of favors it wants from government. Many of these favors aggravate inflation, while others involve resistance to changes in sources and uses of energy. No single interest intends to cause inflation or waste energy, but together

the many favor-seekers combine to weaken government and prevent the differences from being sorted out in the tugs and hauls, pushes and pulls, of the political process.

Those on the following list are a major component of the American government.

THE TOP TEN LOBBYISTS IN WASHINGTON
1. Ronald Reagan

In a public admission to ABC interviewer Barbara Walters, Ronald Reagan boasted that he never received higher than a C in both high school and college. His grasp for foreign affairs is such that he didn't know the name of the President of France and thought Thailand was still called Siam. He persists in calling policies that have created a shocking $100 billion federal deficit and 9 percent unemployment an economic recovery program. Although he makes the hard decisions in the White House, he doesn't like putting in the hard hours and was content to sleep through the emergency involving our aerial combat with Libyan fighters. In warm weather, he can't even stand to be in the White House because he's allergic to the air conditioning.

How is it then that this man has made such an impression on Washington, has established such a commanding presence, and has been compared so favorably to his predecessor, Jimmy Carter?

Because, man on man, Ronald Reagan is probably the most persuasive and effective lobbyist Washington has seen in years.

Max Friedersdorf, the courtly Hoosier who had been Reagan's chief White House lobbyist on the Hill until he pastured himself off as U.S. consul on Bermuda, was one of the best. Vice-President Bush's little-known but extremely effective and professional Capitol lobbying team played a key role in the administration's major 1981 legislative victories. Senate Majority Leader Howard Baker and House Minority Leader Robert Michel earned all the accolades they recieved.

But the lion's share of the credit goes to the lion.

The administration has never had any sweeping national mandate to do what it has done and is still trying to do, but when Reagan goes on television and proclaims such a mandate, it seems very real. When he beseeches Americans for cards, letters, phone calls, and telegrams to Congress, the conservative true believers are almost always the only ones to respond, but they respond in such intimidating numbers as to convince even cynical congressmen they are an outpouring from the nation. When Reagan threatens painful retribution, or offers handsome reward, or leans close like an old, old pal, the lobbyee is invariably terrified, grateful, or charmed. Reagan is the best telephone persuader in the history of the device. It may come from years of selling shirts, hand soap, and coffee pots on television, and it may be the only aspect of government for which he shows any ability, but Reagan is magnificent at lobbying.

Consider it in this light. The predictable and in many cases immediate effects of Reagan's programs included the removal of indigent old people from nursing homes, the refusal of hospitals to accept welfare mothers with problem pregnancies, a terrifying rise in crime rates, drastic increases in transit fares and curtailment of service, major depression in the housing and auto industries, and an inflationary deficit so large as to send the stock and bond markets into hysterics. Yet he got every one of those programs through Congress and a sale of super secret AWACS spy planes to the less than beloved Saudis as well. Consider what would of happened if Richard Nixon, Gerald Ford, or Jimmy Carter had tried this.

With so few intellectual attainments and other presidential abilities, Reagan's stellar performance prompts an interesting question. Who is programming him? Who is telling him what to sell so effectively? As must always be asked about a lobbyist, who are his clients?

At least one answer comes to mind. The Reagan administration adopted some 60 percent of the proposals for change suggested by the right-wing Heritage Foundation, whose biggest single contribution is ultra-conservative multimillionaire Richard Mellon Scaife.

The advice of the oil company and mining consortium regarding the Law of the Sea Treaty did not leave empty echoes.

2. Harlon B. Carter

One of the most effective lobbies in Washington is unfortunately among the most dangerous to your health. With a membership amounting to considerably less than 1 percent of the population, the National Rifle Association has for years been able to frustrate the wishes of what polls invariably show to be an overwhelming majority of Americans for curbs and controls on the circulation and use of firearms. Judging by statistics on the disparity between firearm murders in the United States and those in European countries with strict gun controls, the gun lobby may be responsible for more American deaths than were suffered in all our wars.

Formed in 1871, without much changing its mindset thereafter, the NRA employs some of the most up-to-date and sophisticated computer and mail response technology extant. But then, so do the U.S. Chamber of Commerce and many other well-heeled lobbying outifts. The NRA is so unusually formidable and successful because it has been able to keep its constituency at a constant fever pitch of paranoia and hysteria.

The Second Amendment to the Constitution states: "A well regulated militia, being necessary to the security of a free state, the right of the people to keep and bear arms, shall not be infringed." To George Washington, among other Founding Fathers, this meant a national guard in which all males 18 to 45 would be enrolled.

Instead of urging its 1.8 million members to join the National Guard, as very few of them do, the NRA instilled into their brains a fervent belief in their inalienable right to turn their recreation rooms into arsenals. The NRA has got them to equate gun ownership with patriotism, nationalism, masculinity, Christianity, and invulnerability. The slightest suggestion by any politician that guns might somehow cause harm or ought in some small way to come to the attention of government is treated as a Russian airborne invasion of Texas would be.

The NRA doesn't get its way 100 percent of the time. Despite a barrage of mail worthy of the first day on the Somme, it failed to prevent the confirmation of Congressman Abner Mikva, a gun control advocate, as a member of the powerful U.S. Court of Appeals for the District of Columbia. But it wins nearly all its fights, going to ridiculous lengths. When the Federal Bureau of Investigation wanted to require the admixture of microscopic traceable taggants to explosives to help track down terrorist bombers, the NRA defeated the bill in Congress, arguing it didn't want taggants in the black powder used in muskets in Civil War reenactments.

After the 1968 shootings of Martin Luther King and Robert Kennedy, the NRA grimly accepted a mild federal law restricting the interstate sale of guns, for fear it might get something worse. Since then, it's been working mightily for repeal, and may well succeed. Ronald Reagan supports the notion. Abolition of the Bureau of Alcohol, Tobacco, and Firearms, the only agency with any real effect on illicit trade in handguns, was put high on the list of Reagan's priorities.

Congressmen tend to pay attention when they receive 300,000 letters and mailgrams, especially when they drew only 51 percent of the vote in their last election. Liberal George McGovern eventually got done in by the Gun Lobby in 1980, but to fend them off, the great liberal was cravenly supporting measures to decontrol gun purchases in the late 1970s. Gerald Ford was a longtime supporter of a ban on Saturday night specials—until the 1976 election.

There was an attempt by some NRA leadership in the 1970s to try to transform the organization from a fanatical pressure group to an actual gun club, but these heretics were given the bum's rush and replaced with a more ardent faction in 1977.

The most ardent of them all is Harlon Carter, the NRA's top gun. A bald fellow nearing 70 who bears a slight resemblance to Nikita Khrushchev, Carter is a retired U.S. Border Patrol chief who holds 44 national pistol and rifle shooting records. He has devoted his whole life to guns, he says, because "it's important for the family, and it's important for the country."

Carter's NRA has an annual budget of $30 million, of which at least $4 million is spent on lobbying. It has a staff of 275, administering to the needs of 54 NRA groups and 9,000 local gun clubs. It also publishes three magazines.

The NRA purports to be motivated solely by principle, but there's some economic advantage to their efforts. American handgun manufacturers, a $235 million-a-year industry, need an expanding American gun market (guns aren't very perishable, after all) to absorb the 1.8 million handguns they turn out every year. American handgun manufacturers are big advertisers in NRA magazines.

Though it has skilled lobbyists like Neal Knox and Susan Reece on its staff, and spends some $500,000 on political campaigns in election years, the NRA might as well go off on holiday as long as Ronald Reagan is President. After getting shot and almost killed by a handgun-wielding weirdo in March 1981, Reagan said he still saw no need for handgun controls.

Harlon Carter, incidentally, killed a Mexican youth with a shotgun in Texas in 1931. Though sentenced to jail, Carter's conviction was overturned by an appeals court and the charges were dropped.

3. Clifton Garvin

The U.S. Chamber of Commerce and, to a lesser degree, the National Association of Manufacturers are effective voices for big business in Washington. The Chamber, after all, has a $20 million annual budget and 89,500 corporate members. But, in terms of sheer power, the most important business lobby in town is an almost secret one—the Business Roundtable.

It maintains an office in Washington, but most of its small staff are discreetly headquartered in New York. It wouldn't matter if the Roundtable had no staff at all. Its membership is made up of the chief executive officers of 200 of the biggest corporations in the country—all but a handful of them among *Fortune*'s top 500.

Though the Roundtable occasionally employs professional lobbyists for specific purposes, it most often relies on the singular clout and widespread contacts of its members, the enormous grass-roots pressure it can generate through its employees, suppliers, and stockholders, and, let us never forget, its many PACs.

As columnist Jack Anderson noted, a visit by a Roundtable chap "has an unbelievable impact" on a mere congressman. "No one is likely to turn away the president of DuPont or General Motors when he comes calling," said one lawmaker.

With the advent of Jimmy Carter in 1977, the labor movement hoped to expand upon the many gains they had made during Lyndon Johnson's Great Society years. The Business Roundtable, with a little help from its friends, stopped them cold. And they're prepared to keep Ronald Reagan in line, too.

A native Virginian who earned his chemical engineering degree from Virginia Polytech, Clifton Garvin lives in Greenwich, Connecticut, and does all the things a rich man of his station and six decades would be expected to do. His predecessor as head of the Roundtable was Thomas A. Murphy, head of General Motors. Garvin is chairman of a little company called Exxon.

4. Tommy Boggs

Tommy Boggs, 40-year-old son of Congresswoman Lindy Boggs and the late Congressman Hale Boggs, is one Washington lawyer who admits he doesn't really practice law. He practices lobbying and does it better than almost any other lobbyist, certainly better than any other freelancer in town.

Such regulatory powerhouses as the Federal Trade Commission have always feared him, and he is acknowledged master of The Hill. Most lobbyists are specialists, working specific committees. Boggs is a specialist working the entire Congress. He has been learning its many and mysterious ways since he was a small boy.

Though a Democrat and a supporter of the unpopular Jimmy Carter, Boggs has no end of Republican clients, or of clients, period. His law firm of Patton, Boggs, and Blow, which he founded in 1966, has a list as long as an overly twisted arm. Some recent examples include the Trial Lawyers Association, General Motors, Chrysler Corporation, Westinghouse, the State of Alaska, *Reader's Digest*, Wilshire Oil, the Korea Marine Development Company, the mighty Business Roundtable, the National Associations of Chain Drug Stores and Truck Stops, and the National Pharmaceutical Alliance.

Though given to Louisiana-style cowboy boots and loud clothes, Boggs is very much a Washington product, having grown up in the Federal City and graduated from Georgetown Prep, Georgetown University, and Georgetown Law.

At the age of 29, Boggs ran for Congress himself as an antiwar candidate in suburban Maryland, and lost. Now he's content just to make money, which he couldn't do any faster if he had his own mint.

"Tommy is the type of lobbyist who would slip through your fingers if you tried to pick him up," Ralph Nader once said of him. "But you always have a feeling that if he were a member of Congress he'd be a liberal."

5. William Timmons

Sometimes described as the "rainmaker" for his uncanny ability to change the weather on Capitol Hill, Tennessean Bill Timmons is what you might call a slow talker. But they do well in Washington, too.

Since forming his Timmons & Company with former associate Tom Korologos after they both left the Ford administration in 1974, Timmons has compiled a client list nearly as good as the larger Boggs outfit's. It includes Standard Oil (Indiana), the American Petroleum Institute, the G.D. Searle Drug Company, H.J. Heinz, Northrop Corporation, and Major League Baseball. He also does work for the Trial Lawyers Association and Chrysler.

Chrysler ought to name a couple of new models after Boggs and Timmons.

Born in Chattanooga in 1930, Timmons first came to Washington as a student at Georgetown and George Washington Universities, following service during the Korean War with the Air Force. He went into government almost immediately, working as an aide first for Senator Alexander Wiley and then for Congressman (later Senator) William Brock. He joined the Nixon team in 1969.

A deft political thinker who managed Brock's four congressional campaigns, Timmons was a loyalist who did all an honest man could for Nixon. But there are limits, and he always recognized them. Timmons is one of those who have given lobbying an honorable name.

6. Robert Gray

A Hastings, Nebraska, lad who now rides around in a chauffeur-driven limousine, chatting by radio-telephone with his many friends, Robert Gray knows everyone, especially in the Reagan administration. An establishment Republican (if Gray were a hod carrier, he'd be an establishment hod carrier), Gray surprised everyone by backing Reagan against incumbent Jerry Ford in 1976. Gray was rewarded for that and for helping in the 1980 campaign by being named cochairman of Reagan's regal inaugural, a position that allowed him to make even more friends.

Gray was longtime head of the Washington office of Hill and Knowlton, one of the world's largest public relations firms—public relations in Washington being considerably different from public relations in New York. Their clients—the Health Insurance Association of America, Motorola, RKO General, Uniroyal, and the

Distilled Spirits Council of the United States, among others—do not expect them simply to hand out press releases. Now he has his own firm, Gray and Company, which is just as prestigious.

Born in 1925, Gray served in the Navy in World War II, went to Harvard, and came to Washington in the early 1950s looking for a job. He got one almost immediately with the secretary of the Navy. Ultimately, he became Eisenhower's appointments secretary and then secretary of the cabinet. In 1961, Hill and Knowlton decided to hire the well-connected fellow for their Washington office. It had a staff of four then. It grew to more than a hundred.

"He has a way of watching for every opportunity to gauge who is in power in this town," Tommy Corcoran, the FDR aide and once king of Washington lawyer-lobbyists, once told the *Washington Post*. "He's very presentable."

7. Nancy Reynolds

Robert Gray will never be as close to anyone in the Reagan administration as Nancy Clark Reynolds is to Ron and Nancy. A former Reagan aide, loyal supporter, old and dear friend, the 54-year-old Mrs. Reynolds (divorced) provides a link between the President and the American business community unlike any other in Washington. She also serves as an unofficial but much respected White House adviser on a variety of subjects, but chiefly personnel. The most amazing thing about her is that she performs her role as presidential confidante while holding down a highly paid job as vice-president, national affairs (i.e., lobbyist), for the $4 billion-a-year Bendix Corporation, now an international conglomerate with a big $1.3 billion aerospace division.

A breezy blue-eyed blonde with something of a raw-boned country air about her, Mrs. Reynolds spent a fair amount of her childhood on her parents' ranch in Idaho. As the daughter of Congressman and then Senator D. Worth Clark—a Democrat, of all things—she spent most of her youth in Washington, however, completing her education at Baltimore's Goucher College and settling down as a housewife with three children. When that sort of thing didn't work, they went back to Idaho. After she and her husband divorced, she took a job as hostess of a Boise television talk show, eventually becoming a television news reporter and coanchor at KPIX in San Francisco. Covering Reagan's 1966 gubernatorial campaign, she met press aide Lyn Nofziger, who hired her as an assistant. She quickly became an assistant to Reagan himself, and virtually a member of the Reagan family.

Another failed marriage and a failed Reagan presidential campaign (1976) later, she took the job as No. 2 lobbyist in Boise Cascade's

Washington office. Less than a year later, she accepted a juicier offer from Bendix chairman William Agee (of Mary Cunningham fame), an old family friend.

Mrs. Reynolds virtually introduced the newcomer Reagans to Washington after the 1980 election, setting them up with the right people to know and the right people to know them. Her big black-tie dinner for the Reagans in the F Street Club in November 1980, carefully included some blacks and Democrats on the 50-name guest list. As Mrs. Reynolds made clear to Reagan, the right people in Washington are not just those on The Right.

Mrs. Reynolds also ran Nancy Reagan's transition team, helped the new administration find dozens and dozens of key people for all sorts of agencies, and was Nancy Reagan's constant companion after the President was shot in March 1981. While still looking out for Bendix's many interests, Mrs. Reynolds serves as Reagan's U.S. commissioner to the United Nations Commission on the Status of Women. She enjoys pretty good status herself, having become secretary-treasurer of the all-powerful and largely male Business-Government Relations Council, a sort of high priesthood of Washington lobbyists with only 85 members.

"Whether the press can be counted on not to fret when Bendix next lands a big Pentagon contract remains to be seen," said *Fortune* in a recent article.

8. Bill Hecht et al.

When appearing before tobacco growers back home, Senator Jesse Helms loves to lead them in a rousing chant of "There is no tobacco subsidy; there is no tobacco subsidy." But there is; it is not only one of the most generous in the government's farm vote treasure chest, it has survived even when the Reagan administration was telling the country times were so tough that school-lunch milk might be reduced from eight to six ounces per child and catsup was to be considered half the vegetable portion.

The only real trouble American tobacco interests have faced in recent years was during the brief tenure of Health, Education, and Welfare Secretary Joseph Califano, who had gotten religion about smoking and launched a bureaucratic campaign against it. But with the tobacco lobby so entrenched hereabouts no one expected the crusade to get very far, and it didn't. Neither did Califano, who was bounced from the cabinet. President Carter went down to North Carolina to assure tobacco growers they would all work to make cigarettes "even safer than they are."

Califano is now a lawyer-lobbyist himself, with health care organizations among his clients.

The Tobacco Lobby consists mostly of the Tobacco Institute, which conducts endless studies finding marvelous, wholesome properties in the stuff and endless reasons to doubt the veracity of all the negative reports. Except for an occasional newspaper or magazine advertisement and the usual stream of institutional press releases, the Institute keeps a fairly low profile. It employs one of the best teams of lobbyists in town, including a number of former congressmen: Jack Mills, former executive director of the Republican Congressional Campaign Committee, and Bill Hecht, one of the most effective party givers in town. He threw one not long ago in Tongsun Park's George Towne Club, and guess who showed up? Ronald Reagan himself.

9. Marlow Cook

All Kentucky senators ought to register as lobbyists for tobacco interests, but Republican Marlow Cook kept on being one long after he was defeated for reelection in the GOP's Watergate debacle of 1974.

As a Roman Catholic who grew up in a small town in upstate New York, Cook always was something of an odd duck in Kentucky politics, but he did rather well for a Republican. After serving four years in the state legislature, he was a judge in Louisville's Jefferson County from 1961 to 1968, when he was elected to the Senate.

A single Senate term was more than enough for him to learn the wily and wonderful ways of The Hill, and the lobbying operation he set up after his defeat has prospered mightily, giving him considerably more power than he ever enjoyed as a mere lawmaker. His clients include many more than tobacco interests. As one admiring congressman said, "He'll take anybody."

10. Evie Dubrow

Labor has never been without some strong voices in Washington. The AFL-CIO's Andrew Biemiller was a crafty old master of The Hill, and his successor strategists, notably the AFL-CIO's Kenny Young, are almost as good. Bright labor law specialists like Tom Quinn abound.

But the most effective labor lobbyist in Washington today is the tiniest, Evelyn Dubrow of the International Ladies Garment Workers Union, those people who keep bursting into song on radio and television. At four feet eleven, you don't have to look for the union label to spot Evie Dubrow. As one congressman said, "She's so small she stands out anywhere." She's very good at telling Republicans which piece of labor legislation they can afford to vote for, and at telling Democrats to vote for all of them. In fact, she is now president of the Democratic Club. Now in her mid-sixties, Evie began her

Capitol lobbying career in 1958 and estimates she has worn out 24 pairs of shoes a year since. In the thick of the fight against the Reagan budget cuts, she has no intention of retiring soon.

Many lobbyists are freely generous with Dom Perignon and the like. Evie has at least once served up chicken soup.

The Media

W HEN THE *Washington Star* went belly up in the summer of 1981, the capital of the United States became the largest city in the country to have only one metropolitan newspaper. The *Washington Post,* flagship of an empire four decades in the making, held sway over a market of more than 3 million people.

But even with the *Star* gone, there remain thousands of reporters representing hundreds of news organizations in Washington. The city is the work place of more journalists than anywhere else in the world, and its press corps continues to grow because, come Republicans or Democrats, the most plentiful by-product of a free society is news.

The collecting and processing of news has been a growth industry in Washington that has paralleled the immense expansion of the national government over the past half century. Does it now follow that Ronald Reagan's crusade to reduce the size and influence of the federal establishment on the rest of the nation will also bring a decline in Washington's status as the Spindletop of American news?

Eventually, perhaps . . . if the New Beginning really does return the work of government back to the states and localities. But for now, the very process of trying to unscramble the eggs that FDR and his New Dealers began breaking in 1933 is itself generating more dramatic news than Washington has seen since the death throes of the Nixon Presidency.

The reporting of public affairs, as the journalism schools like to call gathering news about government and politics, is high-status work. The glamor that once attached to police reporters and sports writers—remember Hildy Johnson and Grantland Rice?—now has passed to White House reporters as they fling hardball questions at Presidents, and to diplomatic correspondents as they pursue secretaries of State from the Sphinx to the Wailing Wall and back. But as the kid who ran away with the circus remarked as he swept up after the elephants, it ain't all fame and bright lights. Washington journalism is often as exciting as watching haircuts, and in fact most of its practitioners never get as close to the high and mighty as the barbers in the Capitol.

The Washington press corps is enormous—at least 3,000 reporters, columnists, commentators, editors, and photographers are accredited to the various congressional news galleries, and that figure does not include many hundreds more technicians and other reporters who do their work without ever seeing the inside of the Capitol or the White House.

It also is many-splendored in its diversity. Peng Di, Qian Xing, and their three colleagues are in Washington to report for the Xinhua News Agency of Peking, occasionally crossing paths, no doubt, with Rock Leng and Jasper Hsu of the Central News Agency of Taipei. They all may compare notes with Slobodan Obradovic of the Yugoslavian news agency, Tanjug, but it is unlikely they often run into Jessie Stearns of the Norfolk, Nebraska, *Daily News*, Deborah Strauss of *Hazardous Waste Report*, J. L. McKee of *Furniture Today*, or Peter Ross Range of *Playboy*.

Still, there is fraternization on and off the job. Jon Margolis of the *Chicago Tribune* gave David Broder of the *Washington Post* tips on how to sleep to ease his back pain, and Merilee Cox of UPI Audio and Dick Berkowitz of Cable News Network compete as rival broadcasters but have breakfast together each morning as man and wife. There is, in fact, enough intermarriage in the Washington press corps to have justified an article in the *Washington Journalism Review* entitled "The Two Byline Bedroom."

Washington journalism is bigger but probably more respectable than in the old days, when a reporter might own up to his line of work but add, "Don't tell my mother what I'm doing. She thinks I'm playing piano in the whorehouse."

There still are some epic drinkers and hell-raisers in the capital press corps, but the long bar at the National Press Club is often deserted after the last rush hour bus leaves for Bethesda, and a typical Washington reporter is as likely to be found of an evening tending his tomatoes in a Falls Church garden as trading lies with competitors at the class reunion or sucking up free martinis at an embassy reception.

There are even more former journalists in Washington than working reporters. Every member of Congress has a press secretary, the smallest federal agency has a platoon of people assigned to the care of and feeding of the media (the Pentagon has battalions), and no trade association, political committee, or do-good group is without a "public affairs" apparatus. Most of these people have at some time been in news work or at least in journalism school.

Added to the fact that most politicians and public officials are acutely, often painfully, sensitive to the news, Washington should be a great place to operate a newspaper.

It once was. There were newspapers published in Washington before the first cornerstones were laid for government buildings in the early years of the nineteenth century, and for some time every new administration would be accompanied by an editor who would start a newspaper to disseminate the official word. Just before World War II, Washington had six daily papers.

But those days are gone forever, as the corporate nabobs of Time, Inc., discovered after they plunked down $16 million for the 125-year-old *Washington Star* in 1978. Three years and $85 million later, Time folded the *Star,* concluding that no one could make an afternoon paper pay in Washington.

The *Star,* of course, had been hurt by changing American reading habits—surveys say people get their evening news now from the TV set, not an afternoon paper—and downtown traffic that crippled suburban delivery. But Smith Hempstone, a member of one of the three local families that founded the *Star* in 1862, said when it died, "Had we been a little smarter, more energetic, and less selfish," the paper might have continued to flourish as it had for more than a century.

The *Star* went down with a circulation of about $25,000, but it wasn't selling one-quarter of the advertising that was going to the morning *Post,* and advertising is the lifeblood of daily newspapers.

The local business community that couldn't see the advantage of supporting the sinking *Star* quickly got an example. A few weeks after the *Star* ceased publication, the *Post*—which added about 100,000 papers to its press run—raised advertising rates 10 percent.

The *Post* also bought up the *Star*'s plant and presses, thus preempting anyone who might be thinking about starting a new paper with the old equipment and leaving the morning paper astride the city like the Colossus of Rhodes.

That probably would have surprised Ned McLean, a millionaire playboy of the 1920s who had let the *Post* slip into disreputability and debt while he dabbled in politics (getting caught in the Teapot Dome scandal) and the high life. His wife, Evelyn Walsh McLean, wore the Hope diamond to the auction where the paper was sold to financier Eugene Meyer in the 1930s.

Meyer, his son-in-law, Phil Graham, his daughter, Katharine, and now his grandson, Donald Graham, built the *Post* into a publishing and broadcasting bonanza. The company now also owns *Newsweek* and *Inside Sports* magazines (the latter, a money loser it is trying to sell); a smaller newspaper in Washington State; television stations in Michigan, Florida, and Connecticut; part of some paper mills; half of a flourishing news syndicate that serves several hundred other papers; and, for gravy, a piece of the *International Herald Tribune* in Paris.

Not that all this prosperity has produced happiness at the *Post.* The paper was dogged with bitter labor troubles in the last decade and despite near top-of-the-industry salaries, its editorial staff has been beset with dissension.

Part of this is often blamed on executive editor Ben Bradlee, a profane Bostonian (he told Kay Graham, "I'd give my left one for it" when she offered him the top editorial job), who hires the best talent he can find or kidnap and then pits them against each other in what he calls "creative tension." This does substitute for outside competition on what now has become a monopoly newspaper, but some of Bradlee's staffers also think it encourages news-needling and truth-shading to make stories look better in the daily race for front page display.

Creative tension was assigned at least part of the blame by those who know the *Post* for its 1981 "Jimmy" disaster. Janet Cooke, a young black reporter, brought in a riveting story about an eight-year-old ghetto kid who was hooked on heroin supplied by his mother's dope-pusher boyfriend. The story caused a local sensation and sent the police on a fruitless two-week shakedown of the city's drug scene looking for Jimmy. It also earned Janet Cooke a Pulitzer Prize for feature writing.

It was then discovered that Janet Cooke's real talent was for fiction writing. Jimmy was a figment of her imagination (a "composite") and a product of her declared ambition to succeed in the *Post*'s super-heated competitive environment. When it was learned that Cooke also had invented much of her résumé when she was hired, the *Post* dismissed her as a liar who had victimized the paper.

But, as the *Post*'s own ombudsman pointed out in a lengthy postmortem of the Jimmy affair, Cooke's character did not explain or excuse a long series of lapses in elementary newspaper editing practices that permitted the story to see print, or the initial defensive management reaction to legitimate questions raised about it by the community and members of the paper's own staff.

The *Post* vowed to clean up its act, but it still is not known as one of the country's best-edited papers. Almost a year after the Jimmy flap, it ran a piece on Andrew Young's inauguration in Atlanta, calling him the first black to succeed another black as the mayor of a major city. The next day, it ran a tiny correction noting that in fact the black mayor who had that distinction was one Marion Barry—of Washington, D. C.

The Jimmy affair hurt the *Post*, perhaps as much as it was helped by the 1972-73 Watergate exposé of reporters Bob Woodward and Carl Bernstein, which also earned a Pulitzer. The *Post*'s nearly faultless performance and top-down courage in what became the "All The President's Men" epic inspired some to suggest it had supplanted the

New York Times as America's greatest newspaper. Janet's Jimmy ended such talk, and it is ironic that Woodward was one of the editors involved in the "systems failure" that permitted it to happen.

Some of the *Post*'s more vitriolic critics leaped on the episode to exhume their doubts about the "Woodstein" team's Watergate reporting, particularly their use of an unidentified figure called "Deep Throat." Two points dispose of this carping: first, Woodward and Bernstein used Deep Throat only for leads to be followed and as a check for information developed from other sources; and second, everything they wrote, with one rather minor exception, was correct. There never was a Jimmy, but there was a criminal conspiracy in the White House from Day One of the Watergate saga.

One reason Cooke got as far as she did with Jimmy was that her only local competition came from an understaffed and dying *Star*. Woodward and Bernstein were competing against some of the best reporters in the United States who, short of breaking the Watergate story themselves, would have loved to pin a fake on the two young upstarts who were making them look like helpless cubs. And while the two *Post* reporters did the big job on breaking open Watergate, some of their competition, notably the *Los Angeles Times* and *New York Times* Washington bureaus, contributed significantly to piecing together the entire sordid story.

It is the men and women of these and other bureaus who make up the front line of the Washington press corps. They number several hundred and cover the White House, the Congress, the federal departments and agencies, the diplomatic community, and the wide-ranging networks of partisan politics and special interests.

Behind them is a group of about equal size that concentrates on news that affects the areas served by their own newspapers. To this group, the MX missile is less a story about a new weapons system in the global struggle for nuclear supremacy than an issue of local interest in more jobs and/or environmental disruption.

Finally, there is a herd of reporters who deal with specific subjects—everything from the effect of federal regulations on the anhydrous ammonia industry to the outlook for a constitutional amendment outlawing abortion. This group, frequently writing for trade magazines and newsletters or single-interest pressure groups, is the real lode of expertise in the Washington press corps.

It is often to the specialists that the generalists who work for the daily papers and the networks look for leads on what become major national stories. There are damn few White House reporters who would know a Mediterranean fruit fly from a B-l bomber, but there are a number of agricultural reporters who could quickly supply the information needed to put the Medfly into perspective when it suddenly causes a confrontation between the governments of the United States and California.

Years ago, scores of individual newspapers had their own correspondents in Washington. (In 1913, there were only about 180 reporters accredited to the congressional press galleries, but no newspaper, including the *New York Times, World, Sun* or *Tribune,* had more than 3 in their Washington bureaus.)

Today, a few dailies with less than 100,000 circulation still have their own Washington correspondents. But with the resurgence of newspaper chain ownership—the Gannett, Newhouse, and Thomson organizations lead the field in small papers—most get their news from large bureaus. These often rival in size the Washington bureaus of the companies that still have big-city papers—Knight-Ridder, Scripps-Howard, and Hearst.

In broadcasting, the picture is similar. The networks have very large bureaus (NBC has nearly 160 people, including the news staff of its local outlet, accredited to the radio-TV gallery), some broadcast groups have their own bureaus, and a few individual stations have lone correspondents.

Finally, there are the wire services, United Press International and Associated Press, which form what Stephen Hess of the Brookings Institution has called "the bone structure" of Washington news coverage. Between them, the two wires probably collect, write, edit, and deliver more words of news every day to the print and broadcast media in the United States and abroad than the rest of the Washington press corps combined. AP accredits more than 90 people to the press gallery; UPI about two-thirds that number, with both fielding additional people to take photographs and provide radio reports. Foreign wire services, including the British Reuters, the French Agence France Presse, and the Russian Tass, also cover Washington.

A few years back, a journalism magazine carried an article entitled "Washington's Two Most Influential Newsmen." It named to that distinction the editors of the UPI and AP city wires, both of which run "daybooks" every evening and morning listing news conferences, hearings, scheduled press releases, and a host of other information that make it easier for Washington editors to keep track of what is happening in the capital.

The daybooks are particularly vital to television assignment editors to plan the dispatch of camera crews. Washington press agents are well aware that the way to get their own events covered is to get them listed in the daybooks. So they take pains to cultivate the city wire editors and, back in the days when such things were not frowned upon, frequently reminded them of their esteem with the odd bottle of booze.

The thundering herd that is the Washington press corps has just about the best facilities in the country to help it work. Washington reporters are served—and sometimes used—by an army of flacks that probably outnumbers and surely is better paid than the working press. They run press rooms, ranging from broom closet-sized nooks to posh suites equipped with everything from soft drink machines to video display terminals, and almost everything is paid for by the government or the private organization on whose premises the press rooms are located.

Some news organizations, concerned about potential conflicts of interest in accepting facilities from the people they are writing about, refuse to accept these and other such emoluments as free transportation and room and board for out of town stories. The government, however, makes no provision for reporters to pay for the help they get in covering the news in Washington. One news bureau was told it could not supply its own specialized typewriters in the Senate and House press galleries, but Congress would buy them for it. Another tried to find out what reasonable rent could be paid for the congressional gallery space it used but was told Congress could neither make an estimate of cost nor accept payment. The outfit arrived at a figure on its own and sends a monthly check to the U.S. Treasury.

The press does pay its own way, and sometimes a lot more, to travel with the President, other government officials, and political candidates. The usual charge for press charter flights is 150 percent of first-class air fare, which is also supposed to cover baggage handling and ground transportation.

This charge is generally accepted, but in 1979, news organizations rebelled at the 225 percent of first class that Senator Edward Kennedy's campaign organization wanted for travel with the candidate. Several networks hired private planes to transport their crews, and the Associated Press once sent a reporter by regular commercial airline to follow the candidate. Kennedy eventually went back to the usual charge.

Some who used to watch the Washington press at work on telecasts of presidential news conferences are outraged by the arm-waving clamor from reporters seeking to ask questions. These performances, in fact, also disturb some in the press corps because some of the most obstreperous performers have been people who seldom show up at the White House until a televised conference is announced. They may not have particularly searching questions to ask, but they do get to show their employers back home that they are on the job in Washington.

But the sometimes boisterous atmosphere at news conferences is also a symptom of a bigger problem for the Washington press. It is simply the increasing isolation of the President.

Franklin D. Roosevelt met the White House press twice a week in his office during much of his long tenure. Harry Truman, Dwight D. Eisenhower, and John F. Kennedy held relatively regular news conferences for all who wanted to attend. So did Lyndon Johnson; like HST, he sometimes held impromptu question-and-answer sessions with reporters who puffed along with him on brisk hikes. Johnson patrolled the White House grounds, but Truman liked to stroll around downtown Washington.

Richard Nixon had regular meetings with the press at first, but increasingly withdrew as his Presidency went sour. Reporters had the same problem with Jimmy Carter, who had promised twice-a-month news conferences, and Ronald Reagan had only six open sessions with the press during his first year in office. In addition, his aides made clear that any reporter who tried to ask Reagan questions during such ceremonial occasions as photo sessions with his White House visitors would be asked to remain in the press room thereafter.

All of which adds up to a problem. Reporters are supposed to cover the news firsthand, or if that is impossible, to get information from the best source possible. At the White House, the best source is supposed to be the President, and that is why reporters tend to become overeager on the rare occasions when recent chief executives have invited the press to ask questions.

Restricted access is not a problem in covering Congress. In the House, the Speaker sees the press every day in his office before a session, and Senate reporters go right down to the chamber before the opening gavel to speak to the majority and minority leaders. Most other congressional leaders as well as rank-and-file members are readily available to reporters, who are permitted to request that members be asked to come off the House and Senate floor during sessions to be interviewed.

The problem in covering Congress is one of sifting through the mountain of press releases that piles up every day as members seek to glorify themselves. A champion example was the case of the senator who issued a statement announcing that the President and several dozen of his colleagues and other officials had joined him at a regularly scheduled congressional prayer breakfast one morning.

Actually, it often is easier to uncover the truth of any given situation on Capitol Hill than anywhere else in Washington because the two-party system in Congress creates a built-in check on suppression and self-praise. Experienced reporters know that frequently the way to find out what really happened in a closed-door meeting is to ask the meeting's losers.

Reporters who cover the courts and the bureaucracy sometimes are able to exploit the adversary nature of many situations, but they have another occupational hazard peculiar to journalistic specialists. They sometimes "go native"—begin to identify themselves with the agency they are covering.

The most virulent form of this malady was illustrated some years ago by a wire service reporter assigned to the Justice Department. When his editor called to ask him to get the attorney general's comment on some news development elsewhere in Washington, the reply was: "Oh, I don't think we will have anything to say on that." It came as no surprise when the reporter quit several months later to go to work for the Justice Department.

In general, however, the Washington press corps is a first-class professional group. This is especially true when the Washington press is compared to that in some other countries, where reporters often are primarily motivated by their political leanings. It may well be true that most Washington—indeed American—reporters tend to be liberals, but the overwhelming majority go to pains to keep from letting their copy reflect their personal political preferences.

Sometimes, however, the Washington press gets caught short on a story its members are not prepared to handle. That was the case, sadly, for some of the reporters who were involved in coverage of the attempted assassination of President Reagan in the spring of 1981.

In such a situation, the usually reliable sources of information are not available, and reporters' judgment in keeping rumor separated from fact is crucial. Most of the men and women who covered the White House and George Washington University Hospital that rainy day were very careful, but a few panicked.

There still is controversy over who in the White House was supposed to have said that Press Secretary James Brady had died of his head wound. There is no controversy, however, about the fact that the reporters, primarily on television, who reported Brady dead did not identify the source of their information until it became time to pass the buck.

It is sometimes necessary, especially in Washington, to use anonymous sources to get news that can be secured no other way. But to report that a high-ranking government official has died without attributing the source is to make the kind of blunder that would justify advising a cub reporter to try his hand at selling shoes. The fact that the White House staff was itself in some disarray that day and that the atmosphere was bordering on the hysterical at times made it all the more necessary for reporters on the scene to exercise extreme care in their work.

While the Washington press corps, overall, is very good, it does not at present have the kind of giants among it who dominated the capital's news scene in the past. There is no commentator with the stature of a Walter Lippmann and few reporters with the kind of achievements and respect attained by the likes of James Reston and Peter Lisagor in their prime.

The list that follows is based on the observed excellence and impact of each person's work. If it leans toward political journalism at the expense of top people in other specialties, the authors can only respond that politics, after all, is what Washington is all about.

THE TOP FIFTEEN WASHINGTON MEDIA PEOPLE
1. Donald E. Graham

There is a story about a compulsive gambler who arrived in a strange town and asked the hotel desk clerk where he could find some action. The clerk said he knew of only one place, but warned it had the reputation of being a clip joint. A few hours later, the gambler reappeared and reported that sure enough, he had been taken to the cleaners at the place.

"I told you the wheel there was crooked," the clerk said.

"Sure," replied the gambler, "but you also said it was the only wheel in town."

The *Washington Post,* surely one of the best newspapers in America, is no crooked wheel. But for news-addictive Washington, it is the only one in town, and as publisher, Donny Graham runs it.

Graham was only 34 when he took over the family paper from his mother in 1979. He had learned the business in 10 years of moving between editorial- and business-side jobs, but his test really came in 1981 when the Jimmy hoax broke.

Graham could have sent Executive Editor Ben Bradlee or one of the other hired hands out to announce and try to explain what had happened. But Graham, who had spent 18 months as a beat patrolman on the District police force after college (Harvard) and the Army, had taken a personal interest in the young black reporter and her story of an eight-year-old heroin addict.

So he faced the music himself. Later that week, in an exhaustive reprise by the paper's ombudsman, Bill Green, Graham was quoted as saying, "We can't deny the obvious. The *Post* printed a false story. We ought to ask ourselves what changes to make and make those changes."

Graham actually began making changes at the *Post* shortly after he took over, replacing the editorial page editor of 10 years, Phil

Geyelin, with the deputy editor, Meg Greenfield. If the stories that grew louder after the Jimmy episode have any substance, Graham may be making some other top-level changes at the *Post*. One persistent scenario is that Bradlee, after about two decades in the top news job, will be replaced by Dick Harwood, the deputy managing editor. Those who subscribe to this theory note that Green's long analysis found some kind of fault with Bradlee, Managing Editor Howard Simons, Metropolitan Editor Bob Woodward (who subsequently was shunted off to a "special projects" job), and City Editor Milton Coleman, but contained these words, "Harwood had no role in [the story's] preparation." Other gossips claim that Harwood, who couldn't make a success of the *Post*'s paper in Trenton, New Jersey, was stuck in place. And that Bradlee's successor would come from out of town.

Graham may also be making another major decision soon. When the *Star* went down, reports surfaced that the *Post* would begin publishing an afternoon tabloid for street sale only. Graham denied it at the time, but avoided saying it wasn't going to happen later.

2. David S. Broder

Dave Broder is one of the reasons the *Washington Post* is one of the country's best newspapers. He has been called "The High Priest" of American political reporting, an honorific that probably would evoke a response of "bullshit" from Broder.

The unadorned fact is that Broder, now 52, has been at the top of his craft since the mid-1960s. His presence covering a campaign or a political gathering is enough to give that event its own status in the minds of the rest of the political press. It is not unusual to have a political flack try to lure another reporter to whatever happening he is plumping by announcing that Broder is planning to cover it.

Broder left the *New York Times* in 1966 to join the *Post* and has held the title of associate editor since 1975, which was the year he won a Pulitzer Prize. Despite the title and awards, Broder is no "drop in and drop out" political reporter like some at his level. He sticks with a campaign long enough to get a real sense of its course and tone and will be often found sitting with the "watchman" wire service reporters at some interminable meeting on convention delegate selection rules when the hour has long passed cocktail time.

What really makes Broder different, however, is his devotion to the two-party system. He is, above all, a man who believes deeply in the institution of politics and who, during the "reform" eruptions of a decade ago, sometimes was derided by his peers for doubting that there might be such a thing as too much democracy in the conduct of party affairs.

He also is an exceptionally kind man. It is not unusual to see Broder at a political convention sitting at a bar with a group of young reporters from local papers. At such gatherings, Dave listens more than he talks, and the young ones go away with the feeling that covering a state senate campaign in Dubuque or Deaf Smith County is not all that different from jetting about the country in Air Force One. And, of course, it isn't. In fact, it's usually harder.

3. Roger Mudd

Just as there are those who will tell you that the *Times* lost its chance to establish dominance in political journalism when it let Broder leave, there is a strong faction in Washington that believes CBS blew it when it chose Dan Rather over Roger Mudd for the Walter Cronkite anchor job.

There may be a tad of chauvinism here, because Mudd is very much a product of Washington journalism. He began in print journalism in Richmond, Virginia, in 1953 but shortly switched to broadcasting at a Washington TV station. He joined CBS in 1961 and, with an insight into congressional folkways and rules as deep as any reporter on the scene, covered the great civil rights battles of the mid-1960s colorfully and comprehensively.

Mudd was, like a number of other reporters, close to Robert Kennedy, and there is irony in the fact that it was his early interview with Ted Kennedy in 1979 that is blamed by some for starting that campaign effort off with a plop. But Mudd threw no low blows in asking Kennedy about Chappaquiddick and other personal matters; they were material to the campaign. In the end it was Kennedy's shocking inability to express himself in coherent terms that hurt his candidacy in that interview.

Mudd, now 53, went to NBC after losing the top anchor spot at CBS and, with Tom Brokaw, is anchoring its evening news in competition with Rather and the Reynolds-Robinson-Jennings ABC troika. NBC obviously hopes to reinvent Huntley-Brinkley and regain the ratings lead with its entry. It may not work, but there is going to be a heck of a battle.

4. Sam Donaldson

Donaldson, ABC's White House man since Jimmy Carter came to Washington, doesn't cut quite as much ice since the arrival of Ronald Reagan. But the 48-year-old Texan, "Charlie Hustle" of the Washington television reporters, still is the dominant voice in the cacophonous uproar of the White House press room.

As a reporter, Donaldson is a throwback to the rough-and-tumble days of crime-chasing newsies who would kill for exclusive quotes from eyewitnesses. No one ever demonstrated that better than Sam at the 1976 Democratic National Convention, where he gave party officials and security men palpitations by vaulting up to the podium and interviewing Carter at the moment of his triumph. The rest of the press corps followed, but Donaldson was there first and got the best.

He still is that way and some of his colleagues put Sam down as all brass and no meat. In fact, he is a good, accurate newsman with the same kind of zest for his job that Pete Rose has for his, although he requested a change in assignment after a year of Reagan. He does, however, have a weakness for sharp, sometimes cruel, yak. It could get him in trouble.

5. Mary McGrory

Mary McGrory has been newspapering now for 40 years, but for about a third of that time her employers, the Boston *Herald-Traveler* and the *Washington Star,* didn't know what they had. With the possible exception of *Post* sports reporter Tom Boswell, McGrory is the best writer in the Washington press corps.

"Miss Mary" is a woman of strong liberal opinions, and at times, such as during the Vietnam War and the Nixon Presidency, they tended to overpower her reporting skills. But there is no one in the capital with an equal eye and ear for the texture and sound of a news event and no one with the words to convey both to a reader.

McGrory, who came to the *Star* as a book reviewer in 1947, stuck with the paper to the bitter end although she almost surely could have found a safer berth. Her presence alone was worth the price of the paper, and when she moved over to the *Post,* its management demonstrated its assessment of her value by playing her at the coveted top of page 3. She came through in one of her first pieces with a stunning impression of Supreme Court nominee Sandra Day O'Connor. Her Pulitzer, long overdue, came in 1975.

6. George Will

George Will is not a newspaperman. He is a commentator and an essayist and one of the best in those lines. Will, now just past 40, became a columnist after the senator he worked for, Gordon Allott of Colorado, lost his seat in 1972. It was a tragedy for Allott but a boon for Washington, which gained a forceful, intelligent, conservative voice in the newly-minted columnist.

A former college teacher who was educated at Oxford and Princeton, Will writes formally, sometimes stiffly, but the scope of his knowledge, ranging from the classics to baseball trivia, almost always provides entertainment and illumination.

Just before the 1981 inauguration, Will entertained the Reagans at his home, an event that got a lot of news coverage and signalled to some that the columnist was in the administration's pocket. No sir, Will wrote in a subsequent column and demonstrated his point by climbing on the administration's back several times before the President's first year ended.

A regular panelist on the Agronsky & Company television show (sometimes called "Night of the Living Dead"), Will won a Pulitzer for commentary in 1977.

7. William Kovach

New reporters in Washington often are told to expect something of the following sort to happen to them: A senator's receptionist picks up the telephone and announces to her boss, "There are four reporters and a gentleman from the *New York Times* waiting to see you."

Times reporters, especially during the era of James Reston, did seem to have a kind of aristocratic aura about them. That hasn't been as true lately, especially during the internecine struggle between the *Times* management in New York and the Washington bureau that followed Reston's departure from its day-to-day operation.

New York, that is, Executive Editor Abe Rosenthal, finally won, but it wasn't until rough-hewn Bill Kovach, at 50 a relative short-timer in the *Times* hierarchy, took over direction of the more than 50 reporters, editors, and photographers in the Washington bureau that the backbiting and bickering began to abate.

The *Times* still has the resources, the talent, and the tradition needed to restore its Washington coverage to greatness. Kovach, who retired *Times*man Harrison Salisbury described as a "tough, straight-talking, no-nonsense editor," is the key. Just wait.

8. Meg Greenfield

It is customary to call a newspaper a "voice" in its community. Because it is in Washington, the *Post* is a voice that is heard not only in the capital but in the rest of the nation and abroad as well.

Meg Greenfield, its editorial page editor, not only speaks for the *Post* in her own writing, but decides what other opinion will be given space on its recently-expanded "Op-Ed" and letters pages. That is a lot of power, perhaps more than any other woman in American journalism has.

Greenfield, born in Seattle in 1930, won academic honors at Smith College and a Fulbright scholarship to Cambridge before spending 11 years on the staff of the late *Reporter* magazine. She joined the *Post* editorial page staff in 1968 and 10 years later won a Pulitzer for her work.

9. Walter Mears

If you read *The Boys on the Bus* about the 1972 presidential campaign press corps, you met Walter Mears. He was the Associated Press political reporter over whose shoulder the rest of the newsies supposedly leaned to find out what the lead was on any day's story. It really wasn't quite like that, but Mears was and is a sharp and fast reporter and writer who has an instinct for the headline angle on a breaking news story.

Mears has come a long way since '72. Now 46, he is the chief of the AP Washington bureau—biggest in the city with about 100 people— and an AP vice president. Walter got his Pulitzer for 1976 presidential campaign coverage. In the trade, the word is that he will be getting the AP presidency sometime in the 1980s.

10. Helen Thomas

Helen Thomas learned how to cover the White House from Merriman Smith, the United Press International's man with the President from Roosevelt (Franklin) to Nixon. She turned out to be an apt student, becoming one of the best-connected, most persistently inquiring White House correspondents who ever gave a press secretary fits.

Though just past 60, Thomas still can run for press buses and pool cars with the youngest, and although she is no prose stylist, she gets her stories fast and right. A frequent speaker at colleges and journalism meetings, she probably is the best-known Washington woman reporter.

11. Jack Anderson

This man probably should be called Jack Anderson, Inc. He is the proprietor of the most widely printed Washington column—about 1,100 newspapers in the United States and abroad—and also has regular television and magazine commitments as well as the odd book and frequent speech. Anderson, close to 60, has lots of help: a cadre of experienced editors and a shock troop of green-as-grass intern reporters, all of whom work out of a Charles Addams-style Victorian mansion on 16th Street, well away from the downtown location of most news organizations.

Some in Washington downrate Anderson, but there is no denying his national impact. Some indication of that was illustrated by the reaction of the administration to stories that the White House wanted to dump Secretary of State Alexander Haig. When officials got hold of an advance copy of an Anderson column reporting the story, the author got two telephone calls from Haig and one from Reagan himself to deny it. That, of course, gave Anderson an entirely new column about being telephoned by the President and Secretary of State.

Anderson succeeded Drew Pearson in writing the column and like Pearson gets a lot of his information from disgruntled bureaucrats and politicians working out grudges. Sometimes his tips are spectacularly wrong, but over the years Anderson has turned up a lot of nasty wrongdoing in Washington. He got a Pulitzer in 1972, ironically the same year he printed wrong information about Senator Thomas Eagleton's driving record.

12. Rowland Evans & Robert Novak

In 1963, when "Rollie" Evans and Bob Novak teamed up to write a new Washington column, some had trouble picturing a Waspish, eastern establishment type like Evans eating in the same restaurant with the rumpled and Slavic Novak, but they settled in to a partnership that has done very well indeed.

Evans and Novak are enamored of the inside story—sometimes it seems there is a sentence in every column that begins, "In a development that got little attention at the time . . ." But they have sources, especially when the Republicans are in power, that no one else in Washington can match: during the Nixon years, a writer once referred to Melvin Laird as "the Secretary of Defense, who also writes a newspaper column under the name Evans and Novak."

Some who knew them as reporters (Evans with the New York *Herald Tribune* and Novak with the *Wall Street Journal*) were surprised by the conservative spin their column took over the years. Novak, 51 (10 years younger than Evans), is the more pugnacious of the two and in 1972 was blamed by Senator George McGovern for the savaging the Democratic candidate had taken from E&N. This climaxed with the exile of Novak to the campaign "zoo plane" with TV technicians and weekly newspaper reporters. In *The Boys on the Bus,* Tim Crouse reported that Novak, "in his one endearing comment of the campaign," responded, "OK, no more Mr. Nice Guy."

13. Jack Germond & Jules Witcover

If you think Evans and Novak are an odd couple, you haven't met Germond and Witcover. Jack is bald, rotund, and a lively wise-cracker; Jules has somewhat more hair, less weight, and sometimes appears half asleep. But together or separately, Germond and Witcover are the best "who's ahead" campaign reporting team in the country and among the best connected to professional politicians. If Howard Baker failed to accomplish as much in 1980 as they said he would, we all make mistakes.

Witcover quit a safe berth at the *Post* and Germond chucked a lucrative executive spot with the Gannett organization to take a long chance on the even-then dying *Washington Star* and a column on politics.

Their product was perhaps too oriented to nuts and bolts for many editors outside Washington, but it was must reading in the trade. There was some surprise that the *Post* did not take on Jack and Jules when the *Star* went down, but they were able to move to the Baltimore *Sun,* which has a lot of readership in the capital and in fact has a reputation of reporting Washington better than its hometown. The *Chicago Tribune* helped bankroll them, too.

14. Diana McClellan

Diana is an Englishwoman who many believe had a lot to do with keeping the *Star* alive for at least four years with her unique gossip column, "The Ear." Written in a wicked tone of chatty familiarity, the column specialized in catching Washington's most pompous figures in lapses of hypocrisy or foolishness, and tickled the city's fancy to the extent that some people bought the paper for this alone.

The *Post* hired McClellan when the *Star* went down, and she quickly embroiled her new employer in a controversy almost as embarrassing as the Jimmy disaster. She reported that gossip was circulating that the Carters knew Mrs. Reagan wanted them to move out of the White House before the Inauguration because her conversations at Blair House, the presidential guest quarters, had been taped. All hell broke loose, including a threat by the former President and First Lady to sue the *Post.*

The newspaper's first response was an awkward editorial, which read like it had been dictated by a frightened lawyer, lamely claiming that all the *Post* had done was report an item of gossip, which of course it did not for a moment believe was true. When that didn't satisfy the Carters, Graham apologized and the paper printed what Diana, in her many previous retractions, calls "a grovel."

Diana then became an eye; until recently, she was one of the stars of the revamped CBS morning news program, reporting from Washington.

15. Phil Jones

Phil Jones is the CBS man who covers Congress, and for what it is worth was voted the best TV congressional correspondent in a mid-1981 sampling of officials by *TV Guide* magazine.

Jones followed Rather's stormy tour at the White House, but was moved to Capitol Hill when the Carter administration came to town.

To the more status-conscious among the broadcast journalists, that seemed to be a demotion, but in fact Jones developed Congress as a television news story better than anyone since Mudd.

Newspaper people assigned to The Hill say Jones is a good reporter. They say that about damn few TV people.

Think Tanks

WASHINGTON COULD get along without its think tanks, just as a general might get along without his staff, but not very well, and not for very long. Modern-day Washington, coping with such monstrous complexities as nuclear response, monetary policy, and hemisphere relations, would be unthinkable without think tanks.

For one thing, Washington think tanks function as storage tanks. As much as they supply government with opinions, assessments, and evaluations, even when not asked, they supply government with people. Former Defense Secretary James Schlesinger came into government from a think tank, California's Rand Corporation. When he left his post as energy secretary, it was to go to Georgetown University, which operates all sorts of think tanks. United Nations Ambassador Jeane Kirkpatrick came out of Georgetown U. and the American Enterprise Institute.

Half of government is produced by think tanks, the cerebral consulting organizations that provide intelligence, knowledge, data, computer analysis, historical perspective, and problem-solving techniques—usually for hire, but sometimes just for the historical record.

The two behemoths of the Washington brain business are the business-oriented and largely Republican American Enterprise Institute, much the top dog in town with the Reaganites in power, and the more liberal and Democratic Brookings Institution, which is thriving despite the ascendancy of the New Right and which still has many admirers throughout Congress and the federal bureaucracy.

Founded in 1943 as the American Enterprise Association, the AEI was intended to represent the best interests of the free market economy and the corporate way of life, but since then has expanded into all sorts of new fields, including nuclear rocketry. AEI has established study centers for defense policy, economic energy policy, foreign policy, government regulation, health policy research, legal policy, political and social processes, tax policy, democratic capitalism, and mediating structure.

When the Republicans left office in January 1977, AEI made one of its biggest hauls. Former President Ford himself came aboard as the

Institute's Distinguished Fellow, and 20 other ranking members of his administration signed up as well. The AEI's list of notables now includes former head of the Fed Arthur Burns, resident AEI Distinguished Scholar; former Defense Secretary Melvin Laird, chairman of the defense policy studies advisory council; former White House economic adviser Herbert Stein, now an AEI economic adviser; philosopher Irving Kristol, an AEI senior fellow; and former Treasury Secretary William Simon, chairman of the tax policy studies advisory council. Judge Robert Bork of the powerful U.S. Court of Appeals for the District of Columbia was on the AEI's council of academic advisers, and Federal Trade Commission Chairman James Miller was the AEI's resident expert on regulatory matters. Author Ben Wattenberg is among AEI's Democratic associates and coeditor of its *Public Opinion* magazine.

In addition to its many scholars and advisors, AEI has a full-time staff of 34, led by president William J. Baroody Jr., whose father, Bill Baroody Sr., was president before him and the man chiefly responsible for its existence. In addition to *Public Opinion*, AEI puts out 3 other magazines and produces some 130 other publications. Its weekly television show, "Public Policy Forum," airs on more than 400 television stations.

It won't, of course, touch a penny of government money, getting about 40 percent of its $10.4 million annual budget from corporations and the rest from foundations. In 1970, its budget was only $800,000. It has, to say the least, kept pace with Big Government.

Brookings dates back to 1927, when it was formed as an amalgamation of several small policy analysis outfits that was inspired by civic-minded St. Louis lumberman Robert Somers Brookings. It is the larger of the two giants, with a staff of 50, led by president Bruce MacLaury (a Republican!), and some 50 guest scholars. Its budget, which has always been big, totals $10.7 million, of which 15 percent comes from government grants and nearly all the rest from foundations, although MacLaury took in some $800,000 from corporations in 1979 and since has been working hard to up their ante.

Like AEI's, Brookings' opinions are rendered with all the thunder and lightning of revealed truth. The Reagan administration obviously didn't think much of Brookings' notion that the B-1 bomber (at $250 million each, a gargantuan waste of taxpayers' money designed chiefly to perpetuate obsolete pilots in the Air Force) ought not be built, but the White House must surely have warmed to Brookings' call for abolition of the Agency for International Development. If there's any international development to be done, Reaganites are much keener on the likes of the United Fruit Company and Exxon.

Brookings has uttered the definitive word on Soviet foreign policy, which it said was largely based on Soviet military power, and which, it noted, has been called upon 190 times to achieve foreign policy goals since World War II. Another Brookings study found that the Congress is not a branch of government coequal with the Executive, and shouldn't be. Brookings' Stephen Hess produced a tome on Washington journalism in 1981 that found that 93 percent of Washington reporters had college degrees, compared to 51 percent in 1963; that 65 percent of Washington news people come from the Northeast or Midwest; that 90 percent of high-ranking federal officials read the *Washington Post* while just 62 percent read the *Wall Street Journal* and only 45 percent read the *New York Times*; and that those three newspapers are in Washington's "inner circle," while the *Los Angeles Times* and *Chicago Tribune* are not.

Brookings weighed in with great authority on Reagan's supply-side economic recovery plan, accepting that the tax cuts were overdue but warning that the program could have dire consequences in the form of runaway inflation.

It has also opined on such topics as U.S. economic policy for Southeast Asian countries, international aspects of banking regulation, regulatory reform at the Environmental Protection Agency, salary and retirement for federal workers, economics of the property tax, the financing of community colleges, urban decline and the future of American cities, dynamics of the party system, the futility of family policy, decentralizing urban decision-making, blacks and the military, exports of manufactures from developing countries, preparing for the next oil shock, and U.S.-Mexican free trade—all that and more just in 1981.

Brookings contributed economist Charles Schultze and four other notables to the Carter administration; when the denouement came, Brookings took only Schultze and economist Henry Owen back, but times can get tough.

It's not much of a television power, but Brookings' radio show, "Focus," plays on more than 150 stations. It only brings out about 35 publications a year, but at least half of them are books. Page-turners like *Conservatives in an Age of Change: the Nixon and Ford Administrations; China's Economy in Global Perspective;* and *Nontariff Distortions of International Trade* are typical.

The most interesting thing about Brookings at the moment is that it is becoming more and more like AEI and vice versa. As the two shun ideological cant for pragmatic problem solving, they draw closer to the center. To call AEI conservative Republican and Brookings liberal Democratic 10 years from now might well make no sense whatsoever.

The Rand Corporation has headquarters in California and is

basically a consulting firm, but it has a most important Washington office and is as much a think tank as the rest of them. Also, it more or less runs the Pentagon, which ought to count for something. Rand, now chaired by former Defense Secretary Donald Rumsfeld, brought the American military into the computer age doing preparatory work for the DEW line radar network in Canada and Alaska, and has since made itself indispensable. The American military seldom attempts any new weapons system unless Rand has thought about it, or at least has run it through a computer.

Conservative think tanks of every specialty have come into a prominence they never quite enjoyed until the Reagans moved in. Probably the most respectable is the Hoover Institution of Palo Alto, California, a kind of right-wing, West Coast Brookings. After the election, Reagan's team ordered 52 copies of Hoover's *The United States in the 1980s*, a 916-page collection of scholarly essays on just about everything. Hoover, whose director, W. Glenn Campbell, was picked personally by the late Herbert Hoover in 1960, kindly made Ronald Reagan one of its fellows. White House domestic adviser Martin Anderson and his wife, Annelise, associate director of the Office of Management and Budget, both came from Hoover.

Georgetown University's Center for Strategic and International Studies, which gave the world Richard Allen and became a post-public life haven for Jim Schlesinger and Henry Kissinger, is a right-leaning outfit that had a heavy hand in the Reagan transition.

The most rightward-leaning of the tanks (so much so it's almost horizontal) is Reagan's beloved Heritage Foundation, started in 1973 by its current president, Edward Feulner (former aide to Congressman Phil Crane), and Paul Weyrich, the baby-faced fellow who had such fun bullying radical leftists like George Bush and Howard Baker after the 1980 election as head of the totalitarian Committee for the Survival of a Free Congress. Financed by such rightos as beer king Joe Coors and the mean-minded Richard Mellon Scaife, among others, Heritage has formulated policies and opinions that prompted the head of one of its think tank rivals to remark: "Anything to the right of the Heritage is the fringe."

But the Heritage is listened to and read by the Reaganites, including the No. 1 Reaganite himself. Perhaps the best read of Heritage publications was its 3,000-page blueprint for Reaganism, *Mandate for Leadership*, on which it lavished 250 contributors and $100,000. Among its recommendations: cut agriculture spending by 15 percent, nearly all in food stamps; increase defense spending by 20 percent; support tuition tax credits for private schools; abolish the Energy Department; freeze hiring for the Department of Housing and Urban Development; weaken influence of environmental groups over public land use; remove the Justice Department from busing cases and rescind curbs on the FBI; cut the budget for the Comprehensive Employment Training Act (CETA) programs; provide more military aid to anti-Communist Central American regimes; allow local discretion over uses of Transportation Department grant money; cut income taxes 10 percent across the board; and unleash the CIA. They sound almost as though Reagan wrote them himself.

Reviewing *Mandate*, OMB Director David Stockman said: "Leaders in both the new administration and Congress will find in this work all of the tools they need to hit the ground running." "Very impressive," said presidential counselor Ed Meese. "The Reagan administration will rely heavily on the Heritage Foundation." Soviet news agency Tass denounced Heritage as "the nerve center of American neoconservatives." No one could ask for more. Although Heritage complained Reagan's first year was "disappointing."

New York's Hudson Institute has had some bad guesses, such as when it wrote one of its famous "scenarios" predicting that the increase in Japan's gross national product would be 10 percent a year until the year 2000. But it's had some very good ones, predicting in the early 1970s that gold would be revalued, and calling the Iranian revolution six weeks before it happened. Headquartered in New York's Westchester County in offices overlooking the Hudson River, and run by a very bright lady, Mrs. Gail Potter, Hudson commands a lot of respect in Washington, if mostly because of the corporate clients it gets: Xerox, Rockwell International, Westinghouse, General Motors, General Foods, Royal Dutch/Shell, Boeing, Ford Motor, and Coca-Cola.

Not content with the monumental Brookings, some Democrats have created their own think tank forum, the Center for National Policy, as a foil to AEI, raising more than $1 million for it with the avowed goal of taking the White House away from the Reaganites in 1984. Creation of this outfit involved such Democratic heavyweights as former domestic policy adviser Stuart Eizenstat, Congressman Michael Barnes, former Labor Secretary Willard Wirtz, and arms control negotiator Paul Warnke, as well as such lightweights as former State Department flack Hodding Carter and his wife, former State Department human rights czarina Pat Derian.

Georgetown University, under the leadership of Father Timothy S. Healy, S. J., operates a vast catalogue of think tanks. In addition to its world-famous Center for Strategic and International Studies, Georgetown has the Institute for the Study of Diplomacy, the Center for Contemporary Arab Studies, the Center for Immigration Policy and Refugee Assistance, the American Language Institute, and the Kennedy Institute of Ethics.

Then there is something in Washington called the Advanced International Studies Institute, affiliated with the University of Miami, which has predicted Russia a head-count winner in a nuclear war and sent forth news releases with such gripping headlines as: "Africa is the Proving Ground for Soviet Premise that Continued Pressure Against the West Will Result in World Hegemony, Expert on Soviet Union Asserts in Latest AISI Monograph: The USSR and Africa: New Dimensions of Soviet Global Power."

There is doubtless a think tank in Washington called the Institute for Institutional Thought. There may well be one that thinks Upper Volta will win the nuclear war.

But the very, very best of the Washington think tanks, in terms of intellectual attainment, purity and usefulness of purpose, and objectivity, is (logically enough) associated with and housed in the Smithsonian Institution. It is the Woodrow Wilson International Center for Scholars. Its trustees have included William Baroody Sr.; Judge Robert Bork; White House aide James Baker III; former White House aide Bryce Harlow; the late Senator Hubert Humphrey; Henry Kissinger; Senator Daniel Patrick Moynihan; Allan Nevins; Elliot Richardson; Caspar Weinberger; Dean Rusk; and Cyrus Vance.

Its scholars and fellows have included the *New York Times'* Neil Sheehan, Mario Vargas Llosa, former General Edward L. Rowny, Professor Kenneth Waltz, journalist Henry Bradsher, Bereket Selassie of the Ethiopian Selassies, Avery Dulles, and Professor Wanda Corn of Mills College, a world-renowned art expert. Its umbrella encompasses the Kennan Institute for Advanced Russian Studies, a Latin American program, international security studies, an East Asia program, and an environmental studies program, as well as academic advisory panels on historical and cultural matters, and social and political studies, the latter including Elliot Richardson.

Perhaps the most useful function of the Wilson Center is its "evenings," better known as "evening dialogues." One such memorable occasion in 1980 brought together former Secretary of State Dean Rusk as speaker and Senator Richard Lugar and journalist Neil Sheehan as panel respondents for a rehash of the Vietnam War and the press's role in losing it. Among those in the discussion group were former CIA Director William Colby, General Rowny, Undersecretary of State Richard Holbrooke, and Senate foreign relations expert Jeffrey Bergner.

Other "evenings" have featured Paul Nitze, George Ball, Senator Claiborne Pell, Congressman Paul Findley, Senator Henry Jackson, and Max Kampelman. Daytime discussions have brought forth the likes of the *New York Times'* Harrison Salisbury; Michael Forrestal;

William Hyland, Henry Kissinger's Rasputin; Israeli Ambassador Ephraim Evron; and George F. Kennan.

Subjects taken up at the Wilson Center have ranged from Bolshevism vs. Leninism and America's response to longer life, to revisiting the Peruvian experiment and the survival of Cambodia. They even found time for nationalism and social change in Transcaucasia.

The Wilson Center is devoted to encouraging, not ideological cant, corporate greed, Latin American totalitarianism, liberal orthodoxy, or party-line Republicanism, but thought—a rare but we think admirable trait in a think tank, especially a Washington one. What

THE TOP FIVE WASHINGTON THINK TANKERS

1. William Baroody Jr.

One of the biggest catches the American Enterprise Institute made from the exiting Ford administration was Bill Baroody Jr., son of its own late guiding genius, Bill Sr.

Born in Manchester, New Hampshire, in 1937, Baroody the Younger studied English at Holy Cross College and political science at Georgetown University, which gave him quite a fancy for Washington. He became a legislative assistant and press secretary to then Congressman Melvin Laird in 1961, was made research director of the House Republican Conference in 1968, joined the Defense Department as assistant to the secretary (later deputy secretary) in 1969, was made a White House aide to President Nixon in 1973, and came to the Ford team as assistant to the President in September 1974. He joined AEI in 1977 as executive vice president and succeeded to his father's throne in 1978.

If he went back to the White House, the Big Four of Baker, Meese, Clark, and Deaver would have to be expanded to five, but Baroody seems content running the city's chief Republican and preeminent think tank.

2. Bruce K. MacLaury

The weightiest opinions of the Brookings Institution are its economic ones. It is well that Brookings' president, Bruce K. MacLaury, is an economist.

Born in Mount Kisco, New York, in 1931, deep in the heart of oh so Republican upper Westchester County, MacLaury got a B.A. in economics from Princeton, and an M.A. and Ph.D. in economics from Harvard. He joined the research department of the Federal Reserve Bank of New York as an economist, was made manager of the Bank's foreign department in 1963, and became vice president in charge of that department in 1965. Ever the Westchester Republican, he joined the Nixon administration as deputy undersecretary of the Treasury Department in 1969, dealing mostly with debt management and international finance. In 1971, he went out to Minneapolis to become president of the Federal Reserve Bank headquarters there, and joined Brookings as president in February 1977.

A Phi Beta Kappa man who belongs to the elitist Cosmos Club and lives in McLean, MacLaury was a draftee GI in the 1950s and belongs now to the Council on Foreign Relations and the Trilateral Commission, as befits a Brookings man.

3. Donald Rumsfeld

The Rand Corporation's president, Donald Rice, is a brilliant chap who has the biggest say in running the joint, but the Rand fellow with the biggest clout in Washington is its new chairman, Donny Rumsfeld, also remembered as former secretary of defense and the White House power who survived the Nixon administration best.

After the Ford administration fell to Jimmy Carter in 1976, Rumsfeld, once the boy wonder congressman of Chicago's suburban North Shore, took over the then failing but now prosperous G. D. Searle drug company out there, and bided his time. The Reagan election, transition, and inaugural came and went, and Rummy was still biding his time, though people had been talking about how he wasn't going to accept mere Defense this time but would hold out for something spiffier, like secretary of state.

Born in Chicago in 1932, Rummy was a Princeton wrestler before he became a congressman and head of Nixon's war on poverty, Nixon's war on inflation, ambassador to NATO, and Ford's White House chief of staff. He was a good secretary of defense and, even if biding his time, does stand an excellent chance of getting his old job back or moving up to secretary of state should Reagan ever reshuffle the cabinet.

Rummy might even be given the directorship of the CIA, the job he stuck George Bush with when he was running Ford's White House. Bush could tell him how to survive that, too.

4. Richard Mellon Scaife

The Heritage Foundation and eight zillion other right-wing causes would be nothing without the handsome Richard Mellon Scaife, great-grandson of the founder of the Mellon empire. Himself worth $150 million, he is chairman of his mother's Sarah Scaife Foundation, which he has spun around ideologically, despite his sister Cordelia's efforts to confine the foundation to Mother's interests in population control and art. A huge contributor to Richard Nixon, he provided the Heritage Foundation its start-up money and has contributed a total of $4 million to it since it was organized by his friends Joe Coors and Paul Weyrich in 1973. He has also been a bankroller of the Pacific Legal Foundation, a right-wing public interest law firm that has gone to court to fight for unrestricted use of moth pesticides, private development if not ownership of California's beaches, and removal of pregnant women from welfare rolls; and the Mountain States Legal Foundation, to which he is the largest donor and which gave the world Interior Secretary James Watt.

A Yale and Pittsburgh University graduate who is one of the towering figures of western Pennsylvania, the 48-year-old Scaife is not always a gentleman. We quote the following from an article in the *Columbia Journalism Review* in which former *Wall Street Journal* reporter and Columbia faculty member Karen Rothmyer attempted to interview him:

> Rothmyer: "Mr. Scaife, could you explain why you give so much money to the New Right?
> Scaife: "You fucking Communist cunt, get out of here."

Curiously, Scaife's wife Frances is a great benefactor of animal protection work and one of the sweetest and gentlest women in America.

5. James Billington

Historian James Billington, a Princeton and Oxford man who taught at both Princeton and Harvard, has been director of the Woodrow Wilson International Center for Scholars since 1973, when he left Princeton to try to introduce thought to the nation's capital. Now in his 50s, he grew up in Merion, Pennsylvania, served as an Army officer attached to the CIA in the 1950s, and wrote what has become the standard work on Russian classical history, *The Icon and the Axe.* He also studied in Finland on a Fulbright, learning to speak the almost impossible Finnish language, which has, incidentally, 15 cases. A man who finds libraries the most exciting places on earth, he seems to enjoy the Center's "evenings" more than anyone in the room. He is hard at work on what he considers his life's work, a study of Russian in the seventeenth century. He must be counted as one of Washington's 10 most intelligent and educated individuals, and the town is damned lucky to have his presence.

Flacks

IN SIMPLER TIMES, everyone knew what a press agent did: he got your name in the papers if you wanted it there; he kept it out if you didn't. Nowadays, press agents don't even exist. They are called public relations counselors, public affairs officers, information specialists, media liaison coordinators, and press secretaries. There are thousands of them in Washington. Most don't like it and many don't deserve it, but all of them often are simply called flacks.

One estimate in 1979 placed the government public relations payroll at 19,000. That may go down as the Reaganites carve away at the federal work force, but it seems sure that the largest number of flacks in Washington will continue to be supported by the taxpayers.

In truth, they are an essential link between the government and the public. Without them, the press corps probably wouldn't be able to report a tiny fraction of what the government is doing for and to the people. And it is also true that they tend to isolate government officials and sometimes cover up their blundering and wrongdoing.

There is not even a ballpark estimate of how many people work at public relations in Washington for nongovernment employers. Hundreds of companies, trade associations, labor unions, charitable organizations, and other cause groups have their own p.r. staffs in the city. And finally, there are almost two full pages in the Washington classified telephone directory of individuals and firms offering public relations services. The industry supports its own wire service in the city and is a big customer of the many private courier services operating in the capital.

The sum of all this government and private p.r. activity is a daily flood of press releases, information kits, brochures, reports, and other printed material that flows into Washington news offices by mail and messenger and leaves, often unopened and unread in trash baskets. Washington reporters spend as much or more of their time each day reading as they do listening or watching the news develop, but there are few who can do any more than skim their daily harvest of handouts.

188

And there is a lot more to public relations in Washington than papering the city with press releases. Some flacks do nothing but keep their agencies in touch with what is going on in the industries they are regulating; others only monitor the agencies that regulate the industries they are working for. They also write speeches and testimony for congressional hearings and agency appearances, plan and run seminars and conventions, set up press conferences, lay on cocktail parties, and take clients and contacts to lunch and dinner. The last has done wonders for the restaurant business in Washington.

The best of the Washington flacks do none of the above. Whether they work for the government, for companies, or for p.r. firms, they spend their time talking to people. At one end of the process, they advise their principals on how best to present themselves and what they are doing to the press and/or the public. At the other, they are the public voices of their employers, most often as nameless "spokesmen" for this official or that industry, but often on the record in print and on the television screen in person.

The President's press secretary is the number one flack in Washington. Whether he is a James Hagerty, who knew what was going on in the Oval Office because he often had something to do with it, or a Ron Ziegler, who knew only what he was told was going on, the press secretary has Washington's most demanding public relations job.

Because no President since Lyndon Johnson has had any personal link to the press corps, the press secretary has become a crucial figure in the presentation of the administration to the media. If the White House press believes the press secretary is both informed and honest, he can successfully speak for the President. That same credibility is tested daily all across Washington in the offices where government p.r. officers brief the press and answer its questions.

That also is the case in nongovernment public relations. Bob Gray, one of Washington's most successful public relations and lobbying men, told an interviewer just after Watergate: "Get caught telling an untruth once in this town and you're through." Another man, vice president of a relatively small p.r. firm, said, "I figure I'm doing my job if reporters accept me as a reliable source."

Yet every reporter knows every flack is going to do all he can to make his client, be it a huge government agency or a multinational conglomerate, look good in all things. Some Washington reporters think government p.r. people, because they are paid with public funds, should tell the worst about their bosses. Few do.

However, most of the misconceptions about Washington public relations appear to be harbored by people who hire capital flacks. "Some of our clients think all they have to do to get what they want in this town is hire a good p.r. firm," one agency man said. "It doesn't work that way, and we even have trouble convincing our people in other cities of it."

Another public relations man told of trying to get the president of an organization he was working for on a network interview program. When he contacted the producer of the show, he found out the client also had retained a personal p.r. man to make the same pitch, which also failed.

Public relations in Washington can come close to outright lobbying, and some firms register their people as lobbyists. However, because the line between trying to influence public opinion and official action on an issue—say, a tax cut for business—is so blurred and the registration law is so broadly construed, few bother.

Because they frequently are quoted in the newspapers and seen on TV, top government p.r. people often become better known than private practitioners. The State Department's Hodding Carter was in American living rooms daily for months during the hostage crisis in Iran, and Reagan Press Secretary Jim Brady, before he was shot, was rapidly developing into a media star. Yet some of the best remain faceless. Joe Laitin, a top flack for the Treasury and the Pentagon in both Democratic and Republican administrations, remained all but anonymous during his long career; and who but a few lawyers and reporters would recognize Barrett McGurn, the longtime press officer for the U.S. Supreme Court?

Some Washington p.r. people do make their own splash, however. Gray got a lot of press attention during the Nixon years as a frequent companion of the President's longtime secretary, Rose Mary Woods, and Steve Martindale, a young member of the big Hill and Knowlton Washington staff, was the subject of a searing profile in the *Washington Post* some years back when he told reporter Sally Quinn how he planned to become one of the capital's leading party-givers. He never made it.

THE TOP FIVE IN WASHINGTON PUBLIC RELATIONS
1. David Gergen

As noted, Jim Brady would be in this spot had he not been cut down in the attack on the President in the spring of 1981. Gergen takes his place because, as White House communications director, he has become the most authoritative official voice in the White House pressroom.

Gergen, just 40, worked in both the Nixon and Ford White Houses and was not regarded as a major figure in the Reagan operation until after the shooting removed Brady from the scene. Until then, he was involved mainly in speech writing (he was the man who suggested

Reagan end his debate with Jimmy Carter by asking the audience if it was better off in 1980 than 1976), but now he is in charge of both that function and press relations.

Gergen, who has no trouble attracting attention when he stands up to his full six-foot, five-inch height, is from North Carolina. He was educated at Yale and Harvard Law School, worked for both Nixon and Ford in the White House, and spent the four-year Democratic interregnum as editor of a magazine for the conservative think tank, American Enterprise Institute.

2. Robert K. Gray

Bob Gray, the proud owner of his own public relations firm after 20 years as head of Hill and Knowlton's Washington operation, is a man who knows how to get attention.

Gray, although a confirmed Republican—he was Dwight Eisenhower's appointments secretary and has been a big GOP fund-raiser for years—makes a point of associating his interests with the opposition. At Hill and Knowlton, he hired for a top job Liz Carpenter, Lady Bird Johnson's former press secretary, and in his new firm, Gray and Co., he has installed Gary Hymel, Speaker Tip O'Neill's longtime aide.

He also was the cochairman of the Reagan inaugural committee and, as if to show his connections extend to the other end of Pennsylvania Avenue as well, recently was host at a giant outdoor party for Senator Paul Laxalt, Reagan's good friend, under a circus tent on the Capitol lawn.

Trim and white-haired, Gray is always impeccably dressed, and so are the employees of his new p.r. firm, quartered in a renovated power station on the Chesapeake and Ohio canal in Georgetown. They have to be—Gray does not countenance pantsuits for women or shorter than calf-length stockings for men.

3. Bob John Robison

With a name like Bob John, the head of the largest public relations operation in Washington might seem to be a leftover from the Carter administration. Not so. Robison, a former top naval aviator, has been in high-level corporate public and governmental relations for years and left another Washington corporation job in 1981 to take over the helm of Hill and Knowlton's Washington office.

Although some clients left with Gray, Hill and Knowlton still is considered to have the biggest show in town, with about 50 people on staff. It also is the nation's largest public relations firm, with more than 1,000 employees in offices across the country. Hill and Knowlton was purchased by the J. Walter Thompson advertising giant in 1980, one of the reasons Gray says he decided to strike out on his own. It was one of the last of the major p.r. firms to become tied in with a big advertising agency.

Hill and Knowlton is one of the Washington public relations companies with a major lobbying component. Eight of its executives are registered. It also takes on foreign governments but will only represent them on economic matters. (This is a most sensitive issue for p.r. firms: Carl Byoir & Associates, another of the major companies, represented the German railroads before World War II and, despite a clean slate from congressional investigators, suffered for years under charges that it had been a propaganda outlet for the Nazis.)

But Washington public relations companies get into plenty of controversy, and Hill and Knowlton is no exception. It was deeply involved in the hassle over the banning of saccharin and trucking deregulation. It also was retained by Metropolitan Edison after the Three Mile Island reactor accident, and suffered the embarrassment of having a couple of reporters eavesdrop on a closed meeting at which its Washington staff was trying to teach the Pennsylvania utility's executives how to handle themselves at a congressional hearing.

4. John M. Meek

The career path of Washington public relations people often starts in government, as it did for Gray and Robison, or news work, as it did for John Meek, the head of the Daniel J. Edelman firm's Washington operation.

Meek, an Oklahoma native in his early 50s, started out as a newspaper reporter in Texas and New York State, but switched to politics and government in the 1960s. He came to Washington to work for Oklahoma Senator Robert Kerr, one of the real power brokers of his day, took part in Robert Kennedy's 1964 Senate campaign in New York, served with the Democratic National Committee and as a speech writer for Lyndon Johnson until 1968. He then joined Edelman.

Meek's shop was deeply involved in the long-running campaign against the required use of air bags in automobiles and handled the successful effort to secure American landing rights for the Concorde SST. The company also has had a number of foreign clients, including some, such as Haiti, that have involved it in disputes with human-rights advocates.

5. Victor Kamber

Vic Kamber, who is one of the young and upcoming people profiled in David Broder's look at future leadership, *Changing of the Guard*, got started in Washington in the Nixon-Agnew campaign of 1968.

He worked for a New York Republican congressman for several years, but then made an abrupt career change, moving to the staff of the AFL-CIO Building Trades Department. Kamber directed the labor federation's struggle for the big Labor Reform bill in the later 1970s—it got through the House but died in the Senate—and then decided to open his own shop to represent labor clients. He staffed his new firm, the Kamber Group, with such well-known Washington figures as Allen Zack, a top AFL-CIO flack, and John Leslie, for years the chief information man at the Labor Department.

Although Kamber's is not the only labor-oriented p.r. firm in Washington—Maurer, Fleischer, Anderson & Conway is one that has been in the field for years—the new entry has made something of a splash by straightaway taking on the New Right. Backed by liberal activist Pamela Harriman, socialite wife of the former New York governor and veteran diplomat, the Kamber Group produced a series of TV ads attacking Terry Dolan and his National Conservative Political Action Committee when NCPAC launched its own 1981 broadside against Democrats in Congress who opposed the Reagan economic program. It will be necessary to wait for the results of the 1982 elections to learn the outcome of that battle royal.

Mouthpieces

HOLLYWOOD MAKES MOVIES. Pittsburgh makes steel. New York makes women's clothes, entertainment, books, and bank loans. St. Louis makes barge gunk. Washington makes laws.

The United States has two-thirds of all the lawyers in the world, three times as many per capita as are found in England, from which we derive our basic law. America's lawyers serve only about 30 percent of the American population with any adequacy, according to the American Bar Association. Ninety percent of our lawyers serve only 10 percent of the population. In the 1970s, corporations were spending $24 billion a year on legal services, more than 10 times the budget of the entire Justice Department.

Washington has more lawyers proportionately than any other city in the country, even if you don't count lawyers who work for the Justice Department. "I have concluded in my old age that the city is too full of two kinds of people: lawyers and press people," CBS's Eric Sevareid once said. "It is quite clear now that the lawyers paralyze everything. That's what lawyers are for, to keep things from happening."

Chicago has 20,000 lawyers, two times the number of doctors in the entire state of Illinois. Chicago is a city of 3 million people. Washington has only about 637,000 people, yet it has 20,000 lawyers in private practice alone, and another 12,000 working for the government.

There are 535,000 lawyers in the country, an increase of 50 percent from 1970, for a ratio of one lawyer for every 410 persons. In West Virginia, the ratio is one for every 1,100 residents. In Washington, it's one for every 64 persons, the highest concentration of lawyers anywhere in the country or the world.

They make a good buck. The total legal take in Washington in 1980 was just shy of $1 billion. Covington & Burling, the city's largest firm, took in $40 million. Starting salaries for a lawyer at Covington & Burling are close to $40,000 a year. The average income for all lawyers practicing in the country is about $33,000 a year. Incomes of $500,000, $600,000, and $1 million a year for the top partners in the

194

city's major firms are now commonplace. Joseph Califano made $505,000 in 1976, the year before he joined the Carter administration. He's doing much better now. Lawyers keep up with inflation. They have to. Their lust for office space in downtown Washington has driven the cost up from $10 to $12 a square foot in 1976 to $26 or more now.

For all this, Washington does not have a lot of big law firms: none among the top 25 in the country. Its largest, Covington & Burling, with just under 200 attorneys, is 27th largest in the country. Its next biggest, Hogan & Hartson, with just under 150 lawyers, is 47th largest in the nation.

What's happening is that big firms in other cities are opening branches in Washington. In 1978, 33 of the country's 50 top firms already had offices in the city. By 1981, this had increased to 47 out of 50. The impetus has come largely from the greedy desire not to split fees. Why hire a high-priced freelance mouthpiece when you can move in your own and keep things in-house, and possibly save some dough? Of course, trying to keep things in-house at such a far remove can be confusing. Winston, Strawn, a curmudgeony, conservative Chicago Republican firm that sponsored and put most of its political chips on Illinois Governor James Thompson, went and hired former Vice-President Mondale when he left office. It is presumed they knew he was a Democrat. What else did they know? Chicago's huge Kirkland & Ellis, which maintains a 74-lawyer office in Washington, got into big trouble a few years ago when its Washington office turned out to be on one side and its Chicago office on another side in the same case.

Washington attorneys tend to be specialists—in areas of government. Some know only regulatory law. Some know only international trade law. Others know only some friendly congressmen. Except for occasional aberrations like Watergate and Abscam, most of the criminal stuff in Washington is left to low-priced lawyers.

There's another peculiarity to the Washington legal community. Though the city is nearly three-quarters black, only four black attorneys have become partners in big Washington firms.

There's an actual lawyer shortage in Washington in one regard. In large part because of all the branch offices of big firms here, there aren't enough small, general practitioner firms typified by so many Jimmy Stewart movies. A recent seminar on how to open your own Washington area law office drew just 100 people. But the shortage wasn't so acute that the courts were willing to further suffer Fred Owings Sullivan, the champion amateur lawyer of Washington with 110 lawsuits filed, all on behalf of himself.

In one, his official complaint scrawled on both sides of a paper bag, he asked $500 billion in damages from the Walgreen's drug store at the New York Port Authority bus terminal because a clerk threw him out. In another, he sought $500,000 in damages from a Connecticut laundromat because he was allegedly refused use of a dryer. In yet another, he asked "$100 zillion" from a suburban Maryland roller rink because he was refused admission. If he wanted $100 zillion, he should have passed himself off as a procurement officer from the Pentagon.

Finally, an exasperated Federal Judge George Hart had Sullivan declared an official nuisance and barred him from the U.S. District Court here "permanently and forever."

Many wish he would do the same to about half the lawyers in Washington, though certainly not to anyone on the following list.

THE TOP FIVE LAWYERS IN WASHINGTON

1. William French Smith

Attorneys general are not selected with the care and screening that Supreme Court or Appeals Court justices are. It may be the single most important lawyer's job in the country, but the country is largely at the mercy of the presidential whim. For every Elliot Richardson or Edward Levi, there's a Bobby Kennedy, John Mitchell, or Richard Kleindienst.

From all the hundreds of thousands of attorneys, judges, and law professors in the country, Ronald Reagan picked his family lawyer, William French Smith, a man whose legal opinions had not been much discussed at Harvard Law.

French Smith has surprised many. He turned out not to be just another Los Angeles society lawyer catering to the film crowd, but a pillar of the Western Establishment, Harvard Phi Beta Kappa, a man of affairs with an abiding interest in the arts and international relations. And a pretty fair lawyer who has run a pretty good shop. In fact, French Smith has proved to be one of Reagan's better cabinet choices.

He's had a peculiar difficulty trying to wed Reagan's brand of laissez-faire conservatism to the activism that has been tradition for Justice Department attorneys for two decades now, and vice versa, but he seems to have taken a moderate, accommodating course, and achieved some success. If no Ed Levi, he's at least a Richardson.

2. Edward Bennett Williams

Known to many only as a baseball and football sports impresario, Edward Bennett Williams is the best trial lawyer in Washington, which may not be saying all that much, and one of the very top trial lawyers in the country, which is saying a lot.

The long and not entirely savory list of clients he's successfully defended include former Treasury Secretary John Connally, mob figure Frank Costello, the presumed late Jimmy Hoffa, Adam Clayton Powell, Dave Beck, and Bernard Goldfine. He couldn't save Bobby Baker from the slammer, but who could?

On the side of the angels, he represented the *Washington Post* and the Democratic National Committee during Watergate. According to one of the notorious tapes, with the expletives deleted, Nixon said, "We are going to fix . . . [Williams] because he's a bad man." We all know who got fixed.

Williams' 60-lawyer firm dabbles in other things than criminal law. If it didn't, there'd be an awful lot of pin-striped vested suits down in those grungy Washington police courts. But it remains his lucrative passion. Some lawyers brag about making $500,000 a year. Williams reportedly earned $500,000 just for defending John Connally in his bribery trial. He now charges $200,000 and more in advance before people even walk through his door.

They get their money's worth. The character witnesses Williams produced for Connally included Lady Bird Johnson, Barbara Jordan, Dean Rusk, Robert McNamara, and Billy Graham.

As well-connected as he is talented, rich, and successful, Williams counts Ben Bradlee of the *Washington Post* and columnist Art Buchwald among his close friends, and has pals almost as close all over The Hill. And in the White House. And everywhere else. According to Saul Pett of the Associated Press, LBJ wanted him to run for mayor of Washington, and Ford wanted him to take over the CIA. Being one of the shrewdest men in town, he naturally declined both offers, but it wasn't bad for a poor kid from Hartford, Connecticut, who got through Holy Cross on a scholarship.

3. Lloyd Cutler

One of the few smart things Jimmy Carter did in his forlorn and mostly forgotten term as President was hire superlawyer Lloyd Cutler to replace White House counsel Robert Lipshutz in 1979. The Carter White House needed counsel. The sage Cutler gave the crackers more than they ever heeded, but he kept Carter out of a lot of trouble. If he couldn't keep Carter in the White House, it certainly wasn't for lack of advice to keep Brother Billy the hell out of Libya.

Senior partner in the big, powerful, and prestigious firm of Wilmer, Cutler, and Pickering, Cutler is *a*, if not *the*, Mr. Establishment of Washington law. His outfit has represented General Motors and corporations representing every kind of industry in the country. It's wired on The Hill and nimble in the courtrooms. If the Democrats ever come back, it could be, arguably at least, No. 1.

Born in New York City in 1917, the distinguished Cutler is a magna cum laude Yale man who practiced law in New York before World War II and moved on to Washington immediately after it, seeking, perhaps, a somewhat smaller pond for the big splash he was going to make. Active in civil rights causes and a former trustee of the Brookings Institution, Cutler was busy in government matters before joining the Carter White House, serving as a special representative on U.S.-Canadian boundary problems and as a lobbyist for SALT II.

4. Clark Clifford

Born in 1906, Clark Clifford is the resident sage of the Washington legal community, and a few other Washington communities. He was the onetime special counsel to President Truman (1946 to 1950) who helped teach old Harry how to master the "Do Nothing" Congress and stay on the top of the capital heap. He was the World War II Navy captain who became Lyndon Johnson's secretary of defense and who warned of the disaster that would ensue if LBJ didn't abandon the idiocy that was American war policy in Vietnam. He was the old Washington hand who came forward with the good advice that let Carter budget director Bert Lance get out of town gracefully. He is the senior partner of Connecticut Avenue's prestigious firm of Clifford, Warnke, Glass, McIlwain & Finney. A Kansas-born, St. Louis Democrat before he came to the Federal City, he will doubtless be a valuable resource for the next Democratic President.

5. Joseph Califano

Joe Califano came into the job of secretary of Health, Education, and Welfare in 1977, viewing it as the crowning triumph of his career. He was rudely fired by a scapegoat-seeking Jimmy Carter two years later, but that only enhanced his career. He is one of the few veterans of the Carter administration who still commands respect on The Hill.

And other places. A Brooklyn-born Harvard man just past 50, Califano joined the Kennedy administration as a Defense Department lawyer and rose to become LBJ's top assistant. It was he who pulled off the neat trick of creating the Transportation Department. Between the Great Society and whatever it was that Carter gave us, Califano labored as a ranking partner of Edward Bennett Williams' all-powerful Williams, Connolly, and Califano, functioning as the manager of the firm and earning more in one week in 1975 than the average American did all year.

Already the author of three books, Califano paused after his dismissal to write a hefty tome that happily savaged Carter and his clan, but he's likely to emerge a major presence in Washington yet again. He gave up his half-a-million salary to serve Jimmy Carter.

Now he can give that sort of thing up for a cool million in salary.

And, in Ronald Reagan's administration, it doesn't hurt to have Republican friends, such as Alexander Haig. It was Califano's shrewd counsel that kept Haig from going down with Watergate in Nixon's final days and that eased the way for Haig's confirmation as secretary of State when hostile senators were trying to unleash the Watergate beast all over again.

Honorable Mention—Sol Rosen

Sol Zalel Rosen is a bald, bespectacled fellow who keeps pens in his shirt pocket and works out of offices in a seedy section of town that would make a Philip Marlowe character feel uncomfortable. He is one of those very non-pin-striped barristers who hang around the Superior Court at Fifth Street and Indiana Avenue representing indigent clients who qualify for public defense funds. Though he once landed Bernard Welch, the despised burglar and murderer of revered celebrity doctor Michael Halberstam, as a client, Rosen's customers more usually run to the likes of prostitutes, junkies, and thieves.

So he won't be called upon for advice by any President or big corporation. But there is a great big Washington out there that the white enclave never pays any attention to, and Rosen is the only kind of lawyer most of the people there can afford. Known as "the King of Fifth Street" lawyers, Rosen symbolizes justice for the better part of Washington, and that is not a fact to be overlooked.

Society

T HE SECRET to society in Washington is that there isn't any.
  "In Des Moines, there are probably 25 established families who determine the character of the place," a retired foreign service officer and longtime observer of and participant in the Washington social scene told us. "In Washington, forget it. There are 'old families' here, but they're not rich enough, not influential enough to make other people feel like strangers. In other places, it takes two generations to feel at home. In Washington, just two years. Actually, anyone who's been here six months has been here as long as anyone else."

Washington has money. Fairfax and Montgomery Counties are among the very richest in the nation. It's expensive. The cost of living is the third highest in the country. But it's a matter of a lot of people having some money; there's practically no one with a whole lot of money.

The other cities of America are their own versions of Boston, New York, Philadelphia, and Charleston, their "society"—whether of the Yves St. Laurent or Johnny Carson double-knit variety—the same sort of established aristocracy. Washington has more in common with the old mining-camp towns of California and Colorado; it is a transient place attracting the governmental equivalents of prospectors, drummers, whores, gamblers, speculators, swindlers, adventuresses, and whiskey merchants, the "society" determined by whoever is flush at the moment.

America's "great" families are so because of great fortunes, and, however squalid their beginnings (Commodore Vanderbilt's first command was a Staten Island garbage scow; Gustavas Swift first sold meat from a pushcart), great fortunes mean major industries—steel, railroads, meat packing, automobiles, oil, even hamburger chains.

Washington doesn't have any. There are a railroad and a candy bar company with main offices here, but the largest industry in Washington is printing, and it's quickly being rendered obsolete by computers—from California.

An industry that initially had as much to do with the building of Washington as government was slavery. During the first half of the nineteenth century, it was one of the largest slave markets in the nation, its vast slave pens visible from the windows of Congress. When slavery was finally outlawed in the District in 1850, it became a mecca for free blacks. It remains a largely poor and overwhelmingly black city, its white sections only enclaves. The black community has its society, but not one the white community recognizes.

Washington only started to become a really big city in 1965, when Lyndon Johnson's Great Society program gave a big spurt to the growth of government and thus government's dependencies: law firms, consultants, lobbyists, think tanks, printing firms, French restaurants. Government salaries are big, sometimes handsome, but not enough to support anyone beyond the upper-middle class. Senior partners in law firms can knock down $500,000 a year and much, much more. They can afford million-dollar houses. But they live off salaries, money earned with their grubby little hands, or minds, or friends, not interest earned on capital. The few people who *do* do that in the Washington area are what one Massachusetts Avenue toff sniffingly referred to as "parking lot magnates."

There are some old family names around Washington—Mellon, Cabot, Harriman, Amory, Roosevelt. But they are names that first became famous in Pennsylvania, Massachusetts, New York, and other places. Washington has always been a comfy nest for third-, fourth-, and fifth-generation descendants; distant cousins; the last born; remittance men; peripheral aristocrats who were underfoot and in the way in Newport, Philadelphia, and Chicago but became instant grande dames and great lords in aristocracy-starved Washington. Sometimes, they don't even become that. The most famous Roosevelt in Washington today, albeit a gracious, charming, and accomplished credit to the clan, is a newspaper reporter, the *Washington Post*'s Margot Roosevelt Hornblower.

Washington is also a great place for utter nobodies to become somebodies. Joe Allbritton, basically just your run-of-the-mill Texas millionaire, would have had trouble getting a headwaiter's attention in New York. Instead, he moved to Washington and became a titan. Hodding Carter, scion of a small newspaper holding in the rearmost backwoods of Mississippi, got a job with the State Department and became a great personage—in Washington. No one can remember where Barbara Howar came from, or where she went.

Washington society has no means of regulating itself. In Boston, Philadelphia, or Chicago, the Old Guard exerts rigid control over who gets into local society and how far they rise within it because they exert rigid control over residence, charity and arts boards, and exclusive club membership—the principal measures of local social status. Jackie O. may seem the Queen of the May to the masses, but there are buildings in New York where she and her millions would not be welcome (recall the fate of Gloria Vanderbilt). The masses think that Bonnie Swearingen, wife of the chairman of Standard Oil, is the top of Chicago society, but she isn't, because the stuffy grande dames won't let the Alabama preacher's barefoot daughter get on any of the "prestigious" local charity and arts boards. The newspapers have made much of President Reagan and Vice-President Bush belonging to the "exclusive" Bohemian Club, but the Bohemian Club is not among the handful of clubs listed in the *Social Register*.

In Washington, there is no Old Guard, certainly no hereditary one. As long as they have the scratch, people can live wherever they want, without fear of mean-minded home-owners' committees and other lynch mobs. Labor Secretary Ray Donovan, New Jerseyite pal of the Teamsters, moved into a house on the best hilltop in McLean. The arts boards in Washington are prestigious and include their share of "rich bitches." But they are quasigovernmental entities controlled largely by politicians. The boards are ridden with politicians. There are as many congressmen's wives on them as there are high society la-dee-dah ladies. Egalitarianism reigns, after a fashion.

The show is constantly changing, like the movies in a small town. The aristocrats of John Quincy Adams' administration were chased out of Washington by the backwoods nabobs brought in by Andrew Jackson and the bed-hopping Peggy Eaton. Jackson's protégé and successor, Martin Van Buren, brought in toffs and dandies. His first lady, daughter-in-law Angelica Singleton Van Buren, was the first mistress of the White House to fancy herself a queen, and took up sitting on thrones and wearing feathered headdresses to prove it.

The stodgy boardroom, officers' club, country club Washington society of Dwight Eisenhower was replaced by the glamorous Camelot of the Kennedys, which was just as abruptly replaced by the mile-long barbecue pits of the Johnsons. The Washington society of Jerry and Betty Ford, which enjoyed such entertainments as Bob Hope telling bathroom jokes in the East Room about Abraham Lincoln, was replaced by the Washington society of Rosalynn and Jimmy Carter, who served cheap wine.

The Carter bunch were louts and slobs, but they never really pretended to anything else. The Reagan bunch pretend to a reincarnation of Versailles, but within some of them are really louts and slobs fighting to get out, and often they do.

Nothing so typifies the "class" that the Reagans are so applauded for bringing to Washington than the cover of the September 1981 *Dossier* magazine, a publication that purports to be the bible or at least the scrapbook of Washington society.

The cover story, entitled "For a Healthy America," was about

Richard Schweiker, the once-liberal Republican senator from Pennsylvania who jumped ship to join the Reagan "ticket" in 1976 and was rewarded with the secretaryship of Health and Human Services (HAHS?) four years later. The article treated him as a sort of Mother Theresa of the Reagan administration, rambling on about his "life-long desire to help others."

The cover photo that accompanied the article was one only Nicholas and Alexandra could have loved. Schweiker was dressed in white tie and seated in a gold-backed banquet chair. Mrs. Schweiker, the original "Miss Claire" on television's "Romper Room," stood next to him in what looked like Elizabeth I's burial gown, with enough gold jewelry wrapped around her neck to keep every child in America in catsup for a year (with hot water, it makes a sort of soup). The table before them was strewn with fine china, gold-rimmed crystal, and other niceties. "Class," as they say.

One waits for the *Dossier* cover photo showing Ronald Reagan handing his horse's reins to a small black jockey.

Fine china is de rigueur wherever the First Lady feeds, which posed a problem when she moved into the White House. The china there, acquired by various Presidents over the centuries, was something of a hodge-podge, not enough left of any single design to provide the same setting for each of the guests Mrs. Reagan routinely invites to state dinners. So she dashed out and picked up a little something to make do, a nifty red and gold on ivory number featuring the presidential seal. It came to $952 for each place setting, or $209,440 for the whole 220 place settings. At a time when school-lunch milk was being cut by a quarter, the taxpayers might not have been so happy about such an outlay, but they hadn't to worry.

The Congress had appropriated $50,000 for Mrs. Reagan to use to redecorate the White House when she moved in, but she declined this generous offer of public moneys. Instead, she embarked upon an interior decoration fund-raising drive in the, er, private sector. The total quickly reached $822,000, with $270,000 kicked in by 23 oilmen, who certainly must have appreciated Reagan's having not long before decontrolled gas and oil prices. China, of course, is quite decorative.

The dishes are washed in the kitchen. The money was laundered in the White House Historical Association. And they can hold the state dinners in the Oil Room.

It's legend now that the Reagans brought back such refinements as limousines, hard likker, and after-dinner dancing, not to speak of menus in French—or sort of French. They keep lapsing into English, as in "Lobster en Bellevue with Sauce Remoulade." Why? After all, Nancy Reagan oversees the White House menus personally, and she went to Smith.

What the Reagans really brought back to Washington society were troops. At times the White House seems in mid-coup. There are military trumpeters on the balcony, the Marine band to play "Hail to the Chief," color guards, honor guards, sentries, and military social aides to escort VIPs.

The Reagans also brought back some really big high-society names, the kind of toffs and swells who were seldom invited to Jimmy and Rosalynn's do's and probably wouldn't have come if they had been. Amidst all the trumpeters and military social aides one might catch Mrs. Cornelius Vanderbilt Whitney, Blanchette Rockefeller, Evangeline Bruce, or Brooke Astor. But, in all fairness, the Reagans are much more egalitarian than that. Their inner inner circle runs to the likes of the invitees to Reagan's first White House birthday party: Francis Albert Sinatra, James Stewart, Charles Z. Wick (born Zwick), the ever present Jerome Zipkin, Walter and Lee Annenberg, and "The Eight"—Betsy Bloomingdale and seven California women just like her.

In even more fairness, the Reagans actually did bring some social class to Washington, in the form of such truly gracious ladies as Barbara Bush, wife of George; Patricia Haig, wife of Al; and Sue Block, wife of Agriculture Secretary John. They're not often seen dripping in mink, $25,000 evening frocks, or half of Tiffany's but, even in Reaganite Washington, class will out.

If Washington society lacks the traditional means of determining its own membership—rigid control over charity and arts boards, residence, and clubs—it does make a few feeble efforts at exclusivity, none of them very successful.

One is the *Green Book*. A family business, published by founder Helen Ray Hagner from 1930 to 1942, by daughter Carolyn Hagner Shaw from 1943 to 1977, and by granddaughter Jean Shaw Murray since, the *Green Book* purports to be the *Social Register* of Washington. It is not.

The *Social Register* has standards. Some of them aren't very savory, but it sticks to them nevertheless. Jewish people, for example, can't seem to get into the *Social Register* except by marrying some socially prominent non-Jew who's already listed. The *Social Register* frowns on divorce, and will not suffer theatrical people. The *Register* recently dropped the once preciously social Junior League from its listings of exclusive clubs, reportedly offended by the League's too-passionate embrace of social causes. The League's been teaching slum children needlepoint and taking convicted criminals out on pass to tea, for heaven's sake.

The *Register* was founded (like so many family fortunes) in 1887, the good old days of robber barons. The *Green Book* came more than four decades later, in the good old days of the New Deal. The *Register* has fallen on times sufficiently hard to be taken over by *Forbes* and have all its lovely little local editions compressed into one thick volume not unlike a hardware store catalogue. But the *Register* does not accept advertising.

The *Green Book* shamelessly accepts advertising, from Harry Winston and the Meyer Davis Orchestras, to be sure, but also from A. C. Electric and Ralph Brown Buick. The *Green Book,* never wishing to offend, lists all the senators and congressmen, including the likes of the Honorable John Jenrette and the Honorable Richard Kelly, he of the C-note–packed midriff. In its "Social List of Washington," the *Green Book* lists mere newspapermen. If the same social standards were applied to New York and Chicago, Jimmy Breslin and Mike Royko would find themselves in high society. The *Green Book* lists mere colonels, captains, and commanders; the assistant director for energy research and the principal deputy assistant secretary of state, and all manner of third-level White House employees, including the person who mails news releases to small newspapers out in the boonies. During the Carter administration, it even listed Hamilton Jordan, until his Amaretto-and-cream-spitting bouts proved too much even for the *Green Book,* and congressional liaison Frank Moore, who liked to take his shoes off at black-tie dinners. On one occasion, someone made off with them and he had to leave in his stocking feet. It lists Sarah McClendon, comic relief at presidential press conferences, but not Ben Bradlee or Meg Greenfield. We'll never understand why it doesn't include G. Gordon Liddy.

The other major arbiter of Washington society, such as it is, is *Dossier* magazine, chronicler and photographer of all the parties; purveyor of high-toned, uninteresting, and out-of-date gossip; and defender of the faith. It was founded in 1975. James Fallows, former Carter speech writer gone straight, wrote less than favorably about *Dossier* magazine in the *Atlantic Monthly:* "Each month's issue depicts the elected and appointed tribunes of the people at an endless whirl of galas and receptions, the men in dinner jackets and the women in evening gowns, provender from foreign governments and private corporations laid before them on banquet tables."

Dossier snapped back, denouncing Fallows for his "hothouse mentality."

"Such misconceptions amuse more than insult Washingtonians who still enjoy the capital's cornucopia of charity events, national days, testimonials, fund-raisers, benefits, cocktail and dinner parties and other social diversions," *Dossier* said. "Washington's social life is the most interesting and complex medium in America."

When *Harper's* jumped in, too, *Dossier* let out all stops:

> The *Dossier* is not a mass medium. Look elsewhere for a record of plebian pursuits and an avalanche of clotted words like those that fill spaces between the ads in the local mass media. *Dossier*'s turf is unique in America and most of the participants in our social chronicle have been well-educated in the rough-and-tumble school of American success . . .
>
> What they share is the simple discovery that mobility and opportunity are the only ingredients that hold the system together. What would America be if there did not exist the possibility that, through the manipulation of opportunity, one could move from poverty to riches, from obscurity to notoriety, from ignorance to enlightenment, and ("this truth may hurt") from caste to caste and class to class? . . .
>
> If we catch them in moments of laughter or leisure, dressed to the ears, sipping and supping from bounteous boards, pompadoured and pampered, raise up a cheer for America, kids!

The Reagan crowd loves *Dossier* magazine.

"Washington has always had two or three crass, commercial Welcome Wagons, like *Dossier*," our longtime Washington socialite friend concluded. With a slight yawn.

Washington always had two or three newspapers, too. Society coverage may have been a major factor in the death of one of them, the *Washington Star*. Under publisher Joe Allbritton and editor Jim Bellows, the *Star* quickly attracted a following as a smart (some said "smart ass"), sophisticated, sassy, and surprisingly antiestablishment alternative to the *Post*. When Time, Inc., took it over in 1978, it brought in its chief of correspondents, Murray Gart, as editor. He immediately transformed it into a miniature, cheapo version of the *New York Times*, filling it with a global potpourri of little news stories, many of which often seemed to have already appeared in the *Post* that morning. If Washingtonians were interested in that, they would have said so. The circulation of the *New York Times* in the Washington metropolitan area is only about 28,000.

Worse for the *Star*, Gart had social ambitions. And then some. He and his limousine prowled the party circuit like a beat cop in a squad car. He became the personification of the *Dossier* vision of America. And he ordered up a feature section to match. The *Star* began covering the party scene as lavishly and lovingly as the Republican National Committee's house magazine covers Republican conventions. He resurrected Betty Beale, who seems to have broken into journalism as a typist for a telephone directory publisher (or was it the *Green Book*?). But the "A" team comprised the three ladies known as Murray's Angels: Nancy Collins, who had tried and failed to be the *Post*'s answer to the *Star*'s Ear Column; statuesque Jurate Kazickas, a society type herself who had been working at the AP seemingly for the fun of it; and favorite Judy Bachrach, who came to be known as the Queen of the Section. Bachrach managed to offend the entire George Bush family while covering his 1980 campaign, and got the freeze from press corps regulars on the Bush bus as a result. But otherwise, *Star* society coverage was everything Washington society could ask. And Murray Gart became as popular as he could ask. But, as the *Washington Monthly* noted prophetically two months before the *Star* went el foldo, the circulation of *Dossier* is only 40,000.

The *Star*'s demise left the *Post*'s Style section in a monopoly position on society news, which was nothing really for Washington society to cheer about, even though the *Green Book* carefully informs its readers of the names of everyone working for Style. The big splashy play in Style is much more likely to go to an article about movie stars like Sissy Spacek or Siamese twins or best-selling authors than to who showed up for what ball.

Post society reporter Elisabeth Bumiller can still have her pick as to which embassy mahogany doors will be flung open for her at any given moment, but top dog on society matters is Diana McClellan of the Ear. Given the nature of Washington society, this is fitting. Mrs. McClellan, who chased the uncuddly Maxine Cheshire from the *Post* when she was plucked from the sinking *Star,* covers society this way:

> . . . a faintly shocked flash from the Big Ap: Last weekend, Protocolette Lee Annenberg zipped up for the big OSS dinner at the Waldorf. [The OSS, remember, was the baby CIA.] She *insisted* on a High-Visibility Seat on the Raised Dais among the OSS officials. 'Totally unprecedented,' clucked one OSSer, profoundly shocked. Ear was rather shocked itself. What kind of OSSers sit on a Raised Dais? No wonder everyone's digging holes and picketing parties. Ear will not watch those spaces.

Murray Gart had one thing right: Parties are basically all there is to Washington society, which further explains its sorry social reputation.

An Organization of American States bash (the OAS at times seems nothing more than one long party) might draw stars like the Bushes or Al Haig. A Heart Association luncheon might bring Barbara Bush, Sue Block, and Juliette Clagett McLennan, who herself may turn up dancing with Austin Kiplinger at a ball where you might also find the Japanese ambassador and Elliot Richardson and his wife.

But at other do's given feature play in *Dossier,* guests could include Paula Parkinson, the lobbyist with a publicly proclaimed passion for "horizontal sports," and G. Gordon Liddy, even if he wasn't listed in the *Green Book*. Another spread in *Dossier,* devoted to a party at the country home of Kiplinger, showed a guest dancing barefoot—an elderly male guest. The prestigious Eva Gabor and her husband threw another headliner at the Metropolitan Club that drew Haig, Senator Charles Percy, and the ambassadors of England, Ireland, Hungary, Jordan, and Tunisia all right, but the entertainment was all of them and the 33 other guests making speeches.

As for Washington manners, Betty Beale wrote up a little Georgetown dinner thrown by retired columnist Joe Alsop with a guest list that included Caspar Weinberger and his wife, the British ambassador and his, British philosopher Isaiah Berlin and his, Evangeline Bruce, Robert McNamara, Katherine Graham, and lib columnist Clayton Fritchey and his wife. At one point, Fritchey got excessively lib and began pressing Weinberger about the accuracy of Russian missiles. Alsop exploded. "You can't be rude to a guest at my table!" he snapped, being rude to a guest at his table. According to Beale, Fritchey rose and said, "I am not at your table. I'm leaving," and stormed out with his wife. A bit later in the evening, someone remarked: "You can't depend on your allies," at which, Lady Henderson, Mrs. British Ambassador, hiked up her skirts and stormed up the stairs. Beale said she was just funnin', and everybody laughed. Berlin must have thought it quite something to be among such great minds.

Perhaps the best Washington society party in recent years was thrown in New York for Nancy Reagan. The hosts were columnist William Buckley and his wife, Pat, who is a dear friend of the ubiquitous Jerome Zipkin, who is an even dearer friend of Nancy.

Zipkin was among the 30 guests, as were Nancy's dancer son Ron and Ron's wife, Doria; Cliff Robertson and wife, Dina Merrill; Kandy-Kolored writer, Tom Wolfe, and wife, Sheila; Brooke Astor; John Chancellor and wife, Barbara; Bill Blass; public policy mogul Richard Clurman and wife, Shirley, wearing Oscar de la Renta pants; Oscar de la Renta himself; Ted Graber, Nancy's personal interior decorator; film director Alan Pakula; and Henry Grunewald, editor-in-chief of Time, Inc. Murray Gart didn't show.

The high point of the evening occurred almost immediately when it was discovered that hostess Pat Buckley was wearing exactly the same Oscar de la Renta pants as Mrs. Clurman. Someone suggested they stand at opposite ends of the room. Oscar de la Renta himself laughed. Otherwise, nothing untoward happened.

Perhaps it wasn't such a good Washington party.

Some Washington society figures seem to linger on forever. The peerless Alice Roosevelt Longworth hung around until 1980, when she died at 96. The aristocratic Adelaide LeRoy Tottle Morgan died in her Chevy Chase home in 1979 at 81. Georgetown's Lorraine Cooper is still hanging on. Horsey Oatsie Charles still comes and goes, but she's as much a Newport and Southampton society figure as a Washington one, nice Alabama lady that she may be.

But when most Washington society figures disappear, they just disappear. *Who's Who*'s last listing for Barbara Howar, once the hottest stuff in town, had her in New York. Vicki Bagley, who with her Reynolds tobacco heir husband, Smith, was The Society Figure of the Carter administration, is still in Washington, but not the way it counts. Her most recent showing in the news was when she dropped her $9 million libel suit against the *Star* for a number it did on her. Complaining the press became tired of her, she said: "They have used us up. They have made us boring simply because they overexposed us. They created the monster and then decided that the monster was boring and went on to something else."

Then there was Page Lee Hufty, a great-granddaughter of a president of Standard Oil and a goddaughter of a president of Quaker Oats, was a Washington society queen in the mid-1970s. When she finally married a Baltimore investment banker named Ben Griswold IV in 1979, Betty Beale, unable to contain herself, proclaimed the proceedings "the wedding of the century." This would put it in a league with the Prince Charles–Lady Di affair, if not Grace Kelly's. But Betty explained, asking who could "remember another wedding reception in a private house big enough to accommodate dinner and dancing for 500? And nuptial music from a built-in organ? And afterwards, rockin' and twirlin' like mad in the same 'music room' to Lester Lanin's orchestra, with lots of the guests wearing those little Lanin hats, as in the old debut days, that Lester is still giving out?" Betty's Washington nickname is "Gush."

Page Lee and Ben IV "made a glamorous exit at midnight in an open coach drawn by a pair of horses that took them only down the long driveway to the gate house at cousin John Archbold's estate on Reservoir Road. There, they switched to a car and headed for the Fairfax Hotel before flying to Bermuda the next day." After that, they settled into the Baltimore area and Page Lee has not been heard from again, though Baltimore is just 40 miles away.

Blonde Tandy Dickinson was described by *Washingtonian* magazine as "one of the most glamorous creatures in Washington society. Had F. Scott Fitzgerald lived fifty years later," it said, "and written about Washington, he would have found Tandy Dickinson and understood her." Even if he was drunk. A belle of Lynchburg, Virginia, the then Tandy Meem came to Washington in 1960 to attend prestigious Mount Vernon Junior College, and decided to hang around. While hanging around, she married a Maryland real estate developer twice her age, divorcing him three years, six minks, and a sable later. The divorce settlement provided her with 200 grand in walk-around money. She then burst into the big time as the constant companion of Tongsun Park, who quickly rose to the top of the Washington social heap by virtue of his lavish parties, where Tandy got to meet such worthies as Spiro Agnew, Tip O'Neill, and the great Ardeshir Zahedi. When the newspapers took to summing up Tongsun's social and business life with the word "Koreagate," Tandy's big time turned into a pumpkin. Worse, Tongsun had "borrowed" most of the 200 Gs, she said, and she had to sue to get it back.

Tongsun still shows up in Washington throwing parties, but Tandy has vanished, even if still present.

Few now recall Joanne Herring, a Texas "TV personality" who had married the chairman of Houston Natural Gas, swept into Washington in 1976 and parlayed a few parties into friendships with Ardeshir Zahedi, Henry Kissinger, and the King of Morocco. This led to her becoming (woweee) honorary consul of Morocco and Pakistan. In Houston. She did most of her consuling in the Federal City, however, which by 1979 led to her being dubbed "La Herring" by the *Star* and accorded top-of-the-page society queen coverage. How does a Texas TV personality turned honorary Houston consul get to be a Washington society queen? It doesn't matter. You don't even see her in *Dossier* anymore.

There are some society ladies in Washington you never see very much about. Because they're black.

Washington is a city of more than 600,000 population of which more than 70 percent is black. A decade ago none of them were listed in the *Green Book*. In 1971, two got in. Now a dozen or so are listed—out of five thousand listings. There is, of course, a substantial difference between black and white society in Washington: the blacks are the only ones in town who run their society along the traditional lines of Boston, Philadelphia, and Chicago society. Their top society figures come from the oldest and most prominent families. They work their way up through local charity boards. They tend not to be flamboyant. Black Tandy Dickinsons don't rate for quite so much. And they don't rely on splashy party invitations and newspaper society stories to define their own status.

Washington's white society brings a lot of mystery names to the public eye. One keeps seeing the names, but never learns why. Someone named Craig Spence, for example, throws parties that major personae flock to in trickles, at least, but no one knows who he is. "I wear a lot of hats," he told an interviewer at one of his parties. "It's hard for people to figure out what I do."

Not everyone can make it in Washington society, however. One fellow named Francis Albert Sinatra has been trying to crack it since 1960, through such prestigious friends as Jack Kennedy, Hubert Humphrey, Spiro Agnew, and Ronald Wilson Reagan. Though Kennedy, apparently, allowed him access up the back stairs, Sinatra mostly got stiffed, especially when Kennedy's friend Judith Exner proved to be not only the friend of Sinatra but the friend of Sam "Momo" Giancana.

After the 1980 election, it looked like Sinatra was finally going to make the big time, just like La Herring and Tandy Dickinson, because Ron and Nancy Reagan actually were his good friends. At inaugural time, Sinatra zipped around town with as much czarist aplomb as the other toffs. He was host at the great inaugural gala that featured black dancer Ben Vereen shuffling and groveling before his new President. Though Sinatra was not invited to sit among the VIPs at the inaugural ceremonies, he bluffed his way in anyway by putting on a monkey suit and waving a standing-room pass at one of the guards. When he checked out of his posh, luxurious suite at the Madison Hotel, he tipped owner Marshall Coyne with an 18-karat gold Piaget watch.

But check out he did. Though he occasionally gets invited back for parties, he's been kept at arm's length, just as he came to be by Kennedy, Humphrey, and Nixon. He didn't get his Medal of Freedom, even though Jimmy Carter was handing those out to his staff like Cracker Jack prizes. Sinatra didn't even get an ambassadorship, even though Reagan was handing those out like Cracker Jack prizes.

The Reagans have a little class. So, in fact, do most of the leading society figures in Washington.

THE TOP FIFTEEN SOCIETY FIGURES IN WASHINGTON
1. Alice Roosevelt Longworth
Yes, Alice is dead, having tired of it all for good in 1980 at 96. And yes, unlike Calvin Coolidge, you can tell. Washington without her is like a saloon after closing the night after the morning after the Fourth of July. Washington just isn't much like old Washington anymore. Jackie O.s, Barbara Howars, and Page Lee Huftys come and go, but when they go, they're just gone. They don't take anything with them. Alice Roosevelt Longworth took all that remained of old Washington with her, leaving a void that new Washington will never fill.

From the very beginning, Alice had nearly all the usual attributes of a Washington society figure: she came to Washington from somewhere else (New York). She was a lesser-known (initially) member of a well-known family (the Long Island Roosevelts). She had important friends (she came to know every President from Benjamin Harrison to Gerald Ford). She was pretty (some very popular songs were written about her). She loved parties (Mrs. Longworth holds the Washington record for parties attended and thrown). She loved gossip (hearing it and causing it). She married well (the very rich and powerful House Speaker Nicholas Longworth). And she didn't mind taking advantage of others (her much-remembered remark about Thomas Dewey looking like the man on the wedding cake was pirated from someone else).

Her attributes went far beyond that, of course. She had wit to match her beauty and intelligence to match both (she was studying quasars in her 80s). She despised the stuffy, arrogant, and pompous, and would not suffer the ill-bred and bad-mannered. She was extremely unfond of people who drank too much, but neither could she stand goody-goodies like her cousin Eleanor. She liked living at DuPont Circle when it was one of the most exclusive addresses in the city and still liked it when it had been taken over by hippies, gays, and worse. She had her own style, shooting revolvers from railroad trains and jaunting off to the Philippines with then Secretary of War William Howard Taft in her youth, making a face at Woodrow Wilson and playing poker in Warren G. Harding's White House in more sedate years, going to see *Hair* and calling her mastectomies "going topless" in her old age.

Scads of Washingtonians have owned Cadillacs. Mrs. Longworth acquired a Cadillac in 1945—and kept it for 25 years, along with the chauffeur, a wartime taxicab driver who had struck her fancy. She lived in a five-story mansion, one of the most opulent in the city, but let it become so overgrown with ivy, bushes, and trees that one could scarcely tell there was a house there.

She had a dark side. She was obsessed with politics. She could be excessively cruel to people she did not like. Though she later doted on her granddaughter, she neglected the daughter she had, almost as an afterthought, at 41. The daughter died at 31 of a drug overdose. But people with dark sides do very well in Washington.

Mrs. Longworth's chief attributes were staying power and self-confidence. She was the capital's champeen hanger-around. Her husband's death in 1931 and the Depression impoverished her and almost cost her her home, but she hung on, publishing her autobiography in 1933 and using the proceeds to keep out of debt. She got the freeze from Eleanor and Franklin but bounced back as a favorite of Harry Truman. She almost perished of boredom during the tranquil Eisenhower years, but was reborn as the grandest Grande Dame of Kennedy's Camelot. She was a pal of LBJ. She loved Richard Nixon, but loved even more the circus of Watergate. She didn't care much for Jimmy Carter, but then, who did?

Her own wedding, a far more tasteful and elaborate affair than Page Lee Hufty's (there were more than two horses), was also called the wedding of the century, young as the century was. She didn't care. She never really cared what people thought about her, and certainly not what they said about her. So she said whatever she wanted about them.

William Howard Taft was "great in girth . . . but great in nothing else." Coolidge looked "like he was weaned on a pickle." As for Franklin Roosevelt and his mistress Lucy Mercer: "Every man in Washington has a 'summer wife,' and Franklin deserves one because he's married to Eleanor." When LBJ showed the world his gall bladder operation scar, she said: "Thank God it wasn't his prostate."

When her car was sideswiped one night, the white driver leaned out and shouted at her chauffeur, "You black bastard." She put her head out the window and said: "Shut up, you white son of a bitch!"

A friend, Michael Teague, interviewed her not long ago for a book of her remembrances. She summed up her notion of the capital this way: "When I look back from my vantage point of advanced age, I can see why I made Washington my home. I think I would have found anything else rather dull in comparison. But Washington is a small, cozy town, global in scope. It suits me."

Alice Roosevelt Longworth dominated the top spot in Washington society so overwhelmingly, so uniquely, and for so long that the number should be retired with her. We leave No. 1 an unfilled and unfillable vacancy as one of her many monuments.

2. Barbara Bush

There's a rule of thumb that the First Lady should be at the top of the social heap in Washington. Thumbs get bent and broken a lot in Washington.

That the gracious and totally unaffected Barbara Bush has little or no interest in where she might rank on someone's society list is just one reason why she belongs at the top. Another is that there is no one in Washington who could get away with trying to look down on Mrs. Bush socially. Another is that there's no one, including the First Lady, who can't help but look up to Barbara Bush socially, no matter how unhappy it makes them.

Mrs. Bush has Smith College, devotion to her husband, and politics in common with Mrs. Reagan, but little else. Daughter of *Redbook* and *McCall's* publisher Marvin Pierce, she was a Westchester County girl who grew up in Rye, New York, just across the state line from

Greenwich, Connecticut, home of young George Herbert Walker Bush. They met at a dance in Rye in 1942, when she was sixteen. He shortly after went off to war as the youngest combat pilot in the Navy. Two weeks after he returned from the Pacific on Christmas Eve, 1944, they were married. She went with him to Yale, to Texas, to Congress, to the United Nations, to China, to all the crummy motels along the 1980 primary route, and ultimately to the Vice-President's house on Observatory Hill, which suits her well.

"I'm square," she told an interviewer shortly after moving in. "I love my husband. I love my children. I love my country. I love God. I have no great gripes. I am boring! I'm not protesting. That's not to say I think the world is perfect. I'd like to work to make it better. That's why it's boring, because there's nothing that gripes me. I have a great theory that you ought to be happy with what you're doing."

Quite attractive in a fresh-faced, wholesome, wind-blown way as a girl in Westchester, she was just as attractive as a young woman, and a not-so-young woman, and is just as attractive now as a middle-aged matron. She dislikes people making a big deal out of it, just as she dislikes people making a big deal out of anything, but she is wholly unlike most of the ladies in the Reagan crowd. She has no entourage of potion-toting hairdressers, couturiers, jewelers, and ring bearers. Her hair is the white it naturally became. She doesn't drape herself in $15,000 gowns or drag around $1,600 handbags. She doesn't need to.

As might be expected from someone as secure and content with herself, Mrs. Bush has what her preppy husband might call a really neat sense of humor. There may even be an impish, mischievous little trace of Alice Longworth in her. At one White House luncheon, people at her table were talking about a televised faith-healing show in which people came forward to display parts of their bodies that had been healed. Mrs. Bush, recalling the somewhat scatological ailment that most discomfited Jimmy Carter while in the White House, wondered aloud what might happen if he came forward. Then she hid behind her napkin.

3. Nancy Reagan

Had her husband picked anyone else for Vice-President, Nancy Reagan would perforce be at the top of this list, not only because it's supposed to go with the job but also because she is a tough, courageous, elegant lady with considerable style.

The style came somewhat late and a little hard. Born, according to Smith College records, in 1921 (her press office says 1923), she was the daughter of an unsuccessful used-car salesman and a struggling young actress, Edith "Dee Dee" Luckett. Her father deserted the family just after she was born, and she was sent to live with relatives in Maryland at age two so her mother could work on the road. Mother never made much of a splash, but within five years had met and married Dr. Loyal Davis, a rich Chicago neurosurgeon whose ultra-conservative politics can best be summed up by saying: "If they have no bread, let them become neurosurgeons."

Though she was not legally adopted by Davis until she was 14, she was given all the advantages of a genuine society girl—the prestigious Girl's Latin school, a debut at the exclusive Casino Club, Smith, and all the goodies. Contemporaries have described her as prim, straight-laced, something of a homebody, and a little embarrassed by her past. Following in her mother's footsteps, she became a largely unsuccessful actress, her best work being in the "B" flicks, where she met her husband. As with Barbara Bush, she has made her husband her real career. If possible, she's been even more devoted to Reagan than Mrs. Bush is to Bush, but that isn't possible.

Her children, dancer Ron and singer-actress Patti, didn't turn out much like the Bush's brood of blazered all-American blue bloods. They didn't turn out much like Nancy, either. Even her friends look upon her as the quintessential '50s woman, but since her husband is trying to turn the entire country in that direction, there's nothing wrong with that.

Mrs. Reagan is far from the political busybody her predecessor, Rosalynn Carter, was. There's none of that ruling-the-Free-World-from-the-bedchamber business. Nancy likes to keep her mind on more pleasant things (as does, some say, the President). She did intercede in the 1980 campaign at a couple of critical moments, and probably ensured herself the First Lady's role as a direct result. It's a role she fully enjoys, the ceremonial life-style, the unparalleled status, the glittering parties, the glory to share with her friends.

If some complain about her luxurious life-style at a time school lunches are being shrunk and poor people are being told to get packing, no one can say the Reagans promised anything else. And, as Reagan might put it, her life-style says something about the American way. Where else could the daughter of a ne'er-do-well used-car salesman and the son of a drunken shoe salesman rise to the top of Washington society, not to speak of the leadership of the Free World? But it says something about Washington society, too.

4. Jerome Zipkin

For all the intensity of her devotion to her husband, Nancy Reagan has another man in her life. As regards her social life, he is without doubt the second man in her life, and logically follows after her on this list, as he does so often in expensive department stores and restaurants.

His name is Jerome Zipkin, a.k.a. called "Baby Zip." He is what *Women's Wear Daily* calls a "walker," a fellow whose chief function in life is to escort, advise, and generally keep amused the wives of busy (if Ronald Reagan can be so described) rich men.

In a remarkably understated article, the *Washington Post* noted that he "reeks of sandalwood perfume." Truman Capote, who is considered a rival of Zipkin's (at least in the Hamptons), got away with saying Zipkin's face looks like "a bidet." Zipkin was a frequent guest and close friend of the late W. Somerset Maugham. Nancy Reagan describes him as "a sort of modern-day Oscar Wilde. He has more depth than a lot of people in our lives." He certainly has more cuff links. According to the *Washington Post,* he once took 86 pairs with him for a weekend out of town. He also wears velvet evening slippers with little red hammers and sickles on them.

Born in 1914, the son of a New York real estate man, Zipkin went to Princeton, but never graduated. Instead, he just moved back to his millionaire parents' Park Avenue apartment, and began making friends. He never wrote an *Importance of Being Earnest* or *Ballad of Reading Gaol;* he just kept making friends, from Maugham to the Duchess of Windsor to Claudette Colbert and Paulette Goddard.

His stable of friends is quite large, including such Nancy Reagan chums as Betsy Bloomingdale and Patricia Buckley. But the First Lady is Zipkin's First Friend. Before the inaugural, which he attended almost as a member of the family, he used to take her to the hairdresser, the ballet, museums, shopping, and to supper. He was with the Reagans the night Ron won the nomination. He partied with them after the election. He was an honored guest at the White House birthday party for the President. He advises them on family matters. At one very public Washington party, he was seen zipping up Nancy's dress.

Zipkin is not always amusing. According to the *Post,* he's been described by longtime acquaintances as "nebulous, bitchy, very, very pretentious and affected," and "snide, haughty, contemptuous, and sneering." Anyone with social ambitions in Washington who crosses him could be in big trouble, at least for the duration of the Reagan administration. Nancy is said to be delighted with the gossip he tells her and is highly respectful of his social opinions. Zipkin has so much power he makes Truman Capote look like a, well, wimp.

5. *Jackie Ted Gore Ethel Nina Joan Janet Lee Okenvidkenstraightkenauchinradz*

They're all at the same high level of Washington society. They all live, or lived, on or near the same posh hill in McLean. They're all somehow related. Except for Nina, it is often very hard to keep them straight.

Jackie O. is now over 50, still has caviar and champagne and practically nothing else for lunch, still pops up at the oddest places in New York, still pops up in *W* (a "Beautiful People" newspaper put out by *Women's Wear Daily*), sometimes with as many as three pictures on a page, and has become czarina of Martha's Vineyard, where she dwells in reclusive splendor in digs that cost so many millions the toilets have hot water in them. She was recently photographed with a man who was believed to be superrich mineral king Maurice Tempelsman, who was believed to be her latest fling. It turned out that the man in the picture was Tom Walsh, the Kennedy family accountant, and that Mr. Tempelsman wasn't a fling but a friend. Jackie O. still wears size 10 shoes.

Teddy is just now crossing the half-century mark, is still in the Senate, is still living in the big house off Chain Bridge Road, is still going up to Hyannisport, and is no longer with Joan. He has put Chappaquiddick behind him, along with any real chance of getting elected President, though he's still trying. If you don't think so, why did he invite 300 political writers up to Hyannis for an intimate weekend just 10 months after the 1980 election?

Gore is still writing books. His last one, a historical novel about the ancient philosophers, hit the best-seller lists like a rocket, then fizzled and died. He was going to run for governor of California (or was it President?). He is no longer feuding with Truman Capote, though if he is too caustic about the Reagans, he may end up feuding with Zipkin. He is still cousin by marriage to Jackie O. and half brother to Nina Straight. He came back to McLean for a party at Merrywood for Nina, but arrived so late no one is sure he was there.

Ethel is still running Hickory Hill, playing celebrity tennis, and being nice to tail-wagging groupies like Art Buchwald. She is still helping people out (she gave a job to the unfortunate wife of defrocked congressman Richard Kelly) and raising money for handicapped children. She has so many children that one of them is bound to be President some day.

Nina (a.k.a. Nini) Straight is still Gore's half sister. Having grown up at Merrywood, that once-great estate on the hill where Gore, Jackie, and Lee grew up, too, she returned recently for a party celebrating the publication of her novel, *Ariabella: The First,* a rattling good yarn about Newport tea dancing. *Ariabella* never did hit the best-seller lists like a rocket, but the party got written up in the papers, even if Gore did arrive late. Nina, who is still a few years from 50, is now studying law. Anything to keep busy.

Joan is still on the wagon, still living in Boston, still going to school, still a blonde knockout, and still, alas, wearing eyelashes that could carry a good-sized pigeon aloft. She is still staying the hell away from Washington as much as she can, which is too bad for Washington.

Janet Auchincloss is still mother of Jackie and Lee, stepmother of Nina, and mother of Nina's half brother Jamie. She is no longer much of a Washington society figure, though, having recently married a New Yorker named Bingham Morris and moved from Georgetown to Southampton, which is roomier. Though someone was saying she's back in Georgetown again. Well, who could resist?

Janet's move occasioned one of the more mirthful tales ever to appear in Maxine Cheshire's column. Daughter Lee warned Mama not to use professional movers, complaining that a professional outfit had charged her seven grand to cart her bric-a-brac from 79th and Park to 78th and Fifth. So, Ma brought in some amateur help, including—according to Maxine—members of a gay motorcycle club caled the Druids. The move-out took three days amidst a great deal of confusion. When it was over, a number of pieces of engraved family silver were missing, each with the Auchincloss family crest. Also, some items advertised as Auchincloss family memorabilia were later auctioned off at a downtown gay bar.

According to the butler, John O'Connor, the Druids were quite respectable folks. "Very responsible people," he told Maxine. "It's more of a fraternal thing. One member is a parole officer in Maryland. Another works for Indian Affairs. There's an Army officer and two Air Force captains. I don't think any of them even owns a motorcycle. They don't even wear leather. They all dress in dungarees." But not in velvet evening slippers with hammers and sickles on them.

Lee is no longer a Polish princess but is still in *W,* though not as much as Jackie and not as much as she used to be. She was supposed to marry this older man in San Francisco, but didn't.

Merrywood, where it all began, was bought on the cheap by some people named Dickerson in 1965, but it's still there.

6. Sir Nicko

The British embassy is the highest-ranking socially in Washington, and the British ambassador is usually treated accordingly, no matter who he is. Longtime ambassador Peter Ramsbotham, a very definite upper-class foreign-office type, was a charming chap and quite the favorite of Washington toffs in the early and middle 1970s. There was sniffing outrage when new British Prime Minister James Callaghan packed Sir Peter off to Bermuda in 1977, for fear he couldn't relate well to Ham Jordan and the down-home Carter boys.

Callaghan replaced Sir Peter with his own son-in-law, British journalist Peter Jay. He got along swell with the hapless Carterites, for all the good it did England, but was a flop with local society. Worse, he lost his wife to Carl Bernstein of Watergate and ABC News fame, whose social status is best defined by the fact that he was thrown out of a *Chicago Tribune* party in 1981.

Margaret Thatcher hastily bounced Jay (who decided to hang around Washington), replacing him with Sir Nicholas Henderson (Sir Nicko, to his friends), a first-rate career man who had served in Washington back in the Truman years.

Born in 1919, Sir Nicko is rather much an Oxford don in thought, word, deed, and appearance, and rules Her Majesty's huge compound on Massachusetts Avenue with more flair than most, though he quickly pulled down the garish modern art Jay had stuck all over the official residence and put up stuffy historical portraits instead. Under Sir Nicko, who is known to have fine French wines served at staff meetings, the British embassy maintains the most exclusive guest list in town, though he occasionally lets in some churlish American newsmen.

Sir Nicko's wife, Mary, is a Greek-born former war correspondent for *Time* magazine. They were greeted with quite a surprise upon their arrival in Washington. Her former husband, British journalist Stephen Barber, was stationed here, too.

7. Bernard Vernier-Palliez

François de Laboulaye, the previous French ambassador, was a Washington fixture. He was born in the American capital during his father's service as French embassy secretary in the 1920s. He returned in the 1930s to attend Georgetown University while his father was serving as *the* ambassador. He knew well how Washington society works (though it's grown uncomfortably large since the 1930s when he said there were fewer than a thousand important people in town), as well as his embassy's place in it, which is right up at the tippy top. If slightly less prestigious than the British one, it's more popular, largely because of the fine feeds.

His successor, Bernard Vernier-Palliez, has a difficult tradition to live up to, especially since he has no diplomatic experience or foreign service background. But he found a warm welcome in Ronald Reagan's Washington. As the longtime chief executive officer of Renault motors, the 63-year-old vice-president is among his very own kind. French president François Mitterand may be a Socialist, but he wasn't foolish enough to send another Citizen Genêt. Even if he had, the local hootie-tooties would still rank the French embassy as top drawer. After all, its menus are in French.

8. *Juliette Clagett McLennan*

After waiting five years for it, Edith Blair, great-great-granddaughter of Kentucky newspaperman and Andrew Jackson confidante Francis P. Blair, got the job of assistant manager of Blair House in 1979. It was a low-paying but highly interesting job because Blair House, until 1942 the home of Edith's Uncle Gist Blair, is the official Washington guest residence for visiting heads of state. When the Reagans arrived in 1981, Miss Blair lost the post. It had gone on the "plum list" and, though a Republican, Miss Blair was a Carter appointee.

Happily, the Reagans gave the top job of Blair House manager to the classic and great Judy McLennan. Herself the product of a top Washington family and the same Kalorama neighborhood where Miss Blair grew up, she is considered one of Washington's most charming yet unaffected hostesses, as pleasant and pleasing a lady enough to set the most churlish and irascible VIP visitor at ease.

A tall, athletic, and elegant blonde who had a career as an international-class ski instructor in Canada before her divorce from her husband and return to her native Washington in 1975, Judy has always been deeply interested in history, especially Washington's. She was a high-ranking and highly valued staff leader in the campaigns of Gerald Ford, George Bush, and the Reagan-Bush ticket. When it came time to hand out the plums, she and the Blair House job seemed made for each other.

Returning home the night before she was to start on the job, she was told to report at once because the Dutch prime minister had already arrived. She dropped everything and did. He was as pleased with his stay as every VIP since has been.

A descendant of super rich Chicago millionaire Marshall Field's original partner, and of the tragic Mary Curzon, wife of the Viceroy of India, Judy McLennan is a niece of the classic and great Oatsie Charles, one of the wittiest women in Washington, when she's in Washington. Active in horse things, Judy is also intensely if curiously interested in Irish affairs, and is said to read the Irish *Times* of Dublin every day.

9. *Muffie Brandon*

Muffie Brandon is not really a real Muffy. As the *Preppy Handbook* notes, Muffie is correctly spelled "Muffy." And, though she has the accent, she's not really British, having been born two-score-and-a-little-more years ago in Boston. And her name is really Mabel Brandon. But she is Nancy Reagan's social secretary, which means she can be anything she wants, in Washington.

What she wants a lot is to be very, very proper. Informed that female Carter staffers occasionally answered the door in clogs, she was aghast. "We do not wear clogs at the White House," she said. Or have barbecues on the roof of the press room, which is more than Carter could say.

Muffie fits right in to the Reagan swim of things, having been a Miss Porter's and Smith girl, but might be a little embarrassed about her shameful past, having been a Democrat. She was, in fact, part of the now despised Great Society, having served as national coordinator for Project Headstart from 1963 to 1964. Previously, she was a museum assistant and, afterwards, a public relations and arts consultant. What made her a Georgetown heavy, though, was her marriage to Henry Brandon, the *Sunday Times* of London's main man in Washington. Through him, she got to be a great chum of Henry Kissinger, Mrs. Sir Nicko, and countless others who don't wear clogs.

The *Washington Post* quoted one critic as saying: "Muffie's ambitious and a bit too much of a hustler for me, but she will subordinate herself until the time when she can put herself forward. Nancy Reagan is very lucky because Muffie knows her way around the city. So Nancy's got herself a plus rather than a minus."

And lucky for Baby Zip that he doesn't wear clogs.

10. Count and Countess Wachtmeister

If you can't snare an invite from Sir Nicko or Monsieur Laboulaye, one from the Wachtmeisters is almost as good. Sometimes better. The Swedish ambassador and his wife operate from a sprawling, in-town estate at Massachusetts and Nebraska Avenues, and they operate in the grandest of styles. Ask around Capitol Hill, the White House, the State Department, or the other foreign embassies, and the parties people always seem to remember best are those tossed (heaved?) by Wilhelm and Ulla Wachtmeister. The decorations at one recent Svensk bash included 2,500 roses.

Born a count, Wilhelm studied for the law, but upon graduating in 1946 joined the foreign service instead. Prior to his appointment as ambassador to the United States in 1974, he served in Vienna, Madrid, Lisbon, Moscow, and Rabat, and for a time as UN Secretary General Dag Hammarskjold's assistant.

Ulla, an appropriately beautiful blonde lady, was born a baroness, the daughter of a Norwegian cavalry officer and the heiress to one of Norway's great fortunes. She married Wilhelm in 1947. An accomplished artist, she has paintings on exhibit in museums and in private collections in the United States, France, and Sweden.

The extravagant entertaining of the Wachtmeisters leaves the same question in the minds of Washington society types as it does in those of State Department dips: What on earth do they hope or need to get out of all this?

11. Betsy Bloomingdale

Nancy Reagan has eight best friends, not counting Baby Zip, but counting Mrs. Jean Smith, wife of Attorney General William F. Smith; former child movie star Bonita Granville Wrather, wife of Hollywood type Jack Wrather; Martha Lyles, wife of producer "Here's Boomer" A. C. Lyles; Betty Wilson, wife of rancher-investor and kitchen cabineter William Wilson; Marion Jorgensen, wife of steel baron Earle Jorgensen; Jane Bryan Dart, once a starlet and now wife of Justin Dart, who once was married to a drugstore heiress; Virginia Tuttle, wife of wealthy Ford dealer Holmes Tuttle; and Betsy Bloomingdale, wife of Alfred.

Betsy, born Betty Lee Newling and old enough to have married her husband in 1946, is Nancy's very best friend, and has been so for some 20 years.

Her husband, of the department store Bloomingdale's, made his pile as a Hollywood and Broadway producer, credit card mogul, and entrepreneur in Florida and California real estate. He reportedly came to Washington having hopes of being made ambassador to France. Well, what are friends for, especially best ones?

12. Evangeline Bell Bruce

The daughter of an American foreign-service officer, the still pretty Evangeline Bruce is the widow of the late ambassador and foreign affairs scholar David K. Bruce; the mother of the tragic Sasha Bruce, allegedly shot to death by her husband; the preeminent hostess currently holding sway in Georgetown; and the highest ranking society friend Nancy Reagan has in Washington.

Mrs. Bruce is most notable for two social institutions: her own famous Georgetown Sunday brunches, at which folks like Sir Nicko turn up, and the very intimate and regular luncheons Mrs. Reagan has with five or six Washington society leaders every month or so in some of the city's poshest digs. What the used-car salesman's daughter derives from holding court in this fashion is hard to say, but swell times are said to be had by all, including the very distinguished Mrs. Bruce. According to *Washingtonian* magazine, Mrs. Bruce is considered a great catch for other parties, too, but usually comes alone and arrives and leaves rather abruptly.

Washingtonian also clucked that Mrs. Bruce "dresses in the most tasteful fashion for social events, but traipses around Georgetown in eclectic combinations of boots and knits." Horrors.

Her boots, at least, don't have little hammers and sickles on them.

13. Lorraine Cooper

Alice Roosevelt Longworth is gone. Lorraine Cooper, wife of John Sherman Cooper, is not. But then, Alice was 96. Mrs. Cooper is but a maid of, well, still fewer than 80 summers.

An elegant socialite divorcée from New York, Mrs. Cooper settled into Georgetown in 1953, meeting and marrying the former Kentucky senator shortly thereafter. Shortly after that, he was made ambassador to India. He was subsequently made ambassador to East Germany. A former schoolgirl in Florence (her mother married the Prince Orsini), Lorraine enjoyed it all immensely, though East Berlin is hardly Florence, or, for that matter, Georgetown.

Mrs. Cooper does enjoy Georgetown immensely, especially her four-story, red-brick, 1768 merchant prince's house that is a highlight of the Georgetown House Tour. A friend of Nini Straight's, among hundreds of others, Lorraine is famous for her 24-person dinner parties, and invitations to them are highly prized. Jack and Jackie came to one shortly after his inauguration.

A lady with a, er, distinctive profile, she was once told by famed photographer Cecil Beaton that "your face breaks the camera," but he took a picture of her that didn't. She still finds it glorious. Mrs. Cooper has an eye for pictures, having contrived to buy two of Salvador Dali's paintings from him for $500 each and having picked up two Raoul Dufy watercolors for $100 and $200 respectively. She says she sends Dior "a small check every month."

14. Elizabeth Taylor Warner

For one of her husbands, movie mogul Mike Todd, Elizabeth Taylor became Jewish. For her latest, Senator John Warner, she became a Republican. Worse, she moved to Washington. They're legally separated now, but happily she still comes back to Washington. Even women of the world get Potomac Fever.

She and John, a native Washingtonian, met in ripping good Washington style, having been introduced at a British embassy bash by Sir Peter Ramsbotham himself. As she stated in an interview, she fell in love with John, a former Navy secretary who had been in and out of the Mellon family, in large part because he was so good in, well, they had lots of fun out at his farm in Middleburg. They've had lots of fun at his pied-à-terre in Georgetown, too. They had not quite so much fun during his campaign for the 1978 Virginia senatorial nomination, during which she was exhibited, pinched, and prodded like a prize hog at a county fair. She was also made to endure what might be called Weight Watchers nonanonymous.

The crowning indignity came when he lost the nomination to right-wing Reaganite Richard Obenshain, attaining it later only as a not overwhelming second choice after Obenshain was killed in a plane crash.

Mrs. Warner spends a lot of time in New York, finding Washington society a trifle dull, though not always. The following account in Diana McClellan's Ear column explains:

Liz Taylor's Deeply Divine Wolf Trap Gala made $200,000 for the Performing Arts Park this week, darlings, and we're all terribly proud of everyone who was in it—Liz, Liza, Johnny Cash, Burt Reynolds, Rod McKuen, Alex Gudonov, et al. Ear's astonished to hear all was not too Divine backstage. Odd doings started when Liz announced to Rod, "I'm going to do my poem now, or not at all," and Burt piped, "Oh, good. She's not gonna do it." Then Liz and Rod got into an Epistemological Scrap. Liz slapped Rod. Rod slapped Liz back. All the stars were enraged with Liz for dragging the Mountain Mission Orphan's Choir into the Gala, to sing off-key for what seemed like hours. Then, they were livid with Johnny Cash, who was supposed to do ten minutes and wouldn't leave the stage for half an hour. (And when he finally did, darlings, he got into a hellacious fight with the Park Service folks, who wouldn't let his car out before the show was over. "I have to get home to a sick child!" he kept bawling.) Liza Minnelli swears she'll never come back. Burt Reynolds, not she, snagged the Star dressing room. As though that wasn't bad enough, she had to stew through five hours of everybody else, mostly the Orphan's Choir, and half the audience had left by the time she finally straggled onstage, around 12:30 A.M. At 12:40, on bustled the Choir with a huge flag for the finale. To make matters worse, after Burt Reynolds and Rod McKuen had rather embarrassingly sung "Baby It's Cold Outside" to each other, one man who'd played a minor role in the decorations wandered around groping all the male guests. When it was all over, just as Liz cooed "Come on, Sen-Baby!" to hubby John, he threw up.

15. Brooke Astor

Such gracious ladies as Patricia Haig and Sue Block probably belong on this list, as might a dozen others we can think of. But we're going to give this last spot to Brooke Astor, widow of the filthy rich Vincent.

Born in New Hampshire (she won't say when), Mrs. Astor has been absolutely everything in New York and New York society—magazine editor, trustee of the Metropolitan Museum, etc., etc., and most especially, president of the filthy rich Vincent Astor Foundation.

Not counting mere advertising people and the like who can be found among Reaganite sycophants, Brooke Astor is the only member of Real New York Society who has had much to do with the Reagan folk. After the election, she found herself at a dinner party sitting next to columnist George Will, who then was styling himself the reigning intellectual of the Reagan administration (he hastily backed off from this when his newspaper colleagues began treating him as just the reigning apologist for the Reagan administration).

In any event, somewhere between the soup and nuts, Mrs. Astor told Will she wanted to do something important for the new Republicans.

"Throw a party," said Will, munching away, and so she did. A real extravaganza, in which she introduced the Reagans to all the New Yorkers who counted. She failed to invite Mayor Ed Koch. A trick like that ought to be worth charter membership in Washington society.

Sex

Sᴇx ɪs the pepper in the stewpot of politics. Nowhere has this been truer than in Washington, a city invented solely for the conduct of government and the practice of politics.

In Andrew Jackson's first term, all but one member of his cabinet resigned in a controversy over the morals of a colleague's wife. Not long after, another President helped a young White House messenger skip town in a fruitless effort to cover up a murder caused by high-level adultery. More recently, the careers of two powerful congressmen were cut short by sex scandals. Another man, a rising star in his own party and a loud champion of moral rectitude, came crashing down when he was revealed to be a habitué of homosexual pickup bars.

Sex also affects politics in less direct ways. There is a man in the Senate today who some believe would never have been elected had he not traded on the fame and sex appeal of his movie star wife to draw campaign crowds. And there is another whose reputation as a rake was so fixed that his account of an accident in which a young woman died was never completely accepted by the public and press—possibly destroying what had been his bright chance to become President.

It is easy to picture Washington as a city that makes Sodom and Gomorrah look like mere tank towns in the annals of depravity. It was Washington that gave the language the term "hooker" as a synonym for prostitute after Civil War General Joe Hooker tried to confine vice in the capital by restricting his division's camp followers (3,900 of them by one count) to a single area of town.

Not that Washington needed Hooker to give it a bad name. Thirty years earlier, Andrew Jackson, the seventh president, had to replace everyone in his cabinet except the postmaster general in order to settle what came to be called "The Petticoat War."

It began when John Eaton, a Jackson protégé, married Margaret "Peggy" O'Neil Timberlake, a young widow with a reputation for entertaining callers in her bed. Jackson appointed Eaton Secretary of War, but soon found that the wives of several other cabinet members would have nothing to do with his friend's wife.

"I will not part with Eaton and those who cannot harmonize with him had better withdraw, for harmony I must and will have," Old Hickory told the cabinet. When the cabinet wives still refused to accept Peggy Eaton, their husbands (with the exception of Postmaster General William Barry) resigned.

This episode had repercussions. The only cabinet member who had supported Jackson and Eaton was Secretary of State Martin Van Buren, who cleverly had suggested the mass resignation and who got Jackson's endorsement as his second term vice-president.

Just before the Civil War, a New York congressman, Daniel E. Sickles, gunned down U.S. Attorney Philip Barton Key (son of the author of "The Star-Spangled Banner") in broad daylight in Lafayette Park across the street from the White House. Although a notorious womanizer himself, Sickles killed Key when he discovered the lawyer had been having an affair with Mrs. Sickles. He beat the subsequent murder charge by pleading the unwritten law and then went on to further fame as the general in the Civil War who almost lost the Battle of Gettysburg for the Union.

Two decades after the Civil War, a Cleveland newspaperman called Washington "one of the wickedest cities of its size in the country," and just after World War II, two tough New York tabloid reporters wrote a book depicting the capital as "the dirtiest community in America . . . a cesspool of drunkenness, debauchery, whoring, homosexuality, municipal corruption, and public apathy."

And it continues. Only weeks after the nation's voters rejected straight-arrow Jimmy Carter in favor of Ronald Reagan, the country's first divorced President, the blonde young wife of a South Carolina Democratic House member broke into print with an exposé of the "congressional fast track"—a moral obstacle course of flowing booze and easy sex that tempted the upright and snared the weak. And just to keep it all bipartisan, a short time later, newspaper stories disclosed that three Republican members of Congress had spent a Florida holiday with a voluptuous blonde lobbyist. This lady, bringing high tech to kiss-and-tell, claimed she had videotaped one of her amorous encounters with a congressman.

A brief pause here in the name of perspective. Despite all of the above, Washington's moral climate probably is no more lax than that of many American cities. Certainly, it is not as wide open a town as New York nor as kinky as San Francisco. But with the possible exception of Hollywood, Washington has two elements in its population shared by no other community. First, it probably has a higher proportion of nationally prominent men and women in residence than any other. And second, it has the highest concentration of reporters in the world, all focused on the government and the people who run it.

Actually, the Washington press corps is not particularly scandal-oriented. Most in the city take the position that they are in Washington to report what the government is doing for or to Americans and that the personal lives of federal officials and politicians are irrelevant unless their actions affect their conduct of the public's business. As a result, highly-placed people who are discreet about their private lives seldom get into the papers. Even those who may down a drink too many or take a lady other than their wives to dinner usually don't read about it in the gossip columns, even though there may have been newspeople at the same bar or restaurant.

But when a prominent person's activities become public record they can depend upon becoming the objects of attention of some of the most aggressive reporters in the country.

There does seem to be an affinity between sex and politics.

Perhaps the best-known theory to explain it might be called The Kissinger Axiom. The former secretary of state said power is the strongest aphrodisiac of all—the ability to move and shake great events holds out more sexual enticement than good looks, fine clothes, or even a fat wallet. In any case, it was Henry The K's stock explanation of how a chubby, near-sighted, middle-aged former college professor with a funny accent could get dates with some of Hollywood's sexiest starlets.

Associated with that is the ego theory: It takes a man or woman with enormous self-confidence and an exaggerated need to win the love or loyalty of others to succeed in politics.

Terri Calabrese, who left a job in Hollywood in the 1960s to work for Representative Adam Clayton Powell in Washington, said the theatrical people she knew were quite different when they were out of the public eye, but politicians always seemed to be on stage and playing for applause. Her boss certainly demonstrated that—even when he died in self-imposed exile Powell had several women fighting for his body.

There is another explanation that draws a parallel between political and military lives. In both, the campaigning requires long periods of intensive, exhausting work, separation from family and hometown ties, and a close association with young and unattached people. Under such circumstances, it is easy for taboos to fall.

And fall they do. Rita Jenrette, the South Carolina congressman's wife, wrote, "There is something about a congressman that brings women out of the woodwork." Before she divorced him, Rita Jenrette wrote that some of her husband's troubles came out of the bottle: "Sex and alcohol become a convenient pit stop on the congressional fast track."

Representative Robert Bauman of Maryland also blamed drinking.

As fierce a crusader against sin as ever wowed a Moral Majority audience, Bauman pleaded innocent to a charge of soliciting sex from an underage man while cruising Washington gay bars. Bauman said he had "homosexual tendencies," but blamed his problems on alcoholism and, when he appeared in court, agreed to undergo psychological counseling. That was the same "first offender" arrangement made a few years earlier with Representative Fred Richmond of New York, who also was charged with a similar offense.

Bauman and Richmond were accused of homosexual activities away from Capitol Hill, but in the case of a third congressman, Representative Jon Hinson of Mississippi, a men's room in the Longworth House Office Building was the scene of the arrest. Hinson had been reelected after admitting he had been at a gay theater where a fire killed several patrons, but resigned after the Longworth Building episode in 1981.

These incidents raised eyebrows in Washington, but their impact was mainly on the individual congressmen and their districts. That was not the case in the 1970s when the alcohol-sex combination was blamed for ending the long career of one of Congress' most influential and prestigious members.

Wilbur Mills of Arkansas had served in the House for more than 30 years. As chairman of the House Ways and Means Committee, he was regarded as Washington's most knowledgeable and powerful voice on taxation, international trade, and the federal role in welfare and health care. It was an understatement to say that official Washington was stunned to learn that the sedate and portly congressman had begun cavorting in public with a South American striptease dancer named Fanne Foxe and had come to police attention when the lady, after an argument, jumped out of the car they were in and into the cold waters of the Tidal Basin. Fanne was fished out intact, but Wilbur was in the soup. After a couple more bizarre episodes, including an appearance with Fanne on a Boston burlesque stage, Mills took the cure. But his political career was over, and leadership on all the important issues that had been his passed to others.

There was a certain amount of sympathy for Mills, but not much when a buxom blonde named Elizabeth Ray blew the whistle on Representative Wayne Hays of Ohio a short time later.

Ray, in a chance meeting with two *Washington Post* reporters, let it be known that she was on the congressional payroll for the sole purpose of supplying sex. She had an office and a desk, she said, but in fact couldn't even operate the typewriter.

Hays, a blustering veteran of the House who loved to cut up opponents in floor debate, was chairman of the House Administration Committee, controlling both patronage and a long list of congressional perquisites, including paper clip supplies, as well as holding jurisdiction over campaign finance legislation and contested elections. With that kind of power, he was an enthusiastic practitioner of Charles Colson's famous formulation of political power: "When you've got them by the balls, their hearts and minds will follow."

So when Hays left Washington, many of his colleagues were as happy as the Capitol waiters, barbers, and doorkeepers he terrorized for years. His fall was the occasion for a particularly grim glee on the part of blacks who recalled that it was Hays who had been given the job of investigating the antics of Adam Clayton Powell in 1966.

As a result of the Hays case, several other instances came to light of congressmen keeping women on their payrolls for sexual service, and the subsequent blast of publicity left some members "scared straight."

More than five years later, Representative John G. Hutchinson of West Virginia frankly conceded he was not about to hire any "baby dolls" for his office and gave an aide the following terse guidelines for hiring women: "Larry—35–40 or older preferably married. If they could stop a clock, qualify for grade A."

Not all congressmen insist on the convenience of having their doxies in the outer office. According to a number of accounts, they have been patrons of free enterprise sex as well for many decades.

Jack Lait and Lee Mortimer claimed in *Washington Confidential* that "The same stagecoaches which carried the first congressmen to Washington . . . also brought the first whores. They and their descendants have been there ever since, an integral, important part of the population." Lait and Mortimer might be guessing, but Frank Carpenter, who was Washington correspondent for the Cleveland *Leader* in the 1890s, was an eyewitness in that era.

Carpenter wrote: "There are more of the demimonde in Washington than ever before. No law is put into force to stop them. They parade Pennsylvania Avenue in scores every bright afternoon, dressed in their sealskins and silks, either walking or driving in some of the best turnouts in the city." It was Carpenter who wrote that he "spotted them in the private galleries reserved for members' families where a Member of Congress must have furnished the ticket for their admission."

Later testimony came from Jimmy Griffin, a congressional employee for 40 years, who commented in the 1960s that the huge Rayburn House Office Building was being erected on the site of a former cluster of "boarding houses that furnished many congressmen bedmates as well as beds."

Robert McCord, staff director for the House Education and Labor Committee in the 1960s, said that 30 years earlier, as a young insurance salesman, he knocked on the door of a row house at the foot of Capitol Hill just two blocks from the Senate chamber and was welcomed by a black madam who lined up a score of girls to buy 50-cents-a-week "casket policies."

The constitutional separation of power definitely does not reserve sexual hijinks for the legislative branch. The White House has the advantage of a high iron fence and usually discreet employees, but enough has been said and written about what goes on there to make it clear that Presidents, to reverse the familiar phrase, also take off their pants one leg at a time.

Most presidential tomcatting seems to have been conducted before the principals were elected, or outside the White House. Gossip about Presidents goes all the way back to George Washington, who was said to have had a young man's crush on Sally Fairfax, a married lady, and, of course, Thomas Jefferson, whose relationship to Sally Hemings, his slave, has had historians in a swivet for decades.

More recently, Franklin D. Roosevelt saw Lucy Mercer Rutherfurd in and away from Washington, and Dwight D. Eisenhower had a friendship with Kay Summersby when he was still a soldier.

But the ladies in at least two other cases—Nan Britton and Judith Exner—claimed to have dispensed their favors to Warren Harding and John Kennedy right there at 1600 Pennsylvania Avenue. Both women wrote books: Britton claiming to have given birth to a presidential love child and Exner describing an affair that was supposed to have continued even while she was the girlfriend of Chicago Mafia don Sam "Momo" Giancana.

Lyndon Johnson also was said to have had a roving eye. Adam Powell once told two reporters that LBJ gave him a White House souvenir cigarette lighter in the Oval Office with the warning, "Now don't lose it in a whorehouse." When Powell replied, "Mr. President, I never paid for it in my life," Johnson responded, "Well, I have."

In his book *Lyndon*, Merle Miller relayed a story, "no doubt apocryphal, but widely circulated," of a young woman on the White House staff who returned from an assignment at the LBJ ranch saying that she had awakened one night to find someone in the bedroom with her but, before she could scream, "heard a familiar voice say, 'Move over, honey; this is yore president.'"

These activities are by no means the exclusive province of the high and mighty in Washington. In recent years, there have been many stories about private businesses, pursuing the federal dollar, furnishing women to government contract officers. Some who have had lunch in one of the congressional cafeterias or witnessed the daily exodus of young men and women from the big departmental buildings are amazed that there is any market for commercial sex in Washington. The capital, with its huge force of office workers and with a number of large military installations nearby, has what must be one of the country's largest populations of good looking, unattached, and lonely people in the prime of their sexual lives. Not surprisingly, Washington and its suburbs also have a thriving singles bar scene . . . and a sky-high abortion rate.

This is not entirely a product of the New Morality. Ben Perley Poore, a newsman in Washington for 60 years during the last century, and Carpenter, covering the post-Civil War era, both wrote of "female clerks" being led astray, entering the capital's "market of human flesh."

Lait and Mortimer, constrained by no Victorian euphemisms, reported that after World War II, "G-Girls" flocked to Washington bars, "where they compete with the harlots, who violently resent them and call them 'scabs.'"

The hookers on Washington's 14th Street sex-for-sale strip do seem to have a militant sense of turf. Not long ago, local police put a number of appropriately dressed young women officers on the street in an effort to discourage men from picking up streetwalkers. Several nights of arrests for soliciting sex from the policewomen put a damper on business on 14th Street until the angry hookers took after the "Flatfoot Floozies" with umbrellas and handbags. Uniformed cops finally had to be called in to rescue the embattled decoys.

THE TOP FIVE SEXIEST WASHINGTONIANS
1. Ted Kennedy

Edward M. Kennedy has spent most of his adult life in a glare of publicity, much of it tragic, all of it fascinating.

Handsome, rich, and charming, the Massachusetts senator, like his dead brothers John and Robert, has been the subject of more sexual gossip and speculation than any regiment of Hollywood leading men. Some of it probably is true; much of it is the product of overheated guesswork, political hostility, and just plain envy.

In Ted Kennedy's case, the truth is almost irrelevant. Whatever his sex life is or has been, Kennedy is perceived as a womanizer by a large part of the American public. Because of that, his repeated denials that there were any sexual overtones to the automobile accident that resulted in the drowning of 28-year-old Mary Jo Kopechne on Chappaquiddick Island in 1969 simply have not satisfied the public and the press.

Kennedy did not seek the Presidency in 1972 or 1976 in part because of Chappaquiddick. When he did make the run in 1980, questions—old and new—about the accident distorted his campaign and dogged him to its dismal end. He may try again, despite his broken marriage, but there are many politicians who now believe that

Ted Kennedy's sex life—real or imagined—has destroyed his chances of becoming President.

It is a perhaps ironic postscript that one President, Grover Cleveland, confessed father of an illegitimate child, was elected twice.

2. Elizabeth Taylor

The movie star with violet eyes and more husbands than fingers of one hand is on this list because she demonstrated in the late 1970s just how valuable a famous and sexy wife can be to a politician.

John Warner is a personable, exceedingly handsome man who was formerly married to a member of the Mellon family and lived the horsey life of the ultrarich around Middleburg, Virginia. Warner was secretary of the Navy and chairman of the Bicentennial Commission in the 1970s, but he never set Washington ablaze with his intellect or political acumen.

More to the point, Warner was all but unknown in Virginia politics when he returned to the state after the Democrats recaptured the White House in 1976. And when he started campaigning for a Senate seat, there were few politicians willing even to predict he would win the Republican nomination.

When they looked again, Warner, with the plump but still gorgeous Elizabeth by his side, was packing crowds in at bull roasts, oyster shuckings, and horse shows all over the state. Just like in *National Velvet,* they won in a gallop.

Elizabeth, by the way, appears to be very conscious that she has established a political presence. Most of the time she avoids any comment on issues, but once took exception to one of the senator's comments on equal rights for women and took him on in public debate. Warner has since been exceedingly circumspect on the subject.

If he seek a second term in 1984, Warner may have to go it alone with his own good looks, charm, and record. In 1982, after she had achieved a long held ambition to make it on the legitimate stage with a starring role in "The Little Foxes," Liz and John announced they had filed for legal separation. That seems to assure that if John returns for a second term his opponent won't be able to say, as one did in 1978, "Viginia has elected three of the biggest boobs in the state to the U.S. Senate."

3. Rita Jenrette

As Rita tells the story, John Jenrette whisked her off her feet with his tenderness, his looks, and his impulsiveness after a chance meeting on Capitol Hill. He was a dashing young Democratic congressman, she was a new young Republican campaign staff worker. It wasn't until after the wedding that she found out he liked to drink and chase skirts.

She stuck with John, despite finding him one morning in Myrtle Beach "drunk, undressed, and lying on the floor in the arms of a woman who I knew was old enough to be his mother." But when John was sucked up in the Abscam scandal and convicted of taking a bribe, the romance that blossomed under the dome of the Capitol (and, according to Rita, was once consummated on the steps of the building's House wing) went sour.

Rita posed topless for *Playboy*—to raise money for John's legal expenses, she said—and went public with her experiences in the magazine, the *Washington Post,* and a quickie book. It is for this body of literature, a steamy firsthand account of what had been only cocktail party chatter about sex on Capitol Hill, that Rita made this list. A congressman, she wrote, "might be paunchy, middle-aged, balding, and dressed in Robert Hall suits, but there always will be women willing to overlook such details. And if he's young, handsome, and flirtatious, trained attack dogs won't be able to keep them away. I know; I tried."

Rita, writing all this when she was 31 and as stunning a woman as the most devoted girl-watcher might hope to see on The Hill, said she was far from the most unfortunate of the congressional wives. She said one woman told her that her lawmaker-husband was using cocaine and making frequent trips to "massage parlors" on Washington's sex-for-sale 14th Street strip. When she rejected his proposals that she accompany him on these excursions, the congressman "invited out-call massage girls to their home and tried to persuade his wife to join in," Rita wrote. At least some folks still believe in togetherness.

4. Paula Parkinson

Like Rita Jenrette, Paula Parkinson is very blond, very attractive, just past 30, and has displayed a lot of skin in *Playboy*. But they differ in one important aspect. Rita really was on the inside in Washington until she wrote her own ticket out of town. Paula, by all accounts, gave everything she had to gain entrée, but never got beyond the bedroom door.

Sleeping with congressmen obviously isn't always the way. The stories told by and about Paula and her brief career as a lobbyist vary, but the figure for the number involved appears to be about the size of a medium-sized congressional delegation.

But then it never was the quantity of her exertions that interested Washington in Paula. Innovation was what got her on the map. By reportedly videotaping a roll-in-the-hay with one of her congressional contacts, she brought the new world of communications technology to the dreary landscape of Washington gossip. Cocktail parties that yawned at such tidbits as who was seen checking into what motel with which secretary fairly buzzed with the word that somewhere up there on Capitol Hill was a lawmaker who had done a star turn for a very candid camera.

Nobody (to date) has seen such a videotape. About the only real information on Paula's activities was contained in confirmed reports that she had shared a cottage with three Republican congressmen during a 1980 Florida golfing excursion. That all three of them had voted against a bill Paula was trying to defeat was enough to cause one indignant (and obviously unlobbied) member of the House to demand a Justice Department investigation to ascertain whether votes had been exchanged for sex.

After six months, one of Washington's famous unidentified sources at Justice told the Associated Press, "She gave us some salacious accounts of purported activities with congressmen, but there was no evidence of federal violations."

Which is what Paula said all along. She told a couple of interviewers earlier there was no quid pro quo in the dispensation of her favors: "I just like horizontal sports."

5. Helga Orfila

Although certainly the most alluring woman in Washington embassy row society, one does not always come away from an encounter with Helga Liefeld Orfila with a vivid impression of her lovely face. Depending on which of her extraordinary party gowns she decides to wear, one sometimes comes away with a vivid impression of her décolletage, sometimes with one of her navel.

The wife of Argentinian Alejandro Orfila, secretary general of the Organization of American States and one of the most socially active dips in the Federal City, the German-born former model must be the most photographed woman in town after Nancy Reagan. A tall, striking blonde, she seems to be in *Dossier* magazine almost every issue. There are men in town who wish she were in *Playboy* magazine every issue.

How attractive is she? Orfila says he first saw Helga at a social funtion to which he had escorted Jacqueline Onassis. He left Jackie temporarily to find out who that gorgeous blonde was.

"My husband is much more conservative than I," she once told an interviewer with wonderful understatement. "Though I've gotten him to wear blue jeans." For the Orfilas, though, it's more usually black tie and navel—and at the fanciest parties in Washington, whether on Embassy Row or in their own palatial digs on California Street in Kalorama.

Honorable Mention—Elizabeth Ray

Liz Ray doesn't live in Washington anymore but the buxom blonde—now pushing 40 and still trying to break into show business in New York—is a fitting representative of every woman who was ever chased around a desk in a Washington office.

Liz, a star-struck poor kid bored with her southern hometown, was one of those who didn't try too hard to win in those pursuits when she found work on Capitol Hill. One congressman paid her to entertain his colleagues and visiting firemen on a Potomac River houseboat; her second boss gave her a desk, a typewriter (which she couldn't operate), and a telephone, which would ring when the old boy's sap was rising. Liz blew the whistle in a chance encounter with two of the *Washington Post*'s reporters, Rudy and Kathy Maxa, and the exposé uncovered half a dozen other cases of congressmen keeping their doxies on the public payroll.

It also threw some light on sexual harrassment in Washington. Most of the women who work in the capital's offices are not trying to earn promotions on the boss's couch or in a corner of the mail room and object to the assumption that they are. Liz Ray's revolt, perhaps perversely, may have helped them by cooling off a few office Romeos, on Capitol Hill and elsewhere in town.

Political Pros

THEY ARE THE MIGRANT WORKERS of politics, following campaigns across the nation like seasonal crops. They work hellish hours at a frantic pace in the busy even-numbered years and scratch for jobs between.

They call themselves "political consultants." Candidates who don't have one and discover their opponents do sometimes call them "hired guns." But they are the professionals of the television, computer, and opinion-polling political age, the men and women who have brought high technology to what has traditionally been regarded as a rather low calling in this country.

There always have been a lot of talented amateurs in American campaign management. McKinley's Mark Hanna was a wealthy businessman; Kennedy's Larry O'Brien was a press agent. And such people still play key roles in the campaign processes, dropping their usual pursuits as elections approach to help their parties or their friends. A lot of them are lawyers: Republican John Sears and Democrat Bob Strauss are leading examples.

But more and more, campaigns are planned and managed by full-time professionals. Although their "industry" can be traced back half a century to the legendary Clem Whittaker and Leone Baxter in California, it didn't really come into its own until sometime in the 1960s.

Many of them, especially at the beginning, got started as campaign volunteers. The best of them have worked at one time or another as full-time employees of political organizations. Some follow their successful clients into government jobs, making room for those who were attached to the latest crop of losers to set up shop in the real world. An increasing number are specialists in market and product research, direct mail advertising, and filmmaking. Many of them concentrate on campaigns in election years and return to the sometimes less exciting but usually more lucrative private sector after the votes are in.

No one knows for sure how many people practice this profession full-time, although there is an American Association of Political

Consultants. Nicholas Lemann estimated their number nationally at "perhaps a thousand" in a *Washington Monthly* article in 1980. Daryl Glenney, head of a company that supplies experts to firms and groups that want to form political action committees, lists 57 of the best-known consultants on her Campaign Works roster.

Political consultants set up shop all over the country, but most of those who work in statewide or national campaigns have some link to Washington. But some of the best known—David Garth in New York and Stuart Spencer in California—have reputations that bring the candidates to them. The pollsters also are exceptions to this: Top people like Pat Caddell, Dick Wirthlin (the 1980 Carter and Reagan pollsters), Bob Teeter, and Lance Tarrance all are based elsewhere and are involved in commercial as well as political polling work.

Almost all of the political professionals handle either Republican or Democratic candidates exclusively, but most do not draw the lines between the parties' liberal, moderate, and conservative factions. Very few are strongly committed to single-issue politics as such.

There are some noteworthy professionals who concentrate on causes. Richard Viguerie, who brought direct mail fund-raising and advocacy to a high art in the 1970s, works only with candidates and issues he perceives to be sufficiently conservative. He has been involved in the presidential races of Democrat George Wallace, Republican Phillip Crane, and Democrat-turned-Republican John Connally, declaring all to meet his ideological standard.

Another conservative who makes his living in politics is Terry Dolan, the enfant terrible of the New Right. He has raised sacks of money to finance attack campaigns against liberal candidates across the nation. He operates as an independent under the federal campaign finance law, so his National Conservative Political Action Committee (NCPAC) cannot formally link itself to the conservatives it supports. But Dolan, who has frequently clashed with Republican officials because of the free-swinging nature of his campaigns, nonetheless claims to have elected a raft of staunch conservatives in 1980.

The Left also has its political pros. Russell Hemenway of the National Committee for an Effective Congress provides campaign expertise to dozens of liberal candidates. The AFL-CIO Committee on Political Education (COPE), run for years by gruff, cigar-smoking Al Barkan—succeeded by his longtime associate John Perkins—has been a mainstay of "in-kind" aid to Democrats and a few Republicans whose records hew to the labor line.

As might be expected, the largest concentration of political professionals can be found in the major party committees. Both national committees have had pros as chairmen at various times, but for the most part, the Democratic chairman is more likely to be in the talented amateur category. The current Democratic chairman, Charles Manatt, is a banker and lawyer with a lifelong association with politics, but he is no technician. That also was true of his three immediate predecessors, John White, Kenneth Curtis, and Bob Strauss.

But GOP chairman Dick Richards, although a lawyer, made his living in politics for some years and is regarded as an accomplished professional. So was the late Ray Bliss, a no-nonsense Ohioan who served the GOP full-time for many years in his state and then came to Washington after the 1964 Goldwater debacle to rebuild the national organization.

Less well known than the national committees but more deeply involved in actual campaign work are the House and Senate committees supported by both parties on Capitol Hill. They began as incumbent protection societies, but in recent years have been expanding to help candidates who are challenging opposition senators and House members.

American political consultants are by no means limited to campaigns in the United States. A number of them have worked in campaigns abroad, including Venezuela, Peru, Spain, and France. This, of course, is a somewhat touchy business, and in some cases—as when consultant Joe Napolitan advised Valery Giscard d'Estaing—the presence of an American professional is kept quiet.

That has happened in the United States as well. When Maynard Jackson first ran for mayor in Atlanta, Boston's Mayor Kevin White sent one of his aides south to help out. To avoid the charge of carpetbagging, the adviser from Yankeeland was quartered in a black motel, and for some time went unnoticed.

The arrival or departure of a well-known political consultant during a campaign frequently becomes hot news by itself. When Ronald Reagan sacked John Sears just before the 1980 New Hampshire primary, it was the signal for a lot of punditry about the deep trouble the former California governor was in. Sears was in trouble, all right, but Reagan was not. George Bush proceeded to wound his campaign during the Nashua debate with Reagan and opened the door for Reagan's straight run to the GOP nomination.

Any ranking of political professionals is bound to provide arguments among the cognoscenti, because the best of them have some flops on their records. The list that follows is based on accomplishments and reputations of consultants operating mainly out of the Washington area.

THE TOP TEN WASHINGTON POLITICAL PROFESSIONALS

1. Richard Richards

Richards leads this list because he is a professional who has reached the pinnacle of his calling, chairman of his party's national committee. A big man in his 40s, Richards' high forehead and strong chin give him a fleeting resemblance to Gerald Ford, but he has been a Reagan partisan for years.

He started in politics, like so many others, in his party's youth auxiliary, but moved up shortly to head the Utah GOP, ran unsuccessfully for the House, and got on the Republican National Committee as a paid staff member. He worked for the RNC as a deputy chairman and director of its political division, and in two winning presidential campaigns—1972 and 1980—headed operations in the western states.

When Reagan tapped him for national chairman, Richards knew just what he wanted to do. He quickly abolished a number of semi-autonomous ethnic and minority offices that had managed to do not very much for the GOP or its candidates and then quelled howls about what he had done by appointing a Hispanic as political affairs director of the national committee.

Richards was not a favorite of Lyn Nofziger, who ran the White House political operation in the administration's first year, nor of Ed Rollins, Nofziger's successor. Their disfavor partly resulted from differences in style and from the almost inevitable strain that comes from differing priorities. The Nofziger-Rollins operation is concerned about making the President politically secure; the national committee chairman is responsible for the fortunes of the entire party and has to exert himself to avoid becoming a mere extension of the White House.

However, Richards did some talking out of school about the Richard Allen case and was embarrassed by revelations that he was deeply in debt to the Small Business Administration. Things like that could send him back to Utah.

2. Ann Lewis

Both major political parties have had women at the head of their national committees, but neither Democrat Jean Westwood nor Republican Mary Louise Smith had made their living in politics.

Ann Lewis, who has been supporting herself as a political technician and adviser for years, became the political director of the Democratic National Committee in 1981. The title puts her at the second level of the senior DNC staff, but she in fact is responsible for the national committee's involvement in federal, state, and local campaigns—heavy combat politics.

Now in her mid-40s, she has been working in politics since the late 1950s, first as a volunteer doing campaign scoutwork but then quickly moving into the substance of helping her former husband Gerald get elected Florida state controller. She was involved in Democratic presidential campaigns from 1972 on and moved to the DNC after several staff jobs for Democratic House members. Her brother is Representative Barney Franks (D-Mass.), and she helped him get elected, too.

Lewis is a liberal Democrat, but her approach is thoroughly pragmatic. Like others in the new staff Manatt brought to the DNC, she realizes the GOP is well ahead in the use of new campaign techniques and technology and is determined to close the gap.

3. Douglas Bailey and John Deardourff

Bailey, Deardourff, and Associates have the best record of any Republican political consulting firm. All but 3 of the 29 statewide candidates they worked for during the 1972–78 span were winners, and in 1980 they helped win governorships in Missouri, Delaware, and Indiana as well as assisting the pro-Reagan political action committee, Americans for an Effective Presidency.

Both men come out of the GOP's liberal wing. Bailey, a Ph.D. from Pennsylvania's Fletcher School of Law and Diplomacy, worked for Henry Kissinger at Harvard and for Nelson Rockefeller's 1964 presidential campaign. He is regarded as a TV advertising whiz and was credited with helping Senator Charles Percy come back from what looked like certain defeat in 1978.

They also have lost some big ones, most recently the governorship in Republican Virginia.

Deardourff, also a Fletcher grad and former Rockefeller staffer, was the man who thought of using Joe Garagiola in commercials for Gerald Ford in 1976. Political professionals still marvel that Bailey and Deardourff, with Stu Spencer and Bob Teeter, engineered a 31-point surge for that campaign in the final months. It was, of course, one point too few.

4. Matt Reese

In 1960, Matt Reese was one of the two paid staff members of John Kennedy's primary campaign in Reese's native West Virginia. In 1980, Reese went back as the head of the most consistently successful Democratic campaign consulting firm to secure Jay Rockefeller's reelection as governor . . . and a place in the presidential nomination picture of the 1980s.

White-haired and a more than a little oversized, Reese served as operations director at the DNC during the Kennedy administration, returned to West Virginia for a state post, and then came back to Washington to set up shop as a political consultant in 1967. That makes him the senior man in the profession, but he demonstrated in 1980 that he is not the proverbial old dog by introducing a complex computerized system for targeting voters in telephone-bank campaigns. Phones, letters, and door-to-door canvassing were the features of one of Reese's most remarkable victories: reversing a 60–30 deficit in 1978 in Missouri to defeat a right-to-work initiative opposed by his union clients.

5. Bill Sweeney

Sweeney, just past 30, is something of a prodigy in politics. He became the deputy director of the Democratic National Committee for planning and organization in 1981 after seven years with the Democratic Congressional Campaign Committee—the last four as executive director.

Sweeney's job is vital to a political party that has just absorbed a nasty defeat. He must try to restore some of the unity among the disparate groups (minorities, labor, ethnics, small farmers, southern racists, etc.) that kept the Democrats in the saddle for most of the five decades after the Great Depression.

Perhaps the toughest part of the job will be to forge some stronger links between the House and Senate campaign apparatus and the DNC, not to speak of fostering coordination between their leaders. That is one big reason Manatt plucked Sweeney off Capitol Hill, and it will be the big test of his capacity.

6. Charles Bailey

Chuck Bailey, like RNC chairman Richards, is from Utah, and was the national committee's deputy chairman during the first year of the Reagan administration after 10 years in fieldwork and political training. He was succeeded in the job by Rich Bond, a George Bush political protégé sent to keep an eye on the national committee for the White House. This move had more to do with Dick Richards' problems with the White House than with Bailey's competence.

In 1980, Bailey ran the national committee's Senate campaign operation, which helped bring in the first Republican majority in 28 years. He was directly involved in GOP victories in the Iowa and South Dakota Senate contests and in 1982, having left the committee for private practice, will be working for the reelection of Republican Governor Albert Quie of Minnesota and Senator Orrin Hatch in his home state.

But Bailey, an energetic and enthusiastic man in his early 50s, is best known as a political teacher. He was involved in the creation of the national committee's "campaign management college," and is one of the founders of a unique new program at Westminster College in Salt Lake City to train future campaign managers. The American Institute of Applied Politics opened shop in 1980 with a faculty drawn from both parties, including Richards, Reese, Spencer, and former Democratic National Committee executive director Mark Siegel.

7. Peter Hart

Peter Hart's expertise is public-opinion polling, and he has done that work for such high-profile Democrats as Ted Kennedy, Walter Mondale, Bill Bradley, Hugh Carey, and Jay Rockefeller.

But Hart is more than a numbers man. In his *Washington Monthly* article on the political consultants in 1980, Nicholas Leeman recounted how Hart, with ace advertising man Bob Squier, did such a good job for Mississippi gubernatorial candidate Bill Winter in countering the strengths of his strongest primary opponent that several other challengers overtook her and a whole new strategy had to be created. It was, and Winter won. Hart also is the ranking national expert on a vexing old problem—nonvoting. He does the principal polling for the Committee for the Study of the American Electorate, the authority in the area of voter turnout.

8. Eddie Mahe

Like so many of the Republican political pros, Eddie Mahe is a westerner. That might have had something to do with his decision in 1980 to lead the campaign of John Connally for the GOP nomination. The campaign raised so much money that it was the only one in either party to be able to turn down federal subsidies, but that didn't exactly get former Democrat Connally many delegates in the Republican primaries. His delegation totalled one woman.

Still, Mahe did have some noteworthy successes—Gordon Humphrey's New Hampshire Senate win and Dick Thornburgh's successful run for governor in Pennsylvania. He also has some impressive credentials: former deputy chairman and executive director of the RNC under Mary Louise Smith and field director for both the House and Senate Republican campaign committees.

9. Robert Goodman

Bob Goodman is based in Baltimore, just up the line from Washington, and he is a television specialist, but he has left his mark on contemporary campaigning.

Goodman was George Bush's media man in 1980 and, with the aid of actors in a commercial depicting an airport campaign rally, made the Bush bandwagon appear to be rolling a lot faster than the subsequent vote totals justified.

But whether they sniff at his work or not, a lot of other pros concede Goodman is a hell of an image-maker. His classic was in the 1978 Wyoming campaign, where he put a Yale-educated, New York-born son of English parents into cowboy togs on top of a horse and elected Malcolm Wallop to the U.S. Senate.

10. Marvin Chernoff

Political consultants don't give each other a lot of points when they draw good candidates and easy campaigns. It is those pros who rescue the losers that make a reputation.

Marv Chernoff was running an office equipment store when he helped Carl Stokes become one of the first black mayors of a major city, in 1967 in Cleveland. Nine years later, in the campaign business full-time, Chernoff drew a congressional candidate whose wife had just filed for divorce, naming a dozen or more examples of marital infidelity. With Chernoff emphasizing his congressional work, the candidate still won.

By 1980, the same candidate was laboring under bribery charges, but Chernoff got him through his primary just the same. However, not even Chernoff could save John Jenrette by the time of the general election. He lost, but Chernoff still is regarded as something of a magician.

III

THE HABITAT

The Actual City

THERE ARE TWO WASHINGTONS. Most Americans know one: that of the sweeping lawns and neoclassic architecture of the White House, the great gleaming dome of the Capitol, the vaulting obelisk of the Washington Monument.

Fewer know the other Washington, a city of more than half a million people that is the centerpiece of a metroplex housing nearly 3.2 million. For them, the reality is much the same mix as it is for millions of other Americans—the amenities of big-city life and the comforts of suburbia interspersed with neglect and decay in the old neighborhoods and cheap and ugly development in the new outlying communities.

Not so different from the rest of the country, but still unique. By location, Washington is a southern city, and for nearly 150 years its life-style and folkways more resembled Richmond than Philadelphia. But the Great Depression and World War II propelled it into the role of workshop of national recovery and hub of global politics. The result, in the words of John F. Kennedy, was a city "of northern charm and southern efficiency."

The central fact of Washington's local political life is that it has the highest percentage of black population of any major American city. Washington's black majority, 70.3 percent of its 637,651 total population, has not only had a profound effect on who governs the District of Columbia and how, but on the politics of the 11 surrounding counties and cities in Virginia and Maryland that comprise the national capital's metropolitan area.

Race was a political issue in the District long before blacks outnumbered whites. The city was created from the land of two slave states, and until 1850 blacks were sold at auction at a market where the National Archives now stand.

It also was a haven for many freed blacks, and that scared the white population. The city had strict laws controlling the lives of blacks for nearly half a century and was segregated until the 1950s. Its race relations hit bottom with a five-day riot in July 1919, which was not

247

quelled until the cavalry and the Marines were called in. And that was blacks against whites, unlike the outbreak of burning and looting directed against property in black neighborhoods after the murder of Martin Luther King Jr. in 1968.

For all of that, until it became a black majority city in 1960, the black population of Washington never exceeded 35 percent. But the trend was upward from the end of World War II, when blacks surged out of the rural South and Washington's whites fled to the newly developing suburbs.

Except for a brief period in the 1870s when it was given territorial status, the District of Columbia has been controlled to some degree by the federal government. In the mid-twentieth century, when it had become a major city, Washington was run by three commissioners appointed by the President, and its municipal ordinances were passed by Congress. More often than not, the commissioners were political cronies of the President, and the members of Congress willing to spend any time on Washington affairs were southerners intent on keeping political power out of the hands of the growing black population.

This was achieved by allowing no one, black or white, to vote. It was 1964, 163 years after the city was founded, before residents of Washington could vote for President. Four years later, with the power of the southern chairmen of the House and Senate District committees beginning to crack, an elected school board was approved by Congress, and in 1974, Washingtonians elected a mayor and city council.

The first elected mayor was Walter Washington, a benign bureaucrat who had been the head of the appointed commissioners just before home rule. He was beaten four years later in the Democratic primary—Washington has no Republican Party worth the name—by Marion Barry, who had come to town a dozen years earlier as an organizer for the Student Nonviolent Coordinating Committee, organized a youth self-help group in the late 1960s, and served on both the school board and city council.

Both Washington and Barry had all the problems of trying to keep a city together under the stress of growing crime and poverty and a fleeing affluent citizenry. They also were saddled with a bureaucracy left over from the city's days as "America's Last Colony," a municipal work force of both blacks and whites that had been selected and promoted on the basis of passivity and obedience to the city's masters on Capitol Hill.

As a result, Washington had, and to some extent still has, a city government that, to quote Lyndon Johnson, "couldn't pour sand out of a boot if the instructions were printed on the heel."

Barry and the younger and sharper administrators he brought with him improved some city services, but a lot of the basics are still embedded in molasses. The new regime also found that the city, which spends about $1.5 billion a year, had a long-term cumulative deficit of $409 million that no one had done anything about retiring. To get a start on that, and with federal aid becoming increasingly difficult to come by, Barry began cutting payroll and services.

The schools are in the worst, and most tragic, plight. Segregated by law until 1955 and by white flight since, the school system has been starved for funds, equipment, and teachers and overwhelmed by kids who are lucky to get breakfast at home, let alone help with their schoolwork. The school board has seen some of the most disruptive hassling this side of Teheran and has cashiered or lost half a dozen superintendents who had tried to cope with a system that was obliged to flunk half the children in grades one through three two years ago.

The city council has demonstrated a little more class, although one recently defeated member was charged during his term with sinking his teeth into a tow truck driver who was blocking the councilman's car in the city hall parking lot. Still, the council tackled and found at least a partial compromise in the volatile area of rent control and condominium conversion and, after some backing and filling, rewrote the city's archaic sex offenses law.

The last illustrated the fact that even with an elected municipal government, the District remains on a tight congressional leash. The city's home-rule legislation gave Congress the right to veto local legislation on grounds that the national government had to protect its security in the capital. Veto the sex law it did.

That does not explain, however, what the federal interest is in the age of consent for sexual intercourse, or, in an earlier attempted congressional intervention, what business the national government has deciding whether the District of Columbia should have a lottery.

The lottery issue provided an example of the extent to which the suburbs still try to wag the Washington dog. Maryland has a lucrative state lottery that gets a lot of play from District gamblers, and it was that state's congressional representatives who expressed concern about the propriety of gaming in the national capital.

The Washington suburbs, including five counties in Maryland and four counties and the city of Alexandria in Virginia, generally are wealthier, whiter, and much more Republican than the District. Virginia's Fairfax and Maryland's Prince Georges counties, rivaling or surpassing the District in population, are run by Republican conservative executives whose interest in the city sometimes seems to end with making sure their taxpayers have good roads to get to town and pick up their paychecks. In any case, another fruit forbidden to the

District is a commuter tax, the very mention of which causes battle flags to be run up in Maryland and Virginia.

With all of this, the city and its suburbs do manage to cooperate in some areas. They jointly run the area transit system, including a new and (thus far) clean and safe subway that has helped ease horrendous traffic and air pollution problems that were overwhelming the city in the 1960s, although its rising fares drove many commuters back to their cars.

The city and the Maryland suburbs also have been able to combine resources on sewage disposal, changing the Potomac from a river called "an open sewer" to a waterway that may soon be fit for swimming for the first time in decades.

The Washington area is widely regarded as recession proof, which is based on the premise that when the private sector in the rest of the country goes sour, the government will expand to help it out. In the Reagan era the premise may be a myth, because he claims the way to expand business is to shrink government. Thus, in the summer of 1981, when national unemployment is under 7.5 percent, joblessness hit 10 percent in the District of Columbia.

Still, there are many signs of prosperity in Washington. With the subway in and running, much of the dilapidated old downtown shopping area is under renovation and redevelopment. A new, block-square convention center was rising near downtown, and hotel builders, as well as other entrepreneurs, were jacking up land values in an area that had barely been able to support used-tire shops and tattoo parlors.

As the 1980s began, Washington found itself with 165,000 fewer inhabitants than it had 30 years before when the suburbs were just starting to take off. Its housing stock rose slightly between 1970 and 1980, and its black-white ratio held just about steady. The census also showed that while the city population declined 16 percent during the 1970s, three times as many blacks as whites moved out. That could presage an increase in white voting impact in a city that now is almost entirely black-led.

Some blacks are convinced that the whites intend to take back political control of Washington. It might be "Chocolate City" now, they say, but the scoop of vanilla usually ends up on top.

Here are the blacks and whites who run local government in and around the national capital.

THE TOP TEN IN WASHINGTON LOCAL GOVERNMENT
1. Marion Barry
Back in 1965, anyone who came to Washington wearing a dashiki and talking about civil rights was viewed by the local establishment,

black and white, as trouble. Barry, then 29, came to the capital to head the Washington office of the Student Nonviolent Coordinating Committee and remained to become the second elected mayor of the District of Columbia in 1978.

Born in Mississippi, raised in Memphis, and educated as a chemist there and in Nashville, Barry is one of the most successful of the young Southern blacks who came to prominence in the civil rights movement that began with the student sit-ins in 1960. He became the first national chairman of SNCC, but after two years as its Washington contact man, Barry switched his attention to the community and shouldered his way through the city's black bureaucrats and politically-active ministers to the top of the heap.

When Barry beat incumbent Walter Washington and local Urban League leader Sterling Tucker in the 1978 Democratic primary, his promise was efficient operation of the city. He got some results, but the local bureaucracy, which some have compared in speed and efficiency to that of India, still maintained a glacial pace in many areas.

Despite his arrival in the city as a street activist, Barry got some of his strongest support in 1978 from the white precincts in the city. He also courted the vote of the city's sizable and politically-active gay community. A poll at the end of 1980 showed Barry had an approval rating of only 33 percent—31 percent among blacks and 37 percent among whites.

He is a hard-working politician, hopping around the city, dropping in at neighborhood celebrations and meetings, and walking (prudently, with police accompaniment) the dope-selling corners to assure shopkeepers and residents that they will get help. He also went to dinner at the White House to welcome the Reagans and establish contact with the new administration, which thus far has shown few signs of a wish to break its back for Washington, or any other city.

Barry had some luck the first time out when Washington and Tucker split the black establishment vote. Washington is out of it for 1982, and Tucker is said to have lost some of his base. Councilman John Ray (an on-and-off Barry ally) and others of the mayor's generation may try their luck, but so far Marion Barry has been drawing the good cards in Washington politics.

2. Elijah B. Rogers

Elijah B. (for Baby) Rogers is a short, dapper man with a booming voice who drives a silver Alfa Romeo convertible and runs the District of Columbia government. As the $53,000-a-year city administrator, Rogers, former city manager of Berkeley, California, and at one time leading contender for the $92,000 job in Dallas, Rogers is the top professional in the Barry administration.

As the superintendent of the city's day-to-day operations, the job Rogers does has a lot to do with Barry's political fate. So Rogers rides herd on the city's struggle to provide housing for its poor (some small signs of progress), and repair the streets (lots of activity), and tries to keep vital services functioning in the face of heavy debt and gloomy prospects for help from the White House and Congress.

Rogers also is the man who speaks for the Barry administration when it gets into trouble. So far, he has handled that part of the job with considerable aplomb.

3. Walter Fauntroy

Walter Fauntroy has two things going for him as an urban black politician. First, he is a minister, which gives him recognition in the voting community and an audience every Sunday in the church-going community—the same formula Adam Clayton Powell had for years in Harlem. Second, Fauntroy is a veteran of the civil rights movement of two generations past: just as Marion Barry was the SNCC presence in Washington, he was Martin Luther King Jr.'s representative in the capital.

Fauntroy, 48, has been pastor of the New Bethel Baptist Church for more than 20 years and, in 1971, when the District of Columbia was given the right to elect a nonvoting delegate to the House of Representatives, walked away with the job. With the help of what is considered to be the only political organization worthy of the name in Washington, he has kept the job and pulled a lot of Democratic strings for the past 10 years.

Fauntroy, who backed Sterling Tucker in 1978, probably could beat Barry for mayor, but that's not what he wants. He was a prime mover of the proposed constitutional amendment to give the District voting representation in the Senate and House, and if it should get ratified, he would like to be one of Washington's senators. He shouldn't hold his breath.

4. Sterling Tucker

There still are a lot of people who can't figure out how Sterling Tucker managed to lose the 1978 mayoral race. As the longtime head of the local Urban League, he was at least as well known as any of the other candidates. He had been chairman of the city council, and he had the Fauntroy organization behind him.

What happened is that Tucker split the support of the black preachers of Washington and their flocks with Walter Washington, and simply didn't turn on blacks or whites elsewhere in the city.

He served as assistant secretary of Housing and Urban Development during the last two years of the Carter administration, and while that kept him in Washington, he was out of the flow of city politics. He is expected to try again for mayor, if he can reassemble his support. If the polls that rate Barry low are right, Tucker might well make a local comeback.

5. John Ray

John Ray, 39, is a bit of a political high-roller. In 1978, he figured the city's politics were fluid enough to give a total newcomer a chance and plunged into the mayoral race. He subsequently dropped out in favor of Barry and was repaid with the mayor's support when he ran for an at-large seat on the city council.

Now Ray seems to have walked off with a number of Barry's financial supporters and campaign workers, which points to a battle between them in 1982 for the same constituencies. Ray also has been working the same areas of the city that gave Washington and Tucker their main support in 1978, and he may be more popular among municipal employees who gave Barry a lot of backing but since have come to believe the mayor is trying to solve his problems by dumping them in budget cutbacks.

6. Arrington Dixon

Dixon, the city council chairman, is another young and ambitious but relatively inexperienced politician. As head of the council, Dixon has a better shot at media attention than do at-large members John Ray and Betty Ann Kane, one of the three white members, and all share the advantage of having run and been elected citywide.

Dixon, also 39, probably would be getting in beyond his depth if he runs for mayor this time around, but making a few feints toward a race to assess his support could pay off later.

7. Ivanhoe Donaldson

Had this been written when Marion Barry had just become mayor, Ivanhoe Donaldson probably would occupy the second spot on the list. A college and SNCC associate of Barry's, Donaldson is listed as assistant to the mayor, and when the new group took over, he was deeply involved in government operations.

But Barry needed experience more than loyalty and willingness to work, so Rogers became the effective operating chief of the municipal machinery. Donaldson was assigned to troubleshoot another of the District's snarled programs, the summer youth job effort that Barry wanted to use as a showcase of his administration. In the first two years of Barry's term, the program all but floundered, but Donaldson's stroking produced improvement in 1980—at least the kids got paid. Donaldson remains Barry's chief political strategist, which makes him a key man in 1982.

8. Jack Herrity

Herrity, who looks something like a tall version of Ed Asner, has been chairman of the Fairfax County, Virginia, Board of Supervisors for six years, and in that role has a strong voice in Washington-area government.

Herrity, a staunch conservative Republican, heads a suburban government for a county with almost 600,000 residents, nearly as large as the city across the river it feeds on. With that size constituency, it was no surprise that Herrity tried for a seat in Congress in the 1970s, though he fell short of victory.

He has a political soul mate across the river in Maryland, where Larry Hogan, a former FBI agent and GOP congressman holds sway as county executive of Prince Georges County. Hogan, presiding over a county even bigger than the District in population, might be expected to swing as much weight as Herrity, but the Virginian has a much richer jurisdiction, counting scores of members of Congress, federal judges, and government and military officials. Hogan is running for the Senate.

9. Alfonse D'Amato

That the newly-elected junior senator from New York is on this list is an example of how fast things can happen when power changes hands. D'Amato was presiding supervisor of the Town of Hempstead on Long Island in 1980 when he beat veteran Senator Jacob Javits in the GOP primary and then Democrat Elizabeth Holtzman in the general election.

With the Republicans suddenly in control of the Senate, D'Amato became more than a freshman member of the Appropriations Committee—he was given chairmanship of its District subcommittee. Both the House and the Senate act on the vital "federal payment" from the U.S. Treasury to the District to help offset the federal government's huge tax-exempt presence in the city. In practice, few senators bother to concern themselves with the District and its problems, so D'Amato is almost a one-man band and has much to say on how much Washington gets and how it is spent.

D'Amato is counted among the Senate's new breed of strong conservatives, but Barry and other District officials say they are happy to have drawn a former local government official as the city's Senate monitor.

10. Ronald Reagan

There are people who would say the President of the United States ought to lead any list of the most important people in Washington local government; others who would say Reagan appears to have scant time for the problems of the nation, let alone the capital city.

Some Presidents have taken an active role in the governance of Washington. Franklin Roosevelt (and Eleanor) tried to clean up the city's slums and improve the quality of its governing commission; Lyndon Johnson went to bat himself for home rule and appointed the first black commissioner; Richard Nixon publicized the crime problem and backed modernization and expansion of the then pitiful police force.

Washington's fate is tied more closely to that of other big cities under Reagan's overall policies than to his specific feelings, if any, about the capital. But the White House can do special favors for special cities—witness Westway in New York. At the minimum, Washington needs the goodwill of the family at 1600 Pennsylvania Avenue.

Cops

A RESIDENT of a Virginia suburb of Washington overslept one morning and had to make an extra fast run into town to get to an appointment on Capitol Hill. "I broke the speed limit in six different police jurisdictions to get here on time," he reported on arrival.

He wasn't exaggerating. The tardy commuter had to drive on roads patrolled by the Fairfax County, Virginia highway, Alexandria city, U.S. Park, District of Columbia Metropolitan, and U.S. Capitol police forces. "Russian roulette on wheels," he called it.

The Washington metropolitan area has 25 different federal, state, county, city, and special purpose police forces. One police official, running down the list, said it was entirely possible that there were more people with arrest powers in the Washington area than any place this side of Moscow. A study some years ago of the area law enforcement rosters concluded that there were 10 or 11 police officers per thousand civilians, compared to about 6 in the Boston area. A police union official estimated in 1981 that, apart from private "rent-a-cop" agencies, there were 18,000 law enforcement men and women in Washington and its environs.

The area police forces range in size from the District of Columbia's 3,600 to fewer than 30 in the suburb of Rockville, once a small Maryland country town but now a burgeoning city with high-rise buildings, multilane highways, and law enforcement problems it never dreamed of.

An example is the experience of two top cops. Burglars broke into the city home of D.C. Police Chief Burtell Jefferson in 1980 and made off with $1,600 in cash and goods. The haul was undisclosed, but the same thing happened a short time earlier at the suburban Virginia home of H. Stuart Knight, then head of the U.S. Secret Service.

As it is almost everywhere else in American urban areas, crime is a serious problem in Washington. It is aggravated by the peculiarly transient nature of the area's population. The tensions of race (the familiar pattern of a black inner-city surrounded by white suburbs) and the clash of poverty living next to wealth—a couple of the suburban counties have median incomes among the nation's highest

256

while the city has an unemployment rate that was nearly 50 percent higher than the national average in the summer of 1981—only heighten the problem.

And, of course, Washington crime gets an inordinate amount of attention. When an elderly man gets robbed and shot on the street anywhere, the community is alarmed. But when the victim is a John C. Stennis, dean of the U.S. Senate, it makes the network news shows and headlines across the country.

There is an appalling number of guns in Washington. The city has what has been called the toughest firearms laws in the nation, but it is only a short ride across the line to places in Virginia where guns can be bought and used in the same day. The National Rifle Association, which at one time considered moving its headquarters out of Washington because of the street crime, was quick to note that President Reagan was shot in a city with stringent gun laws, but neglected to add that the accused attacker bought the weapon he used and a backup arsenal elsewhere.

Also not mentioned was that the attack on Reagan was the first attempt on a President in Washington in more than 30 years (during which real and would-be assassins were blazing away at chief executives with depressing regularity in such places as Texas and California) and the first to draw blood in the capital since James Garfield was shot in 1881.

In any case, although it never has been the worst in its population category in crime statistics—sixth in homicides in 1980, for example—Washington has been called the "crime capital" of the nation by Richard Nixon and many other politicians. Washingtonians, who must deal with the problem for the most part without the benefit of high iron fences around their houses and phalanxes of bodyguards, note only that the politicians, especially Nixon, have done their part to uphold the city's criminal reputation, as in Abscam and Watergate.

There is one place in Washington, at least to date, where crime has not been a problem. That is, to the surprise of most, in the Metro subway system that began operating in 1976 and in its first five years suffered no killings, 2 rapes, and only 1,000 crimes of any description. The 40-mile (and growing) system, which was carrying about 300,000 passengers a day in 1981, is policed by a force of about 300 cops headed by a veteran military policeman, Angus MacLean.

MacLean and his force are aided by a subway design that provides very few isolated areas for criminals to hide or wait for victims and a closed-circuit television system that keeps most of the stations under constant surveillance. They also have the power, held by no other nonfederal police agency in the country, to make arrests in three jurisdictions: the District, Maryland, and Virginia.

There also is a crime that is almost impossible to get away with in Washington—illegal parking. In the early 1970s, the city, with no rapid-transit system worth the name, was all but choked by cars, trucks, and buses. It had monumental traffic jams every workday rush hour, half a dozen or more air pollution alerts every summer, and scores of streets all but closed by triple as well as double parking. Tickets were cheap and often ignored, and towing was rare.

No more. The District police and Department of Transportation now ticket more than 10,000 cars daily and tow and impound some 30,000 a year. The risk and hassle of being towed is so high that one entrepreneur started a service called Humiliation Elimination, Inc., which for a fee will pay a motorist's fines and reclaim his car from the city impoundment lots. And drive the motorist to the lot in a limousine!

Washington does have some policing problems shared by few other cities. In the 1960s, early 1970s, and once again in the 1980s, Americans by the hundreds of thousands have converged there to protest social conditions or government policies. The city has seen crowds of 500,000 or more in the past two decades as civil rights demonstrators were followed by antiwar marchers, who were followed by antiabortionists, protesting farmers, and angry union members. Add to these the gigantic crowds that attend inaugurations, Fourth of July celebrations, and the occasional visit of a Pope or King, and you have a traffic and law enforcement problem that has given Washington police chiefs some memorable headaches, and their rank and file some bulging overtime checks.

The cops in Washington have also suffered some memorable scandals. In the 1950s, investigations turned up widespread payoffs, and Odessa Madre, a black bootlegger and madam, told an interviewer 20 years later that she had white cops, many of whom she had known since childhood, on her payroll for years.

Vice, of course, begets vice. Some years back, when Washington police, like others, regularly hounded homosexuals, the public was treated to the spectacle of a local vice-squad man and a plainclothes member of the U.S. Park Police arresting each other in the Lafayette Park comfort station. Each claimed the other had made the first move.

More recently, half a dozen D.C. cops were disciplined when their superiors discovered they had hired a couple of hookers off the street to provide the entertainment at a bachelor party in a local hotel for one of their number about to be married.

A bigger problem was race. The Metropolitan Police had only a tiny representation of black officers until well into the 1960s, although blacks by that time were in a majority in the city. Like the rest of

Washington government, the police force was treated as an extension of congressional patronage, and much of the roster was drawn from rural areas of Virginia, Maryland, the Carolinas, and Pennsylvania. Head-busting was the order of the day in Washington police work.

It took one of the North Carolinians, a bald, mild-looking high school graduate named Jerry Wilson, to turn the local police department around in the late 1960s. He recruited and promoted more blacks than all of his predecessors and began the process of linking the cops to the community—the only known way of successfully fighting crime.

In 1978, with the District force about 45 percent black, the city got its first black chief, Burtell Jefferson. Linked to the old black bureaucracy of the city, notably former mayor Walter Washington, the 32-year veteran clashed with Mayor Marion Barry and retired after three years. He was replaced by another black, Maurice Turner.

Turner has the biggest police job in the area, but problems are growing as well for the forces in the neighboring suburbs. Prince Georges County, northeast of the District, has taken the brunt of low-income migration from the city in recent years and has the largest suburban force, about 800, under former FBI agent John McHale. The P.G. force also has the reputation for being the toughest in the area, with a number of charges of brutality, especially in cases involving blacks, lodged in recent years.

Fairfax County, Virginia, and Montgomery County, Maryland, Washington's generally white and affluent bedroom suburbs, each have police forces of about 750. Fairfax chose a 40-year-old native son, Carroll Buracker, as its chief, but Montgomery went to the District for a top-ranking Metropolitan cop, Bernard Crooke, after a short and litigious go-around with former Boston police chief Robert DiGrassia.

About the same size as the suburban county forces is the U.S. Park Police under Lynn Herring. It works in all three jurisdictions, policing highways, parks, and memorials in a wide area around the capital. The Park Police also had something of a head-knocking reputation, but since it suffered serious embarrassment in the early 1970s when its officers busted scores of people, including some subteen kids, for flying kites on the Washington Monument grounds, it has tried to improve its image. Now it sponsors a yearly kite-flying contest there.

The second largest police agency in the Washington area is the Federal Protective Service, an arm of the General Services Administration. It supplies about 3,000 guards and patrol officers for federal buildings in Washington—a job so big it has to subcontract to private security firms for about a third of its work.

The place that gets the most intensive policing in Washington, with the exception of the White House, is Capitol Hill. Chief James Powell, a veteran of the old District force, commands about 1,200 officers to protect about 225 acres of land. Powell now has professionally-trained officers under his command, but for years the Capitol cops were mainly patronage appointees. Georgetown, George Washington, Maryland, and other area universities have hundreds of graduates who worked their way through school toting guns on Capitol Hill (and often doing their studying at guard posts in its buildings).

There is nothing amateurish about the policing at the White House. That is the mission of the Secret Service, both the plainclothes agents who protect the President and his family, and the uniformed officers who protect the White House grounds.

There are 1,535 Secret Service agents, but most of them spend their time chasing counterfeiters for their employer, the secretary of the treasury. There also are more than 800 members of the uniformed Secret Service, which has the additional job of mounting guard over foreign embassies in Washington.

The Federal Bureau of Investigation, headquartered in an architectural monstrosity on Pennsylvania Avenue that has been called J. Edgar Hoover's last erection, has thousands of employes and hundreds of agents in Washington. In addition to the headquarters staff, there is a big FBI field office in Washington and a smaller operation across the river in Alexandria, Virginia.

There are also many specialized law enforcement agencies in and around the capital—alcohol agents (revenooers, to mountain folk), Drug Enforcement Agency "narcs," customs officers, State Department security agents, and Federal Aviation Administration police at National and Dulles Airports.

Washington's most important cops are those who work in close, protecting the monumental and working heart of the government and the people who pass through or toil there.

THE TOP FIVE WASHINGTON COPS
1. Maurice T. Turner

Turner, appointed chief of the big District police force at 45, is a Washington native who joined the force in 1957 after a stint with the Marines in Korea. A bear of a man—six feet two inches tall and 215 pounds—Turner came up through the ranks, walking a beat in the tough southeastern section of the city in his rookie days. He still believes in foot patrols and says he will get more cops out of their cars and on to the pavement.

Turner is regarded as a tough but fair cop, less concerned with connections and protocol than Jefferson and more inclined to direct action. Shortly after he took over the force, the police began heavy patrolling on the streets where drug peddlers had been operating openly day and night. That dispersed but did not rid the city of them.

As chief of the District force, Turner technically does not have to worry about the high-visibility protection jobs at the White House, Capitol, federal buildings, and embassies. But when big trouble erupts, as it did during the days of the Vietnam war protests, the Metropolitan police always are called upon. That is when Turner will find himself with a national audience.

2. William H. Webster

Art Buchwald used to have fun with the idea that J. Edgar Hoover had been director of the FBI so long that anyone who took over the job after the original G-Man died had to adopt the name alaung with the title. No one, however, has ever mistaken William Webster for J. Edgar Hoover.

Although he was Jimmy Carter's second choice to head the FBI (Judge Frank Johnston, the first, withdrew because of health problems), Webster has done much of what Carter wanted with the federal government's first-line law enforcement agency.

Mainly, he has kept its 7,800 agents out of the kind of trouble they became involved in under Hoover—the "black bag" break-ins—and kept himself from being drawn into the kind of high-level political intrigues that ruined L. Patrick Gray as Hoover's successor. He also has continued the process started by Clarence Kelley, his predecessor, of opening the FBI's ranks to minorities and women and eliminated much of the agency's lock-step image and director-worship.

Webster, born in St. Louis in 1924, graduated from Amherst College and Washington University in his hometown. After practicing law for 20 years, he was appointed to the federal district court bench in 1971 and after 3 years moved up to the appeals court for 5 years. He succeeded Kelley in 1978.

3. John R. Simpson

John Simpson moved up to be director of the Secret Service at the end of 1981, when Stuart Knight got caught in the bureaucratic switches. Knight, a 30-year veteran with the SS, once clashed with a California agent named Robert Powis and tried to fire him. Powis became deputy assistant secretary of the Treasury Department when the Reagan administration came in and Knight decided to retire, taking an upstairs job in Treasury himself.

Simpson, a 49-year-old Boston native, joined the Secret Service during the Kennedy administration and moved up to head of protective services—that arm of the agency responsible for the life of the President, his family, and other present and former luminaries.

The protection job is like place kicking for a football team. It doesn't call for constant action, but the action better be done right when the time comes to perform. The main job of the SS is to protect U.S. currency, but the agency is judged on how well it protects the President. What that can mean was illustrated by agent Tim McCarthy, who stepped directly into the gunfire of Reagan's assailant in 1981.

Simpson's job is going to be tougher because the SS is now swallowing up the Alcohol, Tobacco, and Firearms Bureau's 1,200 agents under Reagan budget-cutting mandates. That means the Service henceforth will be chasing not only counterfeiters and potential assassins, but bootleggers and gun nuts as well.

4. James M. Powell

Tennessee-born James Powell, like a lot of the 535 senators and House members he works for, is well beyond regular retirement age. Born in 1914, he joined the District police force in 1940 and moved up through the ranks to deputy chief in 1965, when he moved to the Capitol force.

Even with a $22 million budget and more officers than Atlanta, Georgia, Powell has a problem. He has to deal with a complex of buildings that must be kept open to the public—his bosses insist on it—and try to keep out the crackpots and terrorists. That hasn't always been possible—in 1954 a group of Puerto Rican nationalists shooting from the House visitors' gallery wounded five congressmen, and in 1971, someone bombed a restroom in the very center of the Capitol.

For that reason, Powell has been able to gradually professionalize the Capitol police force, keeping 30 D.C. officers on the rolls (including himself) and requiring a 16-week training course at a police academy for rookies. He also has been able to install metal detectors in the entrances to the Capitol and the galleries overlooking the House and Senate chambers.

Even so, members of Congress tend to think of Capitol policemen they have sponsored as their own gofers. An extreme example of this was former Representative William Ayres of Ohio, who once took a child's wading pool to a Capitol Hill party for then Attorney General Robert Kennedy, whose Hickory Hill poolside social events were getting a lot of press attention. Ayres brought along the Capitol cop he had placed on the force to inflate the pool.

5. *Lynn H. Herring*

The U.S. Park Police is not a huge force, but it is highly visible in Washington. Except for the White House and Capitol, Herring's 660-member force guards most of tourist Washington, and its blue-and-gold clad officers—including a mounted patrol—are the police sight-seers are most likely to have contact with in the capital.

The Park Police have primary jurisdiction over the two-mile-long Mall from the Lincoln Memorial to Capitol Hill and thus have to deal with everything from lost kids to demonstrations with as many as half a million participants and, a few years back, a Roman Catholic mass celebrated on the Mall by the Pope.

In addition to their work in the tourist heart of the capital, the Park Police are the traffic cops on a number of the parkways leading into Washington and also have jurisdiction over federal areas in Georgia, New York, and California.

Herring was in charge of the California patrol until taking over command of the Park Police in the fall of 1981. At 52, he is a 22-year veteran of the force, having learned the ropes in Washington during the hectic decade of the 1960s.

Museums and the Arts

UNLIKE OTHER WORLD CAPITALS, Washington is definitely the nation's second city as concerns the arts and, in fact, is listed as such in the 1982 *Places Rated Almanac*. Its National Gallery of Art may be the second best art museum in the Western Hemisphere, as some say, but it is not the great institution that New York's Metropolitan Museum is justly considered. The National Symphony is not in the same league as the Chicago Symphony. Washington actors have to make it to Broadway to become successes. The city's best ballerina, Amanda McKerrow, had Moscow audiences enthralled, but she's not quite as good as New York's best.

As concerns museums in general, however, Washington is without question the museum capital of the country. There is indeed a spirit of grandeur and empire in the Federal City, having not to do with the nouveau-riche White House crowd, the nabobs of The Hill, or the pin-striped warlords who run the cabinet departments, but with Washington's vast collection of museums, which is mostly to say, with the unique, wonderful, and sprawling cultural and scientific enterprise known as the Smithsonian Institution.

Its secretary, the haughty, bemused, and brilliant Dillon Ripley, rules his realm as absolutely as a Manchu, and as elegantly. Fittingly enough, the Smithsonian's principal offices are in a castle. If the National Gallery is in second place, the Smithsonian's Air and Space Museum is without peer and the most popular museum in the world. The American History Museum is by any standard the best of its kind.

The Smithsonian possesses more than 78 million objects. They range from Rodin's "The Burghers of Calais" to Edward Hopper's "People in the Sun" to the world's largest stuffed elephant to George Washington's dentures to an actual photograph of Dolley Madison to the plane that dropped The Bomb on Hiroshima to an 1836 railroad car to a camel saddle equipped with Gatling gun to an F. Scott Fitzgerald telegram seeking money to the deadly Hope diamond to the Wright Brothers airplane to the Apollo 11 moon capsule to Chinese pandas (live) to a Chou dynasty tiger (bronze) to the world's longest beard to a World War II army latrine to . . . .

264

Suffice it to say, presuming the Enola Gay is not pressed into action again, Smithsonian-goers a century from now will doubtless come to marvel at President Reagan's cabinet room jellybean jar.

The Smithsonian empire encompasses six major art museums, including the separately administered National Gallery of Art, and two art galleries and a museum of design and decorative art in New York. In addition to the mammoth Air and Space and American History Museums, it has a first-rate natural history museum, arts and industries museum, and neighborhood black culture museum. It owns the National Zoo and a huge wildlife preserve in the Blue Ridge Mountains. It has a center for environmental studies in Chesapeake Bay and owns a number of islands. It has a center for marine studies in Florida, and another for anthropological studies and is home to the Woodrow Wilson Center for International Studies, where some of the nation's greatest minds gather together and still yell at each other about Vietnam. There's a conservation analytical laboratory, a horticulture office, an astrophysical observatory, a radiation biology laboratory, a tropical research institute, and a center for folklife studies that sponsors an annual American Folklife festival that is one of the very few living museum exhibits in the world. It also owns 25 million dead insects.

The Smithsonian's libraries and archives could be mistaken for those of the Congress. Its peripheral industries include one of the country's most profitable magazines, an enormous mail-order gift business, a chain of gift, souvenir, and bookstores, a travel service, restaurants, and a merry-go-around. It conducts symposiums and seminars, sponsors expeditions, operates a cultural and scientific exchange service with similar establishments all over the world, and awards six annual Smithsonian medals, whose recipients have included Charles Lindbergh, Pope John Paul II, and Queen Elizabeth II. It produces all manner of radio and television programs and its Division of Performing Arts puts on music, theater, and dance productions seen by more than 500,000 a year. Its cocktail parties, receptions, and other soirées are among the very most socially prestigious in the capital. To dine in the banquet hall of The Castle is to dine in the style of Lorenzo the Magnificent.

The Smithsonian's operating budget is rapidly approaching $200 million a year, with the federal government picking up 60 percent. The total might not seem much by Pentagon standards, but it's a pretty penny for an outfit that likes to bill itself simply as "the Nation's Attic."

The amount certainly would have confounded the man initially responsible for it all—James Smithson. Born in 1765 the illegitimate son of the Duke of Northumberland and one Elizabeth Macie,

Smithson managed to grow up a London gentleman nevertheless, a fairly rich chap dabbling in the rather volatile and exciting pastime known as eighteenth century chemistry. According to the *New Yorker* magazine (but not, officially, to the Smithsonian), Smithson completed some middling experiment without blowing himself up and submitted the findings to the Royal Academy in hopes of a rapturous reception. When it was not forthcoming, Smithson waxed very angry, and, as legend has it, plotted his revenge. When he died in 1829, he left his estate to his nephew, but with the curious proviso that, if the nephew should die without an heir—as he did shortly—the money would be given to the United States for the establishment of an institution "for the increase and diffusion of knowledge among men." To the English intellectual of that day, this would have seemed the nastiest and sourest of bad jokes. In modern-day terms, it would be like establishing a major center of knowledge and learning in Peoria.

The money came to more than $500,000, an enormous sum in those days, and, frankly, it bewildered the American government. While the Congress pondered and quarreled over what to do with it, the money was unfortunately invested in what proved to be unsuccessful bonds. By the time Congress finally agreed upon a bill creating the institution, sponsored by former President and then Congressman John Quincy Adams, in 1846, it had to sheepishly replenish the original bequest out of taxpayers' funds. But it went ahead, as it has with every other boondoggle since, and The Castle was what resulted. The site on which it was built was then in a remote area over which wandered goats, chickens, sheep, and murderous gangs, and which was separated from Washington proper by the pestilential Tiber Creek canal (now Constitution Avenue).

But Smithson got his wish—and revenge—having assured "my name shall live in the memory of man when the titles of the Northumberlands are extinct and forgotten." We can just be thankful his name was not James British Museum.

There are also museums not connected with the Smithsonian in Washington, at seemingly every turning.

The Phillips Collection just west of DuPont Circle is the oldest museum of modern art in the country. Consequently, a lot of its stuff dates back to the nineteenth century. The Corcoran, just north of the White House, has a great deal of contemporary American art but its collection dates back to the eighteenth century.

The Navy, the Army, the Supreme Court, the Congress, Ford's Theater, and myriad other Washington institutions each have their little museums, and in aggregate constitute a historical collection unrivaled in the nation. The National Park Service, the best-run federal agency in the government until James Watt became secretary, has within a 100-mile radius of Washington an open air museum displaying what amounts to most of the Civil War.

Just south of the White House, in a Beaux Arts building worthy of the most megalomaniac Newport robber baron, the Daughters of the American Revolution have amassed a sort of attic's collection of early Americana that includes a George Washington exhibit replete with George's bedsheets and tumblers in which his visage stares at you from the bottom of the glass. The 35,000 pieces also include Benedict Arnold's wife's white satin bridal shoes.

There's also the National Geographic Museum, for those who like primitives but don't want to walk all the way to Congress; the B'nai B'rith Museum; the Stephen Decatur House; the Folger Shakespeare Library; the Hillwood Museum, originally the home of the late Marjorie Merriweather Post, which her executors could not get rid of; the Library of Congress, originally the library of Thomas Jefferson; the Museum of the Building Arts; the Museum of Modern Art of Latin America; the Goddard Visitor Center; the National Archives, which may well include Rita Jenrette's memoirs, or should; the National Historical Wax Museum; the Octagon House, the post-War of 1812 White House; and the Woodlawn Plantation, which shows how Washington's black population lived before emancipation.

Thanks to the generosity of the Mellons and the genius of J. Carter Brown, its director, the National Gallery is the crowning jewel of Washington culture, a far cry from the old days when, according to Edgar Applewhite, arts fancier and author of *Washington Itself*, the "whole function was polite custodianship." The old days were not so good. The Corcoran, founded long before New York's Metropolitan or anything in Boston, suffered from arrested development in part because it kept its endowment in the stuffy conservative hands of the Riggs Bank. The joke was that, between 1901 and 1950, the endowment grew from $1 million to $1 million. According to Applewhite, the Corcoran was also quite skittish about modern art, and refused to show much of it until a group of free spirits formed the Washington Gallery of Modern Art, which proved that people would actually come to see the stuff. The Corcoran subsequently took the Modern Art gallery back under its wing, and got with it.

Being No. 2 in the arts isn't all that bad.

Ten years ago, there was New York and there was everyplace else. Now there's New York, then Washington, and everyplace else. And New York is getting a little nervous. People are beginning to talk about a rivalry, asking whether Washington might some day overtake the Big Apple. It's nonsense, of course, but the fact that there is such talk is extraordinary. Good grief, the *New York Times* has printed two very long articles on the subject.

In fact, New York has become so nervous that it's begun to sneer, a sure sign of creeping fear. Washington has art, but no artists, critics say. Where are its opera, its writers, its Greenwich Village? Said sniffling New York art critic Robert Hughes of Washington's Hirshhorn Museum: "It looks like the setting of *The Guns of Navarone* without the guns."

Washington is occasional host to visiting opera companies, but has none of its own in a league with the Met. First-class opera companies are grotesquely expensive to maintain and the city simply can't afford it. "The costs are astronomic," says Kennedy Center's Roger Stevens. "It's not in the cards."

Except for a few good novelists like Herman Wouk and resident journalists and political types who turn out occasional books, Washington hasn't much of a literary community, and the only publishing company of real consequence is the government.

It has no ballet company worthy of international competition. It has some fine theaters, but no great pool of resident acting talent and no avant garde or off-Broadway theater to cultivate promising players and playwrights. Its promising young musicians go to school at Juilliard, in New York. They seldom come back, except on tour.

The National Gallery is a first-rank museum and the Corcoran, Hirshhorn, and Freer, among others, are very, very good. But Washington is shamefully miserly when it comes to supporting local artists. As the saying goes, Washington snobs would rather buy their paintings on 57th Street than 7th.

And if architecture is art, Washington is a disaster.

Yet, it makes Chicago, Los Angeles, Boston, Philadelphia, San Francisco, and all the others look like cultural tank towns. Occasionally, it makes New York look like a tank town, as when La Scala came to the United States in 1976, played to boffo crowds at the Kennedy Center, and skipped New York entirely. Washington is, after all, the nation's capital. If, like Joe Hirshhorn, you give your collection to a Washington museum or to the government, you are giving it to the nation, and the American people. It beats giving it just to the people of Toledo or Pittsburgh.

Washington, happily, hasn't much in the way of local high society, which in too many locales has been to the arts what constipation is to the digestive system. Chicago is typical in that rich people give to the arts largely to get on the boards to improve their social status and donate their collections largely for the tax deduction. In Washington, the boards are mostly appointed by the President and the Congress. The society types, such as there are, are mingled with political types and people genuinely devoted to the arts.

The board of the Kennedy Center, for example, includes socialites

Frank Ikard, Mrs. Edward Breathitt, Tricia Nixon Cox, Mrs. J. Willard Marriott, Mrs. Donna Stone Pesch, Mrs. Jean Kennedy Smith, and Mrs. Jack Wrather. It also has Senator Charles Percy, Mrs. Howard Baker, Melvin Laird, Ron Nessen, Senator Edward Kennedy, and Mayor Marion Barry. But it also has S. Dillon Ripley, lord protector of all Smithsonia; Daniel Boorstin, librarian of Congress; J. Carter Brown, National Gallery director and chairman of the government's Fine Arts Commission; and William Rumsey, director of the District's Department of Recreation.

This "mixed economy," as Applewhite calls it, prevents the capital's arts scene from becoming "just another hymn to capitalism." It also provides what many society types are notoriously chary with: money. The federal government picks up three-quarters of the Kennedy Center's maintenance and utility costs. Lincoln Center gets only 8 percent of its revenues from government subsidies.

As the nation's capital, Washington is an obligatory stop for touring companies and exhibits from abroad, often the first stop and sometimes an exclusive one. Not only La Scala but the Vienna Opera came to Washington without stopping in New York. So did the extraordinary Chinese Exhibition of archeological relics in 1975. And the foreign governments usually pick up the tab: $1.3 million for La Scala, $1 million for the Comedie Française, and $1.6 million for the Vienna Opera.

Washington benefits from its proximity to New York. When New York is booked up, as often occurs, shows go to Washington instead. And zillions of shows start in Washington. Some, like *Charlie and Algernon*, S.R.O. in D.C. but blasted by the New York critics, shouldn't. But others, like the immensely successful revival of *Oklahoma*, Arthur Kopit's brilliant *Wings*, and a number of Tom Stoppard's works, made it big in the Big Apple only after conquering Washington.

Washington also comes into a lot of foreign largess. The Japanese shelled out $3 million to finish the Kennedy Center's Terrace Theater as a Bicentennial gift. Sweden chipped in with 18 crystal chandeliers in the Grand Foyer. Finland contributed the china for the restaurants.

As the *New York Times* noted, Washington does best as a "packager of culture," a producer of theme shows, a creator of festivals. Its 1975 Haydn Festival had 72 events, including all 12 of his masses. "Paris: A Romantic Epoch" in 1979 was a two-week extravaganza that involved the Kennedy Center, the National Gallery, and the Library of Congress. J. Carter Brown's brilliant Rodin exhibition in the National Gallery's new I. M. Pei East Wing in 1981 was the most impressive and successful exhibit of the great sculptor's works in the history of the United States.

Washington's Kennedy Center, which celebrated its tenth anniversary in 1981 and which in many ways is the superior of Lincoln Center, isn't as pretty as Lincoln Center. Designed by Edward Durell Stone, the marble-mad Albert Speer of American architecture, the Kennedy is outsized to the point of, well, as one of its biggest champions, composer-conductor Leonard Bernstein, put it: "I don't think it's so ugly to look at. I take exception to that. I've grown accustomed to it." Its roof perennially leaks. It adjoins the Potomac in one of the most scenic and least convenient locations in the city. It does not have eight resident performing companies.

But at times it seems it has all the world's performing companies. One recent season saw the Kennedy Center host to the orchestras of Boston, Philadelphia, Pittsburgh, Cleveland, Detroit, San Francisco, Buffalo, and New York. The orchestras of London, Prague, Leipzig, and Toulouse came, too. There were present, of course, La Scala and the Vienna Opera, and also Moscow's Bolshoi Opera, the Paris Opera, and the Deutsche Oper of Berlin.

The Kennedy also has standards. New York producers and critics have railed at the Ken Cen's Roger Stevens for his arbitrary rejection of such hot Broadway properties as Neil Simon's *California Suite*. In fact, Neil Simon has never had a play produced at the Kennedy. Stevens said only of *California Suite* that it wasn't a good play. As czar of the Ken Cen, he is Washington's most effective critic.

If people don't like the Ken Cen, they can always go downtown to the National Theater, which has been a going concern since 1835 and is no longer under the thumb of Stevens. Consequently, it puts on a lot of Neil Simon stuff. Also, hot properties like *A Chorus Line*, *Ain't Misbehaving*, and even Liv Ullman's *Anna Christie*.

The Warner, another theater put into the big time as an alternative to the Ken Cen, plays hot properties, too. Ford's Theater, host to the unfortunate scene in 1865, is a wonderfully cozy place that is host to some marvelous one-man shows, experimental stuff, and such frolics as "A Christmas Carol" done as a musical. The Folger provides meticulous Shakespeare; the Arena puts on Shakespeare, Shaw, Edward Albee, and Tom Lehrer. It also has presented seemingly forever, thank heavens, a marvelous one-man show called "Banjo Dancing," of which there certainly is no other.

Washington has a great many people in the arts of whom there are no others. Alice Denney, described as grande dame, enfante terrible, maverick, and all sorts of other things, used to raise some really wonderful hell with the Washington arts establishment in the 1960s and 1970s, staging, among other things, the city's first avant-garde art festival in 1966. "Alice put Washington arts people on roller skates," said one admirer.

Washington may not have produced a sculptor equal to the Rodin works it so marvelously exhibited, but it does have people like Phillip Ratner, whose sculpture goes for $5,000 and up and has been featured in one-man shows in the National Academy of Sciences, among other places. His Samson has hair you'd love to cut. Ratner did study at New York's Pratt Institute, the visual arts' version of Juilliard, but he came back to the city of his birth.

Washingtonian Judy Mussoff's acid-colored lonely faces have spell-bound every collector who's looked at them, including Joe Hirshhorn, who went to a showing of hers at Gallery K and snapped up three of her paintings. She's only 27.

Washington has Manny Azenberg, a onetime Madison Square Garden promoter, flack, and David Merrick assistant who took the National Theater away from "pro-British" Roger Stevens and took the capital by storm with such hits as *Children of a Lesser God* and Neil Simon's *They're Playing Our Song*.

Washington has the Wolf Trap Opera Training Program, which has not produced a first-class opera company but some good singers. It has the New Playwrights Theater, which has never been darkened for want of theatergoers but which occasionally gets shut down by city inspectors.

Thank Heavens, Washington has the Commission of Fine Arts, which kept Richard Nixon from recreating the Tivoli Gardens on the Capitol Mall and stopped a hospital project planned by the Veterans Administration for Arlington Cemetery. J. Carter Brown, who ought to be granted a $100,000 pension for life by a grateful capital, heads the outfit.

Washington has had a few people around with big bucks who made a point of throwing some of them culture's way. The late Morris Cafritz's foundation has dropped millions into the local arts till, Cafritz having worked at odd local jobs as a poor boy in Georgetown. Wolf Trap would have been impossible without Mrs. Jouett Shouse; the National Symphony of today was made possible largely by the late Marjorie Merriweather Post; and the Arena Stage would have been nothing without super generous David Lloyd Kreeger.

Even with such generosity and the munificent influence of government, Washington arts have a tough time. Soloist fees these days range up to $40,000. In 1981, the National Symphony found itself needing $11 million in permanent endowments and $2.5 million just to get through the year, faced as it was with a $1.8 million deficit. The Washington Opera was putting on cheapo, reduced-scale productions in the Ken Cen's little 513-seat Terrace Theater. Livingston Biddle's National Endowment for the Arts, the fairy godmother of much of American artistic creativity and sometimes known as the National

Bureaucracy for the Arts, was hit with Reaganite budget cuts of about half its federal funding.

The arts, the Reaganites decided, were something for rich people in the private sector to support, especially since the Endowment had been throwing around sums like $3,000 to pay for projects like the map of Washington some local artist sandblasted onto a dull brick wall on 14th Street.

It was something less than an immortal work. The air in Washington being what it is, the map quickly began fading into the brickwork again.

The reputations of the people on the following list will be quite a bit longer lasting.

THE TOP TEN MUSEUM AND ARTS FIGURES IN WASHINGTON
1. S. Dillon Ripley

Since it was created by Act of Congress in 1846, the Smithsonian has had only 8 secretaries. In the same period, the United States has had 28 Presidents.

The eighth and mightiest secretary, Dillon Ripley, is descended from a nineteenth-century railroad robber baron who was present at the 1869 joining of the Union Pacific and Central Pacific to form the nation's first transcontinental line (he has the spike on his desk). Ripley, whose Connecticut family eventually became so unquestionably eastern establishment it didn't matter if it had any money (which is fortunate, because his father didn't really), is now master of an empire that far transcends the wildest fantasies of any nouveau riche Reaganite, not to speak of his robber baron great-grandfather. Not bad for someone who might well have ended up just another bird-watcher.

The "Sun King," as he is sometimes referred to, was born in New York City in 1913. He boarded and prepped at the best schools in New England as a child, travelled to Europe and lived in India, went to Yale and Columbia, and sailed 30,000 miles around the South Pacific and the world—all before he was 25. Returning to Yale as an assistant professor, he embarked on what was almost a lifelong career as ornithologist and zoologist. He remained at Yale with only brief time-outs as curator of birds for the Smithsonian, and as spook for the Office of Strategic Services in World War II, later adding on the duties of ornithologist at the Peabody Museum of Natural History.

When the Smithsonian started searching for a new secretary in 1963, it remembered Dillon for his exemplary wartime service as bird curator, thinking his brilliance, drive, cleverness, and charm might be just the ticket. It proved much more than just the ticket. When he arrived, the Smithsonian had just seven museums, plus the Museum of History and Technology (now Museum of American History), which was nearing completion. By 1976, Ripley had added seven more, was goading his art collectors to greater and greater triumphs, and was plunging the Smithsonian into extraordinarily successful commercial ventures, such as its highly popular magazine. He sent forth more expeditions than Ferdinand and Isabella, established the wildlife park in the Blue Ridge, and thrust the Institution headlong into the field of environmental and ecological survival.

A masterful politician who would have survived in the court of the Byzantines, Ripley was the cleverest part of the plot that parted a Jewish immigrant, self-made millionaire Joe Hirshhorn from his superb modern art and sculpture collection—creating the Hirshhorn Museum on the site of the Armed Forces Medical Museum (it held Civil War General Dan Sickles' leg and Mussolini's brain) on the Mall. More amazingly, he convinced Congress to go along with the scheme, which was highly controversial at the time.

A tall, egghead-bald, erudite, and frankly arrogant fellow, his greatest success was nevertheless bringing the Smithsonian closer to the American people, adding loud bells and whistles to railroad exhibits, instituting English double-decker museum-to-museum shuttle buses, making exhibits of American sports heroes, and in every case explaining everything—simply, effectively, and very intelligently. Before him, many if not most of the exhibits were little more than piles of things, arranged largely for the convenience of scholars. He got dubbed "P. T. Barnum" by sneering academics for his train bells and the like, but he saw the need in egalitarian America for something more interesting than the stuffy likes of the British Museum.

Using the Smithsonian's inspiring real estate as the setting for all manner of dinners, parties, receptions, and grand balls, Ripley also ingratiated himself with Washington's hoity-toity social set, even if it is at least two cuts beneath his own.

Occupying a regal suite of offices in The Castle, filled with enough rare objects to constitute a museum collection in their own right, and stocked with the finest of wines, Dillon is eccentric enough to have become lost one day in his Museum of Natural History just across the Mall and fun-loving enough to have installed the public merry-go-round just across the street, but he's no one to slap on the back.

It should always be remembered that when the Pope visited Washington in 1979, he had an audience with S. Dillon Ripley.

2. J. Carter Brown

The National Gallery is a great museum because of two men: Andrew Mellon and J. Carter Brown.

Museums often win their reputations with the contribution of a single great collection. Bertha Palmer's great haul of Impressionists made the Chicago Art Institute. Nelson Rockefeller's house was one of the great museums in the world, and the Museum of Modern Art owes him much. Andrew Mellon's Rembrandts, Vermeers, Raphaels, Valesquezes, and Goyas struck Franklin D. Roosevelt as the makings of a terrific fine arts museum for the then rather culturally backward Federal City. There's a story, perhaps apocryphal, that Mellon was in some trouble with the IRS before he donated his collection to the Smithsonian, and afterwards, not. But who would believe that?

In any event, Mellon was a first-rate act in one regard. Despite the trend in philanthropy that has seen donors' names put on plaques affixed to hospital doors and window frames, Mellon kept his name off the museum his collection made possible so as not to deter other rich collectors from handing over some of their goodies. The same cannot be said for Mellon's chief rival in the Washington great art collection game, Joe Hirshhorn. In 1938, when the Congress voted to create a National Gallery of Art to house Mellon's stuff, it also authorized the President to set some space aside on the Mall for another museum if needed. By the time of Lyndon Johnson's presidency, it was decided Washington needed its first grand collection of modern art. Hirshhorn, a onetime penniless immigrant turned uranium millionaire who owned one of the finest collections of contemporary art in the country, seemed just the man. Queen Elizabeth and Nelson Rockefeller, who wanted his stuff for their own bailiwicks, thought so, too, but got out-charmed by the patrician Dillon Ripley and the down-home LBJ. Charmed he may have been, but Hirshhorn held out for the following: a $15 million museum building on the Mall, government support for its staffing and maintenance, a big say in appointing the board. And his name on the building. Many in Congress thought that terrible form, but LBJ was persuasive, and prevailed.

A bureau of the Smithsonian that is run as a separate, independent, fiefdom, the National Gallery has become a major rival of the Hirshhorn's in the field of modern art, especially since the construction of the I. M. Pei East Wing, specializing in twentieth century art. Carter Brown, who has placed great emphasis on contemporary pieces, used the East Wing for his greatest coup—his 1981 "Rodin Rediscovered."

Brown, who first suggested the Rodin exhibit to his board in 1969, worked for more than a decade to assemble through loans and whatnot a 400-piece collection of Rodin's best, pulling off what was probably Washington's best cultural show—with attendance figures to match. The Hirshhorn, which had balked at lending Brown Rodin's "Burghers of Calais," ultimately relented.

Born in Providence, Rhode Island, Brown is the quintessential careerist. Graduating summa cum laude from Harvard in 1956, he went on to study with Bernard Berenson in Florence and acquire a number of other superlative academic credentials from Munich University, the Ecole du Louvre in Paris, and NYU (NYU?). He joined the National Gallery as assistant to the director in 1961, became assistant director in 1964, deputy director in 1968, and director in 1969. If there is a logical heir to the "Sun King," it is this mastermind of masterpieces.

He is also a high pedigreed aristocrat. As with Nelson Rockefeller, rich American arts figures tend to come from families who made their pile in the late nineteenth century. Brown's ancestors were filthy rich in Colonial days. The Ivy League's Brown University is named for one of them. The John Carter Brown Library had similar origins.

A handsome devil, Brown is more aristocratic looking than the Duke of Windsor ever was, and he has a wife to match. The elegant Pamela Brown is considered one of the most beautiful women in Washington.

3. Roger Stevens

As theatrical producers go, the awesomely powerful Roger Stevens is no Minsky. Great heavens, the man sneers at Neil Simon. He doesn't sneer at Leonard Bernstein, who more or less worships Stevens, absolute master of the Kennedy Center since it opened in 1971.

Bernstein's celebrated "Mass" was to be the first orchestral work performed in the Ken Cen, but as opening date approached, completion did not. Bernstein was having composer's block. Stevens had suffered a heart attack just then and was recovering in an intensive care unit. Bernstein visited him, asking: "Is there anything I can do for you?" "The best thing you can do for me is to finish the 'Mass,'" Stevens said. "I went home and I finished it, by God," said Bernstein, whose "Mass" played the Kennedy again on its tenth anniversary.

To appreciate Stevens' power, imagine what New York would be like if one man decided what one-half of its plays, concerts, operas, and ballets would be at any given time. If the one man were Stevens, it wouldn't be at all bad. His autocratic style and refusal to countenance the works of the world's most successful living playwright sparked a brief but noisy rebellion against him in the Congress. Senators Bill Bradley of New Jersey and Alan Simpson of Wyoming, among others, complained that the Kennedy Center had become "an exclusive artistic club" that "consistently refused" to play the works of Simon, David Mamet, David Rabe, and other worthies. Charging

Stevens with the crimes of being "discriminatory and provincial," and worse, favoring European playwrights over American ones, they demanded a congressional hearing into Ken Cen management. New York Senator Daniel Patrick Moynihan, chairman of the Public Works Committee, talked them into an informal meeting in his office instead, and the controversy eventually blew over. "I do not intend to involve the Congress in making or second-guessing artistic judgments," Moynihan wrote Stevens, who seemed hardly fazed by the matter. Said the American Film Institute's George Stevens on a later occasion: "Roger Stevens has no interest in the democratic process."

Born in Detroit in 1910, Stevens was a Choate, University of Michigan, and Amherst man. As a real estate broker involved in all sorts of profitable hotel deals, Stevens made a tidy fortune, even in the Depression. But he made his mark as the producer or coproducer of more than 200 Broadway shows, including *West Side Story*, *Cat on a Hot Tin Roof*, *Bus Stop*, *Tea and Sympathy*, *Sabrina Fair*, and *A Man for All Seasons*.

Made chairman of the Ken Cen board back in the planning days of 1961, when it was just a gleam in then President John F. Kennedy's eye, Stevens also served as assistant to the President on the arts, chairman of the National Council on the Arts, chairman of the National Endowment for the Arts, president of the National Opera, chairman of the American Film Institute, chairman of the National Book Award committee, and, in 1956, chairman of the finance committee of the Democratic National Committee.

He is now also a trustee of the American Shakespeare Theater, and a director of the Metropolitan Opera Association, of Wolf Trap, of the Folger Library, of the Circle in the Square Theater, etc., etc., etc. He's been awarded enough foreign arts medals to make it impossible to see he's wearing white tie when he's wearing white tie.

His wife, Christine, another remarkable person, is the capital's leading defender of wildlife causes, which in Ronald Reagan's Washington is a job as tough as being Neil Simon's agent in Roger Stevens' Washington.

4. *Amanda McKerrow*

All right, Amanda McKerrow is not as good as New York's Cynthia Gregory—yet. But the 18-year-old Rockville, Maryland, dancer may just possibly be the second-best ballerina in the country, and certainly the best and most famous living artist Washington has produced.

The blonde, five-foot-four, 92-pound sparrow was one of 13 Americans in a field of 150 dancers from 17 countries competing in the contest, considered the world championship of dancing, for a prize that goes to Soviet dancers with amazing regularity. Despite the brilliance of her performances for *Sleeping Beauty* and *Les Sylphides*,

Amanda was sure the 1981 first place would go to a Russian yet again. It did, to ballerina Natalia Arkhipova, but it also went to Amanda. A member of the Washington Ballet for only a year before the Russian competition, Amanda drew eight curtain calls from the Soviets. Her feat put Washington arts on the map as nothing any of its culture barons have done has. Because of it, Amanda will be a very old woman before anyone knocks her off this list.

Rather single-minded in her approach to ballet, she has been dancing seriously since the age of seven and even dropped out of high school to pursue her career, attaining her diploma through correspondence courses. She said she had wanted to dance at the Bolshoi since she was seven—hardly an ambition to endear her to the Reagan set, but so what?

One of the Washington Ballet's 20 regular and 6 apprentice dancers who work mostly at the Lisner Auditorium of George Washington University, Amanda says she plans to stay in town, though there will surely be attempts to lure her to the Big Apple. If she does leave, Washingtonians won't like it, but they'll understand.

5. Roger G. Kennedy

The National Gallery of Art is the Smithsonian's most prestigious museum and the National Air and Space Museum the most popular, but its most interesting and (arguably) its best is the Museum of American History. Roger Kennedy, a Minnesota-born Yalie who came to the Smithsonian after careers in television, government, and with the Ford Foundation, has been its much-admired director since 1979.

Formerly the Museum of History and Technology, the massive structure at 14th Street and Constitution Avenue is at once the most fascinating and functional of Washington's museums. Objects are not merely put on display but made to work. The Tower of London stacks its ancient arms in great racks and cases. So does Kennedy's museum, but there are working, illuminated, moving diagrams, showing how matchlock, wheel-lock, and flintlock firearms actually sent bullets spinning into space. The "Nation of Nations" exhibit, which eloquently and delightfully makes the point that all of us including Indians are immigrants, has a continuous movie roll showing, among many others, a young Frederick Austerlitz (Fred Astaire) dancing. It also has the "Colored Only" door sign from a Jim Crow–Deep South washroom. The maritime exhibit has a reconstructed sailor's tattoo parlor. The nineteenth century one-room schoolhouse in the "Everyday Life in the American Past" exhibit has an indentation in its glass panel that allows museum visitors to sit down at a couple of the desks and look up at the blackboard.

Roger Kennedy has the mind and imagination to equal such a place. Born in St. Paul in 1926, he emerged from Yale and the University of Minnesota with a law degree, served as a Justice Department attorney, and then became a Washington correspondent for NBC News. He went on to become a muckity-muck in the Department of Labor, a bank executive, and vice-president of the Ford Foundation. He also sings a first-rate baritone, as he occasionally does at museum do's.

A bluff, cheery fellow with a voice to command the attention of the exalted ones across the Mall in The Castle, this former investment banker is the man who thought up the idea of putting hotels on top of Broadway theaters to keep the legitimate stage financially viable. He's always thinking of something, whether it's making wine available in the staff dining room, or creating exhibits to make Henry Ford's first American production line and Harriet Beecher Stowe's *Uncle Tom's Cabin* come alive. Thanks to Kennedy, the John Bull, America's first railroad locomotive, spent its 150th birthday pulling an 1836 passenger car up and down the Chessie tracks along the Potomac.

6. Kay Shouse

Now well into her 80s, Catherine Filene Shouse is no longer chairman of the executive committee of the Wolf Trap Foundation. But she continues as chairman of the program committee and, painful arthritis or no, she still pretty much runs the place. As well she should.

A Democratic Party activist who came with her first husband, Alvin Dodd, to Washington in the 1920s, she lost him to divorce and most of her wealthy father's money to the stock market crash. She held onto enough to buy, in 1930, a Virginia country estate for $5,200. Now worth several million, Wolf Trap belongs to the nation, having been given to the Interior Department by Mrs. Shouse in 1966 for use as a national park for the performing arts. She became Mrs. Shouse in 1932, marrying Jouett Shouse, a Kentucky newspaperman, lawyer, congressman, and ultimately assistant secretary of the Treasury. And, of course, a Democrat. In fact, a national party leader.

The best outdoor/indoor country concert hall and theater of its kind, Wolf Trap has been run by Mrs. Shouse with, er, highly individualistic style, having had more than eight executive directors since it opened in 1971. But her feistiness has kept the federal bureaucracy at arm's length from it. There would never have been a Wolf Trap without her, and there wouldn't be the Wolf Trap there now if it weren't for her. If she hasn't been the most pleasant of persons, she has been a very successful Washingtonian.

7. *Charlton Heston*

The National Endowment for the Arts has never kept the federal bureaucracy at arm's length. It is one. Founded in 1965, the Endowment's first budget was only $8.5 million, but it kept increasing at a rate of sometimes 50 percent a year after that. In his first year in office, Richard Nixon, who may someday be rightly recognized as the country's most liberal President since Roosevelt, doubled the Endowment budget, and then doubled it again the following year. It reached $124.5 million in 1978 and $156 million in 1980, all to be lavished on the arts, keeping them alive come what may.

Some of the arts it got lavished on should have been starved to death. A grant of $500 funded a poem that consisted entirely of the word "LIGHGHT." Federal money supported Erica Jong in some of her more profane efforts, and a $6,000 grant produced a "space sculpture" that amounted to the sculptor dropping colored streamers from an airplane. In January, it helped bankroll a Washington erotic arts show that also accepted contributions from the Pleasure Chest, a store selling leather items, electric vibrators, and such like. When told this, NEA spokeswoman Kathy Christie said: "Oh brother."

However, the Endowment has supported some more serious endeavors—sending the Boston Symphony to China was typical—and may be credited with cultivating a full spectrum of artistic activities in all the many tank towns of America. Through its matching grant activities, it brings as much as $1 billion a year to the arts from private contributors, Ronald Reagan's favorite kind.

Were it still the palmy days that preceded Reaganism, the Endowment's former chairman Livingston Biddle would be an automatic inclusion on this list. One of those snooty Philadelphia Biddles, St. George's, Princeton, and all that, he was once an aide to the equally superior Senator Claiborne Pell. Biddle actually lobbied for the Endowment chairman's job as one befitting an actual Biddle.

He got it in 1977, but the Endowment's low esteem (and budget) in the Reagan administration deflated Biddle's status significantly.

The real power in this neck of Washington's arts woods is a Malibu man, actor Charlton Heston, appointed by Reagan to lead the White House Task Force on the Arts and Humanities, a 32-member panel that has also been described as the White House Task Force Against the Arts and Humanities. As *Dossier* magazine put it, the mission of the Task Force was to find ways "to do more with less," but, despite Heston's best intentions, it mostly found out only how to do less with less, but that at least put an end to the colored streamers dropped from airplanes.

Less hardly bothers Reagan; his idea of fine art is "Little House on the Prairie."

Born in Evanston, Illinois, in 1924, Charlton (his real name) was a TV actor himself, after having apprenticed as a stage actor in the 1940s and before becoming a movie star in the 1950s. A student at Northwestern University until he left to join the Army Air Corps in World War II, Heston has had bureaucratic experience as a member of the National Council on the Arts, trustee of the Los Angeles Center Theater, and chairman of the American Film Institute. Like Reagan, he is a past president of the Screen Actors Guild, the only union whose pickets wear Guccis.

Heston has played some godlike roles before, but nothing quite so powerful—as far as the arts are concerned—as this one.

8. Noel Hinners

Much of the credit for making the National Air and Space Museum the most popular in the world goes to Michael Collins, the Apollo II astronaut who served as its director from 1971 to 1978 and oversaw its establishment in its wondrous new building on the Mall in 1976. Never before has so much been seen by so many in an enclosed space. And who but former Air Force officer Collins would have liked the idea of displaying a World War II Spad upside down?

The Collins tradition has been continued and improved upon by his successor, Dr. Noel Hinners, who took over in 1979, adding such touches as exhibits honoring pioneer women aviators, and expanded space technology exhibits.

A product of Rutgers, the California Institute of Technology, and Princeton University, Hinners is a space man, having served as head of lunar exploration for Bellcomm before joining the National Aeronautics and Space Administration. He became NASA's associate administrator for space science in 1974, and was one of those responsible for thinking up new things for astronauts to do once they got to the moon. He received NASA's Distinguished Service Medal in 1977, 1979, and 1981.

9. Harold Pfister

Considering that it usually exhibits only pictures, the National Portrait Gallery has acquired a remarkable following in Washington as one of the most intelligent and entertaining museums in town.

The core of its collection is its treasure of early American drawings and daguerreotypes (including one of Dolley Madison) and its hall of presidential portraits, including Norman Rockwell's mealy-mouthed Richard Nixon. Its genius, though, shows up particularly in its temporary exhibitions. "Return to Albion" depicted and chronicled Americans returning to mother England, including the genius painter and inventor Samuel F. B. Morse, the pretentious Henry James, and the social climbing Chips Channon of Chicago, bosom buddy of Edward VIII. "Scott and Zelda" brought the Fitzgeralds back to life, showing off such artifacts as Scott's flask and Zelda's amateurish, tormented paintings. The Henry Clay exhibit featured a recording of his old presidential campaign songs.

Maurice Sadik, who took over the Portrait Gallery shortly after it opened by Act of Congress in the old Patent Office Building in 1968, resigned in 1981 to become a consultant to collectors.

The Smithsonian undertook a months-long, nationwide search for a worthy successor, but there was always an excellent choice right under Dillon Ripley's nose—Harold Pfister, Sadik's extremely bright right-hand man. Born in Evanston, Illinois, in 1947, Pfister graduated magna cum laude in fine arts from Harvard, and quickly made a reputation for himself as an expert in early American culture. After serving as the Portrait Gallery's head of program management, he became assistant director in 1980.

10. Elizabeth Taylor Warner

The *Washington Post* recently ran a special Sunday "Show" section boasting of the cultural competition Washington was giving New York but devoted in large part to whining about how local performers still feel they have to move to the Big Apple to be successful. That's certainly not true of one local performer.

Though now a maid of more than 50 summers, Elizabeth Taylor Warner remains one of the most popular and preeminent theatrical personalities in the country. Though her long-lasting superstardom is based on a talent that occasionally gets stretched a little too thin, her name can still sell out a theater in 24 hours (if not always a movie theater).

Yet the legendary Liz chose to dwell here among the rubes of the Potomac, eschewing the big-time glitter and glamour of Hollywood, Manhattan, London, and other show-biz centers she used to favor. And, from time to time, she'll even clamber onto the local boards and perform, selling out the Kennedy Center or Wolf Trap in a lot less than 24 hours. Her performances at local Republican dinners with husband Senator John Warner rival anything she's done on stage or screen.

She would be a major presence wherever she might decide to roost, but she's indisputably the show-biz queen of Washington, even though she and John are separated and she spends much of her time in Los Angeles and New York. With her new repertoire company, she'll remain a regular fixture in the capital. Liz is nothing if not loyal.

Sports

WASHINGTON never really has been a big-league town.
True, it has had a few champions over the years, but for the most part, the place of the capital in the national sports picture was summed up in the crushing verdict passed long ago upon the late baseball Senators: "Washington . . . first in war, first in peace, last in the American League."

Alas, the Senators. Twice born to represent the national capital in what is supposed to be the national pastime, the local baseball team was twice abducted by proprietors salivating at the prospect of greener outfields and perpetual motion turnstiles in, of all places, Bloomington, Minnesota, and Arlington, Texas.

Usually, when a team is in trouble, the owner fires the manager. But Calvin Griffith, inheritor of the original Senators, and Bob Short, purchaser of an expansion club formed to replace them, fired the town.

Griffith, miffed because he couldn't control the hot dog and beer concessions in the city's new stadium (and, as he admitted years later, unwilling to stay in a town with a black majority), shipped the team that had been a charter member of the American League to Minnesota, where under the name of the Twins it shortly won a pennant with the players who had developed their skills in Washington. In this, Calvin demonstrated that sentiment never was a Griffith family trait—his step-father, after all, once traded his own son-in-law to the Boston Red Sox.

Short, a Minneapolis trucking magnate and political amateur who some said bought the Senators as a favor to Hubert Humphrey, dumped the team like a frame-sprung rig a few years after taking it to Texas. On the Senators' last night in Washington, the customers hanged Short in effigy and raised such general hell that the game had to be forfeited.

In fairness to the two emigré owners, it should be said that attendance before they left was not good. In fairness to the fans, it must be said that neither were the teams.

282

Part of that, at least for the Griffith-owned teams, had to do with a personnel policy that resembled nothing so much as the nation's Asian foreign policy in the 1950s and 1960s. The United States took the position during that time that there was no such thing as Communist China; the Senators operated on the apparent premise that there were no American blacks who could play baseball.

The Senators hired a number of Hispanic players during that period and some of them were black. But as the southernmost major league franchise in the East, the Senators appeared to be more concerned about the sensibilities of the Virginia and Carolina audiences who were part of their broadcasting market than they were about the quality of the team.

Washington's football Redskins went through much the same charade during that period, once signing a Hawaiian player and claiming to have broken the color barrier. But until the Kennedy administration made it clear to owner George Preston Marshall that a lily-white team was not going to play in a stadium built with public funds, the Redskins were exactly that, and *Washington Post* sports writer Shirley Povich was able to report each fall that Cleveland's Jim Brown or some other black opponent had "integrated Washington's goal line . . . again."

In the decade that followed the departure of Short's Senators, organized baseball repeatedly promised Washington a new team, but that proved to be as illusory as the balanced federal budget pledged by every new President.

The last time it looked as if Washington might get a team was in 1979, when Edward Bennett Williams bought the Baltimore Orioles. But Baltimore, suspicious of the big lawyer from Washington, extracted a promise that Williams would not move the team if Baltimore fans supported the team. They did and he didn't.

So Washington baseball fans commute 40 miles to Baltimore—which of course helps keep the Orioles there—and spend their time mooning about Senator greats of the past—the World Series winners of 1925, the legendary fastballer Walter Johnson, home-run sluggers Harmon Killebrew and Frank Howard, and batting champions Goose Goslin and Mickey Vernon. A threadbare legacy at best.

Washington football fans still have a team and a fresher memory of great days. Under Marshall and behind the running, passing, and kicking of Slinging Sammy Baugh, the Redskins won five division titles and two National Football League championships in 1937 and 1942.

They also suffered the worst embarrassment in the history of the game when in 1940 they met the Chicago Bears for the title. The

Bears picked that game to unveil a new offense, something called the T-formation, and humiliated the Redskins, 73 to 0.

Better days came again when Williams, a minority stockholder, took over operating control of the team in the 1970s, hiring Vince Lombardi to coach and, after Lombardi's death, the controversial George Allen. Allen, proclaiming "The future is now," traded away a generation of draft choices to get proven players and propelled the Redskins into a series of play-offs and the 1973 Super Bowl. Miami beat them, 14-7.

Williams made Allen—about as beloved in some Washington circles as Nixon—general manager as well as coach and came to regret it.

"I gave him an unlimited expense account and he exceeded it," Williams said before he fired Allen in 1977 after a long and nasty contract dispute. When Allen left to second-guess other coaches from his press box seat as a CBS television commentator, his creaking "Over The Hill Gang" was dismantled, partly by his successors and partly by opposition teams.

But a losing Washington football team is not the same kind of bad news at the gate as a turkey would be in most other sports. Redskin games are as much social occasions as sporting events, and Robert F. Kennedy Stadium's 55,000 seats have been sold out to season ticket holders for a decade. One reason is that lobbyists and big law firms often hold blocks of seats, using them to keep out-of-town bosses and clients happy.

Redskin games can be a celebrity show. Most Presidents make at least one home game; some government big-shots always are in the stands, and there is always the chance of spotting a celebrity like Art Buchwald, munching a hot dog in Ethel Kennedy's box seats.

This is not a recent phenomenon. Reporters covering the Redskins on December 7, 1941, were alerted that something momentous was happening when the public address announcer began paging dozens of generals and admirals to call their offices.

Washington's entries in professional basketball and hockey are the creations of Abe Pollin, who decided to become a sports mogul after building his family's plumbing firm into a successful construction company. Pollin bought his basketball team in Baltimore (one more reason that town is uneasy about Williams) and then built an arena for it and the major league hockey team he started in the Maryland suburbs of Washington. Interestingly, the Capital Centre was erected in the area's blackest suburban area, which, along with Pollin's own record, washes out any suggestion of racism.

The basketball Bullets had one championship year in Washington, but age also caught up with them as the likes of Wes Unseld, Elvin Hayes, and Phil Chenier were overshadowed by the Julius Ervings, Larry Birds, and Magic Johnsons of the new generation.

Pollin's hockey team, the Capitals, skated around in aimless circles for seven years before they could beat Montreal, but they recently came within a whisker of making the National Hockey League play-offs, and that may keep hope alive at Cap Centre.

The city also has had several professional soccer teams in recent years, including one or two that have been able to give the New York Cosmos—the class of American soccer—a run. But despite Washington's multisplendored ethnic mix, it has never made soccer a paying sport.

Actually, it is possible to see good soccer free in Washington, as well as cricket, polo, and rugby. With so many embassies there, the Sunday stroller in the parks along the Potomac River can often watch amateur teams in all those sports playing for the fun of it.

The University of Maryland, just to the north of Washington in College Park, has in the past given the capital its best in collegiate sports, especially basketball but also including lacrosse. More recently, Georgetown University has built up its basketball image under former professional John Thompson. Georgetown could become the DePaul of the 1980s with Thompson's recruitment of some of the most widely sought high school players in the East.

The list of Washington's movers and shakers in sports is not long.

THE TOP WASHINGTON SPORTS FIGURES

1. Abe Pollin

Pollin, 54, has been in Washington since he was 8 and lived a few blocks from Griffith Stadium. He was hot for the Senators and says he went to the first Redskin game in Washington in 1937. He is a sports fan who was able to make his dream come true by becoming the owner of two major league professional teams, the Bullets and the Caps, as well as the landlord of a commodious sports and entertainment arena he built in record time with $20 million of his own money.

Despite a triple coronary bypass operation, Pollin is an active and visible team owner and, after the Bullets won the 1978 NBA championship, personally shepherded the team on a tour of Israel. When a local magazine asked if he was interested in bringing baseball back to Washington, Pollin replied: "I have no desire to own any more teams. Two is enough. It may be too many, but it certainly is enough."

2. Sugar Ray Leonard

Born and reared in the suburbs near Abe Pollin's Capital Centre, Sugar Ray is Washington's only authentic sports hero of the 1980s. He may be the best looking boxing champion since Muhammad Ali was still Cassius Clay, but his gritty battles with the fearsome Roberto Duran and "Hit Man" Tommie Hearns for the welterweight crown demonstrated that there was skill and strength behind the pretty boy façade.

Leonard made Washington into a boxing town when he won a gold medal in the 1976 Olympics. The city had only one championship fight up to then—Joe Louis' 1941 battle royal with Buddy Baer—although Ali did fight at Cap Centre during one of his comeback campaigns. But since Sugar Ray came back from Montreal in 1976, little black kids in Washington are as likely to be seen shadowboxing as trying slam dunks on the city's playground basketball courts.

Leonard, who made $21 million in his first four years as a professional, had exceptional help. At first, it came from Janks Morton, his coach in Palmer Park where he grew up; then from the veteran manager Angelo Dundee and a young local lawyer, Mike Trainer, who negotiated the first million dollar nonheavyweight bout on Sugar Ray's behalf.

3. Sonny Jurgensen

Christian Adolph Jurgensen (now you know why a grown man doesn't object to being called Sonny) is a lot thinner and a lot more subdued than the pot-bellied, hell-raising quarterback who led the Redskins to football respectability in the 1970s. As a sports commentator for WDVM, CBS's top-ranked Washington outlet, Jurgensen has problems with the names of French-Canadian hockey players, but when he talks about football, Washington listens.

Jurgensen is a genuine sports hero—the town promptly forgot all about Billy Kilmer, Jurgy's arch rival for the quarterback spot for years, and has not yet adopted Joe Theismann, their successor. But more important, his judgments about the football team probably have more influence in the city than the combined opinions of all the sportswriters of the *Post* and the blow-dried video jocks of the TV stations. Sonny seldom criticizes the Redskins openly, but viewers can tell when he thinks the coaching staff is making mistakes. His dispassionate commentaries on the job done by Jack Pardee, Allen's successor and his own former teammate, probably had as much to do with preparing the town for Pardee's ouster as the team's plummet in the NFL standings after 1979.

4. Bobby Beathard

Beathard has been general manager of the Redskins since the 1978 season, but it was something that happened after the 1980 season that made him a heavy hitter in Washington sports.

With team owner Jack Kent Cooke as referee, judge, and counting for knockdowns, Beathard won a debate over the near and probably distant future of the team against coach Pardee, the well-liked former

Redskin linebacker who had succeeded Allen. Pardee was canned; Beathard was left to select a new coach—Joe Gibbs, late of San Diego—and in a very real way to become the top man in Washington football.

Beathard, at age 42, became Redskin general manager after four years as personnel chief for the Miami Dolphins, where he made a reputation for spotting promising professionals in the roulettelike football draft. It was disagreement over the player development function, Beathard's forte, that led to the showdown with Pardee after the team completed a dismal 6-win, 10-loss season in 1980.

Beathard felt Pardee, who had been one of the supposedly washed-up veterans Allen had coaxed some additional fine playing years out of, was trying to reinvent the 1970s in Washington. He winced when good young prospects were dropped by Pardee in favor of battle-seasoned veterans—in effect disposing of seed stock in hopes of reaping an immediate harvest. After a series of conferences with both men at his estate in the Virginia hunt country, Cooke decided to continue with Beathard and drop Pardee, who had twice been NFL Coach of the Year in a short career.

So Beathard, a five-foot nine-inch college quarterback who had never made it in the pros, prevailed. But Cooke, who lets his people do their thing as long as his teams are winning, is watching from Upperville.

5. Edward Bennett Williams

The Orioles' owner, although listed as president of the Redskins, owns only 14 percent of the football team and was foreclosed from an active management role by NFL Czar Pete Rozelle's rule against the kind of multisport mogulism that Pollin represents.

But the big 61-year-old lawyer remains a strong presence in Washington sports. There are many who believe he will return big league baseball to the capital—either in the uniform of the Orioles or some other team in one of the astonishing deals that shift professional sports franchises from place to place. Failing that, with Cooke getting on in years, Williams might well return to the helm of the Redskins, who, after all, are the team that Washington loves best.

Real Estate

COME ALONG to a Georgetown cocktail party. The 200-year-old house, elegantly restored, is crowded with people whose faces you have seen on television, in the newspapers, and in *Dossier* magazine.

Over by the buffet is that senator who ran for President, deep in conversation with the former secretary of defense and a young White House aide. Are they discussing the Middle East? No. The subject is real estate.

In a corner, a congressman and the columnist who was on "Meet the Press" last week are listening to a handsome, well-dressed woman. Is she a feminist pitching for the Equal Rights Amendment? A svelte lobbyist for a big oil conglomerate? No. Real estate.

Let's leave and cross town to a small rowhouse on Capitol Hill. This party is younger and livelier. Over there, two young men are chatting with two young women. Romantic talk? Forget it. Real estate.

What *is* this all about? Well, the senator is explaining how he made $350,000 on the Wesley Heights house he bought six years ago for $110,000. The lady with the congressman and the columnist is explaining the real estate market—she is a congressman's wife who has hit $1 million a year in sales for the past several years and in the process earned more than her husband.

At the Capitol Hill party, the young lawyer and his architect friend, having made several hundred thousand dollars buying and selling old houses as a sideline, are telling the two young women how it is done. The women, congressional staff members, have just paid $125,000 for a 14-foot-wide house in what was once an alley near Lincoln Park. They didn't get stung; an agent already has told them he can sell the place for $134,000.

Real estate may be a fixation in Washington because it is one of the capital's few yardsticks of affluence. A title may connote power in Washington, but it says nothing of wealth. As Vice-President, Nelson Rockefeller went home to his own immense estate; Hubert Humphrey, in the same job, lived in an apartment.

Speculation in real estate began in Washington shortly after Pierre

L'Enfant sketched the city plan in 1791. Davey Burnes and Daniel Carroll were the first to make a bundle.

Burnes, a crusty Scottish farmer, held most of the swampy land that was to be the governmental and commercial core of the city from Georgetown on the west to the foot of Capitol (then Jenkins) Hill on the east. Carroll, an already well-to-do descendant of Lord Baltimore, owned much of the high ground from the Hill eastward to the Anacostia River. Washington dickered with them and a handful of other landowners for about 5,000 acres. They were to donate the land needed for streets, parks, and public buildings, receive $66 an acre for half of the remainder, and keep the other half to hold or sell themselves. They got a bit of a shock when they discovered L'Enfant's expansive plan required them to give away about 3,600 acres, but did very well on the rest of the deal.

Washington had hoped to peddle the $66 acres to raise cash to build government buildings, but could sell only 100 lots at auction. The government finally got out from under by dumping its land on one James Greenleaf, who has the distinction of being one of the few people ever to go broke in Washington real estate.

Things picked up after 1800, but disaster was soon to come. In August of 1814, the British sacked the city—burning both the White House and the Capitol, causing Margaret Bayard Smith, wife of the editor of the *National Intelligencer,* to write: "I do not suppose government will ever return to Washington. All those whose property was invested in that place will be reduced to poverty."

But the government did come back and rebuild, and real estate prospered. By the 1880s, Frank Carpenter, reporting from Washington for a Cleveland newspaper, noted that a boardinghouse that had been built at the start of the Civil War for $4,000 had just been sold for $64,000 and that a building on F Street, just then emerging as the downtown retail center, had gone for $80,000, a profit of 1,500 percent.

And the boom, with a few pauses, has continued. In 1980, a trade association paid $530 a square foot for a parking lot on the northern edge of what had been Davey Burnes' farm. If the old farmer had been able to get that from George Washington, the price would have been $23 million an acre.

Washington went through some tough times on the way to that kind of land values. In 1842, Charles Dickens visited and called Washington "The City of Magnificent Intentions" that lacked "only houses, roads, and inhabitants" to fulfill its promise.

A political freebooter named Alexander Shepherd pulled Washington out of the mud in the 1870s. A crony of President Grant, Shepherd put in miles of sewers and pavement and dozens of parks, overrunning by $11 million the $10 million debt limit imposed by Congress on the city. That provoked Congress to withdraw Washington's home rule, but by then the capital was on the way to becoming a real city.

About the same time "Boss" Shepherd gained power, the first full-time real estate agent showed up. A former government clerk, Brainard Warner, opened shop in 1869 and shortly became a power in the city's business community.

By 1885, Warner had more than 100 competitors; today, the industry, sustained by the market created every time the Presidency changes hands, employs thousands in the city and the still-expanding suburbs. Several of the real estate companies in the area are among the largest in the country, and it takes 30 pages of classified telephone directory to list all the companies in the Washington area.

There are some prodigious salespeople among Washington's real estate agents. One firm, Long and Foster, advertises that it has 114 people who have sold $1 million or more a year, and one of the Town and Country firm's legendary producers, a woman known only as Bathsheyba, turned in some stunning individual sales, including the $35 million Nelson Rockefeller estate, before moving on to the West Coast. Another famous agent is Dorothy Newman, who sold a whole hotel and adjacent apartment building to the Peoples Republic of China for an embassy in the late 1970s. That $5 million deal capped a career that included more than 40 sales of buildings and houses to foreign countries or their diplomats.

Women do very well in Washington real estate and few better than congressional wives. Among the best known in the field are Pat Derwinski, wife of the Illinois House member, Antoinette Hatfield, wife of the Oregon senator, and Corinne Conte, wife of the Massachusetts congressman.

Nothing makes a capital grow more than a war, and it was the Civil War that pushed Washington past the boundaries of L'Enfant's original city plan into the farmland of the District of Columbia. It was not long before people were moving into houses built on what had been Joseph Bradley's farm, called Chevy Chase, on the far north-western edge of the District.

The population doubled to nearly 200,000 between 1860 and 1880, and by the end of that decade, 2,500 buildings a year were going up. Land shot up from six cents a square foot to more than 48 cents.

As the century turned, there arrived on the scene a remarkable Englishman named Harry Wardman. A self-taught staircase builder, the hustling young Brit quickly saw the opportunity for an enterprising builder. He started contracting for single-family dwellings, and before his construction empire went smash in the Depression had built 5,000 homes in the city.

But Harry Wardman had bigger dreams. He built 250 apartment buildings, including the sprawling and elegant Broadmoor and Northumberland, and half a dozen hotels, several of which still are among the capital's best. These included the present Hay-Adams across Lafayette Park from the White House, the Sheraton-Carlton a few blocks uptown, the Roosevelt and the Annapolis (both converted to other uses), and his masterpiece—the 1,250 room Wardman Park on Connecticut Avenue above Rock Creek Park.

Some called it "Wardman's Folly," but the hotel, which for many years had the largest ballroom in the capital, prospered, and it wasn't until 1980 that the Sheraton chain tore it down and replaced it with the 1,500-room Hyatt-style Sheraton-Washington. The company did retain an adjoining apartment hotel and brought back the builder's name, calling it Wardman Towers.

Between 1930 and 1950, the District's population increased from 497,000 to 832,000, which was to be its high point. By that time, the once bucolic suburbs of Maryland and Virginia were teeming with development. New housing, encouraged by government mortgage subsidies, improved highways, and lots of cars drew newcomers and old residents alike far across the District line. The pull of whites to the open spaces was accelerated by the push of thousands of southern blacks heading north for what they hoped would be better living.

The white flight brought the District down to a population of 637,000 by 1980, but the black population had doubled in three decades to more than 70 percent. The Washington metropolitan area, now reaching 30 miles or more beyond the limits of the District of Columbia, had passed the 3 million mark.

Like so many other old cities, Washington suffered grievously during the 1965-75 decade. But despite the crime, the blight, and the bug-out of middle-class families, it had in federal government an industry that wasn't shrinking, and by 1980 there were unmistakable signs of rebirth in the capital.

Money tells part of the story. Between 1970 and 1977, median household income in the Washington area rose from $11,237 to $19,800, an increase of 13 percent *after* inflation. The key was the living standard of the bureaucracy, which was held through most of the 1960s to pay levels below the $22,500 congressional salary. Since then, many federal workers have more than doubled their income as the pay of members of the Senate and the House rose to $66,000.

In the '60s, Washington's old downtown and center city commercial areas looked like goners. The riots that followed the murder of Martin

Luther King Jr. in 1968 left three shopping corridors of the city looking as if the British had returned, and the big stores of once-bustling F and 7th Streets downtown were rapidly closing in favor of mammoth shopping malls in the outskirts.

A new subway system, designed specifically to discourage crime and graffiti, helped stem the decline, keeping such "anchor" department stores as Woodward & Lothrop, Hechts, and Garfinckel's alive in the shopping heart of the city. When they held, a number of developers such as Oliver T. Carr moved in to buy old buildings at low prices and begin a renovation and rebuilding process that promised to transform the center city by the mid-1980s.

This process was aided by the approval of a big new convention center near downtown and the decision of some major organizations, such as the American Medical Association and the National Association of Counties, to build new headquarters in or near the center of town. It was the National Food Processors Association that paid the record-breaking $530 per square foot—$9.5 million—for less than half a block of land in the downtown in the fall of 1980. Within six months, a one-acre area—a block close to the convention center site—went for $615 a square foot, or $40 million, to a Canadian company.

The same upward movement of real estate prices continued in the suburbs. In May of 1981, a 117-acre tract of land adjacent to the big Tysons Corners shopping center in McLean was auctioned off at $35 million to developer Theodore Lerner. That was one-third more than its appraised value only two years earlier.

Despite its depression-proof reputation, these prices had some people in Washington worried. William A. Regardie, publisher of a slick magazine that chronicles the area's business activities, wrote at the end of 1980: "Damn it, people, stop and think. Washington, D.C., may well be the golden goose, but it seems very clear that the goose better watch where it walks and what it steps in."

Scores of men and women have grown wealthy from Washington's golden goose, but the following people have gathered the most eggs.

THE TOP FIVE IN WASHINGTON BUILDING AND REAL ESTATE
1. Oliver T. Carr

"In the land of the blind, the one-eyed man is king." As it happens, Oliver T. Carr has been blind in one eye since birth. As it also happens, Carr is one of the few Washington developers who didn't cut and run when the city was torn by riot and fire after the murder of Martin Luther King Jr. in 1968.

"The role of the city as the confluence of government, finance, and communications wasn't going to change just because we had a little social unrest," the veteran but still youthful-looking Washington developer said 11 years after the riots sent most of his competitors into the suburbs.

Their flight left Carr to become king of downtown Washington. The company that bears his name may not be the largest in the area, but most observers of the real estate scene in the capital agree Carr is the leader in the rejuvenation of Washington's commercial heart and close-in residential areas.

Carr has been involved in commercial development in the capital since the early 1960s, but it wasn't until the 1970s that he emerged as top dog downtown. By the end of the decade he had developed and owned or was managing about 30 major buildings between George-town and the White House and in the '80s was moving into the fading old shopping center of the city.

His biggest ventures in the 1970s were development of an area called the West End near George Washington University and an immense complex called International Square north of the White House. The Carr developments frequently combine offices, stores, and apartments, a mix planners and local officials feel will bring life after dark back to the center city.

There have been some bumps in Carr's road. He was pressured to retain the neoclassic façade of a building he wanted to replace across the street from the U.S. Treasury, and he was repeatedly picketed and heckled at public appearances by preservationists who objected to his plan to tear down the ramshackle building housing a souvenir store that once housed Rhodes Tavern. The structure was one of the oldest in the city and had served as the headquarters of Admiral Cockburn, the British commander who put the city to the torch in 1814.

2. Foster Shannon

The Irish did much of the hard labor in building the national capital, and Foster Shannon's father, a carpenter, was one of them. But in 1906, Herbert Shannon went into business with real estate agent Morton Luchs, and together they built a company that has sold or erected more homes and commercial structures in Washington than any other.

Foster Shannon is president of Shannon and Luchs; Kenneth Luchs, grandson of the cofounder, is vice-president. The firm, with about 1,200 employees, does an estimated $1 billion of business a year, tops for the city. It sells about 5,000 units of housing—homes and apartments—a year, leases about a million square feet of commercial space, and manages 18,000 apartments and 30 office buildings. It also is involved in insurance and mortgage financing.

Though better known in the city than in the suburbs, the company has had a good piece of the recent boom in outlying real estate.

Shannon and Luchs acquired the land for Reston, one of the nation's best-known "new towns" in the Virginia suburbs near Dulles International Airport.

3. A. *James Clark*

The Washington Monument dominates the skyline of the national capital, but in recent years the great stone obelisk has been rivaled by towering construction cranes.

More often than not, the signs at these building sites in Washington proclaim that the work is being done by the George Hyman or Omni construction companies. What many Washingtonians do not know is that these companies are under the same ownership, Clark Enterprises, headed by A. James Clark.

Hyman and Omni are more than the same cereal in different boxes. Hyman, a 75-year-old firm that has erected some of the capital's major buildings, employs union labor and thus gets government and other construction contracts from owners whose interests require a union label on their buildings. Omni is nonunion, and its sign is seen on buildings being put up by investors to whom price is paramount. What is interesting is that Hyman and Omni are often working on the same street, a block or less apart.

Clark actually is a national company, with jobs from coast to coast. Its annual revenues were estimated last year at $450 million with about 2,500 people on its payrolls.

The Clark firms dominate Washington, with competition from the Blake and Donohoe construction companies. In years past, it was not uncommon to have an out-of-town construction firm build a major government structure. Thus the Matthew McCloskey firm, the namesake of the then treasurer of the Democratic National Committee, was in evidence during the Kennedy and Johnson administrations, while the John Volpe firm, owned by the family of the former transportation secretary and Republican governor of Massachusetts, did a lot of work in the city during the Nixon years. Probably just a coincidence.

In any case, in recent years it has become less possible to tell which party is in the White House by looking at the construction company signs at the big Washington building jobs.

4. *Wes Foster*

A couple of years ago, Wes Foster had one of those experiences that struggling businessmen dream about. He was ushered into the plush New York office of one of the country's richest companies but told its president, thanks but no thanks, my outfit is not for sale.

"The thought of selling was almost like selling my child," Foster said of the offer from Donald Regan, now Secretary of the Treasury, but then head of Merrill, Lynch. The big brokerage firm was just moving into real estate and wanted to buy out Long and Foster, the Washington area's biggest real estate agency for residential property. Henry Long, who started the firm with Wes Foster in the late 1960s, had been leaning toward the deal with Merrill Lynch but eventually sold out to Foster instead.

Now Foster leads an army of more than 1,150 agents in 31 offices in and around Washington, producing nearly $950 million in business before high interest put the kibosh on real estate everywhere. Foster does it by going after the hot agents—it is his company that boasts more than 100 people who have sold more than $1 million a year in real estate once or more during their careers.

5. *Theodore Lerner*

On a warm day in May of 1981, Ted Lerner spent $35 million in a hot and stuffy courtroom in suburban Fairfax County, Virginia. Lerner, a 56-year-old Washington native, spent the money in outbidding Boston developer Mortimer Zuckerman for 117 acres of land adjacent to the huge Tysons Corners shopping and commercial center about a dozen miles from the White House in a booming suburb.

The $7 a square foot Lerner paid for the Tysons II tract was the largest price ever for suburban Washington land (downtown lots cost 100 times that amount), but it surprised few who had been watching his career in the past three decades.

Lerner truly towers over the world of suburban shopping in the Washington area. His Lerner Corporation developed 4 of the 10 largest shopping malls in surrounding Maryland and Virginia. These range, in addition to the existing Tysons Corners layout, from sprawling Landover Mall in the middle-class and heavily black Prince Georges County suburbs of Maryland to the ritzy and pricey White Flint Mall (Bloomingdale's, I. Magnin, Lord & Taylor) in mostly white and upper-middle-class Montgomery County.

Lerner also is developing Washington Square, an office complex in downtown Washington that may be the most costly place in the capital to do business. Business and real estate publisher Bill Regardie, noting that downtown lots have sold as high as $650 a square foot in public, guesses that the land under Lerner's project touched four figures—near Manhattan prices. Washington has arrived.

The Good Addresses

WASHINGTON's elite tend to live where the elite everywhere live— as close as possible to each other and as far as possible from the common folk. In the District and its Virginia and Maryland suburbs, that tends to be near the Potomac River along its upriver stretches, though there are a number of farther-flung elite enclaves. In a town with so many people going to work in limousines, extra distance doesn't matter quite so much, although you occasionally hear fellows driving past the White House complain: "If we lived there, we'd be home by now."

The District of Columbia itself occupies 66 square miles but comprises only 20 percent of the metropolitan area's 3-million population. About two-thirds of the city is home to poor and working-class blacks. The city is considerably more integrated than it was 20 years ago. Carl Rowan, the black columnist, came to town from Minneapolis to work in the Kennedy administration in the early 1960s, and moved into an all-white neighborhood in Northwest Washington.

As he has told it, Rowan was mowing his new front yard a short time after moving in when a white woman stopped on the sidewalk and asked how much he would charge to do some yard work at her home down the block.

"Well, I work here for nothing," Rowan replied.

"Nothing?"

"Well, I get to sleep with the lady of the house," he said.

Divisions do remain. Northwest Washington west of the natural barrier that is Rock Creek Park still is almost entirely white and extremely expensive. What amounted to a military picket line of police patrols, some of them with dogs, were all that kept a drugs and prostitution district from spilling over into Kalorama and other affluent white sections east of the park several years ago. Now, with the kind of gentrification rampant east of the Capitol, it's the white folks who are invading black neighborhoods.

296

Washington's Metro subway, still incomplete, will be the key to future neighborhood renaissance and a further blurring of traditional black and white sections. The sleeper in this could be Anacostia, in the far southeastern quadrant of Washington, where small but comfortable homes perch on hills that offer some of the area's most impressive views of the Potomac and the "monumental city."

Washington's suburban elite are for the most part people who simply have a lot of money. Except for a slim scattering of "great family" names and a few recognizable from the anchor desks of network news, the owners of most of the big digs are the people who make the really big bucks in Washington: lawyers and lobbyists. Those who lay claim to fame, power, and prestige, but nothing else, are usually out of luck unless they can come up with the scratch.

When Reagan's nominee for labor secretary, New Jersey's interesting Ray Donovan, hit town in early 1981, he plunked down more than $750,000 in cash and acquired a lovely domicile nestled among the Kennedys, Robbs, and (at the time) Dickersons just off McLean's Chain Bridge Road overlooking the Potomac.

Energy Secretary James Edwards, a dentist and former South Carolina governor and a man of much more modest means, asked only to rent some nice place for between $400 and $500 a month. Real estate dealers' eyes rolled, discreetly, of course. Edwards ended up paying $625 a month for a modest townhouse around the corner from Montgomery Ward in Falls Church.

Washington is no Palm Beach or Beverly Hills, no mecca for the superrich, so the sky really isn't the limit on housing prices, no matter how much it seems that way. Consider the case of Potomac House, a 200,000-square-foot brick mansion in McLean long considered the most expensive in the area. Started in 1973 and never fully completed, the house has such amenities as wine cellar, bomb shelter, three kitchens, ballroom, marble fireplaces, elevator, and escape tunnel.

Put on the market for $2.25 million back when that was "real money," it was ultimately valued at over $3 million. (A columnist once suggested that, instead of spending $200 million in taxpayers' money to built the new Hart Senate Office Building to house 25 senators, $100 million could be saved by building each senator a Potomac House mansion instead.) But it didn't sell, not for years. Finally, it was picked up at auction for $1,150,000 by Carol and Climis Lascaris, interior decorators who have never been near a White House cabinet meeting.

The elite suburbs in Maryland tend to be older and more settled than those in Virginia. Until a few years ago, downtown McLean was little more than a couple of shopping centers, an old house converted into a real estate office, and four gas stations. It's coming to resemble overdeveloped Tysons Corners. On Kirby Road just outside McLean and only eight miles from the White House, there's still a cow or two and a number of cornfields. Chevy Chase, in contrast, seems indistinguishable from the Northwest Washington it's an extension of, and in fact lies partially within the District.

Liberals seem happier in Maryland suburbs, though a surprisingly large number seem willing to brave the traditions of Virginia, defiantly pasting "I'm a Virginia Democrat" stickers on their bumpers. The ostentatious fur-coat set also seems to prefer Maryland suburbs, while preppies choose the Old Dominion.

The Mercedes-Benz appears to be the most popular car among the Washington suburban elite in both states, with the Volvo and BMW probably running second and third. A good index of elite land in the suburbs is the number of diplomatic plates to be seen in the shopping center parking lots. The Giant Food lot in McLean is never without them.

The appeal of proximity to the Potomac is largely theoretical, incidentally. The river is polluted for long stretches upriver from Washington by deposits of farmland silt, coal mine seep, the discharge from six major factories, and 100,000 gallons of untreated sewage dumped every day at Ridgeley, West Virginia, a state unregulated beyond Ronald Reagan's wildest dreams. Also, the view of the Potomac from many homesites includes much more of a view of the George Washington Parkway, but status is where you find it.

What follows is our ranking of the 5 best District neighborhoods and the 10 best suburbs in the metropolitan area. The assessment is based on such considerations as home values, per capita income, educational level, proximity to the river, access to downtown, quality of schools, and nearness to decent (Neiman-Marcus, Saks, Garfinckel's, Bloomie's) shopping. But, this being Washington, what counts most is who lives there and what they do.

THE FIFTEEN BEST WASHINGTON ADDRESSES

THE CITY

1. Georgetown

When Alexandria was returned to Virginia by a Congress that didn't think the national capital needed all that land, Georgetown remained as the only part of the District that was in existence as a city before the District of Columbia was formed. It was a thriving Maryland tobacco port and milling center when Washington was just a gleam in George's eye and a few scratches on Pierre L'Enfant's sketch pad.

Georgetown has survived with a few of its eighteenth-century buildings intact and, with a couple of exceptions, has resisted recurring efforts to "Manhattanize" it with high-rise buildings and improved—for which read "widened"—streets.

But despite the traffic and the hordes of tourists and weekend hippies from the Maryland and Virginia suburbs who posture on its sidewalks, Georgetown is the "best" address in Washington. On its quieter back streets, in the walled gardens of the old houses, and on its uneven brick sidewalks, it has managed to retain some of the peaceful ambiance of the little Potomac River village that was swallowed up by the District of Columbia 180 years ago.

If you want to buy in Georgetown, come with at least $225,000, which was the median price paid for a house in the neighborhood in 1980. If you want something special, such as the house that used to belong to Mrs. Hugh Auchincloss, Jacqueline Kennedy Onassis' mother, it would cost something in the neighborhood of $1.1 million, which is what was paid by Laughlin Phillips, the former owner of *Washingtonian* magazine and inheritor of the capital's finest private art collection.

The problem is to find a place for sale in Georgetown. People like former Ambassador Averell Harriman, Senator Charles Percy of Illinois, novelist Herman Wouk, and *Washington Post* chairman Katharine Graham are typical longtime residents and not disposed to move.

Still, newcomers with cash, such as former HEW Secretary Joseph Califano, Kennedy Center impresario Roger Stevens, and Virginia Senator John Warner and his wife, actress Elizabeth Taylor, all found houses in Georgetown in recent years.

Along the Potomac waterfront in Georgetown, there is some new housing, mostly new and renovated condominiums replacing the flour mills and cement works that once represented Washington's heavy industry. Even the small units in these developments go for $150,000 and up per copy.

2. Spring Valley-Wesley Heights

On the far western edge of the District, Spring Valley is an area of substantial homes, mostly in the traditional style but built after World War II with lots of land. They never were cheap and they go for at least a quarter-million dollars now. The area was a favorite of rising members of Congress and the government when it was developed and has had both Richard Nixon and Lyndon Johnson among its residents. When LBJ was vice-president, the Johnsons lived at "The Elms," a mansion once the scene of Perle (The Hostess With The Mostest) Mesta's lavish parties.

Spring Valley now is home for Art Buchwald, David Brinkley, and

Jack Valenti, head of the Motion Picture Association.

Wesley Heights is somewhat closer in than Spring Valley and smaller in area, but probably is more secluded for being bounded by parks and the American University campus. These neighborhoods, with homes also in the quarter-million-dollar range, have convenient shopping at branches of Lord & Taylor, Neiman-Marcus, Saks Fifth Avenue, and the local quality department store, Garfinckel's, just short runs by limo or sports car.

Just off Foxhall Road, which connects Georgetown to Wesley Heights, is the intersection of 49th and W Streets. It is a usually quiet, affluent neighborhood, but it got some heavy traffic back in 1980 when FBI agents decked out as Arab sheiks were entertaining members of Congress in a rented house and taking home video movies of half a dozen swallowing the bait that became the Abscam scandal.

3. Cleveland Park-Woodley

These two are adjoining older, tree-shaded neighborhoods with massive homes about three miles north of the White House and just west of Rock Creek Park.

Woodley, where the median 1980 home price was at the city's top—$265,000—is a small area just west of the zoo and north of the big Sheraton Washington and Shoreham Americana hotels. The larger Cleveland Park neighborhood just to the north extends from Connecticut Avenue west to the towering Washington Cathedral (Anglican) on Wisconsin Avenue and is somewhat less pricey.

J. Willard Marriott, who began in business with a hot dog stand in downtown Washington and now presides over a hotel and food service empire, lives in Cleveland Park. So do Senator William Proxmire of Wisconsin, who jogs to work at the Capitol about six miles away, and Benjamin Bradlee, executive editor of the *Washington Post*.

Before he abandoned Washington for New England, the late Walter Lippmann used to live a block or two from the Cathedral, whose booming bells reportedly came near to driving the great man bonkers.

4. Capitol Hill

When a neighborhood gets hot, it gets bigger, particularly for real estate people. Capitol Hill, a short decade ago, was considered to be the four, perhaps six, blocks directly east of the Capitol grounds. Everything beyond that was terra incognita, at least for white folks.

Today, Capitol Hill extends 20 blocks eastward to the very turnstiles of Robert F. Kennedy stadium, and fortunes have been spent renovating the once-shabby row houses and detached dwellings of an area that was among the city's least esteemed. Houses that could be bought for $20,000 or less when Lyndon Johnson was President have been upgraded and now go for six times that. Pennsylvania Avenue east of the Capitol is becoming a stretch of trendy bars and restaurants, as is Massachusetts Avenue near Union Station.

The march of gentrification has caused some problems—displacement or huge tax assessment jumps for the black residents and crime in the form of burglary and muggings for the newly arrived whites. But Capitol Hill is on the upswing. In addition to hundreds of congressional staffers living on The Hill, a number of members of Congress are settling near to their jobs as well. Senators Daniel Patrick Moynihan of New York and S. I. Hayakawa of California live there; Alaska Senator Ted Stevens lives on Lincoln Park; and dozens of House members are sprinkled throughout the area, including House Minority Leader Bob Michel. Capitol Hill has its own resident gossip: Diana McClellan, the wicked wit behind the *Washington Post*'s Ear column, is a neighbor.

The neighborhood also has its own resident military garrison. The Marine Barracks, housing a complement of crack troops for ceremonial occasions, adds color and, some feel, security to The Hill.

5. DuPont Circle-Kalorama

This is the least residential of the top five neighborhoods, but still a prime area. It was the center of dissent and counterculture in the 1960s, but the condo craze has resulted in the conversion of many old apartment buildings and the influx of a much more establishment-oriented population.

Some of the city's grandest avenues—Massachusetts, Rhode Island, and Sixteenth—intersect at or near DuPont Circle, and some of their huge mansions remain as private homes or formal residences for ambassadors.

Alice Roosevelt Longworth held forth in her home just off DuPont Circle until her death in 1980, as did General Phil Sheridan's daughters in a house on the Circle named for the famous Civil War cavalry general. Today, the Circle is home for a new generation, people like Ralph Nader (a renter); Monsignor Geno Baroni, former Carter administration housing official; columnist Nicholas von Hoffman; Pulitzer Prize-winning reporter William Eaton of the *Los Angeles Times*; and Benjamin Cohen, one of the last of FDR's "Brain Trust."

Kalorama, just to the north of the Circle, is somewhat more residential, and its big houses are as costly as Woodley's. In mid-1981, a house on Kalorama Road sold for $950,000. The area also is a favorite for writers like James Reston and Douglass Cater, but its residents also include defense secretary Caspar Weinberger, oil lobbyist Frank Ikard, Juliette Clagett McLennan, and former airline president Najeeb Halaby, whose daughter became Queen Nour of Jordan.

It also has one of the biggest and quietest embassies. The Peoples Republic of China bought an entire hotel, raised the red star flag, and holed up behind shuttered windows.

Honorable Mention—The Watergate

Unless you were in a coma from 1972 through 1976, you've heard of the Watergate, which is a huge complex of Orwellian high-rise residential and commercial buildings set together on the Potomac River next door to the Kennedy Center and about seven blocks from the White House.

The Watergate isn't in the list above because it isn't really a neighborhood (although it has a full complement of shopping for both staples and luxuries and its own police force), and the neighborhood around it—Foggy Bottom—doesn't quite make the top five.

Even when the Nixon plumbers were burgling the Democratic National Committee headquarters in the Watergate office building, the residential sections were among the toniest in town, with several cabinet members owning apartments. And if you've got the money, it doesn't make any difference what your politics are: former Democratic National Chairman Robert Strauss has lived there since 1973, along with present and former Democratic Senators Russell Long of Louisiana, Richard Stone of Florida, and Stuart Symington of Missouri.

But Watergate really is the hangout of rich Republicans, and the Reagan administration loves it. The Walter Annenbergs, Justin Darts, Charles Z. Wicks, and Alfred Bloomingdales all have rented quarters at Watergate. All have the money to buy in, but the price tags might even make some of these ultrawealthy temporary Washingtonians blink: a Watergate executive was quoted recently as saying, "One two-bedroom recently sold for $750,000. And it wasn't really that nice."

THE SUBURBS

1. McLean

As *Dossier* magazine has pointed out, McLean is not Georgetown, Old Town Alexandria, Cleveland Park, or Middleburg. But the point is, neither are any of those McLean.

Located in an unincorporated area of north Fairfax County

between Falls Church, Arlington, and the great sweep of the Potomac beneath Great Falls, McLean is to Washington what Greenwich, Connecticut, is to New York and much of Marin County is to San Francisco. Rolling hills, horse farms, and large estates comingle with expensive tract homes, town-house developments, and even high-rises.

Camelot came here in the 1960s, Ethel and Teddy Kennedy still have homes just off McLean's Chain Bridge Road. Jackie Kennedy O. grew up not far from either. The community is now rich in powerful Republicans and such *Social Register* and *Green Book* names as J. William Middendorf and Elliot Richardson.

In 1981, $200,000 homes were considered low to moderate housing in McLean, with prices $250,000 to $500,000 typical and $500,000 to $1 million not at all unusual.

The dollar amounts are also remarkable when you consider that the areas covered by the McLean postmark south of Chain Bridge Road include many sections of old, lower-class housing, complete with carports with motorcycles and vans in them. Also occasional Confederate flags.

On one recent drive north of the village, the authors came upon a county convict-labor gang and armed guard repairing a road. All that was lacking were actual chains and a hound or two.

In addition to those already mentioned, McLean's present or recent residents include Supreme Court Justices William Rehnquist, Byron White, and (until his recent and most unpublicized divorce) John Paul Stevens; Deputy Defense Secretary Frank Carlucci; NBC news anchor Roger Mudd; CBS weather czar Gordon Barnes; columnist Patrick Buchanan; former Chief of Protocol Henry Catto; Gilbert Grosvenor, president of National Geographic; James Shepley, former board chairman of the *Washington Star;* columnist and television commentator Edward P. Morgan; social whiz Aliki Bryant; ultraconservative direct mail whiz Richard Viguerie; columnist Roscoe Drummond; Senators Robert Byrd, Richard Lugar, Patrick Leahy, Lawton Chiles, William Cohen, Strom Thurmond, Dennis DeConcini, J. Bennett Johnston, Dan Quayle, and Malcolm Wallop; Representatives Philip Crane, Morris Udall, Margaret Heckler, E. Kika de la Garza, and Kent Hance; former Admiral Stansfield Turner, late of the CIA; former Interior Secretary Stewart Udall; Watergate developer Giuseppi Cecchi; and Egyptian embassy minister Dr. Mohamed Shaker, among hordes of big-time diplomats.

2. Chevy Chase
Like McLean, Maryland's Chevy Chase used to be a far-off country place to which people went to escape the heat, smell, and pestilence

of summer in the city. To get to McLean, they built a railroad. To get to Chevy Chase, they built a trolley. Now you drive in a Mercedes-Benz, Volvo, BMW, or better—as thousands of women do every day en route to the shopping paradise at Chevy Chase's Friendship Heights, commonly referred to as Washington's Rodeo Drive.

Wisconsin Avenue leads to the shopping paradise. Connecticut Avenue leads to Chevy Chase Circle and, thence, to the ultra-exclusive Chevy Chase Club—admission to which was a major achievement of Henry Kissinger's life. Beyond, to the northwest, is Bethesda. To the northeast, up the District line, is Rock Creek Park, which provides a convenient buffer against the middle and lower classes of Woodside and Silver Spring.

Not quite a Beverly Hills, Chevy Chase is akin to New York's Scarsdale and Chicago's Wilmette or Winnetka. Though it has some dumps, and lacks $1 million and $2 million estates in such abundance as McLean, its $4-a-square-foot property cost is comparable, and house prices ranging between $300,000 and $500,000 are commonplace.

The major landmarks of Chevy Chase are the glittery shopping emporiums that run in a row along Wisconsin Avenue, centering on the intersection with Western Avenue. The centerpiece is Mazza Gallerie, which houses Neiman-Marcus and all its $5,000 doodads; Williams-Sonoma, a culinary store where you can buy the finest almond oil; the Sterling Gallery, which seems to have amassed as much silver as the Hunt brothers; Saville of London; La Boutique Française; the Game Boutique, specializing in electronic war and fantasy games for the adult and not-so-adult rich; and Swensen's Ice Cream Factory, where people can be seen wearing cashmere jackets and L. L. Bean outdoor shoes in perfectly warm weather as they line up for the rare available table.

On the north end of the row is what many consider the finest Saks Fifth Avenue store in the country, not to be confused with the Saks Jandel store just across Wisconsin Avenue, featuring such designers as Gucci, Ungaro, Yves St. Laurent, and Valentino.

Chevy Chase is thick with rich lawyers, lobbyists, doctors, and *Social Register* types. Its more famous notables include Pulitzer Prize–winning columnist George Will, Senator Charles Mathias, John Willard Marriott Jr., columnist and radio commentator Tom Braden and social whiz and Rockefeller friend wife Joan, CBS correspondent Phil Jones, former White House domestic czar Stu Eizenstat, renowned obstetrician Dr. Elijah Titus, and Pierre Gustave Toutant Beauregard III.

It was Pierre Gustave Toutant Beauregard, you'll remember, who led the Confederate Army at the Battle of Bull Run, but that, of course, was in Virginia.

Chevy Chase was once included in Maryland's Prince Georges County, and that today must be upsetting to some.

3. Bethesda

Bethesda and Chevy Chase have proved quite attractive to high-rise developers, with most of Bethesda's having gone up in the vicinity of Old Georgetown Road and East-West Highway, its historic center. In large part, though, Bethesda is a Chevy Chase with a little more breathing room.

There are not quite so many stately old mansions, and there are substantially more tract homes, but a nice four- or five-bedroom home on two acres in prime location will still set you back $550,000 or $600,000.

If you count everything out to the Beltway as Bethesda, its major landmarks include the posh, famous Burning Tree Country Club, and, closer in, the National Institutes of Health, and the National Naval Medical Center, patronized by so many congressmen.

Though it hasn't as many of the truly moneyed and *Social Register*ed as Chevy Chase, Bethesda can lay claim to a large share of local notables. Its present or recent inhabitants feature such celebrities as House Speaker Tip O'Neill; former adviser to Presidents and lawyer-lobbyist extraordinaire Clark Clifford; United Nations Ambassador Jeane Kirkpatrick; FBI Director William Webster; retired CBS commentator Eric Sevareid; Channel Nine news anchor Gordon Peterson; Senators Ed Muskie, Dale Bumpers, Daniel Inouye, and Bob Packwood; and Representative Jack Kemp.

4. Great Falls

Certainly the horsiest of Washington's suburban communities, unless you count Middleburg, Great Falls lies west of McLean between the Dulles Access Road and the Potomac. Though here and there are a few (large) tract homes, the area is almost entirely hills, woods, meadows, pastures, horse farms, more horse farms, yet more horse farms, some big estates, and a great many large, individually built homes set on very large plots of land.

Great Falls has its own little town center, complete with traffic light, tack shop, and one of the best fresh fish stores in the Washington area. L'Auberge Chez François, a French country inn that is possibly Washington's best restaurant and certainly its best French one, is in Great Falls. So are the Falls themselves, although McLean people also lay claim to them. The posh, exclusive Madeira

School for young ladies, of Jean Harris–Dr. Tarnower fame, is also in Great Falls, though McLean claims that, too. Wolf Trap, with all its music and summertime high jinks, lies just to the south.

Housing in Great Falls tends to run 20 to 25 percent less than in McLean, but $200,000 and $300,000 homes abound.

As there aren't many government heavies aside from the Reagans who have a big thing for horses, Great Falls drips with social prestige but not with power. Some would describe Ed Meese's digs as being in Great Falls rather than McLean. Powerful Representative Guy Vander Jagt is a Great Fallsian, as is one of the most respected federal judges in Washington, Joyce Green. As other Great Falls residents remember with a shudder, notorious cat burglar and murderer of celebrity doctor Michael Halberstam, Bernard Welch, was a resident himself, though he told people he was in stocks and bonds.

5. Potomac

Nearly as wealthy, horsey, and exclusive as Great Falls—though a trifle more suburban—is its Maryland neighbor across the river, Potomac. Once called Offutts Crossroads and the scene of a spurious post-Civil War gold rush that drove up local real estate prices, Potomac now has real estate prices that go up all by themselves. Its village shopping complex also has a tack shop, but its restaurant is no L'Auberge Chez François. On balance, Potomac seems more appealing to the Jacuzzi set, while Great Falls is more attractive to country gentlemen and CIA operatives.

The chief landmarks of Potomac are Glen Echo Park, a defunct amusement park downriver that was taken over by the National Park Service and is about to go defunct again; the Cabin John Regional Park, which is not a collection of rustic outhouses; the less spectacular Maryland side of Great Falls of the Potomac; and the Chesapeake and Ohio Canal, the towpath of which resembles an interstate highway for joggers and bicyclists on most weekends. Potomac is also home to the Congressional Country Club, which Kissinger never seemed very interested in joining.

A five-acre estate in Potomac will set you back $875,000 or so, but you can buy a nice big house for $250,000.

Potomac is home to superlawyer and sports mogul Edward Bennett Williams, *Time* magazine's Hugh Sidey, columnist Jack Anderson, and artist Jill Cohen. Real estate titans Foster Shannon and Kenneth Luchs live there, too.

During the last gasoline shortage, a well-dressed man was seen terrorizing one of the Potomac gas station lines with a tire iron, demanding a place up front. But civilization never runs deep, not even in horse country.

6. *Old Town Alexandria*

Often called a poor man's Georgetown, Old Town Alexandria, six miles downriver from the Lincoln Memorial, is the most interesting of Washington's well-heeled suburbs and a city unto itself.

Founded in 1747, the City of Alexandria is in fact the oldest in the area, and was for a long time the only one. George Washington, who lived just down the pike at Mount Vernon, hung out there a lot, especially in the public room at Gadsby's Tavern. Robert E. Lee lived there more primly, with his mother. Even now a mooring for ocean-going cruise ships, it was for two centuries a major seaport. Many of the more expensive Old Town houses near the river were originally owned by sea captains.

By the end of World War II, the place was in decline, and many parts of Old Town, frankly, were a mess, looking about as chic and historic as Hammond, Indiana. Some historic pieces of Gadsby's had even been made off with by out-of-town collectors.

But some rich and public-spirited citizens joined together to change all that. After more than three decades of effort, and aided by some handsome bequests, they succeeded in restoring Old Town to its historic grandeur. It's all so picture-perfect Washington might not recognize it. The local Holiday Inn more resembles the House of Burgesses than a hotel.

In terms of real estate values alone, Old Town would be at the head of this list. Land prices average $25 a square foot, fully one-third those of Georgetown. But despite the magnificent ambiance, wonderful shops (including one called "L'Elephant Blanc," jeez), and $250,000 and $500,000 brick town houses, a Georgetown it's not. Georgetown is surrounded by affluent Northwest Washington. Old Town is surrounded by the rest of Alexandria, including some railroad yards, a gritty black slum, an endless strip of car dealers and fast-food huts, and acres and acres of, frankly, middle-class housing.

Old Town also has a somewhat kinky underground life. Some years ago, police found that one of those staid old townhouses had been rented for conversion into an S-M parlor. Subsequently, there have been a couple of murders along those lines.

But its nightlife is very Georgetownesque among the restaurants and pubs along King Street and around the central square. Taverna Cretekou is the finest Greek restaurant in the Washington area, and Patrick Troy's highly Republican All Ireland Pub opposite the square next to Gadsby's is unrivaled, though it would doubtless startle George Washington.

The most noticeable monument is the Confederate War Memorial, if only because it sits in the middle of Highway 1 where it passes through Old Town and challenges thousands of commuting motorists every morning to make it to work alive. Take that, Mr. Lincoln.

Old Town and its environs may not have the chic folk of Georgetown, but it has think tank impresario William Baroody; authoresses Gay Montague Moore and Mrs. Hugh Cox; Charles Hooff III, representing 10 generations of Alexandria Hooffs; Joseph McLaughlin, major power at the National Governors Association; Murray Chotiner and Donald Santarelli, of Nixon-era fame; and columnist Jerold ter Horst, of brief Ford-era fame.

Then there are all those Time-Life people. Time-Life Books, Inc., gave up the Big Apple to come to Alexandria several years ago.

7. Country Club Hills-North Arlington

Arlington, once the estate of Robert E. Lee's wife's family, is the most ethnically and culturally diverse of Washington's suburbs. It has black and white slums, black and white nice neighborhoods, expensive high-rises at Rosslyn and Crystal City, acres and acres of singles' apartments (including one once occupied by bachelor Gerald Ford), a large Vietnamese and Asiatic community, colonies of military apartments, and a vast sea of Virginia cracker bungalows.

East of Old Dominion and north of Lee Highway, running up to the Fairfax County line and the Potomac, lie Country Club Hills and the rest of North Arlington, one of the most prestigious locations in metropolitan Washington, even if the address is Arlington.

Broad, boulevardlike streets wind among steep hills and enough big old trees to make a national forest—or at least a James Watt-size national forest. The houses are old, ranging from big to huge, especially on the bluffs overlooking the river. Mercedes, Volvos, and BMWs poke out of seemingly every garage, sometimes nestled next to Rolls-Royces.

Land prices run around $9 a square foot, and $200,000 to $220,000 can be a bargain price even for one of the older homes. This is the closest of the affluent suburban areas to both downtown Washington and Georgetown (and the Chevy Chase shopping paradise is just across the river and up the hill from Chain Bridge), and people are willing to pay, and charge, for that access.

Among those who do or recently did reside in or near this community are Chief Justice Warren Burger, supercolumnist David Broder, the once and future James Schlesinger, Reagan white-tie, antiwelfare czar Richard Schweicker, former CIA mandarin and master spook James Angleton, and Representative Edward Derwinski.

Many a McLeaner driving up the Parkway or Old Dominion has looked out his window at the luxurious houses of North Arlington and said: "If I were smart, I'd be home by now."

8. Falls Church

One of the best-kept secrets in the Washington metropolitan area is Falls Church, a community of 9,400 population located to the west of Arlington and to the south of McLean.

Suffering from a lack of proximity to either the river or major transportation routes into the District, Falls Church has not been part of the Washington-area real estate boom, having the slowest population growth of any Washington suburb. The ritzy like to think of it as dreadfully middle-class.

But it is one of the wealthiest cities in the nation. Its $20,000-per-capita income is the highest of any incorporated community in Virginia and twice the average for northern Virginia.

Land costs in Falls Church are $.90 per square foot. Half the housing in the city consists of detached homes ranging from $60,000 for a shack to $200,000 for a first-class house, with many going for much higher. Town houses can be had for from $70,000 to $180,000.

Falls Church's more notable residents include syndicated cartoonist Patrick Oliphant, Senator Robert Stafford, and former Representative Richard Kelly of Abscam fame. Just north of Falls Church's city limits but within its postal service area live Senator Paul Laxalt, Representative Henry Hyde, former Secret Service Director H. Stuart Knight, First Lady Press Secretary Sheila Patten Tate, and enough generals, admirals, and high-ranking diplomats to make the area attractive to Russian spies. As it might be, if Falls Church weren't such a well-kept secret.

9. Mount Vernon

Judging by the *Washington Post* real estate ads, you'd think the 86,000 people who live in Mount Vernon are all $15,000- to $20,000-a-year civilian employees at nearby Fort Belvoir, grateful for the moderate price of housing there. But these are the folks who dwell in the stretches of Mount Vernon inland from the river and the southern leg of the George Washington Parkway that terminates at the Nation's Father's plantation.

But along the Parkway are $200,000 and $300,000 homes that could just as easily be in McLean or Chevy Chase. As Treasury Secretary Regan discovered, they possess some of the best views of the Potomac in the metropolitan area. The area can also lay claim to a yacht club, chamber orchestra, and Daughters of the American Revolution chapter. Eyebrows might rise over Springfield, Vienna, or Silver Spring, but the Mount Vernon shoreline brings a respectful nod. And George Washington liked it a lot.

10. Leesburg-Middleburg

Leesburg, county seat of Loudon County, isn't quite yet a Washington suburb but will be as soon as the suburban sprawl that is marching inexorably up four-lane Highway 7 reaches it, which may be at 8:36 A.M. tomorrow. Loudon is now the fastest-growing county in the Washington metropolitan area.

Middleburg, a small village of 900 straddling Highway 50 a few miles southwest of Leesburg, doesn't seem a suburb at all, and wouldn't be, if such residents as Senator John Warner and wife Elizabeth Taylor didn't treat it as one in their comings and goings from Washington.

Along with the Fauquier County town of Upperville, Leesburg and Middleburg are the chief population centers of Virginia's famous horse and hunt country, a superwealthy vast expanse largely owned by American grandees with names like Mellon and host to so much yoicks and tally-ho that the numerous, prestigious local hunts seem like just one big long one.

Yet most of the big horse farms and estates lie within 35 and 40 miles of Washington, as do both Leesburg and Middleburg, a commuting distance comparable to that between Chicago and Barrington Hills, Illinois, or Manhattan and Mount Kisco, New York, where the horse also reigns. CIA folk at Langley frequently lunch in Middleburg. A growing number of affluent but not equestrian Washingtonians are buying full-time residences in the area, especially in Leesburg, once home to General George C. Marshall.

The general cost of individual homes ranges from $50,000 to $250,000 in Leesburg and from $90,000 to $150,000 in Middleburg. As for the cost of the big farms and estates, wander along Middleburg's main street just down from the Red Fox Inn, glance at some of the real estate office bulletin boards, and gasp. A farm in Leesburg with 280 acres and only a six-stall barn was recently listed at $965,000. Another with only 7 acres and no stables went for $485,000.

Country living was never like this.

The Good Eats

WASHINGTON IS ONE OF the nation's great restaurant towns, a little heavy on the French cuisine, perhaps, but surely in a class with San Francisco, Philadelphia, and New Orleans, if not New York.

Washington is a lousy club town. It has nothing at all like New York's Century, Knickerbocker, or Union Clubs, or Chicago's and Philadelphia's Union League Clubs, or San Francisco's Bohemian Club. It has the downtown Metropolitan Club, which is small by big-city standards, does tend to "go with the job," and does allow people with loud pants. It has the supposedly elite Cosmos Club up on Massachusetts Avenue, the chief distinction of which is that it doesn't accept women. Cosmos does allow nearly everyone else. It has an enormous crowd of 3,000 members (more than Chicago's 23-story-high Union League) and even (egad!) admits journalists.

Then there's the Army and Navy Club, which badly needs dusting; the National Press Club, which is packed with flacks; and the International Club, which resembles an airport restaurant. The F Street Club, Federal City Club, and George Towne Club are lunch joints that might as well be restaurants. Washington's University Club has even less prestige than Chicago's University Clubs. In fact, there's not a single Washington club listed in the national *Social Register*. The only truly exclusive club listed in the *Register* is the Gridiron, which is limited to 60 members and hasn't a club house.

Where then do Washingtonians go who seek genuine clubdom, the conviviality of fellows, the fawning attentions of loyal staff and retainers, the feeling of belonging? Why, they go to their restaurants. As former bureau chief Richard Dudman of the St. Louis *Post-Dispatch* once put it: "Mel Krupin's is my club."

The clubdom of Washington restaurants was probably taken to its most ridiculous extreme during the Carter administration, when Interior Secretary Cecil Andrus, who, like many, used Dominique's on Pennsylvania Avenue as a club, was embarrassed by a subordinate who went to lunch there himself. Finding rattlesnake—a vanishing species—on the menu, the subordinate hurried back to the office and fired off an official letter demanding that snake be removed from the

311

bill of fare. When told of this by Dominique D'Ermo, owner of the joint, the grievously offended Andrus instead removed the subordinate from the staff. He was compelled to reinstate him, when the tale received public currency on network news, but the point was made: In Washington, a man's restaurant is a man's club. And a woman's, too, especially since they can't get into Cosmos.

If the snake incident was the most extreme example of this, the most egregious example was the long, sorry saga of Sans Souci, the cramped little French eatery on 17th Street hard by the White House. Born in the days of John F. Kennedy's Camelot, this snobbiest of Washington's slow-food joints flourished because of its proximity to the First Address, despite rubbery lobster and other iffy food that seemed curiously smothered with heavy sauces.

The draw at Sans Souci, though, was not eats but names. Kennedy aides Ken O'Donnell and Pierre Salinger were the first "stars" to lunch there. The Johnson administration brought Bill Moyers and George Reedy. With Richard Nixon and Gerald Ford came Haldeman and Erlichman, and Henry Kissinger, who sometimes came five times a week. Jerry Ford showed up himself for a birthday luncheon.

Sans Souci might have continued in this fashion for yet another generation, but was hit with three blows. One was the loss of Paul de Lisle, for 15 years its maitre d' and probably the most skillful headwaiter in America, to the sedately chic Jockey Club in 1979. Another occurred when a number of its key personnel defected to open the triumphantly rival Maison Blanche. The most devastating blow, which in fact prompted the other two, was the election of Jimmy Carter.

What with Hamilton Jordan, and Frank Moore taking off his shoes, it was probably just as well, but the Carter White House shunned Sans Souci the way Robespierre, Marat & Co. did Versailles. High-roller Robert Strauss was about the only Carteriste, as "Ear" calls them, who showed his face. Clientele declined, and the lobster got even bouncier. Sans Souci made a desperate last stand by becoming an official club, turning its facilities over to the Federal City Club at lunchtime. But it was not enough. In September 1980, Sans Souci closed its doors—as some said, the only real accomplishment of the Carter administration.

Seemingly the easiest kind of restaurant to start is the French kind. There are easily as many in Washington as there are federal agencies, if not stars in the firmament. Blaise Gherardi started Georgetown's Rive Gauche in 1957, and imported a superb French chef, who went off to open his own restaurant. As fast as Gherardi could import them, new Parisian chefs kept coming and going off on their own, giving birth to such classy institutions as Le Bagatelle and Jean-Pierre, named for Jean-Pierre Goyenville, who also started Lion d'Or. Washington's best French restaurant, though, is not in Washington, but far out in the Virginia countryside near Great Falls and very hard to find. It's L'Auberge Chez François, and hordes of people manage to find it all the time.

Washington has two of the country's very best Italian restaurants, the snooty Tiberio and the divinely tasty Cantina d'Italia. Its Szechuan, though a one-flight-up joint on a slightly seedy stretch of I Street Northwest, is a Chinese eatery equal to if not better than anything in San Francisco. Suburban Arlington, the Vietnamese capital of the nation, has restaurants to match. Taverna Cretekou in Alexandria is favored by ranking dips who've acquired a taste for things Greek. Germaine's, on Wisconsin Avenue just north of Georgetown, is almost an adjunct of the British embassy, whose many dips acquired a taste for spicy oriental cuisine while keeping wogs in their place out there on the Road to Mandalay. David Gilliland, Britain's leading Northern Ireland expert, hangs out in Germaine's when he's not in Belfast.

Go to any of the restaurants on the following list and you're sure to see someone.

THE TOP TEN RESTAURANTS (CLUBS) IN WASHINGTON
1. Dominique's

This is perhaps the strangest elegant French restaurant in Washington, after James Angleton's roller-skating La Niçoise. Located on Pennsylvania Avenue beneath the Secret Service Washington headquarters and just three blocks from the White House, Dominique's is enjoyed with equal favor by the White House, the State Department, big-time lawyers, big-time journalists, assorted bureaucrats, and visiting show-biz celebrities. Presidents Reagan, Ford, and Carter have dined here. So has Liz Taylor, who had a dessert named for her.

Hedrick Smith of the *New York Times* is a regular. The late Aldo Beckman of the *Chicago Tribune* used to be. Ranking dips like Robert Funseth, a former Kissinger lieutenant now in charge of Northern Europe, are familiar faces. Former Vice-President Mondale and wife Joan are regulars. The kingpins of the five Nordic nations, Sweden, Norway, Denmark, Iceland, and Finland, hold regular confabs there. Counselor James Sharkey of the Irish embassy goes there. Pearl Bailey, a Washington college student recently, comes by. So do hundreds of other stars. Patrick Oliphant did the cartoons on the wall of the "Star Room." Everybody in Le Tout Washington is a familiar face.

Dominique's is, however, a little strange. It has rattlesnakes and buffalo meat on the menu and moose heads and street signs on the walls. Its entranceway looks something like a supermarket seafood section. But it is a marvelous restaurant. The meals are very French, yet light and healthful. Dominique D'Ermo, formerly of the French Resistance, is a very friendly if slightly bizarre fellow, and his delightful blonde manager and hostess, Dianna Damewood, is the greatest charmer in Washington. Wherever one sits in Dominique's one never feels one has been shunted aside, and one almost always leaves feeling very good. It is the best.

2. Maison Blanche

Owned by Tony Greco, whose restaurant bankrolling successes have included Rive Gauche, Tiberio, Le Bagatelle, The Big Cheese, and Le Steak, Maison Blanche plays shamelessly on the White House connections; witness its name. It likes to call itself "next door" or "across the street" from the White House, but it is actually farther away than was Sans Souci, about a block and a half or more in the Federal Home Loan Bank Board Building on F Street, west of 17th Street, where it opened in 1979. Nevertheless, it was not too far away to be discovered by the White House Troika of Ed Meese, Jim Baker, and Mike Deaver.

Spacious, where Sans Souci was like a submarine galley, Maison Blanche is big on seafood, beef, and veal, and has entrées running to $30 and more. It is unique in that its summertime outdoor café converts to ice skating in the winter. It also has a très cher cafeteria that converts to pop music and dancing in the evenings.

The big thing about Maison Blanche, though, is the names on the reservation pad. On any day of the week you're likely to find, in addition to Baker, Meese, and Deaver: Vice-President George Bush and Barbara; CBS reporter Leslie Stahl; White House aides Martin Anderson and wife, Annelise; big-time lawyer Edward Bennett Williams; reigning Washington matron Ethel Kennedy; Defense Secretary Caspar Weinberger; movie czar and LBJ vet Jack Valenti; Henry and Nancy Kissinger; CIA Director William Casey; Attorney General William French Smith; and Reaganite heavy Lyn Nofziger.

3. The Class Reunion

This quintessential Washington joint functions as a restaurant at lunchtime and a saloon at night, and helps rule the world in both capacities. Located on H Street just down from the Metropolitan Club—and not far from the White House—the Class is noted for its attractive waitresses, its excellent bartenders (who pour the best if most expensive drinks in town), and its clientele, who include David Stockman and all manner of White House staffers, the *Chicago Tribune* bureau, and the *Los Angeles Times* bureau, large contingents from the *New York Times*, *Washington Post*, and—at one time or another—most of the reporters in Washington. White House press secretary Jim Brady, before the tragic Hilton shooting, was a regular. Good grief, even Jody Powell still comes by.

A creation of former CIA man Jack Smiegel, the Class Reunion has been very fond of Republicans. Four from the Nixon White House put it on the map when, going for a stroll around the block after a heavy lunch at Sans Souci, they discovered this inviting bar and ended up spending the rest of the afternoon.

In the Class, one will find Ronald Reagan's movie posters, Jimmy Carter's Annapolis graduation photograph, a young Jerry and Betty Ford, and a great many other amusingly arcane wall decorations.

It's also known as a hell of a place to start, or end, an affair.

4. The Monocle

Located opposite Union Station on the Senate side of Capitol Hill, the Monocle has been the site of more legislative transactions than the Congress. It is host to such spectacular Washington celebrities as Elizabeth Taylor Warner and powerhouses like Armed Services Committee chairman Senator John Tower, who keeps a regular table. But it ranks so high, notwithstanding its comfy surroundings and dandy eats, because its most important customers are the people who really make Congress work: lobbyists and congressional staff. It is a place where you can see the top staff of top leadership slurp a succession of triple Jack Danielses on the rocks after work, a place where at lunch the people who really run big-time committees like Foreign Relations munch across the table from attractive blonde ladies representing the White House, or some big corporation. Or both. Southern accents abound among the clientele, with good reason. Southerners still run the Senate and the Monocle is very nice to people who run things.

The very best restaurant on chic yet still shaky Capitol Hill, the Monocle and its owner, Conrad Valanos, serve up some terrific eats that more than justify the constant expansion the place seems to be undergoing. Soon, the Monocle may have more dining rooms than the Senate has office buildings, as impossible as that may seem. At the very least it will have more justification for them.

5. Mel Krupin's

Washington's version of Runyanesque Lindy's in New York was for years Duke Ziebert's at Connecticut Avenue and L Street. Mel Krupin, Duke's onetime manager, took Duke's reputation to Paul Young's location on Connecticut after Duke's was bounced for a demolition project. Nothing was lost.

A great place for steak, soup, chopped liver, and beer, Krupin's uniquely soft and comfortable multilevel eatery is restaurant, club, and home to a legion of Washington's major powers, including ABC News anchor Frank Reynolds, big-time lawyer Joseph Califano, Democrat Robert Strauss, the ubiquitous Art Buchwald, perennial vice-presidential aide Vic Gold, and scores of top journalists. Before his death, former Ohio Governor Mike DiSalle used to have his own permanent table at Mel's.

"When I walk down the street and somebody says, 'Hi, Mel,'" says the jowly Mel, "that makes me feel good." It should.

Mel's is not quite the sports hangout that Duke's was, which, given some Redskin performances, is just as well. Former Coach George Allen used to have a regular table at Duke's.

6. The Jockey Club

The Jockey Club, just up from DuPont Circle on Massachusetts Avenue in the old but exceedingly genteel Fairfax Hotel, has Paul de Lisle, numero uno among Washington maitre d's. It is far enough removed from the munching mainstream to permit discretion. If you wish to lunch with your mistress and dine with your wife, or vice versa, there's no happier locale. And it is right on Embassy Row, near the superlegations. When the British have some heavy propagandizing to do, the Jockey Club is where they lure their marks. The Israeli, Irish, and all the other hyperactive embassies do a lot of entertaining there, too.

A dimly-lit, leathery, dark-wooded sort of place, the Jockey Club serves up first-class eats, especially soups and crab dishes. Take your mistress or favorite ambassador there soon.

7. Le Lion d'Or

Restaurant critic Phyllis Richman of the *Washington Post* calls Lion d'Or "the king of Washington's French restaurants." With lawyers, lobbyists, high-paid journalists, and others who prowl Connecticut Avenue near K Street, it's certainly that. Washington master chef Jean-Pierre Goyenvalle sure can whip up the old hot rabbit pâté and fresh shrimp in basil sauce. Glance around the room, set in a basement on 18th Street just off Connecticut, and you might find publicist-lobbyist Robert Gray, lawyer-lobbyist Tom Quinn, campaign aide-lobbyist Mary Frances Widner, or almost any kind of lobbyist you can mention. Le Bagatelle, Jean-Pierre, and the others are first-line Frencheries, but the Gold Lion edges them out and remains the headquarters for Washington's American Express card set.

Lion d'Or is also famous for its good house jug wine, a reputation that now extends beyond its basement doors. It has bottled the wine as "La Carafe," subtitled "du Lion d'Or," and is selling it at Cathedral Liquors on Connecticut Avenue, among other places, for about the price of a six-pack of beer. A rare bargain. If you're a lobbyist, give some to your clients.

8. Washington's Palm

One sees Joe Califano eating all over Washington, but one sees him most at the Palm, and for good reason. All that damned French cooking gets to you after a while. At the Palm, Washington's best steak joint, there is Washington's best steak, complete with onions and red peppers if you like. They also have giant lobster, not at all bouncy, if you don't mind hocking the family car to pay for it.

The Palm has Califano's "corner" sort of set aside, but there are lots of comfy seats for everyone else. The wall hangings are caricature's of local celebrities, making the place somewhat reminiscent of New York's Sardi's, except Washington's celebrities are not quite so theatrical—or beautiful. The Palm's regulars include partners from the really big law firms and folk from interesting nearby outfits like the American Petroleum Institute. Which is why you often see actual journalists in the Palm toward the end of the month. Legend has it that the API has a quota of reporters it has to take to lunch.

9. Chez Camille

CIA spooks and high officials have many, many hangouts. James Angleton was fond of the roller-skating-waiter service at La Niçoise. Others appreciate La Mirabelle in nearby McLean, L'Auberge Chez François in nearby Great Falls, and the Red Fox Inn in not-so nearby Middleburg out in the hunt country, which is still just a 35-minute Mercedes limousine ride away from CIA headquarters in Langley.

When they're eating in town, though, the spooks tend to roost at Chez Camille, a discreet, tall-windowed, and somewhat garish joint on DeSales Street hard by the Mayflower Hotel. Perhaps they like the stuffed carp.

Make of it what you will, but *Washington Post* executive editor Ben Bradlee likes to lunch there, too.

10. Nick and Dottie's

Nick and Dottie's comfy, dimly-lit, and very discreet Black Steer Restaurant on 17th Street, just next to what was Sans Souci and also to the McDonald's that so many of the Carter people favored, is a place noted for fast service, hearty food, and relatively inexpensive prices. It is a place near the White House where Washington powers go when they just want to eat—or when they want to work and eat. David Stockman can be found there, upstairs or down, merrily slashing away at budgets while merrily munching on steak, and not paying for it with food stamps, either. Pete Teeley, Vice-President Bush's ever-popular press secretary, is another habitué.

Very soon after the 1980 election, Nick and Dottie's had an organizational chart of the Reagan team stuck up on the back of the door to the closet by the main entrance. It's had a lot of changes penciled in since.

There's a very private booth in a dark alcove off the main dining room on the first floor that's just perfect for cutting deals—or rearranging White House organizational charts.

NOTE: The absence of Tiberio may be noted here. It's a fine restaurant, but is so flush with well-heeled doctors' wives, K Street stockbrokers, and other affluent civilians that it has paid scant attention to Washington's power elite, except passingly during the Reagan transition. It was also insufferably rude to a Washington columnist and the Irish ambassador, which none of the restaurant clubs on this list would have been.

Monumental Egos

A FAVORITE WASHINGTON STORY: A tourist, riding in a taxi down Pennsylvania Avenue toward the Capitol, passes the Greek-revival structure housing the National Archives at Eighth Street, and taps the driver on the shoulder.

"The inscription on that statue back there says, 'The Past Is Prologue.' What does that mean?"

"Oh, that," says the cabbie. "That means, 'You ain't seen nothin' yet.'"

How true. Washington has some of the most beautifully conceived, artistically executed, and historically appropriate monuments and statues to be found in the United States. It also has some of the most misbegotten memorials to obscure events, small-time heroes, and overblown reputations this side of Ozymandias.

Almost everyone has a story, usually involving Washington's Gross Local Product, politics. There is tragedy and comedy, ideology and bureaucracy, egocentricity and sometimes even an example of modesty in the stone, marble, and bronze of Washington's monuments.

For example, the tourist riding past the Archives probably did not see the simple block of white marble set among some shrubs on a tiny parcel of land facing Pennsylvania Avenue. That unadorned stone is the only memorial in Washington to the man who served longer as President of the United States than anyone in its history, leading the nation out of its worst economic disaster, and through its greatest war. The only words on the stone are: "In Memory Of Franklin Delano Roosevelt. 1882–1945."

A few blocks east, on the slope of Capitol Hill, stands an imposing 100-foot bell tower. In front of it is what one critic called "a somewhat undistinguished" 11-foot statue of Senator Robert A. Taft, Republican of Ohio. Elected to the Senate the same year FDR won the Presidency, Taft devoted much of his energy to fighting Roosevelt and his works, and then trying to become the second son of a President to win the office himself. He had some limited success in the first endeavor and flunked the second.

When Taft died in 1953, there were many conservative Re-

319

publicans, especially in Congress, who believed "Mr. Republican" had been euchred out of the presidential nomination by the eastern establishment "liberals" who sponsored the candidacy of Dwight D. Eisenhower. With their dominance in the House and Senate, the Taft partisans moved quickly to set aside the prime piece of land on the Capitol "campus" and raised the funds that produced a memorial within six years, which is downright supersonic speed in the business of erecting Washington monuments.

Some find it ironic that the Taft statue was placed facing toward the White House, which he never achieved, instead of the Capitol, which he dominated. But others find irony in the fact that Taft has his statue and carillon, while there is nothing in the capital to memorialize Eisenhower (other than an office building housing the Republican National Committee and a theatre in the Kennedy Center) or Taft's father, William Howard, who served as both President and Chief Justice.

As for Roosevelt, it may be some form of poetic justice that his memorial has become the victim of the very kind of bureaucracy that flourished in the climate of power-accumulation brought to Washington by the New Deal. It was not until 10 years after FDR died that Congress did anything about a Roosevelt memorial. In 1955, it established a commission to plan and build a suitable shrine to FDR, but all it accomplished in more than a quarter of a century was to demonstrate the truth of the political axiom that if the Israelites had appointed a committee instead of Moses to lead them out of Egypt, they'd still be milling about in the desert.

With offices, a staff, and a sizable budget, the Franklin Delano Roosevelt Memorial Commission got right down to work and in just under 10 years managed to come forth with a plan for a park dominated by a series of towering stone slabs inscribed with FDR's most famous utterances. Quickly dubbed "Instant Stonehenge," it was laughed out of town. A second proposal for a big monument was also rejected as too obtrusive for the Tidal Basin site reserved for FDR, and it wasn't until 1978 that the commission offered a design that wouldn't even break the skyline—a low-lying flower and tree garden with pools and waterfalls built around a long memorial wall of rough stone.

This won the endorsement of the arts bureaucrats who pass on the merit of monuments in Washington, but early in 1979, the Interior Department's money bureaucrats decided the price tag—up to $50 million by some estimates—was out of line. The commission brought back a no-frills, $23 million model, but the critics sniffed that the Lincoln Memorial had cost $20 million less, and it was still no go.

While this was going on, FDR's friends lost patience, raised

$12,000, and placed the plain marble block in front of the Archives in 1965. The justification for this memorial was supplied by the late Supreme Court Justice Felix Frankfurter, who said he once asked FDR what kind of monument he wanted as they were riding together down Pennsylvania Avenue. According to Frankfurter, Roosevelt said he wanted only a simple stone marker and, pointing to the little triangle of land, added: "Right there."

This may have been true modesty, but some who believe Roosevelt didn't have a humble bone in his body think he may have trapped himself as Calvin Coolidge did when he declared, "I do not choose to run." Everyone took Silent Cal at his word, and that may turn out to be what happened to FDR.

The delay in honoring Roosevelt may have contributed to the haste in building a monument to John F. Kennedy. What this most stylish of Presidents got for the people to remember him by was a gigantic and hideously ugly performing arts center, with, some believe fittingly, marvelous acoustics, a leaky roof, and a portrait bust of grotesque size and execution in the main lobby.

The subject of even more malicious glee is the memorial to the World War II exploits of the U.S. Marine Corps in Arlington, Virginia, just across the Potomac from Washington. The huge statue of Marines raising the flag on Mount Suribachi on Iwo Jima, based on Joe Rosenthal's famous photograph, is an impressive tribute to the nation's most machismo-oriented military service. It also is a notorious trysting place for cruising homosexuals.

If the process of building monuments in Washington has a common denominator, it probably is controversy. This began with George Washington himself. The first President was dead 50 years before a decision could be made on an appropriate monument, which was to be a Greek-style rotunda topped by an Egyptian obelisk. When money got tight, the templelike lower structure was scratched, and when a mob of anti-Catholic "Know Nothings" stole a memorial stone donated for the monument by the Pope and chucked it into the river, all construction stopped.

A 150-foot stub stood there for 22 years, when Congress decided to finish the job in time for the 1876 centennial. Once again, there was a hassle about design, with one proposal to decorate the shaft with an icing of statues, friezes, and assorted architectural gimcracks. Somehow, taste prevailed, and the monument was dedicated in its present form on February 21, 1885, only 86 years after Washington's death.

That kind of struggle led to the present system for building outdoor public monuments in Washington. Today, sponsors must get a bill through Congress and signed by the President if the monument is to be on federal land. Then they must get approval from the Commission of Fine Arts, made up of seven artists, architects, and experts appointed by the President. Finally, money must be raised—by the sponsors, in most cases, or appropriated by Congress. Anyone who can complete this process in less than a dozen years probably is more worthy of a monument than the person being honored.

According to James M. Goode of the Smithsonian Institution, two out of every three monuments proposed never get past Congress. This may be fortunate, Goode says, because Washington might otherwise have been treated to the huge image of a German Shepherd dog guarding the Pentagon to honor the military canines of World War II, or a statue of P. T. Barnum, who is remembered for the deathless words, "There is a sucker born every minute."

Congress, of course, can be part of the problem. In the late 1960's, Representative Michael Kirwan of Ohio, who believed no river should remain undammed, undredged, or unbridged, turned his attention to fish. Kirwan bludgeoned Congress into approving what would have been the fanciest and surely most costly aquarium in America for Washington. "Mike's Fish Tank" still has legal authorization, but he died before construction began, and with him went the congressional clout that would have been required to finance it.

But worse, far worse, is what Congress has done to itself and its own.

Senator Everett McKinley Dirksen made some enemies in his time, and people trying to get around the office building named for him on Capitol Hill might readily believe it was no friend of the Illinois lawmaker who so honored his memory. The Dirksen Building has a pseudo-classic façade, but no front entrance. Access to its upper floors was so badly botched that an entire corner of the interior had to be torn up and a new bank of elevators installed some years after its occupancy to give senators a fighting chance to get from their offices to the chamber in time to vote. For the public, it remains a good place to spend a day waiting for an elevator.

But no man's name has been more poorly served by a memorial than that of Sam Rayburn, the longtime speaker of the House. The structure named to honor the veteran Texan, into which was poured more than $134 million over a period of more than six years, is called the Rayburn House Office Building. It is, in fact, a large parking garage surmounted by a relatively small office building.

It houses 9 committees, 169 of the 435 members of the House of Representatives, and 1,600 automobiles. Ada Louise Huxtable of the *New York Times* described its exterior design as "Mussolini Modern," and its vaguely swastika-shaped interior layout makes it, on upper floors, necessary to walk about two city blocks to get between offices whose windows look out on each other. It has a swimming pool in a room with a ceiling so low that the diving board may be used only at the risk of a fractured skull, and, at the end of every wing, swooping formal staircases that had to be shut off by fire doors after the building was completed. Finally, it has a statue of Sam Rayburn that is a spitting image of the old film star, Pat O'Brien.

Dirksen, Rayburn, and J. Edgar Hoover (whose looming, grotesque FBI headquarters rates special mention later in this chapter) were gone when their names were affixed to Washington buildings. In fact, the demise of a namesake used to be the first condition in the process of enshrining someone on the portals of a federal installation, but like other considerations of taste in recent times, that has been increasingly honored in the breach.

Joe Hirshhorn, for example, was alive and strutting in 1969 when Lyndon Johnson scraped up the first shovel of dirt for what was to become the Hirshhorn Museum and Sculpture Garden alongside the other great repositories of history and culture on the Mall. Hirshhorn, a poor boy who literally struck uranium (and got in considerable hot water with Canadian authorities over some of his dealings), used his fortune to buy pictures and statues. As his collection grew in size, value, and fame, Hirshhorn was besieged by curators and politicians on two continents offering suitable sites to house it.

Just as it seemed the collection might go to England, LBJ stepped in. Lyndon didn't know much about art, but he loved the idea of showing the intellectual elite how "Yore President" could win what the elite were about to lose. He laid on the full-press Johnson treatment, but little Joe Hirshhorn was no small-time horse trader. He got a drum-shaped marble museum—distinctive among the squared-off buildings on the Mall—financed by the taxpayers but with his name over the door. (This rattled some teacups in Georgetown inasmuch as the Mellon family built two museums on the Mall and stocked both with priceless art, but put its name on neither.)

Once in place, a monument is hard to displace. But a few have come and gone, including a statue of Frederick the Great of Prussia that attracted so much anti-Teutonic ire during both World Wars I and II (including an attempted bombing) that it was moved to the Army's Carlisle Barracks in Pennsylvania.

And then there were the Social Security eagles. American bureaucrats love eagles, festooning their buildings with the birds whenever possible. So when the Social Security Administration got the go-ahead for a new building at the foot of Capitol Hill just before World War II, the designers provided for a pair of monumental eagles to decorate the façade. Sculptor Heinz Warneke carved them a pair of dandies—two limestone birds each weighing 31 tons. As recounted by Goode in his book, *Outdoor Sculpture in Washington, D.C.*, it wasn't until the eagles were delivered that the builders realized they were too heavy for the structure.

What to do? Why, sell them as surplus, like a gross of canteens or an overstock of GI undershorts. An auction was announced, and a federal employee named Ray Henderson jokingly bid $50 for the eagles, which had cost $6,000 each. The joke was on Henderson—he won.

Henderson hired riggers and a truck to haul the birds to his small house in Arlington, where they were set down in his back yard. But the fierce-looking birds were so tall that they were peering into the second-floor bedroom, and Mrs. Henderson objected. Henderson, unwilling to spend any more money on what was already a costly whim, got a ladder, a mallet, and some chisels and over a period of months reduced the eagles to gravel.

Sometimes memorials are a source of embarrassment to their sponsors, as with the Marines and their Iwo Jima monument. Another such case was the monument built to honor Samuel Gompers, founder of the American Federation of Labor. It is a nice enough little memorial, but it gained a dubious fame a few years ago when it was discovered a gang of burglars had found a trapdoor in its base and were using it to store their loot.

The listings that have gone before this book have ranked the best of their kind. What follows in this section is a departure from that, because memorials and monuments that fail are often as memorable as those that successfully celebrate fame, honor and achievement. Thus, two lists—the best and the worst:

THE FIVE BEST MONUMENTS IN WASHINGTON

1. The Navy-Marine Memorial, on George Washington Parkway.

    Not to be confused with the Iwo Jima memorial, this relatively small monument to sailors and marines lost at sea in World War I is the best in Washington. Erected in 1934, it depicts seagulls flying above a huge wave, symbolizing the spirits of the lost men and the power and danger of the sea. Ernesto Begni del Piatta here created a monument that evokes the maximum of emotion and requires the minimum of explanation. A knockout.
2. The Lincoln Memorial on the Potomac at 22nd Street.

    Daniel Chester French, the sculptor, and Henry Bacon, the architect, found the way to strike awe into the hearts of nearly all who climb the long flight of stone stairs and stand before the 29-foot high pedestal and statue of the seated Abraham Lincoln.

    It is no dead monument, having provided some of Washington's most dramatic events since it was dedicated in 1922. Marian

Anderson, denied the use of the DAR hall because she was black, sang to 75,000 people here in 1939, and Dr. Martin Luther King Jr. spoke the words "I have a dream" from its steps to an audience of several hundred thousand blacks and whites in 1962.

3. The Ulysses S. Grant Memorial, at the foot of Capitol Hill.

This is more than a memorial to Grant. It also honors with consummate artistry and feeling the 750,000 Americans who died in the Civil War. And it is a tribute to Henry Shrady, a self-taught sculptor who worked more than 20 years to complete the monumental three-group memorial and then died of overwork two weeks before it was dedicated.

Originally it was to be built on the Ellipse south of the White House, but Theodore Roosevelt, then President, objected that it would block his view of the Potomac.

The Grant Memorial is one of more than a score to Civil War generals in Washington. It is the best, although some are partial to the almost informal equestrian statue honoring General Phil Sheridan on Massachusetts Avenue.

4. The Jefferson Memorial, on the Tidal Basin.

There was a typical Washington flap when Franklin D. Roosevelt decreed Jefferson's memorial would go on the Tidal Basin, but it now is regarded as an ornament to the area and the favorite of many Washingtonians.

The 25-foot statue by Rudulph Evans stands in a circular rotunda, which has panels inscribed with Jefferson's most famous writings. The memorial had been finished 28 years before a college professor discovered that five words had been left out of the quotation from the Declaration of Independence. It seems there wasn't enough room for them.

5. The Washington Monument.

Because it's there; because it is the symbol of the capital. It was more of a challenge when you could climb the 898 steps to the top, but visitors now are restricted to riding the elevator both ways, because of vandalism perpetrated by stair climbers. But the elevator ride is a thrill and the views of Washington are awesome during summer evenings, or almost anytime.

It is last on this list of the best because there is not much of George Washington to this monument. You have to go outside of Washington to Mount Vernon for that.

THE TEN WORST MONUMENTS IN WASHINGTON

1. George Washington's statue in the Smithsonian Museum of American History.

This was one of the first statues purchased by the government, which commissioned Horatio Greenough to sculpt it in Italy.

When it arrived, there was George, bare to the waist and draped elsewhere in a Roman toga. This apparition caused a Virginia congressman to roar, "No man ever lived who saw George Washington without his shirt." The extended arms of the seated figure inspired another critic to suggest that Washington was saying, "My body is at Mount Vernon and my clothes are in the Patent Office."

Outrage notwithstanding, the half-naked Washington stood 60 years on the grounds of the Capitol until its spot was needed for a driveway. Today it may be seen at the Smithsonian, which after all is known as "the nation's attic."

2. The J. Edgar Hoover Building, Pennsylvania Avenue between Eighth and Ninth.

Hoover was once an authentic American hero, but in his last years was said to have given in to a feeling that people were trying to get him. Among those, he should have included the architects of the block-square behemoth that is the FBI headquarters, named in his honor.

The Pennsylvania Avenue side of the building towers over pedestrians like a stone version of the natives' antigorilla fence in *King Kong*, while the other side of the structure features a bulky T-shaped tower that would have made a suitable backdrop for the filming of George Orwell's *1984*. It also has a ground-level inner courtyard that has all the charm of a training ground for firing squads.

In justice to the architects, the original plan called for a number of ground-level shops and eating places. Hoover nixed the arcade idea for fear someone would be mugged in the FBI's front yard.

3. The National Visitor Center on Capitol Hill.

This used to be Washington's Union Station, one of the most bustling, functional, and beautiful railroad depots in the country. At the instance of one congressman with a half-vast idea and a horde of power-seeking bureaucrats, it was raped, dismembered, and transformed into a cavernous waiting room for bicentennial visitors who never showed up.

Former Republican Kenneth J. Gray of Illinois, a sometime used-car auctioneer and amateur magician, was the congressional villain of the piece; the Interior and Transportation Departments supplied the civil servants to screw up what faint chance the idea had to succeed.

With $117 million down the drain, the building had to be closed because of a leaking roof and falling plaster. Next to it is a gigantic, half-finished parking garage that set cost overrun records even for Washington. And railroad passengers, who have increased in recent years, have to walk around to the back of the building to a cheaply-constructed shedlike depot that would be a disgrace in Antelope, Montana.

Gray, also remembered as the congressman who gave Elizabeth ("I can't even type") Ray her first job on Capitol Hill, has retired and moved to Florida. But he won't soon be forgotten in Washington.

4. The Temperance Fountain on Pennsylvania Avenue near Seventh Street.

This is a monument to what, in Washington at least, is a lost cause. In the 1880s, a California dentist named Henry Cogswell donated "Temperance Fountains" to a number of cities. They were supposed to give parched passersby the opportunity of quenching their thirsts with cool, clean water instead of the readily available beer in nearby saloons.

Functionally, the fountain never was a hit in Washington, which ranks near the top in the nation for liquor consumed per capita. But the gawky heron atop the domed fountain has become a local landmark, and efforts to remove it have always been blocked by citizen protest.

Meanwhile, there is a bar on Capitol Hill called "The Man in the Green Hat" that is a kind of a monument to the Prohibition era that Cogswell and his friends finally produced. The bar is named after the bootlegger who serviced members of Congress in the 1920s operating out of the basement of the House Office Building. And 20 feet from the monument is Apex Liquors, one of the city's busiest retailers of ardent spirits.

5. Major General John Rawlins' statue, 18th and E streets.

You may never have heard of General Rawlins, which is not surprising, since he never won a major battle during the Civil War. But he was on the staff of U.S. Grant and is credited with keeping Grant off the sauce during the crucial periods of the war.

So perhaps he was worthy of a statue, although Rawlins' equestrian monument was rather shabbily treated—moved to five different locations, including one next to a public comfort station, until he was set up in a rather pretty little park near the Interior Department.

6. The Boy Scout Memorial, on the Ellipse near 15th Street.

Here you have a small pool and a statuary group of a Boy Scout standing between two adult figures, who might be his father and mother. Except that Dad is wearing only a breechclout and Mom scarcely more. This may be the explanation of why the Scout manual used to have a section in the back that was entitled "nocturnal emissions."

7. Taras Shevchenko statue, 23rd and P Streets.

    There are two stories about Shevchenko, who was a nineteenth century Ukrainian poet. The first is that he was a fiery anti-Czarist dissident, and as such is regarded as a hero by Communists in the Soviet Union. The second is that he was a fiery Ukrainian nationalist, and as such is regarded as a champion of captive nations by anti-Communists.

    This had everyone shouting at each other, but it was Americans of Ukrainian descent who sponsored the 24-foot statue and turned out an incredible 100,000 people for the unveiling in 1964. It stands peacefully enough today, flanked by a topless-bottomless go-go bar and a park called P Street Beach, a favorite sunning spot for Dupont Circle gays.

8. Albert Gallatin statue, 15th Street and Pennsylvania Avenue.

    How does politics affect the erection of statues in Washington? Back in the 1920s, Democrats got tired of hearing Republicans praise their secretaries of treasury as "the best since Alexander Hamilton." So they put up a statue of Gallatin, who succeeded Hamilton in office and paid off the $4-million national debt he inherited. The Republicans extracted their revenge by blocking public funds for the statue, which was financed privately.

9. Statue of Freedom on the U.S. Capitol Dome.

    This is a very good statue, except for the headdress of the standing female figure, which provides another illustration of ideology run amok.

    When Thomas Crawford designed the statue, he topped it with a Liberty Cap, which in ancient Rome was the safe conduct of freed slaves. But the secretary of war, whose Army Corps of Engineers was building the dome, objected, saying such a symbol would only encourage the Abolitionists, or, God forbid, the slaves. So Freedom was given a headdress of feathers, which offended no one at the time.

    The irony: when the statue was finally raised to the top of the dome in 1863, the rotunda beneath it was being used as a hospital for Union soldiers wounded fighting troops of the Confederacy, then being led by the former secretary of war, Jefferson Davis.

10. Dr. Samuel Hahnemann statue, Massachusetts Avenue and 16th Street.

    Dr. Samuel Hahnemann was the founder of homeopathic medicine, and when this imposing memorial on Scott Circle was erected in 1900, his methods were very popular in the United

States. Today, if all the homeopathic physicians listed in the Washington telephone directory were gathered at the memorial, Dr. Hahnemann would still be alone. This may illustrate the wisdom of letting a decent interval of time pass before a hero or an idea is enshrined in stone.

Afterword

IN THIS affectionately irreverent trip across and, one hopes, into the fabric of Washington, we tried to cast some light on how and by whom this unique place is run.

But more needs to be said. Some have called Washington "nobody's hometown," and said it has no sense of community. Others call it a parasitic place, alien to the nation for which it serves as the seat of the government.

It is true that much is made at cocktail parties when someone is discovered who was born, reared, and remained in Washington. That is partly because people who go to cocktail parties usually don't have anywhere better to be and partly because, if the census is to be believed, damn few Americans stay put where they were born.

But this much is a fact: An amazing number of people who could go elsewhere remain in Washington even after their public or private careers have ended. Multimillionaire Joe Hirshhorn, who could have lived anywhere he pleased, spent his last days in Washington to be close to the princely gift of art he gave the nation.

Six months after the Carters went back to Georgia, a middle-aged woman walking down F Street and lugging a couple of shopping bags toward the subway proved to be Patricia Roberts Harris, who had a limousine to ride in and aides to do her shopping when she was secretary of housing and urban development.

Of course, some people stay in Washington after their turn in the limelight is over because they can make a better living than was ever dreamed of in Little Chute, Wisconsin, but where is it written that you have to go home again?

As for a sense of community, that knock has to come from people who are stuck in the manufactured neighborhoods of the post-World War II suburbs. The amazing fact is that some extremely cohesive neighborhoods exist and thrive in parts of black, white, and integrated Washington that commuters and tourists seldom see. It is amazing because until recently the citizens were never given a voice in local affairs, and because politicians from elsewhere have always taken cheap shots at the city and its people.

Which brings up the image of Washington as the great national leech. We—those of us in the writer's trade—expend a lot of scorn and outrage about bureaucrats sitting on their regulatory butts or lording it over the hardworking citizenry of the rest of the country, but the fact is that the United States has a less corrupt, more efficient, and responsive group of public employees than almost any other country big enough to afford carbon paper. To reduce it to a bumper sticker, if you don't like Washington bureaucrats, try your luck in Paris or Moscow or Ouagadougou.

Nor is there evidence to show that the federal payroll is somehow swallowing the nation. In 1951, there were 2,456,000 federal workers; in 1981, 2,800,000, including the people in the CETA and summer jobs programs. State and local governments, meanwhile, increased their payrolls from 4,031,000 in 1951 to 13,445,000 in 1980.

None of this is intended to portray Washington as Shangri-la even though by one rating it is second best in the nation. Like any major city, it has its stresses, and one lady in a position to know has said that the 300-plus psychiatrists who advertise in the local Yellow Pages represent about as much of the total psychotherapeutic community in Washington as the visible part of the iceberg does of the whole. A recent count put Washington's shrink census at 1,123 more per capita than any other city in the world. But this may be fewer than absolutely needed in a city with 32,000 lawyers.

So that's Washington with, we hope, the warts as well as the beauty marks. It is, as James Fenimore Cooper said, when it was still a young city in 1838, "mean in detail, but the outline has a certain grandeur about it."

Authors

MICHAEL KILIAN, 42, is a Washington-based columnist for the *Chicago Tribune* and the Knight-News-Tribune Wire whose column is distributed to some 115 newspapers in the United States and Canada. He has been covering the Washington scene since 1976, writing about everything from foreign affairs and the environment to presidential politics and White House life-styles, usually in a humorous vein.

Creator and coauthor of a similar work about Chicago, *Who Runs Chicago?* (St. Martin's, 1979), he is also the author of an espionage novel set in Washington and Iceland, *The Valkyrie Project* (St. Martin's, 1981). He is at work on another espionage novel and a historical novel dealing with America from the Jackson to the Polk administrations.

Born in Toledo, Ohio, he grew up in Chicago and in Bedford Village, in New York's Westchester County, attending the New School in New York City and the University of Maryland. He served in Korea with the U.S. Army and is a captain in the USAF Civil Air Patrol. An adviser to Encyclopaedia Britannica's Book of the Year, he is also a radio commentator for CBS in Chicago.

He lives with his wife, Pamela, a magazine writer, and their two sons, Eric and Colin, in Falls Church, Virginia.

Arnold Sawislak has been a United Press International Washington correspondent for 25 years, the last 10 as senior editor specializing in the coverage of politics. He began his wire-service career fresh out of the University of Minnesota in 1949, spending seven years in Madison, Wisconsin, before moving on to the national capital.

He was born in Lansing, Michigan, in September 1927, and lived in Illinois, Iowa, Ohio, and Minnesota—attending 22 schools as his family hopped about the Midwest—before entering the Army for an 18-month tour in the United States, Japan, and Korea as a "geodetic computer" for the Corps of Engineers.

In Washington, Sawislak has covered stories in just about every government agency and department, but put in the longest stint covering the House and the Kennedy-Johnson New Frontier and Great Society legislative programs. He began concentrating on politics in 1968 and has had a hand in covering every presidential campaign since.

A history buff, concentrating on the Civil War and Washington, D.C., he has three children, all widely scattered and none showing the least interest in journalism. He lives in Washington within walking distance of the White House and a very nice neighborhood saloon called The Fox and Hounds. He much prefers the company at the latter to that at the former.

Index

Watergate scandal, 10, 41, 43, 47, 76,
77, 142, 164–165, 189, 197, 199,
257, 302
Watt, James, 9–10, 92–93, 103, 107,
121, 266
Webster, William H., 261
Weidenbaum, Murray, 15
Weinberger, Caspar "Cap," 10, 11,
19–20, 51, 59, 68–71, 72, 73, 121,
128, 131, 184, 208, 302, 314
Will, George, 173–174, 225, 304

Williams, Edward Bennett, 196–197,
198, 283–284, 287, 306, 314
Witcover, Jules, 176–177
Woodrow Wilson International Center
for Scholars, 184–185, 187, 265
Woodward, Bob, 164–165, 171
World Bank, 112–113, 123
Wright, Skelly, 46

Zipkin, Jerome, 204, 208, 215–216